W9-CDS-224

The Mass Media Book

Drawing by Lorenz; © 1971
The New Yorker Magazine, Inc.

The Mass Media Book

Edited by

ROD HOLMGREN
Monterey Peninsula College
Monterey, California

WILLIAM NORTON
California Newspaper Publisher

PRENTICE-HALL, INC., Englewood Cliffs, New Jersey

P92. U5 H6. c.2.

© 1972 by PRENTICE-HALL, INC.
Englewood Cliffs, New Jersey

*All rights reserved. No part of this book may be
reproduced in any form or by any means without
permission in writing from the publisher.*

Printed in the United States of America

ISBN: 0-13-559781-1

Library of Congress Catalog Card No.: 70-39616

10   9   8   7   6   5   4

PRENTICE-HALL INTERNATIONAL, INC., *London*
PRENTICE-HALL OF AUSTRALIA, PTY. LTD., *Sydney*
PRENTICE-HALL OF CANADA, LTD., *Toronto*
PRENTICE-HALL OF INDIA PRIVATE LIMITED, *New Delhi*
PRENTICE-HALL OF JAPAN, INC., *Tokyo*

Contents

The News Media

946039

EDUCATION

The Entertainment Media

Preface

The articles in this book have been chosen to offer the student a critical overview of mass media in America today.

The book is divided into two major areas—news-information and entertainment—following the media's own pattern. Though we spend far less time absorbing news-information than being entertained, the book begins with analysis and comment on the news media.

Some current problems of the media arise from explosive changes in communication technology. Some have been uncovered by research into ways in which the media give us our pictures of the world, and what we do with those pictures. Some spring from what has been called the "glut of information," and our sense of being inundated with more than we can assimilate. Some reflect changes our society itself is undergoing, and the tendency of many Americans to take a fresh, often suspicious, look at all established institutions.

Probes into popular culture provided by the mass media have grown more common in the past decade. The critics argue that the quality of popular art continues to fall despite stereo sound, communications satellites, and the cassette "revolution." The word "revolution," by the way, seems to be used frequently in discussion of the media and their products. The defenders contend that a greater variety of cultural offerings is available today than ever before. The media, they say, have even begun to popularize classical art.

Because the media touch our society at so many points, these essays are directed not only to journalists and students of popular culture, but also to sociologists, psychologists, and political scientists. In the last quarter century, these behavioral sciences have built a considerable body of research on mass communication, especially in the fields of public opinion, propaganda, motivation, and learning.

Not all of us realize how large a part the media play in our lives. While the amount of time we spend reading, listening, or watching varies from time to time—depending on changes in life styles or simply movement from place to place—the figures indicate a great deal of "exposure" at all ages.

Some of these readings are intended to suggest just how important the media are to us. They are big, pervasive, and highly available. The pictures of the world they give us are sometimes sharply focused, multidimensional, and marvelously perceptive, but they are also frequently distorted, exaggerated or under-played, and confusing. So it is urgent that we study the mass media and the processes by which they give us our pictures of the world, as well as the effects of those pictures on our attitudes and behavior.

Rod Holmgren
William Norton

INTRODUCTION

A Look at Modern Media

Media are communication channels that serve people. The mass media—newspapers, books, magazines, radio, television, and film—are channels which address their messages to anyone who chooses to read, listen, or watch.

Size and heterogeneity are marked characteristics of mass media audiences. Before newspapers were sold for a penny apiece in the early nineteenth century, the print media did not belong to the masses. Newspapers, books, and magazines then became available cheaply to almost anyone. All the other important media—television, radio, and films—belong to this century. Radio didn't become important until our century was one-fourth over, and television until it was half over.

The term "mass media" suggests powerful business. And today the media are big. They are almost annoyingly pervasive—institutions which have worked their way into the web of society.

The number of daily papers in the United States has been stabilized at around 1,750 for almost two decades. Their pressrun totals about 62 million copies. Newspapers are read by about 95 percent of the population at least once a week and about 78 percent on an average weekday.

Total newspaper circulation and readership have not risen as fast, relative to population, as total TV set ownership and use. Ninety-six percent of American homes have TV sets, for a total of 85 million in 1970; the sets are watched by 82 percent of all adult Americans for an average of more than two hours every day. More than a fourth of our homes have two or more sets.

Radio is the everywhere medium. Only one home in one hundred lacks a set, and the average home has more than four sets, if we include car radios. While millions of listeners treat radio like wallpaper, in effect saying, "It's just there," about two out of every three tune in more than an hour a day.

Film and the two other print media—books and magazines—draw the smallest audiences, even though the word "mass" is still highly appropriate. For movies, attendance is 13 percent of the population every week, and about 33 percent at least once a month. Well over half the movie-goers nowadays are between sixteen and thirty years old, partly because so much of the movies' content is aimed at youth, partly because free, easy-to-reach television has such an attraction for the over-thirty crowd.

Magazine readers total about 37 percent of the population, who spend $1.3 billion per year for subscriptions. The rest of the magazine industry's $2.5 billion income comes from advertising. This compares to $3 billion spent on television annually, and $5 billion on newspaper advertising.

. Our book-buying habits are not so easy to measure. But more than a fourth of the population spends $2.4 billion yearly on books, and this does not include library users and schoolchildren.

All of this suggests the pervasiveness of the media. They present us with an almost staggering variety of choices. Since the adult American is exposed to one or more of the media for anywhere from a few minutes to several hours a day, the choices we make are important.

Few of these choices are made by chance. We tend to pick the radio or TV programs, the movies, books, newspapers, or magazines that we want to hear, see, or read. And during each exposure period, we tend to tune out those features we don't think are addressed to us individually. We note and remember primarily those ads, pictures, articles, or comments that are individually useful to us. In short, we take from the media what we want, including both information and entertainment. The rest we pass by or forget quickly.

What each of us wants—or needs—from the media from one moment to the next will vary greatly, depending not only on mood, energy level, and time available, but also on such obvious factors as age, education, and economic status.

MEDIA AUDIENCES

For young children, television is the most important medium. But interest shifts to radio in adolescence, and reading of print media—especially newspapers and magazines—picks up rapidly as adulthood approaches.

To suggest one example of how income affects media use, studies show that more than half the adults with annual incomes above $10,000 read magazines, while only 27 percent of those with incomes under $5,000 engage in such reading.

Education, closely associated with income, also plays a part in media use. The more educated the adult is, the more time he spends reading and the less watching television.

However, to say that there are differences in media use according to age, income, and education is merely to call attention to statistical averages. We also know that the individual's media habits vary enormously regardless of these factors.

FUNCTIONS OF THE MEDIA

The ways in which the individual uses the media give us clues to the functions of the media in society as a whole. If we considered only the time they spend on the media, we might conclude that most Americans use them far more for entertainment than for news and information. The conclusion might be wrong, however, for both uses help give us our pictures of the world, and very often we're learning even when we're enjoying ourselves.

We need a continuous survey of our environment, whether immediate or distant. We become uneasy if we do not receive a stream of information, however uneven, about changes taking place on the horizon. More simply, this involves the reporting of news or presentation of information about our world and its people. We might call this the *watcher* function of media, and it is performed especially well by newspapers, television, radio, and newsmagazines.

The same four media provide us with a *forum,* a running series of arguments among rival views and personalities. They give us a basis for what communications theorist Harold Lasswell once called "coordination of responses"—reaching a consensus about issues facing society.

Lasswell also called attention to the transmission of social heritage by the media. This *teacher* function is performed, of course, via both news-information and entertainment offerings. The media also help to *sell goods,* and the advertising industry budgets about $18 billion for this purpose annually.

But it is to *entertainment* that we turn our attention most eagerly; it's so easy to take. Neither radio, television, nor the film demands that we "work" in the sense that all print media do. Nor do they require the same amount of intellectual effort. So we seek entertainment to avoid boredom, to relax, to divert our attention from day-to-day problems, and sometimes —almost by coincidence—to invite intellectual stimulation.

Although when the subject of entertainment comes up, we first think of TV and movies, it's obvious that we are also entertained by books, magazines, and newspapers. Indeed, it's impossible to draw a sharp line between the media as dispensers of news-information and as purveyors of entertainment.

THE TREND TOWARD CONGLOMERATES

A fairly new cause for concern about the media is the trend toward conglomerate ownership. The monopoly newspaper, which publishes without face-to-face competition in its own city, is now often owned by a chain. Half of the 1,750 dailies are owned by 157 chains, which control almost 60 percent of all newspaper circulation in the nation. The accelerated trend toward chain ownership has been complicated by the movement in the sixties toward corporation conglomerates. Eighty-two newspapers own local TV stations and 216 own local radio stations. Radio Corporation of America (RCA), which owns NBC-TV and NBC-radio, and CBS have both bought book publishing houses, and all three networks have worked out interlocking arrangements with movie studios.

Thus, for all the diversity of their offerings, mass media are big business. Many industry critics insist that this fact combines with the essentially commercial nature of the media to put the "free marketplace of ideas" in jeopardy and to debase the media's cultural products.

Of the six media, book publishing is the only one that does not rely on advertising for the bulk of its income. For the TV industry four-fifths of the income is provided by only one hundred giant advertisers, the major corporations which so dominate the national landscape.

However, it does not necessarily follow that the corporations determine the policies of television or any other medium. The journalist or director working in the media makes his decisions to raise or lower the gates on news or ideas, pictures or sounds on the basis of his own professional judgments. He knows that what he offers must, in the end, satisfy the audience, or they will buy a different paper, turn the dial, or purchase tickets elsewhere. In short, he must pay at least as much attention to his audience as to his boss. His boss, in turn, knows that advertisers have a limited number of channels through which to peddle their wares.

As the essays in this book will show, the interplay between the media and their audiences is highly complicated. They will also suggest that there are contradictory tendencies to both overstate and underestimate the influences of the media. These tendencies can perhaps best be summed up in the "model or mirror" debate.

MEDIA: MODELS OR MIRRORS?

Walter Lippmann, the great columnist, wrote in his classic *Public Opinion* (1922) that the mass media "put pictures in our heads—pictures which are representations of the real world," near and far. Lippmann said the pseudo-environment thus created for us by the media consists of a series of man-made fictions which are trustworthy pictures of the world—more or less. What we believe, do, and think all depend on the pictures in our heads.

If we look at the media as pseudo-environment, we see them acting as agencies of social control. The whole communication system, then, becomes an institution which can act either as a mirror of the values and beliefs of society or as a model aimed at changing those values and beliefs. Some analysts have called the model approach the "engineering of consent" and charged that manipulators both inside and outside the media constantly try to change the pictures in our heads to suit their special interests.

The mirror view admits that we all depend heavily on media for information and guidance. But it goes on to contend that media effectiveness springs mainly from the fact that we *already* agree among ourselves as to our basic values and beliefs. The social process, according to this view, prepares the way for the media to operate. And in this process, the most important influences on our values, attitudes, and behavior—far more important than the media—are the small, primary groups to which we all belong—family, friends, church, and the like.

Regardless of whether the pictures put into our heads by the media exercise control over our behavior, values, or beliefs, they *do* give us a large part of our total picture of the world. Without them, each of us would live in a far smaller world, circumscribed by what we ourselves have seen or what friends, relatives, teachers, and others have told us directly.

The News
Media

PART ONE

Critics and Defenders

Introduction

Americans seem to have developed a love-hate relationship with their mass media in recent years. They accept the products of the media eagerly, consuming quantities of print, pictures, and sound. Yet many— perhaps most—Americans are skeptical, suspicious, and nervous about the possibility that tricks are being played on them.

Their suspicion may mean that the average reader, watcher, and listener has become more media-wise than he used to be. His wisdom seems to include the ability to make certain assumptions about the media: for example, that advertising and political oratory contain exaggerations, that TV and radio personalities and ad copy writers often adopt a phony tone of intimacy, and that TV emcees are often insincere. Most audience members seem aware that the media contain a degree of built-in theatrics, or make-believe. However, the growing credibility gap, especially in relation to news, cannot be brushed off by the easy explanation that receivers of bad news always tend toward hasty anger at the bearer, forgetting that he didn't make the news.

Not so many years ago the press shrugged off such attacks, for its honesty was rarely questioned and it dominated the news field. But in recent years its leaders have become deeply concerned about the criticisms, for many reasons. Newspapers are feeling the pinch of sharp competition from newsmagazines, radio, television, and now cable TV. A Roper poll in 1971 found 60 percent of Americans getting "most" of their news from television, while 48 percent of those polled said they got most from newspapers. The same poll showed that if television and newspapers offered conflicting or differing reports on the same story, 49 percent would be "most inclined to believe" the TV version and only 20 percent the press version. Newspaper advertising volume has continued to climb despite competition from other media, but circulation has not kept pace.

The term "credibility gap" was first applied to the Johnson Administration as suspicion grew about Vietnam war information. More recently the uncomplimentary "gap" term has been applied to the press. Result: news-

11

paper leaders are now seeking ways of demonstrating to the public that they take their responsibilities seriously.

The code of ethics is a device many industries have adopted to protect themselves against charges of irresponsibility. Such a code, called the Canons of Journalism, was adopted in 1923 by the American Society of Newspaper Editors. But the Canons provide no machinery for monitoring press performance or for disciplining those who break its rules of ethical practice.

The press council monitoring idea may offer one solution to the image dilemma faced by newspapers. The publishers brushed off the council idea when it was proposed in 1947 by the Commission on Freedom of the Press, which had conducted a ponderous study of the media under a grant from Henry Luce, publisher of *Time*. But now there is widespread discussion of plans for both local (or regional) and national press councils, possibly modeled after those that have worked for years in England and Sweden. Several local press councils have been tried experimentally in the midwest and on the west coast. At its 1971 meeting, the prestigious American Society of Newspaper Editors assigned its ethics committee to explore press council "dry runs."

The growing momentum of the movement toward local and national press councils to monitor press performance is apparently a way of saying, "We don't want the government to police us, and the public doesn't either, but we recognize the need for policing."

Several Presidential commissions in recent years have underscored the importance—and dangers—of the mass media in a culture undergoing such explosive changes as ours. The Warren Commission, the Kerner Commission, the Commission on Causes and Prevention of Violence, and the Commission on Obscenity and Pornography all devoted close attention to the media and their effects.

Neither the commission nor other media critics have limited their attacks to the print media. Assaults on both newspapers and television news analysts by Vice President Agnew in the late sixties and early seventies seemed to find a receptive audience among many discontented Americans. A storm of controversy arose over a CBS documentary, "The Selling of the Pentagon," in 1971, when a television team headed by Roger Mudd presented evidence that the military leadership was engaging in deliberate campaigning to influence political decisions. The tempest subsided some months later when Congress voted down a proposed contempt citation against CBS President Frank Stanton. But the fact that electronic media were regulated by a federal agency, FCC, made radio and TV newsmen feel especially vulnerable to attack.

MAX WAYS

What's Wrong with News?
It Isn't New Enough

Europe never thrilled to what happened in 1492. Columbus' return from the New World set no fast horses galloping between the great cities. No awed crowds gathered in the streets. The news seeped around so slowly that years later most Europeans probably had only a vague notion of the event. Giant leaps in communication are measured by the contrast with 1969 when a fifth of mankind saw simultaneous TV pictures of explorers walking on the moon and could hear and read lucid explanations of how the feat was accomplished along with shrewd speculation as to what it might mean for the future.

Yet today's network of news may serve the times less effectively than did the fifteenth century's. Then, 99 percent of knowledge was far from new. Basic information, basic economic and social skills, basic beliefs and values descended from parent to child. Against this static and familiar background news could be readily isolated; prodigies of nature, interventions by supernatural or political powers, the novel speculations of savants—these exceptions to the normal course were news. But now this kind of news has been outstripped by reality. The pace, breadth, and depth of twentieth-century change have dissolved the static background. Today's novelty is tomorrow's normality, doomed to be soon discarded. A high proportion of the basic information used by society is new information. The father's skill may be useless in the son's time. Even values and creeds are in flux. Where so much is new, what is news?

Journalism has not fully adjusted itself to the transformed situation. Conditioned by its own past, journalism often acts as if its main task were still to report the exceptional and dramatically different against a

"What's Wrong With News? It Isn't New Enough" is reprinted fr ⁓ *Fortune,* October 1969, with permission.

background of what everybody knows. News today can concentrate with tremendous impact on a few great stories: a moon landing, a war, a series of civil disorders. But meanwhile, outside the spotlight, other great advances in science and technology, other international tensions, other causes of social unrest are in motion. Yet today's inadequately reported trends will shape tomorrow's reality.

Again and again the twentieth century has been ambushed by crisis. Looking back from the midst of some tumult, like a race riot, or of some quietly desperate frustration, like the present condition of the cities, we are able to see how disaster might have been avoided by more timely and more effective communication. But we have not yet been able to use such hindsight as a spur to foresight.

The most biting and perilous irony of our civilization turns upon knowledge. Expanding knowledge has multiplied power, which has proliferated into the hands of millions of organizations and hundreds of millions of individuals. Now that everyone has some power to effect change, every aspect of life from economics to religion has been set in motion. But at any moment the significance of any specific change will depend in part upon knowledge of other changes that are in train. If communication lags, then the sum of all the changes will seem random and confused. Obviously, the need for better communication does not fall upon journalism alone. The present challenge to education, for instance, is even more severe. But journalism's role, less discussed than education's, is critical in a society that can no longer depend upon tradition to tell it what it is and how it operates.

Certainly news has not declined in quality. Journalists are better trained, more skillful, more serious about their work than they ever were. They have marvelous new media for reaching a larger, better educated audience, which senses its own dependence upon news. With painstaking care and admirable artistry news today brings information about this change or that one. But in actual life these specific changes are colliding and combining with one another, often in ways undreamed of by their originators—and not alertly reported in the news. A relatively simple compound—automobile plus mass prosperity—brings mass ownership of automobiles, a phenomenon that can ruin cities, alter familial relations, and demand new forms and techniques of government. Adequate news analysis of this particular compound is about fifty years overdue and not yet in sight.

When news fails to add up the permutations of change the best-informed men lack confidence that they know what's going on. Many of those who most confidently assert that they know, don't. Radicals and reactionaries both tend to ignore actual change and to derive their passionately held views from a simpler, more static society that isn't here. The noisiest debates tend to be irrelevant because their informational backgrounds are fragmentary and out of date.

Even the most powerful nation, with the highest production of new knowledge, thus becomes pervaded by a sense of its own ignorance and helplessness because it feels—correctly—that it has no adequate view of its own direction. Lack of confidence in the quality of news could be fatal in our kind of society, as it could not possibly have been in the Europe to which Columbus returned.

A FLY ON THE WALL

In the last few years there has been a noticeable public disenchantment with news media. It's true that the avidity for news increases and the prosperity of news organs continues on a long upgrade. Nevertheless, many consumers of news voice doubts that the news adds up to an accurate picture of what's going on.

The understandable public anxiety about the adequacy of news cannot by itself be counted upon to generate improvement. The public uneasiness now contributes, for instance, to pressure for greater governmental intervention in television news, an irrelevant therapy that would correct no present defects and create new ones. Nor is public criticism of print journalism more shrewdly aimed. It tends, for instance, to overestimate the distorting effect of the commercial motives of publishers, motives that today do not influence news nearly as much as they formerly did. On the other hand, the public underestimates both the objective difficulty of telling today's news and certain rigidities that are deeply embedded in the craft of journalism itself, as distinguished from the commercial context in which most of it operates. . . .

Journalism has been almost silent about its own performance and its own problems. The pretense that it is an unseen witness, a mere fly on history's wall, becomes less and less plausible as the role of news expands. From the demonstrator on the street to the President of the United States the behavior of the actors in the news is affected by journalism. All the subjects of news tend to conform to journalism's standards of what is reportable. . . .

STRANGERS AND BROTHERS

"Journalism" is used here in a broad sense encompassing newspapers, newsmagazines, radio and television newscasts or "documentaries," press services, trade magazines, corporate house organs, labor-union periodicals—in short, the enormous variety of publications that describe or comment upon the current scene or some segment of it. Along with education and the arts, journalism is one of the three great information systems that account for the bulk of "the knowledge industry," the most rapidly expanding part of every advanced society.

One reason why journalism expands is the amazing diversity of contemporary society. All the nonsense about regimentation to the contrary, there has never been a time when men varied so much in their work, pleasures, beliefs, values, and styles of life. In part, this growing diversity in life is a reflection of the specialization in knowledge and in education. To be "an educated man" no longer denotes participation in a common, circumscribed body of knowledge. Though the total of extant knowledge has multiplied many times, that part of it which "everybody knows" has increased much more slowly. Society cannot afford to imitate the university, where communication between departments is either perfunctory or non-existent. Outside the university, the world becomes smaller in terms of interdependence while it becomes larger in terms of the difficulty of communicating between heterogeneous groups and diverse individuals. Every year we become more like strangers—and more like brothers.

To deal with this difficulty, contemporary journalism has developed along a scale that ranges from publications addressed to as few as a thousand readers up to television and magazine audiences ranging around fifty million. Even in a highly specialized scientific journal some subscribers will have difficulty comprehending an article by a colleague who, in pursuit of the scientific goal of precision, may be developing a different vocabulary to express new concepts. The practitioners of each subspecialty also need to know what's going on in the nearest subspecialty, and beyond that one ad infinitum. As the circles widen, the communication difficulty increases.

Fortune, for instance, works in the intermediate range of the scale. Its subject, business, is a valid unit in the sense that its parts are interdependent and have many patterns, practices, problems, and interests in common. A fantastic variety is embraced within this unity. It's a far cry, apparently, from Manhattan's garment trade to the research scientists who developed the laser and the high-technology industries which first used it outside the laboratories. Yet the men on Seventh Avenue needed to be promptly and effectively informed about so fundamental an invention; lasers for cutting fabrics are already in commercial development. To convey such information requires bridging huge gaps between different kinds of information, different habits of mind.

Today every public question—national defense, water pollution, educational policy—involves highly specialized kinds of knowledge. The citizen cannot be adequately informed unless his education and, later, his journalism, give him some access to that essential part of a public question that lies outside his own immediate sphere of interest and competence.

Equally daunting is the journalistic difficulty that arises out of the way contemporary change originates. In a totally planned society (if one were possible) journalism's job would be to focus on the planning authority, reporting its decisions; the sum of these would be the sum of change. But not even the Soviet Union, rigidly authoritarian in theory, works that way. Some shots that the planners call are never made, and new conditions, unforeseen by planners, arise spontaneously.

The dissemination of power implicit in all contemporary society defeats the fondest dreams of centralizers. In the U.S. the decisions of government, important though they are, add up to only a small fraction of the whole impetus of change. Most of the great new government policies of recent decades—social security, welfare, civil-rights programs, increased regulation of business—are secondary changes, efforts to cushion new conditions that had their primary source outside of government. Nor is there in the private sector any one source of change, any establishment of concentrated power, where journalism can find the conscious, deliberate origin of most changes that sweep us onward.

. . . Journalism still clings to the legislative act and the presidential decision because they are relatively easy to get into focus. By contrast, such gradual and multicentered changes as the loosening of parental authority or the increase of consumer credit or public acceptance of a new technology of contraception or the rising resentment of black Americans are much more difficult to pinpoint. They are not "events." They didn't happen "yesterday" or "today" or "last week." They do not fit the journalist's cherished notions of a "story."

LOSING THE THREAD

Insofar as journalism solves the problem of where to look for change, it is then confronted with another set of difficulties: the subject will be more complex, intrinsically harder to tell, than news used to be. A scientific advance, for instance, is harder to convey than an explorer's geographical discovery. . . . The discovery of deoxyribonucleic acid is, to a nonbiologist, more opaque than wondrous. Yet DNA, by unlocking secrets of genetics, may cause more social change than did the age of exploration. . . .

In the last ten or fifteen years journalism, thanks to a few very able science reporters, has made tremendous strides in the techniques of communicating to the public the major advances of pure science. A knowledgeable reporter, skilled in translating scientific languages, can sit down with the discoverer and his colleagues and seek ways to penetrate the opacity that surrounds any scientific discovery. Greater difficulty—and less journalistic success—comes when the new discovery begins to move out into use, mingling with technological, economic, psychological, and even moral factors. As a source of information to the reporter the original discoverer may not be of much use at this point. Members of other academic disciplines may not be interested or adroit in bringing their knowledge to bear on the meaning of the change. Journalism may lose the thread because the change has become complex in a way that goes beyond any academic discipline.

Journalism, for instance, has not done well with the economic and social implications of the greatest technological advance of the last twenty years—the computer, symbol of automation. Since its effects spread out to every part of society, everybody needs to know quite a lot about the computer. In the Fifties, when computers and other devices for automating work were coming in, there was an almost hysterical belief that they would sharply increase unemployment. Thousands of economists and social historians were in a position to know better. They not only failed to reach the general public with a more realistic view of automation's impact on employment, they did not even get the message to the rest of the academic community. Even though U.S. employment has increased 36 percent since 1950, millions of people, including many of the best educated, are still walking around with bad cases of computerphobia.

In 1965, Charles E. Silberman, an economist and journalist, undertook in *Fortune* a careful analysis of the actual and probable future effects of computers on the number and kinds of jobs. It would have been possible —though admittedly difficult—to parallel Silberman's explanation at levels of mass-circulation journalism. Newspapers and television have made little effort to explain the economic and social meaning of the computer. Such a subject simply does not fit their working definitions of news. But if in the years ahead there occurs, for some reason unconnected with computers, a sharp and prolonged rise in unemployment, then the press will feel obliged to carry the mouthings of any demagogue who blames computers for the shortage of jobs. A lot of Americans would fall for this because education and journalism, between them, are not getting over to the public enough timely information about the significance of this sort of change.

THE INVISIBLE AMERICANS

In recent decades journalism has missed changes more important and more complex than the effect of the computer. From the end of the post-

Civil War Reconstruction period to the mid-Fifties, American journalism was virtually silent on the subject of how black Americans lived. Lynchings were reported and deplored, as were race riots and the more sensational crimes committed by blacks against whites. But crimes by blacks against blacks were regularly ignored as a matter of explicit news policy on most newspapers. This was symptomatic of an implicit journalistic assumption that blacks were not a significant part of the American scene. Journalism bears a considerable share of responsibility for white society's disengagement from the Negro and his problems. . . .

In the last few years journalism has been widely denounced for giving undue attention to extreme black militants and to civil disorders arising from racial tension. . . . Black militancy found a way to pass the gate of news standards. In the light of the urban riots and fires, newsmen, especially those with TV cameras, suddenly found blacks eminently reportable.

The contrast in news between the past invisibility of blacks as people and the recent hypervisibility of black militants brings us to certain characteristics inherent in the craft of journalism. . . . Why is journalism still so wrapped up in the deadline, the scoop, the gee-whiz—and so seemingly unable to notice that most of what is new will not fit into a narrative pattern of what happened in the last twenty-four hours?

"The story," and all the bang-bang that went with it, used to be the way "to sell papers" in the days when newsboys crying "Extra" formed the sales force of the press. The business need for this kind of razzle-dazzle has disappeared. The editorial reason for it has diminished to the vanishing point. Yet much of journalism still operates as if its circulation and its usefulness depended on the second hand of the clock rather than the depth of its perception, the accuracy of its report, the relevance of its coverage, and the balance of its judgment.

To understand why news is trapped in its own past, journalism must be looked at in relation to the third great system of social communication mentioned above, the arts. Though most journalists are loath to admit it, what they practice is an art—crude and unbeautiful, but nevertheless an art. Even in the fine arts, where individual originality lies close to the heart of excellence, nearly all artists are influenced by traditions, canons, "schools." Descending the ladder of art toward craftsmanship, originality and novelty become less prominent and tradition becomes stronger. The artifact is acceptable because its design is more or less familiar. This may be especially true of the verbal arts of our day. Language is, after all, a huge network of conventional meanings, a heritage. In slow-moving societies language may have changed as rapidly as the realities it described. In our day, language may be a "conservative" element, lagging behind social change, forcing us to perceive today in terms of the past.

THE ARTISTIC BIAS

The sublanguages of the sciences and other highly specialized activities do change rapidly. But most journalism cannot use these terms because it must transmit information outside the specialized group. In his overriding desire to communicate efficiently, the journalist tends unconsciously to be ruled by precedent in his choice of subject and in the form of presentation. That which is familiar can be communicated more easily than that which is really new. The simple subject is more communicable than the complex. Dramatic conflict, especially when it can be reduced to two sides, is a well established form of communication.

Thus journalism in our time has what might be called a formal bias that causes news to distort reality. Preference for "the story" that journalism *knows* can be communicated leads it to neglect the changes that need to be told but do not fit the standards of familiarity, simplicity, drama. This artistic bias has nothing to do with the ideology or partisanship of the journalist himself. He may take sides concerning the substance of a news story, but such substantive bias will often be overridden by his formal bias. A journalist who sees a story that is attractive—artistically speaking —will tell it even if it runs contrary to his political prejudices, hurts the interests of his friends, and brings sorrow to his mother's heart. This laudable independence exacts, however, a heavy price: if the artistic standards by which the story is selected and shaped are themselves out of phase with reality the consequent distortion may be greater than that produced by a journalist's substantive bias toward one "side" of an issue.

Probably most journalists who handled news produced by the late Senator Joe McCarthy opposed the substance of what he was doing. But McCarthy got enormous attention in the press before he had a large popular following because he played up to the journalistic desire for simplification and dramatization, and had a keen sense of that seven o'clock deadline. On the other hand, most journalists who dealt with John Gardner probably approved of the substance of his influence on public affairs. Yet Gardner, who was Secretary of Health, Education, and Welfare during a critical period, never became a vivid figure in the news. He tended to see life "in the round." Though he recognized the puzzles and problems that engulf government today, he tackled them with an energy derived from a sense of modern society's immense material, intellectual, and moral resources. He did not cast himself as St. George versus the Dragon. He was out of touch with news precisely because he was in touch with contemporary social reality. Gardner's name would have become familiar to every American if, after resigning his post, he had gone along with newsmen who importuned him to launch a series of public attacks on President Johnson.

Ideology and extreme partisanship attract the attention of journalists who are not themselves ideologues or partisans. If news can be simplified into a framework of Cold War or of black extremists against white extremists or of poor against rich, journalists as communicators will be happy although as men and citizens they—along with everybody else— will be depressed at the picture they paint.

BOTH LOCAL AND NATIONAL

In terms of this general view of contemporary journalism's mission, its external difficulties and its internal inhibitions, let us briefly examine some specific media, starting (as a journalistic canon requires) with the most familiar.

Daily newspapers in general do not present an inspiring spectacle of vigorous effort to meet the challenge of change. Most of them go on emphasizing specific events—a crime, an accident, a resolution of the city council—in ways not very different from the journalism of a hundred years ago. Even though crime's incidence has increased to the point where it is a substantial part of the new normality, only a few papers have made a serious effort to explain this change, more important and potentially more interesting than any single crime.

A shift of attention has occurred from local news to national and international news. On most papers this seems to take the heart out of local coverage, while leaving national and international news to the Associated Press and the United Press International, which are the least innovative, most tradition-bound of all journalistic institutions.

Few papers have discovered the category of news that is both local and national. The problems of each city are in some sense unique. Since early in the Johnson Administration, Washington has been aware that decisions made by Congress and carried out by a national Administration will be fruitless unless they are meshed with vigorous and knowledgeable local efforts. Yet each city's problems of transportation, housing, education, poverty, have a wide area of overlap with other cities' problems. The obvious need is for local reporting that will examine what's going on in Pittsburgh and San Francisco in an effort to clarify the problems of Buffalo. Communication, through journalism, between the cities and regions of the U.S. has never been so desperately needed or in worse shape. Efforts to develop a "new federalism" are handicapped by journalism's tradition-bound rigidity that sees national news as one category and local news as an entirely separate category.

The sorry condition of daily newspapers is often blamed on the trend toward local monopoly, a diagnosis that is too easy. In many cities, before mergers occurred, all the papers lacked distinction and leadership. In cities with competing papers journalism is not notably more vigorous than in the monopoly cities. Such notable smaller city papers as the Louisville *Courier-Journal*, the Cleveland *Plain Dealer*, the Minneapolis *Tribune*, and the Charlotte *Observer* are among the very few that really keep trying to improve service to the community.

AWAY FROM THE TRADITIONAL "STORY"

Of yesterday's best-known newspapers the Chicago *Tribune*, the St. Louis *Post-Dispatch*, the New York *Daily News* seem less relevant than they used to be. The most improved large daily (it had lots of room for improvement) is probably the Los Angeles *Times*. In recent years it has developed an ability to cover trends, as well as events, and to relate local subjects to the regional and national scenes. Its intelligent reporting of educational trends, for instance, enabled it to evince clear superiority over the San Francisco press when campus "stories" erupted in the Bay area, at Berkeley and San Francisco State. Because the Los Angeles *Times* was aware of the moving background behind the sensational campus disorders, it reported the events themselves with a far steadier hand than the San Francisco papers.

Two national dailies, the *Christian Science Monitor* and the *Wall Street Journal*, have largely freed themselves from the tyranny of "the story" as traditionally defined. The *Monitor's* interpretive articles are, in fact, more timely than many a front page sprinkled with the words "yesterday" and "today." The *Wall Street Journal's* two leading front-page articles add up in the course of a year to a better report of what's going on than all the bulletins of the wire services. "Kelly Street Blues," a four-part series on a block in a New York ghetto, put together a mosaic of detail that helps one part of society, the W.S.J.'s readers, understand how a very different part lives. Neil Ulman's roundup of protests across the nation against sex education in the schools was an example of the kind of report that conventional newspapers miss. The W.S.J.'s foreign news can discuss basically interesting subjects, such as how Soviet citizens can invest their savings or anti-Franco trends in Spain, that are not pegged to any events.

A long way from the *Wall Street Journal* lies the "underground press" that has sprung up in recent years. Its chief significance is to demonstrate that, economically, the proliferation of many publications is now feasible. Unhappily, it cannot be said that the underground press displays much innovative muscle. Its ideology seems moored in nineteenth-century anarchism, and from that viewpoint it can dislike whatever the "straight" press likes. But that hardly helps the job of reducing the lag between journalism and reality. The underground papers are as similar, one to another, as the square papers. An admittedly incomplete survey of underground papers indicates that none of them has invented a new four-letter word.

In a class by itself stands that most aboveground of American newspapers, the New York *Times*. Its influence is by no means confined to its readers. Most journalists, including broadcasters, start their day with it and each journalist assumes that the others have read the *Times* attentively. In the important matter of day-to-day decisions on which stories deserve top play, the *Times* is the greatest single national influence. Its preeminence goes back a long way and it is still steeped in conventional news judgment and traditional journalistic forms. Nevertheless, in recent years the *Times* has produced more and more innovative journalism. Its development of daily biographical sketches of figures in the news abandons the old elitist assumption that everybody knows who these people are. The new managing editor, A. M. Rosenthal, is among those chiefly responsible for an emphasis on "in depth" reporting that breaks away from yesterday's developments. A landmark of this genre was Anthony Lukas' 5,000-word account of a suburban girl who had been found murdered in an East Greenwich Village basement; Lukas' detailed narrative transformed an incomprehensible horror into a memorable insight into the shifting values and life patterns that touch even the most seemingly secure homes. In August, when 300,000 youngsters suddenly converged on Bethel, New York, to hear rock music, the *Times* reports, departing from the conventional emphasis on the disorderly aspects of the scene, made a real effort to understand what had drawn the kids there, what they got out of it, what their values were.

Because of the *Times'* immense influence on journalism that paper's recent willingness to break out of conventional molds is one of the most hopeful signs of long-range improvement of the press. But it may be years before most papers follow such pioneering. They haven't the reporting staffs to do so. Bright, concerned young men and women are loath to go to work for papers that are clearly not alive, not relevant to the great changes and stresses that are sweeping through society.

BROADENING THE SCOPE OF NEWS

Newspapers have been slow to adjust to the liveliness of good TV reportage and the broad-spectrum coverage of newsmagazines.

From its beginning the great distinction of *Time*, the weekly newsmagazine, was not the much-parodied sentence structure of its early years but its broadened concept of news. For example, it looked at religion as a moving part of the total scene. No future historian of the twentieth century's middle decades could possibly omit from an account of the total change the tremendous shifts of religious and ethical belief that color contemporary life. Yet most conventional newspaper journalism still virtually ignores such subjects, except when they surface as dramatic confrontations. The newsmagazines continue to broaden the concept of news. *Newsweek* has added departments on "Life and Leisure" and "The Cities." *Time*'s recent addition of "Behavior" and "Environment" treats other areas that the older journalism assumed to be static. The departmentalization of news itself is more than an orderly convenience for the reader. The departmental structure forces editors to look where they know news ought to be, rather than passively waiting for news to "flow" at them—an attitude that results in today's news being defined as whatever is most like yesterday's news.

All journalism has something to learn from the pioneers of a new journalism of ideas. The quarterly *Daedalus,* under the sensitive editorship of Stephen Graubard, has reached an impressive circulation of 70,000; it provides for a highly educated readership a forum where voices from many disciplines converge in each issue upon a single subject. *The Public Interest,* another quarterly, edited by Daniel Bell and Irving Kristol, is less formidably academic in style, more directly attuned to current problems. One of the most extraordinary publications is the *Kaiser Aluminum News*, whose editor, Don Fabun, delights in translating, primarily for the company's employees, the most difficult contemporary thought into lucid, poetic words and pictures. Fabun never runs a conventional "audience-building story"; and yet the demand for his magazine continues to build because people are fascinated by what he has to say.

Not one of these magazines pursues an ideological shortcut. All are basically periodicals of explanation. They work on the assumption that relevant truths about contemporary society are difficult—but not impossible—to convey.

THE SPECIAL BIAS OF TV

At the other end of the spectrum lies television journalism with its mass audience. Most of its faults have descended from print journalism; it multiplied its inheritance while finding some distortive formal biases of its own. The artistic bias inherent in the TV medium affects the behavior of the actors in the news. The "demonstration" becomes a dominant form of social action rather than the petition, the political debate, the lawsuit. Other media are drawn toward covering, as best they can, the disorderly scenes that television covers so superlatively. There have been months when a consumer of news might wonder whether anything except demonstrations was going on in the U.S. . . .

Television is exerting another, more indirect, bias upon news. The generation now of college age is the first that was introduced to news through a medium mainly devoted to dramatized entertainment. The drama is usually highly simplified and one side is morally right, the other wrong. The young viewer expects the news to fall into the same dramatic pattern. It is not surprising if he later becomes a recruit to the new anti-intellectualism apparent in the impatience of campus protesters who regard complex facts as distractions from the "gut commitment," which they hold to be a morally superior approach to public questions. Public expectation of moralistic drama presses all media toward defining news in terms of simple conflict. But what the public needs to know may lie in just the opposite direction. Society's ability to avoid ambush may depend on receiving information before the dramatic conflict develops.

Yet some of the most hopeful signs of tomorrow's journalism are also to be found in television. It has an incomparable ability to convey the integrated *quality* of a personality or of a social situation. Eric Hoffer unobtrusively interviewed by Eric Sevareid was an experience in communication that print journalism could hardly match. C.B.S. also recently did a "documentary" (that blighting word) on Japan as interpreted by former Ambassador Edwin Reischauer, which told more people more about the subject than millions of printed words, including Reischauer's own fine books. . . .

Such examples compel the conclusion that television has a great constructive role to play in the journalism of the future. . . .

That poverty in America should have been "discovered" in 1962 by Michael Harrington, an impassioned polemicist, is proof that journalism was not fulfilling its mission. Where were the journalists in the years when Ralph Nader was working on *Unsafe at Any Speed,* an exaggerated indictment of auto manufacturers that is now generally conceded to contain a lot of truth about a matter of universal interest? Nader lately has broadened his attack to other products and services where the buying public is ill-protected and ill-informed. He and Harrington both tend toward governmental remedies for the ills they identify. But the informational problem is more fundamental than the political issue. If society doesn't know about poverty it cannot deal with it governmentally or otherwise; if the consuming public doesn't know enough about what it's buying it cannot protect itself, governmentally or otherwise. The way to defend the market system is to be sure that information, an essential ingredient of any healthy market or any healthy democracy, is adequate.

IT'S UP TO THE NEWSMEN

It ought to be plain, but seemingly it is not, that the quality of journalism depends primarily on journalists—not on government and not on the legal owners of media. Publishers and executives of networks and broadcasting stations now have only a small fraction of the influence on news that owners used to exercise. As commercial bias diminishes, what counts now, for better or worse, is the bias of reporters, cameramen, editors. Their ideological bent is far less important than their artistic bias, the way they select and present what they regard as significant.

Journalism will always need artistry to reach the public's mind and heart. Indeed, what is now required is a higher level of art, a boldness that will get journalism unstuck from forms of communication developed in and for a social context very different from the present. Nobody except journalists can develop such forms. All the public can do is to be wary of existing distortions and appreciative of such efforts as appear to get closer to the current truth.

NORMAN E. ISAACS

Why We Need Press Councils

Behind the drive for a nationwide ethics/
grievance committee: how it began, why it is
resisted, why publishers ultimately may have to
accept it.

For me, it all began with the stress on "good news" in the worrisome, penny-pinching days of the Great Depression. As a young, still untutored reporter in Indianapolis I found it hard to understand why stories about job layoffs should be relegated to short spaces inside the newspaper and why any prediction by any business spokesman about better things to come was almost certain to appear on page 1. As I learned more about newspaper shortcomings and oversights, I swiftly became aware that concerns about newspaper performance were being expressed in many places. It was infuriatingly common to hear the line, "You can't believe what you read in the newspapers."

I also learned a bit about publishers. Young newsmen of that era were impressed and fretful about the surging growth of radio and of *Time* magazine, which had been launched in 1923 by two twenty-four-year-old newspapermen, Briton Hadden and Henry Luce. But the publishers and editors were scornful of these intruders. We young reporters felt humiliated in 1935 when the American Newspaper Publishers Association bitterly opposed the proposed Child Labor Amendment. The publishers wanted laissez-faire for themselves in the use of youngsters to deliver

Norman E. Isaacs, longtime Louisville *Courier-Journal* and *Times* editor, is a recent president of the American Society of Newspaper Editors and Editor in Residence at the Columbia Graduate School of Journalism. "Why We Need Press Councils," originally titled "Why We Lack A National Press Council," is reprinted from *Columbia Journalism Review,* Fall, 1970, with permission.

newspapers and they had not the slightest hesitancy about falling back on the First Amendment. There was also what we considered disgraceful opposition to the Wages-Hours Act in its applications to newspapers; there was long and tendentious argument before a compromise was reached, fixing newspaper executive salaries at $36.

Hence it was little wonder that we perked up in early 1943 when it was announced that Henry Luce had given $200,000 and *Encyclopaedia Britannica* $15,000 for a study into the state of the press and the prospects for its continued freedom. We were buoyed also by the fact the study would be run by Robert M. Hutchins, the lively chancellor of the University of Chicago. We turned resentful later when it was disclosed that Dr. Hutchins had named to the Commission on Freedom of the Press only scholars and had failed to choose even one journalist.

We should have had enough sense, of course, to recognize the capacities of men like Zechariah Chafee of Harvard; John M. Clark of Columbia; Harold Lasswell of Yale; Archibald MacLeish, who was not only a poet of distinction but had served as an Assistant Secretary of State; Reinhold Niebuhr of the Union Theological Seminary; Beardsley Ruml, then chairman of the Federal Reserve Bank in New York; and the senior Arthur Schlesinger of Harvard. Whatever suspicions I had nurtured vanished the moment I read "A Free and Responsible Press," the Hutchins report, in 1947. I was tremendously impressed and moved.

My publisher, Elzey Roberts, was outraged by the report. Even though his St. Louis *Star-Times* was one of the few liberal newspapers in the country, Roberts' visceral reaction was like that of at least 95 percent of his fellow publishers. Up to then, Hutchins had been one of the most influential and effective of citizens; within a year his public standing had been shredded by the distortions of editorial vilification.

What was the heinous crime of which the Commission was guilty? In essence, all it had pleaded for was a press both responsible and accountable. It felt that freedom of the press, while not in immediate peril, was endangered in the long run by the growing crisis in society. The Commission appealed for a moral approach to journalism, saying, "There is a point beyond which failure to realize the moral right will entail encroachment by the state on the existing legal right." While it cast aspersions on the economic structure of communications, the Commission's great sin was in recommending the establishment "of a new and independent agency to appraise and report annually upon the performace of the press." It was a sweeping concept.

Even now—twenty-three years later—people like me who applauded the report feel that the Commission went too far in the task it envisioned for the new agency, which was to be independent of both press and government. It was fine in stipulating that the new body "help the press define workable standards of performance," it was farsighted in wanting "inquiries in areas where minority groups are excluded from reasonable access to the channels of communication," it proposed to serve journalism better in conducting "a continuous appraisal of governmental action affecting communications," it was in proper but risky territory in advocating the investigating of instances of "press lying, with particular reference to persistent misrepresentation of the data required for judging public issues." But the Commission clearly strayed afield when it looked ahead to seeking ways of "supplying service where it is lacking or to provide alternative service where the drift toward monopoly seems dangerous." Unfortunately, because of the fury of the publishers, the nobly worded constructive portions of the report were foredoomed to join the frivolous segments on shelves reserved for small, unobtrusive reference books.

But the need remained for some kind of agency to appraise press performance, or at least to consider grievances against it. For a yawning credibility gap was widening year by year. Less than twelve months after the Hutchins report, for example, there was widespread disillusionment about coverage of the Truman-Dewey campaign. The denouement of that race, of course, was the photograph of the beaming Harry Truman holding aloft an early edition of the Chicago *Tribune* reporting Thomas Dewey's "victory." To its vast embarrassment, the great preponderance of the country's press simply had refused to believe—and report—what its reporters were seeing and hearing: that the "silent majority" of that day were following Truman's campaign and turning out for him. (During the campaign, when a top Kansas City political reporter incredulously told St. Louis colleagues that the "Boot Heel" part of Missouri was Truman country and he was urged to write it, he replied, "My God, no. I'd be laughed out of the state.")

Retrospective unhappiness over 1948, however, turned to professional anger in the 1952 campaign. Adlai Stevenson made his bitter comment about a "one-party press." There were evidences of gross slanting in news columns. The anger surfaced at the 1953 national convention of Sigma Delta Chi. There Irving Dilliard, editor of the editorial page of the St. Louis *Post-Dispatch,* who had been making challenging speeches around the country about one-sidedness, showed as one of his most telling exhibits a copy of the Indianapolis *News'* page 1, made up as a billboard for an appearance by General Eisenhower in that city. The society voted for an investigation of the press' conduct. I was not at the convention, nor did I take part in the public debates. But I was chosen to head the SDX Ethics Committee charged with conducting the examination.

The assignment was not unwelcome. Since 1947, mainly through the Associated Press Managing Editors Association and to lesser degree within the American Society of Newspaper Editors, I had been increasingly involved in the movement for self-examination by newsmen, and principally for higher ethical standards and practices.

(The issue of internal criticism had been one of the chief motivations for the reorganization of APME in 1948. Though the group had been largely a docile appendage of AP, some "young Turks" were pushing for more far-reaching activity. Among the leaders were Kenneth MacDonald of the Des Moines *Register & Tribune*, Lee Hills of the Knight Newspapers, and William P. Steven of the Minneapolis *Star & Tribune*. I had shared their ardor for "action," and quickly joined the movement. After the 1947 meeting, Kent Cooper—for a quarter of a century AP's famed general manager and executive director, who now was facing retirement against his will—advanced the idea of an independent APME. He had incorporation papers drawn up specifically barring publishers from membership, and some twenty of us were among the incorporators of APME, Inc. Out of this came a glowing decade for the "Continuing Studies," the first mass self-examination project in American journalism. They were of varying quality and importance, but they provided individual editors with the opportunity to challenge both specific story coverage and also raise questions of news policy and emphasis.)

The SDX election-coverage study turned out to be both fascinating education and a harrowing experience. What was clearly needed was some kind of intelligent method of assessing performance. It called for study by research experts. "Seed money" for this phase came from the Fund for the Republic, then associated with the Ford Foundation. Raymond B. Nixon of the University of Minnesota and Chilton R. Bush of Stanford collaborated in bringing together virtually every top academic research specialist. Out of this consultation came a moderate, though far-reaching, proposal. It was agreed that it was impossible to pass judgment on election coverage after the fact. The proposal, therefore, was for a widespread on-the-scene study of the 1956 Presidential campaign.

Safeguards were scattered all through the projected study. Editorial pages, columns, and cartoons were to be disregarded. The exploration was to involve merely basic fairness of news coverage. The difficulties of gathering information were to be weighed. Edition schedules were to be taken into account. No judgment was to be passed without direct consultation with the editors involved. The cost was estimated at $700,000.

Repeated consultation with foundation executives made it clear there was no hope of a grant unless at least a majority of the nation's publishers saw merit in the proposal. This meant selecting a list to be polled. It should come as no surprise that one can question fewer than seventy individuals and cover all the major newspaper properties in the United States, as well as many middle-size and smaller ones. After all, when one questions a chain owner, he ticks off a good many big-city dailies in one call. But there is no need to dwell on detail. Only seventeen publishers in the country voted "yes" to having their newspapers studied for fairness during the 1956 campaign. The remainder voted "no"—a number of them vehemently.

It was clear that most of those who owned American newspapers were determined to resist self-examination. I had to conclude that they would not take the slightest step without the greatest of pressures being exerted upon them.

By 1960, however, it turned out that the Sigma Delta Chi experience had not been entirely an exercise in futility. The New England Society of Newspaper Editors voted to have that fall's Presidential campaign coverage studied, and I became chairman of the special committee. Because there were almost no expense funds, it had to be a limited study. Sevellon Brown, then editor of the Providence *Journal* and *Bulletin* and NESNE president, helped as he could. My colleagues were the late Carl Lindstrom of the Hartford *Times* and Ted Rowse of the Washington *Post,* who had written the book *Slanted News.* After considerable thought, we decided to focus on the handling of two stories.

One story was about official Roman Catholic church opposition in Puerto Rico to the election bid of Governor Luiz Muñoz-Marin because of his statements on birth control. The other had to do with a reported loan to Richard Nixon's brother by Howard Hughes. Our reasoning was that if there was going to be any bias in news presentation, including overplays or underplays, it was most likely to show up in these two stories. We thought the first story more likely to capture attention because of the heavy Roman Catholic population in New England and the past attention to birth control, plus the fact Senator Kennedy was a Catholic. The other story stemmed from a Drew Pearson column implying possible future favoritism for Hughes, who was involved in several cases with the Government. AP and UPI had picked up the story, and we felt its handling might disclose bias.

The result startled us. The election coverage in New England newspapers—with only two exceptions—was casual, erratic, and at times incomprehensible. Our report concluded that the general performance had been "so slapdash as to give an impression of bias," even though we could pinpoint none. It was an indictment of newspapering simply on the issue of inadequate news coverage. . . .

Barry Bingham was trying to do something more when he appeared before Sigma Delta Chi in Norfolk in 1963 and proposed the creation of local press councils. He had thought it out carefully and listed the ingredients he thought a council should contain. These included a representative group of a community's citizens, but specifically excluded government officials or political spokesmen of any party. In its purest sense, he was urging local grievance committees which could accept public complaint against the newspapers, study them, ask the editors questions if they so desired, and issue reports on press performance when and if they wished. We tried everything we could at the time to induce Louisville citizens to move on the suggestion. None was so inclined, and we were unwilling to sponsor one on our own, believing that this would properly be considered window-dressing.

The seed did not fall entirely on barren ground. Ben Bagdikian had become president of the Mellett Fund. This consisted of stock left to the American Newspaper Guild by Lowell Mellett of the Washington *Daily News* to "stimulate responsibility in the press while maintaining freedom." It seemed to Bagdikian that local press councils offered just such an opportunity. In 1967 the Mellett Fund offered financing through university sources for press councils in four smaller cities: Bend, Ore.; Redwood City, Calif.; and Sparta and Cairo, Ill.

The Cairo experiment was the only outright failure. "The trouble there," says Bagdikian, who now is national editor of the Washington *Post*, "was that the community's whites wouldn't even sit down to talk with the blacks." The other three turned out to be less than press councils, but nevertheless highly successful. They opened communication between the editors and the citizens on a regular face-to-face basis. Redwood City's effort ran smoothly, but has now been discontinued. Bend, where the *Bulletin* is a daily, and Sparta, which has a weekly newspaper, continue because the publishers in those cities like the idea of informal monthly meetings for frank discussions.

Based on the success in the three smaller cities, the Mellett Fund stretched the move to two major centers, Seattle and St. Louis. Both of these called for a university professor to serve as chairman, to seek systematic examination of facets of news coverage, and to reach out into community problems. The St. Louis experiment is moribund. Only one newspaper was sufficiently interested to take part, and the project itself, Bagdikian reports, was "too unstructured." The Fund learned a lot from the experience, he says.

Seattle is a different story. Henry McLeod, managing editor of the Seattle *Times*, calls it "immensely useful." The Seattle council has been a movement tapping the Negro community. After a few bristling sessions about the newspapers and TV and radio stations in Seattle, the meetings have become educationally beneficial for both sides. There has been examination of the handling of trials in Seattle, and some regular testing of community attitudes. "I do believe," says Bagdikian, "that the existence of the Seattle council has avoided serious trouble for that city." Reports of the editors and the electronic journalists seem to bear this out.

For some months, Philip Geyelin, editorial page editor of the Washington *Post*, has published informative editorial comment on misplays within the communication field, heading these FYI. Now the *Post* has moved further with the appointment of an assistant managing editor in charge of oversight, and some of the early results are encouraging. A yearlong feud between the Honolulu *Star-Bulletin* and the city administration came to an end early this year when a Honolulu media council came into being, under the chairmanship of Dr. Harland Cleveland, president of the University of Hawaii. . . .

Publishers and editors around the United States, however, paid scant attention to these experiments or to the Louisville newspapers' appointing an ombudsman to receive complaints on news coverage. It has been business-as-usual for the press, even though it has been increasingly obvious that the tinder pile has been growing more rapidly. Joseph McCarthy and Governor George Wallace tried putting the match to it, but it didn't burst into flames. There is now some reason to believe they left it smouldering, ready for Vice President Agnew to ignite it.

If the polls are correct—and I do not challenge them—journalism cannot continue to sweep the idea under the rug. One fairly recent Gallup Poll reported that only 37 percent of the public feels newspapers deal fairly on political and social issues. Some 45 percent think newspapers unfair. Listed as not sure were 18 percent. It is significant that the more highly educated the person questioned, the stronger the feeling that newspapers are unfair.

Vice President Agnew has capitalized on serious weaknesses in journalism. (And it is notable that much of Agnew's editorial backing comes from newspapers whose owners and editors are bitterly opposed to any thought of self-examination.) I considered and still consider the Agnew attacks a form of intimidation of the press. Though his more recent approaches stress "sensible authority," it is not inconceivable that a drive for "sensible authority" could be stretched to the creation of an overview agency by government ostensibly to preserve and protect the First Amendment freedoms. Far better, I hold, for the press to create its own protections.

Our troubles in 1968 began well before the Democratic convention. Pierre Salinger had screamed "foul" to ASNE over the Indianapolis *Star's* carving on a New York *Times* editorial to serve its anti-Kennedy purpose. Salinger sent a wire on a Sunday demanding instant investigation and a public report before Tuesday's primary. Vincent S. Jones, ASNE president, rejected Salinger's thrust as a political ploy. But Jones thought it bad journalism and made clear to associates he would have put the matter to the Board if Salinger had invoked the ASNE Code of Ethics. In mid-May Salinger sent Jones a more thoughtful letter, saying:

> [If] ASNE is unwilling to look into the practices of its own members, then who will? Certainly, you would be among the first to admit that the government cannot do this, and that it has to be done by the industry itself.

Chicago was in the offing. That story needs no replaying here. What does bear repeating is the response of the public to what it saw on its TV screens and read in its newspapers—the flood of protests all adding up to the fact people did not believe what they were seeing and hearing.

I believe it fair to question whether we of journalism hadn't been inviting this kind of public response. Each time wise, thoughtful men had asked us as a profession to look into our standards and our practices we had taken refuge in the First Amendment. At various times some of us had challenged publishers' concepts of that Amendment. We had held that it had been written to protect the free expression of opinion, that under it the patriots of early America had created their own underground press. There was nothing in the First Amendment, we had said, that gave a man with a printing press the right to exert a stranglehold on a community's lifeline of information. The press had ignored university poll reports of years ago that showed teen-agers believing that newspapers ought to be under firmer control. We needed to be rebuilding faith in the American press; the shrugging off of inaccuracy and slanting in news columns was the most dangerous course we could follow. An ethics or grievance committee—or, if you will, a press council—seemed to be an effective way to deal with the situation.

What might a grievance committee or press council, under proper auspices, be constituted to do, and how might it do it? Those of us who have been studying the issue believe it should be set up to consider and pass upon serious complaints charging deliberate distortions, unfairness, or grossly inadequate or misleading coverage of news. Clearly, a first requirement ought to be that a complainant must have sought redress and failed to get it from the newspaper. The system of a complainant's waiving the right to use Council findings in a libel suit has been so successfully used by the British Press Council that this concept ought to be adapted to our own uses. There might be panels of editors set up around the country to assess complaints in their regions. All of the discussions have emphasized that there should not be any enforcement powers; that all that is necessary is the expression of approval or disapproval. At the outset, such an agency could well expect a flood of complaints of little or no substance. These can be promptly disallowed or screened out, as has been the case in Britain. William Dickinson of the Philadelphia *Bulletin* has predicted that within a short time there would be only a handful of cases serious enough for investigation and action.

Most of those who oppose press councils on a rational rather than emotional basis customarily raise two warnings. One is the potential impairment of an editor's freedom of action through community pressure as brought through a council. The other is that councils open the door to the licensing of journalists. Erwin Canham of the *Christian Science Monitor* has long held a dour view of licensing. He has argued that a majority given the right to pass on the credentials for a professional might easily be led to deny the right of expression to one with whom they disagreed strongly.

Earlier this year the issue was raised anew by Dr. W. Walter Menninger in a National Press Club speech. Dr. Menninger's comments arose out of his service on the Commission on Violence. Later, in a talk in his hometown, Topeka, Kan., he clarified his remarks. Concerning licensing, he said:

> The phenomenon of the eye of the beholder was dramatically demonstrated in the reactions of some members of the media to the National Press Club address, which included a suggestion of standards for journalists in the form of certification or licensure. While a number of journalists responded thoughtfully and nondefensively, many responded with defensive protestation and emphatic rejection. . . .
>
> What were the provocative comments? "A time-honored question in a free society is, Who shall guard the guards? Freedom of the press is the only guarantee of the Bill of Rights which cannot be exercised by each individual citizen. Practically speaking, this privilege can be exercised only by those in the journalistic profession. . . . In other professions with a public trust—medicine, law, education—laws for licensure and certification assure the public that the practitioner has fulfilled minimum standards, met certain requirements for training and demonstrated competence in the profession. The public is entitled to similar safeguards in the quality of the practitioners of this most important cornerstone in our democratic society, the news media."
>
> Obviously, the thought of "licensing" springs from my medical background. Thus I may have chosen the wrong word to emphasize a concern about professional standards in journalism. It is clear that certification or licensure doesn't guarantee competent performance of professionals. It does no more than assure the public that practitioners have met minimum standards. And there are undoubtedly many legal, constitutional, and procedural problems that would make certification or licensure of journalists by law well nigh impossible. Ideally the question of standards is a matter for the professional journalists to address, but the public has a right to be deeply concerned about these standards.

Dr. Menninger quite justifiably could not resist the temptation to remark about the statement by Sigma Delta Chi's professional development committee in 1966 that "the time has arrived—it is long overdue, in fact

—for the profession of journalism to establish its minimum standards, announce them to the public, and begin enforcing them." Dr. Menninger noted that the proposal had been rejected by the SDX convention and then delivered a tap on our professional Achilles' heel: "It is fascinating to note that none of the discussion of this rejection was reported in the media, despite the presence of the media and their reporting of other convention activities."

As to pressures which might be brought on editors through press councils, the opponents of such proposals often quote the eloquent J. Russell Wiggins, former executive editor of the Washington *Post*, who has said:

> The committee might become in many cities the channels through which the very worst special-interest groups would bring pressures to suppress or withhold news. They might make the collective opinion of the community irresistible at the very moment when that opinion was the most misguided and most in need of contradiction and restraint. . . . The real danger of such committees, of course, is that they might make the press even more subservient to the mores of the community and more than ever the prisoner of the Establishment.

At the risk of sounding cynical, most newsmen can swiftly point out that most middle-sized and smaller newspapers are already, to some degree, prisoners of "the establishment." Although there was a substantive degree of compassionate judgment involved, Wiggins was himself victim at one point of his newspaper's vulnerability to "establishment" pleas. One must also include as parallel victim the Washington *Star*.

This instance concerned the arrest of Walter Jenkins, President Johnson's assistant. The request for "consideration" was made to the editors of Washington's newspapers by former Supreme Court Justice Abe Fortas. The story had been confirmed by reporters in the morning. That day's editions of the *Star* contained no mention of the arrest. The *Post* published nothing of its own, nor had it moved to do so, until UPI carried a story on its wires. None of us in American journalism can claim to have been without guilt, at some point or another, of accommodating ourselves to our communities at some moment of particular stress—or, perhaps, to some individual case, poor or rich, as the episode might have been. I raise the awkward matter of the Jenkins case with full sympathy for all the editors involved simply as an honest offset for Wiggins' fears of what dangers a council might bring in the way of exerting pressures on editors.

By April, 1969, when the wheels of time had ground me into the presidency of ASNE, one of my main goals was to establish a grievance committee. Vincent Jones, vice president and executive editor of the Gannett chain and my predecessor as head of ASNE, became chairman of the small, select committee to try to work out the grievance idea. Committee

members were Barry Bingham; John S. Knight, chief of the Knight properties; Otis Chandler of the Los Angeles *Times;* the youngest of the ASNE
members, James Hoge, Jr., of the Chicago *Sun-Times;* and the present-
day sage of Great Plains journalism, William Allen White's protegé Whit-
ley Austin of the Salina *Journal.* Robert U. Brown of *Editor & Publisher*
had helped counsel in the selection of the small group, and *E & P* carried
a careful supporting editorial about the effort.

At no point in the ASNE's consideration of grievance machinery has
the subject of licensing of journalists been given the slightest consideration. Nor has the possibility of pre-publication pressure entered the picture because this was never the intent. All the effort has been the other
way: to establish a means by which a citizen or organization with a complaint of substance against a newspaper could appeal for hearing. From the
outset it has been made clear that there is not the slightest interest in the
trivia of what we might call civic-club pressures, or in the small omissions
which occur daily as a result of space pressures in daily journalism. The
thrust was summed up well in the statement by Jones when he first assumed the chairmanship in April, 1969:

> Our assignment is to ask whether the Society needs a new definition of
> purpose; whether, in keeping with the noble sentiments of the preamble of
> our constitution and the widely admired Code of Ethics, the Society should
> be able to speak firmly and clearly for the best in American journalism, to
> set standards of behavior and performance, and to function as the top
> leadership of our profession.

In the labors to find the key to unlock the door to approval by the
ASNE Board, Jones's committee went through a series of changes. The
first group (named earlier) served until a meeting in London last fall.
Knight and Chandler asked then to be relieved because of the press of
business and they were replaced by William Dickinson of the *Bulletin*
and Warren Phillips of the *Wall Street Journal.*

The London meeting was the regular fall board meeting. It was called
in England to give the members opportunity to examine the workings of
the British Press Council. Many arrangements were made by H. Philip
Levy, counsel for the International Publishing Corp. (the Mirror newspapers) and author of the definitive book *The Press Council.* A small group
of us drove far into the lovely English countryside to have a luncheon
meeting with Lord Devlin, who as chairman of the Press Council was
credited with a great deal of its success. One thing we learned at this session was of Lord Devlin's introduction of the waiver procedure, under
which the Council declined to accept any serious complaint against a
newspaper unless the complainant signed a waiver stipulating that none
of the Council's investigative findings could be used in legal action

against the newspaper. A quid pro quo was that the editor of the newspaper concerned signed a note agreeing to publish the Council's findings.

Lord Devlin was proud of what had been accomplished under the waiver, and we were to find the leading English publishers and editors agreeing thoroughly. Indeed, the statement was made several times by editors that the waiver had undoubtedly reduced the number of libel actions against newspapers. There was not the slightest doubt that the majority of British journalists were in favor of the Council's work. Indeed, in June, 1969, the *UK Press Gazette* had published a survey showing that 86 percent of newspapermen questioned thought that the spreading of the Press Council movement throughout the world desirable. . . .

Clearly, at some point a proposal is going to have to be put before American journalism. ASNE seems to me the most logical sponsor (though it could come through an organization such as the Association for Education in Journalism, which voted approval of the idea of an oversight agency). The question is, what will move ASNE? [*The ASNE Committee on Ethics has been assigned to explore the Press Council idea further.*] . . .

In the final analysis, what is called for are enough editors willing to put their jobs on the line for what it is they believe in. I know it is asking a lot. But I have done it myself on occasion and so have some others, because we happen to think that's what being an editor ought to mean.

Foreign press councils

There are more than a dozen so-called press councils around the world, most of them variants on the basic themes of upholding professional standards, serving as a type of ombudsman for public complaints, and ostensibly protecting journalistic freedoms. The oldest council is in Sweden, dating back to 1916. Last November it broadened its original scope with the addition of two public members of the board, the appointment of a press ombudsman operating under the council, and the adoption of symbolic fines.

According to Paul Frisch, secretary to the Swedish council, there are no set rules for judging press behavior. "The board considers whether the behavior of a paper has or has not been in keeping with good newspaper practice," he has reported. "The board is guided not by rules, but by what it considers a qualified opinion." He said that if the board's judgment goes against a newspaper, it would be fined 500 Swedish crowns ($100) the first time and an additional 500 crowns for each time thereafter, up to a maximum of 2,000 crowns ($400) in any one year. Frisch said no decision has yet been made on use of the money, but one suggestion is to apply it to a fund for scholarships.

The second oldest council is Switzerland's, which came into existence in 1938. These two were purely voluntary organizations launched by the press in what we can only term urbane, sophisticated countries.

Of the others, it is evident that the journalists of South Africa, West Germany, and India did not adopt their press councils willingly. South Africa's press had faced the alternative of "statutory discipline." West Germany's publishers decided the time had come when the Interior Ministry at Bonn announced its own plans for a council. India's council, patterned on the British model, is described in that country as "voluntary" —an obvious semantic ploy for an overview statutory board created by the federal parliament. Less is known about the councils in Turkey and South Korea, other than the fact both contain lay members on the boards as well as newsmen.

There are five other councils. Two are in Italy and the Netherlands. These two have nothing to do with publishers, confine their activities to the professional standards of journalists. The reverse is true in Denmark and in West Germany's magazine council. These two apply themselves only to publishers and have nothing to do with the working newsmen.

Then there is the British Press Council. It grew out of a demand for a formal inquiry into press performance by a royal commission. The demand had been made by the National Union of Journalists and, after debate in the House of Commons, a sweeping motion was adopted in 1946. It read:

> That, having regard to the increasing public concern at the growth of monopolistic tendencies in the control of the press and with the object of furthering the free expression of opinion through the press and the greatest practicable accuracy in the presentation of news this House considers that a Royal Commission should be appointed to inquire into the finance, control, management, and ownership of the press.

This first Royal Commission report was handed to Parliament in June, 1949. Many times the size of the Hutchins report, it went into specific detail about the nation's newspapers and cited many instances of inaccurate and biased coverage. At one point, the commission termed a *Daily Express* account of an important speech by U.S. Secretary of State George C. Marshall "a travesty." At another, it singled out a headline and noted, "the words in the headline do not occur (in the news account): they are an inference masquerading as quotation." There were scores of such point-blank citations.

The British Royal Commission differed from the Hutchins report in its recommendation for an oversight agency. It called for a "General Council of the Press consisting of at least twenty-five members representing proprietors, editors, and other journalists, and having lay members amounting to about 20 percent of the total, including the chairman." The goals set forth included safeguarding the freedom of the press and improving methods of recruitment, training, and education. The key passage dealt with censure. It called for "censuring undesirable types of journalistic conduct, and by all other possible means, to build up a code in accordance with the highest professional standards. In this connection it should have the right to consider any complaints which it may receive about the conduct of the press or of any persons toward the press, to deal with these complaints in whatever manner may seem to be practicable and appropriate, and to include in its annual report any action. . . ."

The proprietors of the British press dug in for resistance. Only another threatening move in the House of Commons brought the first meetings of the "General Council" in 1953. There were endless, aimless debates. Then, the House of Commons put to work a second Royal Commission, headed by Lord Shawcross. In 1962, the Shawcross report advocated a new constitution for the Press Council; in 1963, the House approved; and on January, 1964, the new Council began work under the chairmanship of Lord Devlin. This is the Council which, for all its shortcomings and lack of enforcement powers, is widely regarded as the model for affording the reading public at least a fair hearing.

JOHN TEBBEL

So What About Our Own Credibility Gap?

In the dark aftermath of the Siege of Chicago, during which thirty-four reporters and photographers were injured, a shocking fact became publicly evident.

When the opinion pollsters asked the electorate how it felt about Mayor Richard Daley's treatment of the press and of the demonstrators, not excluding those convention delegates who were also mistreated in various ways by the police, the people replied in effect that they approved of the Mayor's brutal repression, and by an overwhelming majority.

As the controversy about the Democratic convention deepened, it became even more clear, in remarks by assorted citizens from the Attorney General of the United States to writers of letters to the editor, that Americans have conceived a deep and dangerous hostility toward their press.

It has always been there, of course, and with reason in the eighteenth and nineteenth centuries when the press was first the tool of partisan politicians and later of strong-minded individual entrepreneurs.

LOST ACCEPTANCE

But in this century, when the concept of responsibility and of fair and accurate presentation of the news has developed rapidly, if sometimes imperfectly, the climate has been different. True, liberals raged at the bitter partisanship of some elements in the press during the years of Franklin D. Roosevelt, and there have been other passing phases of overt hostility generated by political events, but by and large, since the Hearst-Pulitzer excesses of the Spanish-American War, Americans had come to accept

John Tebbel is professor of journalism at New York University. "So What About Our Own Credibility Gap?" is reprinted from *IPI Report,* International Press Institute, Zurich, December, 1968, with permission.

41

the press as generally reliable and as their prime source of information.

This is no longer true. Successive surveys have shown that Americans now get their news more from television and radio than they do from newspapers, and believe more in what they see and hear electronically than what they read. Some publishers and professional apologists for the press have tried to push it under the rug, but there is no longer room to doubt that millions of Americans believe the news they read is distorted and biased, and even worse, that publishers, editors and reporters are part of a conspiracy to prevent the truth from being told. They think that newspapers lie, that they manufacture news, that they print only the bad news, that they seek to sensationalize everything they touch, and they entertain a dozen other similar fantasies.

These attitudes exist not only among the uneducated and the uninformed, where such paranoia finds obviously fertile ground, but are frighteningly prevalent among intellectuals and among comfortable upper-middle-class citizens. It is evident in a thousand forms, and among the middle class especially, one senses a hatred that goes beyond simple disbelief, as though people were blaming the press for the ugliness of life in America today.

The basic truth about this situation is that Americans do not want to confront their country as it is. They want to think of themselves as warm, decent, God-fearing people, living comfortably in a society ordained by the Founding Fathers to exist forever in the image created by politicians from the beginning of the Republic to the present.

Thus when middle-class citizens read about riots, the plight of the ghettos and the rise of black militants they believe that newspapers incite the poor and the blacks to make trouble for everybody else because of "all the publicity" given them.

It is the incredibly naive idea of these people, numbering millions, that if the newspapers (and television, for that matter) would just stop talking about the militant leaders and the dissidents of every stripe, and stop printing the news of crime and corruption which saturates the fabric of American life, that much of this activity.which so disturbs the peaceful surface of affluence would wither away from lack of attention.

There are other, more specific, sources of alienation as well. Blacks, for example, do not believe much they read in newspapers about events involving their people. They would not believe it unless it was highly partisan in their favor and reflected their convictions about Whitey. Anything else, in their lexicon, is a lie.

Similarly, there is a widespread disbelief in newspapers among the young. Again this is because newspapers, as business institutions, reflect editorially the largely conservative views of the business community and the middle class in general. That they also faithfully hold up the mirror to most Americans, and to the way they live, means nothing to the student radicals, who do not believe that this is the function of the press in any case. Their view of the press is essentially Marxist-Leninist, or more broadly, authoritarian in the context of thought prevailing in all the Socialist countries today. This view, of course, is depressingly familiar to every student of the world press. "The socialist press," a Czechoslovakia journalists' review once said, "which according to Leninist principles is a collective propagandist, agitator and organizer . . . bases its work on the general line of the communist party, helps to realize the party's decisions, and is guided by its instructions and advice. The party, at the same time, makes sure that the press fulfills its mission, that it does not deviate, that it serves the interests of the working class. . . ."

ROLE OF "UNDERGROUND"

Even those student radicals who reject Marx and Lenin, perhaps because they are not willing to accept this discipline any more than another, regard the press in the same way. It should serve their interests, and it should be a collective "propagandist, agitator and organizer." The radical student "underground" press fulfills these functions; it does not deviate and it serves the interests of the radical Left. Those who read it ridicule the very idea of trying to present the news fairly and impartially. Militant blacks, too, believe this is what the press should be, although the newspapers and other publications which represent the larger black community are not propaganda organs even though they quite naturally reflect the interests of the black world.

As for the slum dwellers, many read no papers at all, either from poverty, apathy, or both, but when they do, they read the tabloids which are written in simplistic language and have an exceptional amount of pictorial coverage. A New York City social worker whose territory is one of the most dismal slums was regarded suspiciously by a client who saw the *New York Times* protruding from her raincoat pocket. "You must be crazy to bring that rich man's paper in here," the client reproached her. "Nobody's going to talk to you if they see that. You come with the *Daily News* next time."

FRUSTRATION

There is a growing irrationality in the population as it surveys the mass media through a haze of frustration and anger which distorts reason. Thus people accuse television of helping to incite race riots and demonstrations of every kind by reason of their presence at these events. A

familiar charge is that the TV crews stage what does not occur spontaneously, and there is just enough truth in this accusation to weaken the
industry's defense. But at the same time, viewers appear to believe implicitly in the reports of newscasters and commentators on both television
and radio—unaware, of course, that a good part of this news comes from
the same news agency reporters who serve the newspapers. Somehow the
sight of an attractive personality, speaking with the voice of authority
directly to the viewer seems far more convincing to them than the words
of the anonymous newspaper reporter, who most often is telling them far
more about the news than the television news show is able to do in its
limited amount of time.

The amount of news conveyed on a thirty-minute television news show
does not begin to compare with what is contained in the pages of a
metropolitan newspaper, yet people want to believe that this thirty minutes, plus the five-minute summaries they hear on radio, plus the kind of
homogenized, highly biased journalism they get from the news magazines, will make them informed.

How to combat these attitudes, and if possible overcome them, may be
the most serious problem newspapers have to face, whether they understand it at the moment or not. For if such attitudes persist long enough,
and if the newspapers do not do a far better job than they are presently
doing of providing the kind of news coverage that only they can supply,
the incredible, the unbelievable may happen and people will simply get
out of the habit of newspapers. The new habit will be radio and television.

SECOND-RATE STATUS?

At the moment this is inconceivable to most people in the newspaper
business, particularly those whose money and entire careers are devoted
to it. With reason, they scoff at the theorists who say the newspaper as a
medium is doomed; there is no reason to believe that this is the shape of
the future. It is surely not doomed, but on the other hand, it is rapidly
becoming a second-class citizen among the media, and public hostility,
combined with public apathy, may well deal it a severe if not necessarily
fatal blow.

There is little, if any, hope that a solution will be found in the Press
Council idea, pioneered in Scandinavia and recently the savior of the
British press (momentarily, at least) when public antagonism toward the
press had become so great that newspapers were suffering excessive libel
awards from courts responding to the often frankly vindictive actions of
juries. Britain's Press Council gave the public an access to the press, and

provided the press with access to those people who tried to interfere with its function of getting the news. Matters are still far from ideal but there is little question that the Press Council, acting as a buffer state between press and public, is an extremely useful device both for improving press morality and reducing hostile tensions among readers.

It would not work in America. The country is too big, the publishers as a body too intransigent to permit such a body to be created, and the state of public morality in America is too far below that of the British public to make such a Council's adjudications effective.

RADICAL REMEDY

A more radical remedy is needed, and it may lie in the coming transformation in the way newspapers are distributed. Television electronics have made newspaper distribution methods seem as old-fashioned and obsolete as they truly are, and clearly, newspapers will not be able to compete ultimately with television unless they abandon these methods and employ electronic transmission itself. This is already technically feasible. News would be brought directly from newspaper to home either by cable, facsimile transmission, present television transmission, or by laser beams operating through satellites. The net effect would be to make newspapers directly competitive with television, and by means of dry-copying slave machines attached to the TV set, would make it possible for the viewer to have any part of the news or feature material being transmitted on a printed page, instantly.

What this will not do, of course, is to restore the newspaper's tarnished image with those people who resent it for various reasons and distrust it because it does not serve their special interests.

It is often said that Americans have a childlike faith in education as the answer to everything, but that may be the only way people can be taught to respect and value their newspapers. For much of the trouble between press and public stems from the fact that people are profoundly ignorant of how newspapers work, how they get their news and how it is processed, how decisions are made about the way the news is displayed, and why the news columns are not extensions of the editorial page, or editorial page syndicated columnists necessarily the voice of the newspaper. One of the few papers to recognize this public ignorance and attempt to do something about it is the *New York Times*, which has produced a booklet describing in detail how the newspaper operates, written by its veteran news editor, Theodore Bernstein. The *Times* advertises this booklet in full page ads in its own columns, and makes a special effort to get it into schools.

PERSEVERANCE

That does not save the *Times* from its critics. At the moment it is under savage attack from both Left and Right, probably because it is the largest visible target. There are people ranging from George Wallace to militants both white and black who refuse to listen to any kind of rational argument about the *Times*. Not much can be done about these people. Education, as the truism goes, is a slow process.

Nevertheless, we need to persevere here in America. Our system of government may not be popular elsewhere (Professor Henry Commager has pointed out that of more than 60 new governments begun in the world since 1945, not one is American in concept) but it is ours and most citizens want it to survive. The Founding Fathers knew what they were about when they made newspapers the only business in America to be given the special protection of the First Amendment. They did so, it must be remembered, at a time when the concepts of responsibility and objectivity were unknown in the press. But Jefferson and the others knew that the press serves a unique purpose in a free society. It is the keeper of that society's values, and it is the forum where all free men may express their freedom.

ROBERT K. BAKER and SANDRA J. BALL

The Marketplace Myth: Access to the Mass Media

The First Amendment presupposes that right conclusions are more likely to be gathered out of a multitude of tongues than through any kind of authoritative selection. To many this is, and always will be, folly; but we have staked upon it our all.

Judge Learned Hand
United States v. Associated Press

Negroes, Mexican-Americans, Japanese, Chinese-Americans, and Indians have more difficulty securing media access than white Americans; yet another barrier exists, this one more from an ideological than from a racist heritage. The outstanding characteristics of ideas that have difficulty gaining access are that they are new, that their proponents lack prominence by traditional media standards, and that they threaten the values of the social group to which the broadcaster or publisher belongs. In the last fifteen years, substantial progress has been made toward providing more coverage of the activities—demonstrations and protests—of minority groups and marginal progress in coverage of their ideas. What is needed, however, is more attention to minority views and less attention to the physical dramatization of conflicting ideas.

Much of the American first amendment, tradition and philosophy is founded, as we have seen, on the eighteenth-century libertarian's assump-

"The Marketplace Myth: Access to the Mass Media" is from *Violence and the Media,* staff report to the National Commission on Causes and Prevention of Violence, prepared by Robert K. Baker and Sandra J. Ball, November, 1969.

47

tion of how the press would function in the search for truth and reason. A press unfettered by government, the libertarian believed, would create a marketplace of ideas similar to the classical economist's marketplace for goods and services. This kind of marketplace, the theory ran, would produce truth in much the same way Adam Smith's classical economics market assured the optimum allocation of goods and services. So long as men were reasonable, and a majority honest, the speculations and abuses of the few would be more than offset by the majority. Truth, justice, and a rational world would inevitably emerge.

Like Adam Smith's marketplace for products, however, certain conditions must be met before the marketplace of ideas can function according to theory. In Smith's marketplace, there had to be a sufficient number of sellers and purchasers that none could affect price; as a corollary, Smith's theory abhors monopolies or conspiracies in restraint of trade. Similarly, one of the underlying assumptions of a smoothly functioning marketplace of ideas is the equal opportunity to take ideas to the public. No control should prevail over access to the marketplace. The government has dealt with monopolization of goods and services through the antitrust laws. There is some evidence the courts are moving toward a theory of the first amendment that will allow the government to act to prevent monopolization in the distribution of ideas. . . .

In 1790, the United States had a total of eight daily newspapers and eighty-three weeklies. When the Constitution was adopted, 97 percent of the population lived in places so small that they were not even called towns. Of the remaining three percent, most lived in towns whose populations were under 25,000—most only a few thousand. Under these conditions, the individual could make his opinions known by giving a speech on Sunday outside the local church or by getting a printer to put up a broadside and by posting it in taverns and in other public gathering spots around town. With relative ease he could have an impact.

Today, unless the individual has access to formal channels of communication, it is almost impossible for him to have an impact. His ability to communicate widely is extremely limited. As a minimum, an effective marketplace requires access on approximately equal terms by all those with messages. Long ago, perhaps, a newspaper might have been started with relatively little capital by one whose views were strong enough to demand that they be aired. Even today, it is probably possible to blanket a city the size of Washington, D.C., with a four-page broadside for about $1,500. Sometimes, television, radio, and newspaper advertising space can be purchased to carry a non-commercial message. . . .

Access to the American public for the message bearer is limited by both mechanical and human constraints. Present mechanical limitations of the media make it impossible for more than a fraction of the potential communications to be carried to society at large.

Mechanical limitations lead to human limitations. Because the media cannot carry all of the messages, someone must select and reject. The process of selection thus becomes a limitation of critical importance, and the media owners and gatekeepers are the first barriers to media access.

The nation's broadcasters, publishers, and editors decide who shall have the opportunity to be heard—an understandable and pragmatically necessary process. But, with the present structure of the communication business, it results in a marketplace far different from the eighteenth-century concept of a marketplace for ideas. The ultimate barrier to communication is, of course, the audience. The significance of that barrier depends in part on how media operators choose to present the news. That the media print or broadcast a message does not guarantee that the audience will pay attention or will retain the message. Yet here, too, the media have some control.

A. ACCESS: THE NEWS MEDIA AUDIENCE

Although the audience is at the end of the communication process, its role as a barrier to new ideas is more conveniently discussed first because audience characteristics that impede communication are also operative, in varying degrees, on newsmen.

There has always been a tendency among journalists to regard the bulk of their audience as not very bright. This makes it relatively easy to excuse themselves of all responsibility when the message is garbled. In theory, the journalist is a professional and the audience is his client. In fact, most newsmen know very little about their audience except that it includes their editors and publishers, their friends and neighbors, and their peers. Moreover, few seem to have any serious desire to learn much about their larger audience. If they devoted more attention to the needs of their real clients, the public, it would become clear that to an important degree journalists must share responsibility when messages don't get through.

Audiences tend to expose themselves to media messages that support their predispositions. A study by Wilbur Schramm and Richard Carter, for example, found that Republicans are approximately twice as likely as Democrats to watch a Republican-sponsored telecast. While those opposed to a particular view have a tendency to avoid such material, the great bulk of what passes for "news" in the modern media is not labeled pro-Republican, pro-Democrat, nor is it attached to any other ideology. The opportunity for selection is far less in the case of news. Moreover, in such media as radio and television, which are linear and fugitive, the opportunity for selective exposure on hard news programs is practically nil. If a viewer watches the news—and two-thirds of Americans regard television as their most important news source—it is difficult for him to avoid a particular segment; his choice is limited to turning the set off. Regular viewers of news programs can be expected, therefore, to receive exposure to almost everything that is broadcast. The decision whether or not to watch a particular documentary program is more likely to be made on the basis of the issue, than on the point of view presented. Again, the opportunity for selective exposure is very low.

In contrast to television hard news programs, a newspaper story is re-garded as highly successful if it is read by 30 percent of the audience. Newspaper stories presented without any predictable slant, however, cannot be sorted on the basis of the reader's predispositions. . . .

The second characteristic that may distort the media's message is selec-tive perception. Some people go to incredible lengths to assimilate infor-mation in a manner that supports their personal prejudices. A group of subjects shown a subway poster portraying a Caucasian, a Negro, and an Oriental, and labeled. "It Takes All Kinds of People to Make a City Run," will tend to interpret the poster to fit their attitudes on racial equality. Those believing in equality tend to see the poster as a strong appeal for racial tolerance; those not supporting equality more frequently inter-preted the poster as suggesting a city needs Negro garbage men, maids, and Chinese laundries. To prejudiced subjects, it is obvious that by performing these functions, members of these minority groups could be good citizens.

It does not follow, of course, that it is pointless to report facts that do not support public preconceptions. That, in any given instance, part of the audience may misinterpret the message only suggests that the media cannot change attitudes instantly. A member of the National Mobiliza-tion Committee has stated: that the amazing aspect of the audience re-sponse to television coverage of the Chicago disorders at the Democratic convention was not that 70 percent of the American people were sym-pathetic toward the police; rather it was that 20 percent thought the police were wrong. Changing attitudes to conform with changes in reality is a slower process than some believe, but the news media must continue to report reality, regardless of how comfortably it fits audience illusions or desires. Every idea begins as a minority point of view.

Like selective exposure and perception, selective retention is also gov-erned by audience predispositions. In one instance, shortly after President Kennedy was elected, two groups of college students were asked to read an article favorable to the President-elect. The pro-Kennedy students learned the material sooner than the anti-Kennedy students.

A third characteristic of audience communication behavior suggesting limitations on the ability of the media to change opinions was well docu-mented for the first time during an investigation of voting behavior in the 1940 election. Many voters who had changed their positions indicated the change was primarily influenced by other people, not the mass media.

Another relevant fact is that there are not merely two classes of people —those who support a particular point of view and those who oppose it. Ordinarily, on any issue, opinion ranges from strong supporters to strong opponents, and somewhere in the middle are those who have not made up their minds.

Similarly, media messages are more likely to influence audience opinions on such issues as student disorders where people have few preconceptions than they are on such issues as national elections, where audiences already may have developed strong opinions.

Among audience members who rank order and obedience to the law high in their system of values, media emphasis on the disruptive and unlawful aspects of dissent impedes the communication of minority views. In addition, at least one study suggests that messages that produce a high level of anxiety—as messages with a high quantum of violence are apt to do—tend to communicate less effectively. Messages that disturb the audience and offer no solution may be ignored altogether.

B. ACCESS: THE NEWSMAN'S PERSPECTIVE

The audience is neither the first nor the most important barrier to access. The newsman's perspective is relevant in at least two respects. First, to the extent that it is responsible for not reporting or biased reporting of the events that frequently give rise to dissent, it creates the need for access. Second, it is an obstacle to the presentation of views by those who are unhappy with the status quo, and when dissidents do secure media coverage, it is only a partial cure because the technique for gaining access (demonstrations and other forms of protest) is frequently emphasized at the expense of the ideas for which access is sought.

Consider the following accounts of the same event:

STUDENT PICKETS MARCH IN CAPITAL

Washington (AP)—Students picketing for peace marched four abreast in spring-like weather to Arlington National Cemetery Saturday, demonstrating their hopes for disarmament and an end to nuclear testing.

STUDENT MARCH ON CAPITAL
TINGED BY BEARDED BEATNIKS

By Robert E. Baskin, Washington Bureau of the *News*. Washington— Left-wing student peace marchers—with a definite beatnik tinge—marched through the streets of the capital Saturday on a pilgrimage to the Tomb of the Unknown Soldier in Arlington National Cemetery.

The first story was written by the Associated Press, the second by Robert E. Baskin, Washington bureau chief of the *Dallas News*. In each case, it appears the reporters were simply holding up [*New York Times* editor] Clifton Daniel's mirror.

Selective exposure, perception, and retention not only affect the audience; they also affect the newsman. Like their audience, journalists bring their own set of preconceptions to their craft, preconceptions produced by their environment, their position in the community, their business relationships, and the requirement that they earn a profit. The biases are both conscious and unconscious. In both cases, however, the remedies are the same: acknowledge the problem exists and, through a combination of conscious effort, changed perspective, and new institutional arrangements, work toward the elimination of systematic distortion.

A gatekeeper is any person who is so situated in the news gathering and disseminating process that he has control over the content and form of the news.

One of the earliest gatekeeper studies was performed by David Manning White and reported in 1950. It was the examination of the editor of a newspaper with about 30,000 circulation in a midwestern community of about 100,000 population, whose job was to select material from the wire services for the front page. During the week analyzed, Mr. Gates (a pseudonym) used approximately 10 percent of the 12,400 column inches received from the three wire services.

The 56 phrases he used in justifying rejection of material divided into two main categories: the story was unworthy of being reported (423 rejections), and the selection from many reports of the same event (910 rejections).

One rejected story had the notation, "he's too red." Another was marked, "Never use this"; it dealt with Townsend Plan, which Mr. Gates felt was of doubtful desirability. Another story was marked, "don't care for suicides."

These were isolated instances, but they do indicate this particular editor had some definite opinions on what news was fit to print based on something other than a neutral standard. In sum, approximately sixteen pieces were rejected as "propaganda," the remainder were apparently rejected for reasons unrelated to content. Gates was found to be conservative both in his politics and his style. He consistently avoided sensationalism and insinuations. Professor White summarized:

> It is a well-known fact in individual psychology that people tend to perceive as true only those happenings which fit into their own beliefs concerning what is likely to happen. It begins to appear (if Mr. Gates is a fair representative of his class) that in his position as "gatekeeper" the newspaper editor sees to it (even though he may never be consciously aware of it) that the community shall hear as a fact only those events which the newsman, as a representative of his culture, believes to be true.

Systematic exclusion was approached by Professor Warren Breed. He compared the content of newspapers with community studies, by examining a book of cartoons rejected by popular publications and by interviewing newsmen.

The subject matter from the community studies was selected on the basis of Professor Breed's opinion of material that might be suppressed. Typically, Professor Breed's study shows that the media have a tendency not to report such items as: elite individuals or groups, usually business, gaining advantage in a privileged manner; negative aspects of religion, such as lack of piety or respect, by parishioners, discontent shown by the clergy, or "human weakness" in church relationships; doctors acting in a selfish, rather than a professional, fashion; national or community pride or integrity in question; shortcomings in mothers, judges, or other institutions which middle-class white society regards highly.

The power and class of favored individuals do not provide a complete explanation, however, because mothers, overseas GI's, members of churches, and unknown soldiers are not normally regarded as elite groups. The dominant cultural patterns and values also provide protection from media exposure. Values such as capitalism, the home, religion, health, justice, the nation, and the community, also receive favored treatment. Similarly, the media's reluctance to discuss social class or social inequality, as the antithesis of the American creed, indicates another bias favoring established values.

Relations with the business community and the process of self-examination indicate a somewhat more conscious form of distortion. Ben Bagdikian has described it thus:

> [Newspapers] are part of a Geneva Convention of Newspaper Warfare which provides that whatever else the parties may do, they shall not escalate their competition to the point where they shall first, expose each other's errors and omissions; second, write about the other's front office problems even if these affect the public welfare; and third, never disturb the business establishment.

In 1966, the Bell-McClure syndicate offered serialization of Ralph Nader's book, *Unsafe at Any Speed,* to over 700 newspapers. None of them accepted.

Frequently, distortion is the product of sloth and indifference. Provided the opportunity to get something for nothing, many newspapers take it. One editorial from the *Industrial News Review* in Portland, Oregon, was published in fifty-nine newspapers. Distributed during the reign of Latin Dictator Trujillo, it began: "Today the Dominican Republic is a bulwark of strength against communism and has been widely cited as one of the cleanest, healthiest, happiest countries on the globe. The guiding spirit of this transformation has been Generalissimo Trujillo." The *Miami Herald* editorialized, "Somehow dahlias, daisies, pine trees, and 65° weather are not the picture that most people visualize when they think of the Dominican Republic, but yet this is what . . ." And two weeks later in the *Hartford Courant*, "somehow dahlias, daisies, pine trees and 65° weather," etc. This editorial was supplied free of charge and was published in fifty-nine newspapers with apparent disregard of whether it was based on truth or the Dominican Government's public relations program.

William Allen White, former editor of the Kansas *Emporia Gazette*, expressed the problem this way:

> If he is a smart go-getting-up-and-coming publisher in a town of 100,000 to 1,000,000 people, the publisher associates on terms of equality with the bankers, the merchant princes, the manufacturers and the investment brokers. His friends unconsciously color his opinion. If he lives with them on any kind of social terms in the City club, he must more or less merge his views into the common views of the other capitalists. The publisher is not bought like a chattel. Indeed, he is often able to buy those who are suspected of buying him. But he takes the color of his social environment.
>
> He is pretty generally against organized labor. He is too often found opposing the government control of public utilities. He instinctively fears any regulation of the stock exchange. The right to strike seems to the rich publisher and his Chamber of Commerce friends to be sheer anarchy. It is inevitable that the managing editor and the editorial writers who want to hold their jobs take their professional views and get their professional slant from their boss, the man who signs the payroll check.
>
> So it often happens, alas too often, that a newspaper publisher, reflecting this unconscious class arrogance of the consciously rich, thinks he is printing news when he is doctoring it innocently enough. He thinks he is purveying the truth when much that he offers seems poison to hundreds of thousands of his readers who don't move in his social and economic stratosphere . . .
>
> The worst of it is that, bad as he is, the crookedest, rich, property minded publisher is vastly better than he would be if he was operating under a government-controlled press. For on seven sides out of ten the most prejudiced, unscrupulous publisher is fair and his columns in those areas are reasonably dependable.

C. ACCESS: NEWS MEDIA STRUCTURE AND COMPETITIVE PRACTICES

By the mid-twentieth century, the structure of the news media as we know it today was largely formed and is the structure with which we must begin our concern. The news media are represented by a multitude of individual examples, but with very few exceptions the major news media share common characteristics imposed by their common economic and business orientation.

Two characteristics stand out. First, many news media are sensitive to their need for large audiences to a degree individual members of their audience may find difficult to comprehend. Second, the media tend toward concentration of ownership, influence, and control, as do other major businesses.

1. THE NEWS BUSINESS

Much of the news media's close to neurotic response to criticism is owing to what Ben Bagdikian has described as the "built-in schizophrenia" of American journalism. The news media "have to be godless, profit-making corporations and, at the same time, be selfless community institutions devoted to the unbiased education of the public." The inner conflict of American journalism cannot be ignored.

Criticism of direct advertising pressures upon publishers is one of the most durable. It is personified in the snivelling publisher who kills the story of a department store owner's divorce under threat of losing the store's substantial advertising revenues. Evidence to prove that assertion is, however, in very short supply. Newsmen asked about it replied that a news operation is most vulnerable to advertising pressure when it is economically weak and, correspondingly, it is most able to resist pressure when it is strong. In a one-newspaper town, advertisers may be more subject to newspaper pressures than vice versa. In at least one instance, a daily newspaper published a list of companies whose news releases should not be printed because they do not advertise in the paper. This, of course, is as objectionable as exercise of influence in the other direction.

On television news programs, direct influence by advertisers is essentially nonexistent. The case is somewhat different for documentaries. Here it appears primarily in terms of the choice of subjects for documentaries.

Documentaries, however, are the most crucial part of the television journalism, because they provide the mass audience with the only kind of programming about vital issues in depth. There is abundant evidence that despite protestations about plenty of hard-hitting documentaries, the networks consistently shy away from subjects which will be unpopular, either by failing to attract large ratings and thus sponsor interest, or by alienating some section of the community.

More important than the influence of particular advertisers is the effect of policies adopted to maximize profits. With high fixed costs, there is pressure to maintain the maximum possible audience. . . .

The effect is for the media to present material of the broadest possible appeal, necessarily aiming at middle America. It is also true that the same high premium is placed on not offending any significant segment of the audience. It is this requirement that makes it more difficult for new ideas to gain access and limits reporting on those conditions which give rise to much of today's dissent.

The need not to offend is greatest for national news media and those with large circulation in metropolitan areas. To limit audience alienation, large circulation media prefer to report ideas of factual stories that are either inoffensive or on which there is relatively broad agreement or wide acceptance.

D. ACCESS: COVERAGE OF PROTEST

The increased frequency of boycotts, sit-ins, picketing, parades, and large-group protest meetings has generated public and governmental concern over the news media's—and particularly television's—coverage of these events. In the late 1950s and early sixties, many southerners believed that if the media would not cover these events, they would not happen. Today many in the North share that view. Some Americans thought such events were one continuous dramatic production staged for and sometimes by the television networks. Criticism has ranged from claims that the media distort the events they report to bald assertions that they incite riots simply by their presence.

At one time, a demonstration, a boycott, a sit-in, or any other form of confrontation, even when non-violent, almost guaranteed coverage by the news media. Today, the greater number of non-violent demonstrations have reduced their efficacy as a technique for access, but still appeal to traditional news values and provide the action desired by television.

Apparent to any observer of the American scene for the past fifteen years is that this technique for gaining access is used by those who have not been admitted through traditional channels. General Motors, the President of the United States, or the Chamber of Commerce do not need a parade or physical confrontation to attract media attention. Dissenters have the problem of attracting not only media attention, but also public attention. The non-violent demonstration is a press conference for those who cannot otherwise command the attention of the media and its public. Although demonstrations would probably occur infrequently if the media did not cover them, press conferences would also occur less frequently if the media did not cover them. Those who object to nonviolent demonstrations may object to the format of the press conference, just as often they disagree with the message.

The criticism that "media coverage of conflict causes conflict" proceeds from an inaccurate assumption: that media coverage is both a necessary and sufficient condition for conflict. It is neither. The causes lie elsewhere, in social conditions and tensions.

One of the earliest accusations that television was the cause of violent eruptions in the process of social change is that of former New Orleans Mayor deLesseps Morrison. Integration of New Orleans schools was less than peaceful. At first he attempted to place the responsibility on Leander Perez, political boss of an adjoining parish. When that met with little success he labeled television the primary villain. Blaming television was an afterthought; the real causes of violence were his own neutrality toward the Supreme Court's desegregation order, the unlawful posture of the governor, the Louisiana state legislature's policy of massive resistance and refusal to support the local school board, and the neutrality of civic leaders. Where government and civic leaders are willing to cooperate in securing orderly social change, it seems clear that the press can be of assistance without seriously damaging its traditional standards of journalism.

The immediate effect of non-coverage of protest would probably be less protest; for those who subscribe to the ostrich theory of journalism, this may be the short-term answer. But protest is an attempt to communicate, to tell the public that the social machine is in trouble.

America continually readjusts its intergroup relations in the pursuit of certain fundamental democratic values. Readjustment, however, can generate severe tension. . . . The alternative to continuous readjustment is massive repression, which would produce a society neither dynamic nor democratic. Without media attention, the tensions of change could not be identified, much less alleviated.

Media performance is subject to criticism on at least two grounds. As suggested earlier, to the extent the media have not focused on the conditions underlying much of today's protest they have reduced the likelihood that these problems would be met before growing to such serious proportions. Even here, however, the failure of the media performance cannot be regarded as the only cause. Some of these conditions were covered but were largely ignored. The second criticism is that the news media slight the causes of protest at the expense of reporting the manifestations of discontent, physical confrontation.

If there were systematic balanced surveillance of the community, the need for demonstrations as vehicles for communication would not be so great. If the news media did not place such a high value on conflict and action, the character of protest might be quite different. If the public and its government had attended to the problems which beset them today, our society would not be in such a state of upheaval.

1. INFLUENCE OF MEDIA PRESENCE

One commentator has said, "Nothing, but nothing, ever happens the same way it was after you put a TV or movie camera on it! The fundamental problem is that TV reporters are so conspicuous that, without intending to, they can't help but influence their own coverage." To the extent his presence is obtrusive, no reasonable and honest newsman can deny that his presence has an effect on the event he is covering. Another has observed,

> A newspaper reporter equipped with pencil and pad subtly influences the event he is covering; a still photographer with his camera dangling about his neck may change it more. And a television camera crew, with their lights and large equipment, can transform the event into an entirely different scene. So much so, in fact, that it is questionable if TV is capable of reporting the news objectively.

Reporting the news objectively, in this sense, means reporting it as it would have happened if the newsman were not present. There is little doubt that his presence has an effect on the behavior of protestors. Consider the following description of television coverage of a picket line:

> By now it was something after 8 p.m. and the television crews needed something to show on the 10 o'clock news . . .
> Up came the three-man television crew: a camera man with a hand-held camera, a sound man and light man. Very discreet in the dark.
> "May as well get it."
> You could sense the disappointment in his voice, because pictorially it wasn't much of a demonstration.
> The light-man held up his 30-volt frezzi and laid a four-foot beam of light across one section of the picket line. Instantly the marchers' heads snapped up, their eyes flashed. They threw up their arms in the clenched Communist fist. Some made a V with their fingers, and they held up their banners for the cameras . . .

Obviously, it was not the same event once the cameras were on.

As on other decisions regarding coverage, it is important to apply neutral journalistic principles in deciding whether to cover an event. What many critics of protest coverage do not acknowledge is that others stage events for the benefit of the press. Yet, was the distortion any greater than the "unreal" hearing which followed the circulation of this memorandum to a congressional committee:

1. Decide what you want the newspapers to hit hardest and then shape

each hearing so that the main point becomes the vortex of the testimony. Once that vortex is reached, *adjourn* . . . .

4. Do not permit distractions to occur, such as extraneous fusses with would-be witnesses, which might provide news that would bury the testimony which you want featured.

5. Do not space hearing more than 24 or 48 hours apart when on a controversial subject. This gives the opposition too much opportunity to make all kinds of counter-charges and replies by issuing statements to the newspapers.

6. Don't ever be afraid to recess a hearing even for five minutes, so that you can keep the proceedings completely in control so far as creating news is concerned.

7. And this is most important: don't let the hearings or the evidence ever descend to the plane of a personal fight between the Committee Chairman and the head of the agency being investigated. The high plane of a duly authorized Committee of the House of Representatives *examining* the operations of an Agency of the Executive Branch for constructive purposes should be maintained at all costs.

. . . The above memorandum was circulated in 1943 by the counsel of a House committee investigating the Federal Communications Commission.

The argument persists that demonstrators holding up clenched fists differ from congressional hearings contrived to focus on a particular point or other public information activities of the government. The demonstrators know what they are doing; they consciously conduct themselves before the camera. If they hold up clenched fists they want to communicate this message to the public. Most of them, however, have some additional message. Although demonstration and confrontation are vehicles for access, something else rides in the vehicles. The media go to a demonstration, make the demonstration the story, but they ignore the message. In doing so they are performing about as well as if they had reported that the President held a press conference, but forgot to tell the public what the President said.

2. MEDIA INCITEMENT TO VIOLENCE

With respect to the possibility that the presence of the media may incite demonstrators to real violence, rather than threats of violence or hostile gestures, the solution does not lie in prohibiting coverage. If the conduct promoted by the media's presence is socially undesirable and not constitutionally protected, a law can prohibit such conduct. Where conduct is unlawful, arrest the demonstrator. But denying all demonstrators access simply because some of them may engage in unlawful activity pre-scribes too broad a remedy for an otherwise narrow problem, and clearly would be unconstitutional. Most demonstrators do not engage in unlaw-ful violence simply to get on camera; less extreme conduct usually suf-fices. Denying coverage to all demonstrators attempts to discourage in-directly that which cannot be prohibited directly: infringing dissident's first amendment right. . . .

Protestors usually have little to gain in the way of access to the media by engaging in unlawful or violent behavior. Indeed, the more violent their behavior, the more likely the media will focus on that to the exclu-sion of the views for which access is sought. Moreover, the revulsion of most Americans to violence means that regardless of the soundness of their view, when the message comes across mixed with lawless behavior audi-ence acceptance is substantially reduced. The dignified 1963 March on Washington, D.C., was a much more effective vehicle for communicating views than the performance of the New York Yippie contingent at the 1968 Democratic National Convention.

Nevertheless, protestors do engage in unlawful or violent behavior for several reasons:

1. Sometimes the grievances of demonstrators include police brutality. To bring the excesses of the police into public view, they may seek to pro-voke them when television cameras were present.

2. The demonstrators may wish to illustrate the depth of their convic-tion in the rightness of their cause by risking jail sentences or other puni-tive action.

3. The demonstrators regard the law they are violating as unconstitu-tional and seek a court test.

4. Frequently, there is a large group that supports the goals of the demonstrators, but is not willing to engage in the extreme tactics they adopt. Under such circumstances, the more radical members seek to gen-erate a confrontation with the police for the purpose of surfacing the "venality" of the "establishment" and thereby convince those on the fringe that any means necessary should be adopted to secure shared objectives.

5. The demonstrators may seek to generate such a massive official over-response as to force a breakdown in the administration of criminal justice and thereby illustrate how corrupt is the entire system.

Media coverage, then, does provide some incentive to violence; but it also provides a disincentive.

First, as suggested earlier, nobody, including demonstrators, wants to have his unlawful acts recorded on camera. Secondly, the presence of the media also tends to have a restraining influence on the use of violence by the authorities. During the late fifties and early sixties, Justice Depart-ment lawyers encouraged media coverage of civil rights demonstrations in the belief that it restrained the police. Former Attorney General Nicholas Katzenbach has acknowledged the constructive role of television coverage:

> The bitter segregationists' view of [the civil rights movement] is that the demonstrators are following the cameras, not vice versa. To them, it is the Northern press and the television networks which seem to be the motive force in the civil rights movement. This idea apparently motivated many of the toughs during the 1961 freedom rides in Selma and elsewhere. Almost their first moves were against the cameras.
>
> Yet news coverage has been a powerful deterrent to racial violence in the South. For every assault on newsmen, many more incidents have been defused by their presence. Reporters and cameras, particularly the network-television cameras, which symbolize the national focus on Southern violence, have had a tempering as well as instructional effect.

In Chicago, many officers removed their badges to avoid identification and frequently smashed cameras to destroy evidence of their misconduct. They did not want the public to know what had happened.

Media coverage thus reduces the immediate violence that results from overresponse by the police. But police violence has a fallout effect that may promote more extreme confrontations or even induce a shift to covert tactics, because they are less risky than public confrontations. . . .

COVERAGE OF DEMONSTRATIONS

Generally, the presence of the media improves the behavior of those present. Most demonstrations involve important political and social issues. Each side seeks adherents. However attractive violence may be to the few, it has little appeal to the vast majority of Americans. In Chicago, the various groups of demonstrators attempted to give dissidents a choice. They tried to warn protestors when a particular line of activity might lead to arrest or violence, and they tried to instruct those who did not wish to participate to avoid these activities. This policy shows that some dissident groups recognize that, if demonstrations are to be successful tomorrow, they cannot lead inevitably to bloody confrontation today; otherwise, the protestors cannot attract people to their movement, people who, while strongly supporting the objectives, either fear or have no appetite for violence. They need such broad support for their success.

The news media can take additional steps to offset whatever incentive they may provide for violence, first by balanced coverage of the confrontation. At least four elements require balanced treatment:

1. The purpose of the demonstration. What is the nature of the grievance? Why are the demonstrators there?

2. The events leading up to the demonstration. Have other remedies

been sought, such as administrative relief or negotiations, either on the grievances or on the right to demonstrate? If so, what has been the response of the objects (city officials, university officials, etc.) of the demonstration?

3. The demonstration. How many people were present? How did they conduct themselves? Do not focus only on the most extreme conduct or dress.

4. What provocations, if any, were directed toward the police? Why were the demonstrators trying to provoke the police? Did the police use more force than was necessary to maintain order? Were there any extenuating circumstances, such as physical exhaustion or security for a presidential candidate?

The issue of provocation presents a special problem. Many provocations are obscenities, not appropriate for either broadcast or for print media. Some people have suggested that the media have an obligation to disseminate the language of provocation anyway. Among those who once subscribed to this theory, at least in reporting on the Walker Report, was Norman Isaacs of the *Louisville Courier-Journal*. But the response from his readers was so overwhelmingly negative that he decided not to do it again. The problem remains, however. . . .

The media can reduce confrontations and demonstrations by giving more balanced coverage to the community, by opening traditional access channels to those with new, different, and minority views. Such changes in media performance will not eliminate protest altogether because other reasons exist. . . .

Where media attention is a positive incentive to demonstrate, it is also a remedial phenomenon that compensates for imbalanced surveillance. The solution, then, is not to ignore demonstrations, but to correct the conditions which, if they did not give them birth, were at least the midwife. Once done, to the extent demonstrations are an access problem they will diminish. Similarly, the standard for determining whether an event will be covered should place more emphasis on the nature of the grievance, the number of people affected, the severity of the grievance, and less emphasis should be placed on the willingness of the aggrieved to engage in violence and the likelihood that they will.

JOHN LOFTON

Pretrial Crime News:
To Curb or Not to Curb?

> *"Under the American system of checks and*
> *balances, the courts and the media both play*
> *roles which are given high priority in our*
> *constitutional system. . . . Neither of these vital*
> *institutions should hold pervasive sway over the*
> *other."*

Should mass media coverage of felony offenses subsequent to arrest be limited by law to the court record until a verdict is rendered? The answer is not easy because both the pro and con sides of this question are in part right. A resolution of the issue is made even more difficult because each side can cite United States constitutional provisions in support of its respective position.

On the one hand, the proponents of limiting media coverage of felony offenses can offer many examples in which the media prejudiced the outcome of criminal cases despite the fact that the United States Constitution in at least ten places[1] contains provisions designed to guarantee the

[1] Article 1, Section 9; Article 3, Section 2 and Section 3; Article 4, Section 2; Article 6; and the Fourth, Fifth, Sixth, Eighth, Ninth and Fourteenth Amendments.

John Lofton, a staff member of the *St. Louis Post-Dispatch,* has taught mass media at the University of Pittsburgh and written many magazine articles and three books, including *Justice and the Press* (Beacon Press, 1966), which deals with the impact of newspapers on criminal justice. He is also a member of the bar. "Pretrial Crime News: To Curb or Not to Curb?" is reprinted from *Current History* (August, 1971) by permission of *Current History,* Inc.

rights of criminal offenders to fair treatment and impartial justice. On the other hand, the opponents of limiting media coverage can offer many examples in which the media helped to protect the rights of criminal offenders and aided the exoneration of the innocent, thus vindicating the media's right to the guarantee of freedom of the press under the First Amendment of the Constitution and under the constitutions of the states.

The case for curbing the media is usually stated most fervently by lawyers, who emphasize the constitutional rights of criminal defendants to be presumed innocent until proved guilty in a fair trial. They add that, without some curb on prejudicial publicity, the accused may be unfairly convicted on the basis of published allegations about him which are not substantiated or which have nothing to do with the crime and which would not be allowed as evidence at the trial.

The case against curbing the media is presented most passionately by newsmen, who emphasize the constitutional right of freedom of the press and claim that any limit on news about criminal cases may interfere with justice by shielding law enforcement officers and the courts from justifiable criticism based on press reports.

The advocates of restriction can show that judicial concern over the outside prejudicing of criminal trials extends back for more than 200 years and that, despite repeated remonstrances, the press in the United States has not mended its ways. In 1742, English Lord Chancellor Philip Hardwicke declared:

> Nothing is more incumbent upon the courts of justice, than to preserve their proceedings from being misrepresented; nor is there anything of more pernicious consequence, than to prejudice the minds of the public against persons concerned as parties, before the case is finally heard.

Lord Hardwicke's decision in this ancient case laid the legal foundation for the present English system under which judges summarily punish for contempt of court newsmen responsible for publicizing evidence or comments which may be inadmissible at trial—that is, such material as confessions of suspects, information as to prior convictions of the accused, comments or accusations relating to past misbehavior or immoral conduct, reports ridiculing the character of the accused, press exposés of purported evidence, or any expression of opinion concerning a pending case.

The English system provides the best example of strict pretrial curbs on the media designed to prevent the prejudicing of criminal cases. Such strictures on the dissemination of extraneous information are intended to allow the law to take its prescribed course with criminal defendants. The law strives to reduce the chances for error by prescribing certain procedures for the handling of criminal cases. An arrested citizen may not be forced to answer questions in connection with a crime. Before making an arrest, the police must have probable cause to believe their suspect committed the offense and, under some conditions, they must have an arrest warrant and a search warrant, if they intend to make a search. The arrested person must be given an opportunity to gain the advice of an attorney.

After the arrest, the suspect must be taken without undue delay before a committing magistrate; he must be charged with a specific offense and given a preliminary hearing. The accused must then be indicted, but only if a grand jury—or in some states, the prosecuting attorney—has found probable cause to believe him guilty. After being charged, the accused must be brought to trial within a reasonable time. These various preliminary procedures are intended to insure that only those persons against whom there is convincing proof are brought into court.

To make the trial itself a reliable mechanism for arriving at the truth, complex rules have been devised as to who may testify, what questions may be asked by attorneys and what evidence is admissible as relevant. The defendant may not be forced to testify against himself. To give effect to the law's presumption of innocence, the state must prove its case "beyond a reasonable doubt."

PRESS DISTORTION

When the media interject into such proceedings information that is designated by law as inadmissible, the processes of justice may be distorted in such a way as to produce an unfair result. Although the focus of concern is usually the impact of the media on jurors, the prejudicial impact of the press can affect policemen, witnesses, lawyers, and judges, as well as jurors who, unlike the others, are at least screened for possible prejudice and who, if the sensational nature of the case seems to make them vulnerable, are sealed off from possible exposure to the media.

In the United States, the press usually does not limit itself to the charges and the other simple facts elicited by the preliminary hearing, but makes a special effort to get *ex parte* statements from the police and the district attorney and makes no effort to get corresponding statements from the defense. This tends to create a built-in bias against the defendant from the start. Such bias is illustrated by frequent news stories to the effect that the police have "solved" a crime with the arrest of a "thug," thus implying unqualified media acceptance of the prosecution side.

Of the various kinds of questionable evidence commonly aired in the pretrial stage by the police, prosecutors, and the media, there are two categories which deserve special discussion: reported confessions and prior police records of suspects. In publishing or broadcasting reported confessions, the media seldom exhibit a cautionary attitude stemming from a recognition that the alleged admission of guilt may not have been voluntarily given. Although the United States Supreme Court has taken an increasingly strict view of the admission of confessions in court, there is reason to believe that physical and psychological force is still widely used in the back rooms of American police stations to extract admissions of criminal offenses over which investigators feel frustrated.

Perhaps the classic example of a well-publicized false confession is that of George Whitmore, Jr., a twenty-year-old semiliterate, itinerant Negro laborer arrested by New York City police in 1964 and reported, after twenty-four hours of interrogation, to have confessed to several crimes, including the widely publicized stab slaying in 1963 of two Manhattan career girls, Janice Wylie and Emily Hoffert. Despite police assurances at the time that they had "the right guy," an assistant district attorney admitted later that the police, by "brain-washing, hypnosis, fright," made Whitmore give "an untrue confession." Still later a state Supreme Court fully cleared Whitmore of the Wylie-Hoffert murders and another suspect was convicted. Whitmore insisted that the original sensationally reported "confession," which could have sent him to the electric chair, had been beaten out of him. There is no way of knowing how many defendants have been convicted on the basis of broadly publicized forced confessions, the false character of which were never proved and brought to light. But there have been at least four book-length studies dealing with more than 100 actual convictions of innocent persons in American courts, some of them involving untrue confessions.

The second kind of questionable pretrial evidence which the media frequently disseminates is the prior police record of the suspect. The police record may even include arrests for which there was no follow-up or no conviction. In many, if not most, cases the past record of a suspect has nothing to do with whether he is guilty of the particular charge for which at the moment he is being held. Yet the existence of such "evidence" often induces the police to believe that suspects are guilty and leads them to try to pin crimes on them. Media broadcasting of prior records is likely to convey impressions of guilt to the public (including potential jurors) who assume that because the suspect was accused in the past, he is probably a chronic offender. Legal scholars who have delved into cases of wrongful convictions have pointed out that the airing of prior police records has often played a part in such miscarriages of justice.

THE COURT OF PUBLIC OPINION

Besides prejudicing cases by the pretrial dissemination of out-of-court opinions of the police and prosecutors and by the publicizing of confessions and prior records, the media sometimes interview witnesses and other trial participants in pending criminal proceedings, thus allowing an unfair "trial" of the case in the court of public opinion.

To avoid the possibility of media negation of the law's presumption of innocence and consequent unjust convictions, it can be argued with considerable cogency that legal prohibitions should be imposed against pretrial release by law enforcement officials or the media of the following kinds of information:

Observations about a defendant's character;
The defendant's arrest or criminal record;
Statements, admissions or confessions attributable to the defendant;
Statements concerning arguments or evidence expected to be used at trial.

Exceptions to these prohibitions would apply only when the release of certain information is necessary to the apprehension of a defendant who is a fugitive from justice.

Such strict curbs on the media can be justified on the grounds that, throughout American history, the press has in countless cases disregarded the principles of due process (fair play) in dealing with criminal cases and, despite exhortations from judges and others and the use of less stringent methods, has shown no overall inclination to reform its practices. As the Warren Commission said in rebuking newsmen for their handling of the assassination of President John F. Kennedy , the

experience at Dallas . . . is a dramatic affirmation of the need for steps to bring about a proper balance between the right of the public to be kept informed and the right of the individual to a fair and impartial trial.

Great Britain, which has imposed drastic restrictions on the media in criminal cases, still enjoys a justifiable reputation as a democracy with respect for freedom of the press.

But the opponents of legal controls on media coverage of criminal cases prior to trial can also make a persuasive case for their position. The media have the function of providing for the public an independent scrutiny of the operation of all governmental institutions, including law enforcement agencies and the courts. If those who staff the agencies of criminal justice were in part shielded from the light of publicity, the society would be saying in effect that they are more entitled to trust than officials in other institutions.

Yet policemen and even judges have been bought by criminal elements in the United States and have allowed the law to go unenforced. In the 1950s, a Chicago *Sun-Times* editorial campaign helped to bring about the murder conviction of a man who had originally been freed by a grand jury through the improper influence of an assistant state's attorney. A miscarriage of justice might never have been corrected had the *Sun-Times* not been free to publish its conclusions.

On the other hand, unjust convictions may be brought about by policemen, prosecutors, and judges who enforce the law carelessly or dishonestly and who are not easily subject to close scrutiny and exposure by the media. In a 1964 New York City case involving Gregory Cruz, an alleged murder suspect, newspaper reporters dug up evidence that helped free him before trial from false police charges. A restrictive policy on the release of pretrial news might have impeded their efforts.

Even the often-condemned pretrial publication of purported confessions can serve a useful purpose—by bringing forth accurate information from others who know that the confession is erroneous or by exposing police resort to duress. Factual accounts of alleged confessions may lead to inferences that coercion has been used and may prompt investigation from a quarter other than the police.

With respect to prior records, a plausible rationale for reviewing suspects' criminal histories in news accounts can be based on a showing that the record, by indicating a peculiar way of behaving or offenses of a similar nature, may suggest the suspect's connection with the new crime. Public knowledge of the record of some suspects, such as racket figures, may also help to deter behind-the-scenes deals with the police to avoid prosecution.

When they play their roles responsibly in the pretrial stage, the media can prevent the conviction of the innocent or unwarranted harsh treatment of the guilty. In a Phoenix, Arizona, case, the investigative work of reporter Gene McLain of the Arizona *Republic* helped substantiate the suspect's alibi claim that he was 500 miles away at the time of the crime and averted the prosecution of the wrong man for murder. In a 1964 case, a Miami *Herald* staff writer found and published the story of two witnesses, unknown to the police, to the effect that a murder defendant was being beaten by two law enforcement officers at the time he grabbed a gun and shot the officers. The disclosure resulted in a reduction of the charge. The American press can cite numerous cases in which unhampered reporting has kept justice on a straight course.

Even though curbs on the media seem on the whole to work well in safeguarding due process in Great Britain, satisfaction with the system is not universal among the British. Critics there have expressed the opinion that restrictions on the media have prevented the exposure of injustice. In any event, Britain is a jurisdiction with a long established and enforced tradition of fair treatment of suspects by the police and courts; in Britain, attorneys, who are not popularly elected to the bench, do not seek political advancement by reputation-building publicity, as they often do in this country. In the United States, elected judges, fearful of the retaliatory power of the press, could not be expected to use their contempt power fairly and judiciously to curb abuses by the media. Those most tempted to use contempt might be the dishonest ones who would see in such power an offensive weapon to divert attention from their own or their accomplices' misconduct.

UNDESIRABLE EFFECTS

Alfred Friendly, associate editor of the *Washington Post*, summed up some of the undesirable effects that could be produced by a flat legal curtailment of all information that might prejudice the outcome of criminal litigation. If police and court authorities in some city connive to railroad an innocent man or to put the fix in for a guilty man who has connections, how is the public to know of evidence never presented or of circumstances kept in the dark? Under a limit enforced by legal sanctions, an insider with knowledge of what is happening would have to risk disbarment, fine, or imprisonment (depending on the specified penalties) for telling the media that a full disclosure of the facts is not being made. An information curb could be used with special effectiveness where the power structure of closed communities, as in some cities in the South, could apply the prohibition to camouflage a double standard of justice—one for whites and another for blacks—with the outside world kept in the dark if the black defendant were being framed and the white law violator were being let off.

Other unwanted results could flow from an absolute barrier against the release of details in the initial stage of a criminal case. An indicted party, whose conduct might be at least partly excused by extenuating circumstances, would be prevented from explaining his side. In some situations, the publicizing of details might bring forth witnesses or information helpful to the defense.

Besides the undesirable direct impact on criminal cases that might be brought about by a tight restriction on information, we must also consider the effect that such a policy might have in general on proper press surveillance of public officials. Under the theory behind the First Amendment's guarantee of freedom of the press, the media should be the watchdog of the judicial as well as the executive and legislative arms of government. It should have maximum freedom to report on and criticize the government, including police departments and courts, which are just as capable of error, dishonesty, and tyranny as any other official agencies. If the power of censorship were conferred on certain officials, these officials might well use it to cover the mistakes or misconduct of law enforcement officers and the courts or to prevent justifiable criticism. The record of biased or lawless law enforcement in the United States does not indicate that police departments, district attorneys' offices and judges should be further removed from the prying eyes of the media.

Despite the fact that some practices of the media are offensive to due process, the proper remedy is not to "try" the offender, to "convict" it and restrict its liberty. Under the American system of checks and balances, the courts and the media both play roles which are given high priority in our constitutional system—the courts, the function of insuring justice for individuals; the press, the function of securing for the public an independent scrutiny of governmental agencies, including the courts. Neither of these vital institutions should hold pervasive sway over the other.

PART TWO

Adversaries

Introduction

The press and the people's governors have been adversaries since James Franklin, Ben's elder brother, used the pages of the *New England Courant* in the 1720s to inveigh against both civil and church authorities. Franklin went to jail for his audacity, but less than fifteen years later, John Peter Zenger was acquitted in a landmark case focused on the right of newspapers to criticize actions of a crown-appointed governor.

The right to act as a critic of government has been used by editors for both high and low purposes since the elder Franklin's time. A cornerstone of the libertarian press system, this right is most likely to be attacked, and is most vulnerable, in periods of national crisis.

The right of free press, imbedded in the First Amendment, is not merely freedom from government interference with publication. It is the right—some call it duty—actively to observe, report, interpret, and comment critically on the government and its officials. By government here is meant *all* government, from the lowliest local commission to the White House, Congress, and Supreme Court.

The word "adversary"—borrowed from the legal profession—has been used only in the last decade to describe the relationship between press and government. But since the beginning the relationship has been one of adversaries—working within the system. When it reports and criticizes government, the press is acting as watchdog for the people. This means that if an official commits a corrupt act, the press has an obligation to report it. When an official violates a campaign promise, the press must call the attention of readers to the turnabout and seek the official's explanation. Moreover, adversary journalism means the voter has ample chance to know everything he needs to know to make sensible choices when he enters the polling booth.

In a way, the adversary system boils down to a duel between the government's attempts to make itself look good and the news media's attempts to report how it really looks—warts, blemishes, and all.

Obviously, the right to look with skepticism on everything the government does and says is crucial to a free press. Every government wants popular approval; every elected official wants high ratings in the opinion polls. If unpleasant facts could be withheld from public view, the ratings would be likelier to stay high. So from White House to Town Hall, the struggle between those who would withhold and those who would disclose goes on—as it has for almost two centuries. In the end, as William Rivers says, "pitiless publicity is the sharpest weapon of a democratic society."

BILL D. MOYERS

Press or Government:
Who's Telling the Truth?

No two callings are more concerned with the public interest or more satisfying to a man's sense of duty than journalism and government. This
bias of mine about the press and government is colored by the fact that I
am a creature of both. I criticize them with affection, having learned
enough about the vices and virtues of these two institutions to know that
neither is totally innocent nor totally guilty of all the charges they heap
upon one another. I have not learned enough about them to propose solutions to all the questions each asks about the other. But our obligation to
each and their great power in a free society compel us all to ponder,
question, and probe constantly whether they are meeting their obligations.

The first point to consider is that credibility is not the government's
problem alone. . . . The press also suffers from the appearance of contradiction, which is the essence of a "Credibility Gap." From my own experience at the White House, the following examples stand out.

First, when Edwin O. Reischauer resigned as United States Ambassa-
dor to Japan, he was interviewed by the press in Tokyo. The headline in the
Washington Post the next day read: REISCHAUER BACKS U.S. VIET
POLICY. The headline in the *New York Times* read: REISCHAUER
CRITICAL OF VIETNAM POLICY. After a debate in the House of

Bill D. Moyers resigned in 1967 as Press Secretary to President Lyndon
Johnson to become editor of *Newsday*. From 1961 to 1963 he had been Associate Director of the Peace Corps. He resigned the *Newsday* editorship
in 1970 to free lance, and in 1971 published the book, *Seeing America*.
"Press or Government: Who's Telling the Turth?" is reprinted from *Television Quarterly*, the Journal of the National Academy of Television Arts
and Sciences, Vol. 7, Summer, 1968, with permission.

Commons on British support of U.S. policy in Vietnam, the headline in the *Washington Post* read: WILSON GETS SUPPORT FOR U.S. STAND. The headline in the *New York Times* read: COMMONS RESTRICTS BACKING OF VIETNAM. Perhaps both were correct, but was one more correct? To reconcile the difference is possible if one could read the full report in both papers, but for most people that is not an option. They do not have the opportunity to weigh the differences between contradictory stories.

Second, the day before the elections in South Vietnam in 1965, one commentator for CBS declared: "the armed forces have been turned loose in the get-out-the-vote movement. In the South Vietnamese army, like any other, an order is an order. But if the voters have to be driven to the polls with guns and bayonets, so to speak, it would appear that the Viet Cong has made its point about the Ky regime's popular support." The day after the election, however, another CBS commentator expressed amazement that so many South Vietnamese turned out to vote against the Viet Cong. "After all," he said, "the Government of South Vietnam is not driving the people to the polls with bayonets. . . ." If the TV viewer had heard both reports, he might have asked: "What's going on here? Was one of the reporters not telling the truth? Was one right and the other wrong?" The answer is probably that each man was partially wrong and partially right, because each man saw what *he* was looking at, or looking for. "Who's telling the truth?" a correspondent friend of mine was asked when he returned from Vietnam. "Nearly everybody," he answered. "Nearly everybody out there bears true witness to his bias and his senses." . . .

I learned at the White House that of all the great myths of American journalism, "objectivity" is the greatest. Each of us sees what his own experience leads him to see. What is happening often depends upon who is looking. Depending on who is looking and writing, the White House is brisk or brusque; assured or arrogant; casual or sloppy; frank or brutal; warm or corny; cautious or timid; compassionate or condescending; reserved or callous. As press secretary, this was repugnant to me. As a publisher, there is no alternative but to accept it.

Does the press really permit its humanity to interfere in the search for truth? For example Richard Harwood, then of the *Louisville Courier-Journal* and now of the *Washington Post*, reported not too long after President Johnson was in office that several long-time correspondents at the White House, when asked why the President's honeymoon with the press had ended, gave this answer: "Although Johnson has made even more of an effort than Kennedy to cultivate and woo the press, most White House reporters don't care for him as a person. They liked Kennedy and enjoyed his company. Johnson hasn't won their affection." In response to this attitude, Ted Lewis, of the *New York Daily News*, asked:

"What sort of journalism is that? It suggests that unless the President wins the 'affection' of the White House press, he is not going to get fair treatment." Ted may be right, yet in my experiences as White House Press Secretary, I rarely found that reporters were intentionally unfair to the President because he had failed to win their affection. No one begrudges a reporter his feelings, but one can lament the righteous indignation he expresses when it is suggested that he is an error-prone human being first, and a journalist second.

All of this is so obvious that the question arises, "Why discuss it?" The first part of the answer has to do with the professional longevity of the journalist. For all practical purposes we are beyond retaliation. We almost always have the last word because we are simply more durable. While the public can turn out officials whose integrity is exposed as unethical, or whose judgments are consistently wrong, or whose talents are proven to be inadequate, journalists do not operate at the end of an electorate's whim. . . .

There is an even more important reason for examining our vision. It has to do with the crisis of confidence in America today. . . . During my recent speeches at several colleges and universities I encountered a biting doubt about the veracity of both government and the press. One student in the Midwest said: "You know, Mr. Moyers, you have served in government and journalism, so it is doubly hard to believe anything you say." That remark says a great deal about the state of America today, and the state of America is disturbing. We seem on the way to becoming a nation of cynics. While skepticism is the mark of a healthy climate in a democracy, cynicism—widespread cynicism directed at the basic institutions of a society—can cripple a nation's will and undermine her spirit. A cynic, Lord Darlington told Cecil Graham, is a man who knows the price of everything and the value of nothing. And that is true of a cynical nation. Cynicism about the press and government ultimately will infect the very core of the transaction of public affairs; it will eat at the general confidence we must be able to have in one another if a pluralistic society is to work.

The fundamental issue, according to James Reston, is the question of trust. He writes: "The most serious problem in America today is that there is widespread doubt in the public mind about its major leaders and institutions. There is more troubled questioning of the veracity of statements out of the White House today than at anytime in recent memory. The cynicism about the Congress is palpable. The disbelief in the press is a national joke. . . . There is little public trust today." . . . Some of my colleagues in journalism say: "Well, they have a point, but most government officials lie deliberately—in the name of national security—while our mistakes are not intended." The reply is that a journalist can lose his credibility in the fashion many ladies lose their virtue: with the very best of intentions.

Many young people constantly point to examples of innocent discrepancy in expressing doubts about what they read. Take, as one example, the coverage last year of the protest in the United Nations Plaza. One headline read: 100,000 RALLY AT UN AGAINST WAR. Another account reported flatly that at least 300,000 had marched. One student told me, "We might forgive journalists for not being able to write, but how can we forgive you for not admitting that you can't count?" Every political reporter knows how difficult it is to assess the size of a crowd, and no one has yet to offer a sure way of improving our estimates. The fact remains that people are not willing to recognize such handicaps in judging whether we are to be believed or not. Virtue can be lost quite innocently.

As citizens we should be worried when millions of people believe the government lies. As journalists we should be equally concerned when millions of people believe the press lies, too. A number of people, especially the young, agree with the assertion that "an ambassador is a man of virtue sent to lie abroad for his country, and a journalist is a man without virtue who lies at home for himself."

If there are growing numbers of people willing to believe the worst about the press, they are supported by quite sincere men in public life ready to convince them that their worst fears are justified. Who was responsible for the plunging fortunes of George Romney last winter? Not George Romney, but the press! "One of the most unfair things that has happened in the last two and a half years," he said, "was the effort by the press to create the idea that I have been inconsistent and wobbly and didn't understand the situation. . . ."

And why do public doubts exist about the Vietnam war? Not because of the tenacity of the Viet Cong, the complexities of a brutish war, or the natural revulsion to the horrors of war. To hear military officials tell it, these public doubts can be traced to a "cynical element" of the press in Saigon. There are always people eager to prove that the press is responsible for their misfortune; the more they succeed in casting doubts on the veracity of the press, the more we have to work to clean our own house.

What specifically can we do? There is no overall cure. My suggestions are obvious and familiar. They simply need to be stated again and again as part of the vigilance that is the price of the power and obligation of the press.

First, the press should act with the same appreciation of candor about itself that it expects of public officials. This would lead to several improvements: an admission of "the subjectivity of our objectivity"; a confession that not even the press can discover the "whole truth and nothing but the truth"—that at best the press can only come up with the "bits and pieces of truth"; and an acknowledgement that its responsibility is greater than its skill.

Second, the press should either be prepared to live apart from tangling alliances with officialdom or be prepared to give up that illusion. There is considerable public skepticism about the cozy ties between the press and governments at every level, and much of this skepticism is justified. In Washington the temptation is often for both government and the press to think of themselves as brokers of the public interest rather than its guardians.

The third suggestion for improving the press's credibility is just as fundamental as a freshman journalism course. It is to make accuracy again the first rule of reporting. Nothing undermines the credibility of the press like sloppy reporting. Bad reporting creates unbelievers. When people read an inaccurate account of their own activities, they will tend to doubt everything else they read, too. It is a sad reflection on the state of our reputation today that far more readers believe the advice they get from Ann Landers than they do the advice of our editorials.

My fourth suggestion relates to one of the most common practices in Washington today—a practice that constantly afflicts the credibility of the press and government. This is the indiscriminate use of "backgrounders" as the source of hard-news stories. In order to correct this misuse, members of the Washington press must adopt some basic ground rules for "backgrounders" and must seek to get government officials to recognize and respect those rules.

The "backgrounder" is an old Washington institution—more endured than revered. The original purpose was to permit a government official to talk freely to newsmen without worry that some offhand remark would embarrass him, his agency, or the government. For that purpose it still has merit. . . .

Individual reporters, . . . constantly seek information on a "background" basis from officials. They want as complete a story as possible, and frequently, in order to receive particular pieces of a story, have to promise not to quote the man they are talking to, or even mention his agency. . . .

Formal group briefings, however, are quite another matter. They tend often to degenerate into a relationship between the public official and reporters not unlike that of an *amanuensis* to his master. The competitive pressure permits little time for cross-checking and thus contributes to uniformity—as if the press corps were a delayed-action Greek chorus. That, indeed, is what the public officials want. Their objective is to get out what the government wants to get out, as the government wants it to get out— a quite natural and understandable ambition.

The dangers in this practice should be clear to anyone. For one thing, anonymity is fearless, and if a public official wants to do so and can find a journalist willing to co-operate, he can hide behind that anonymity to grind an axe or to float a balloon, while protecting himself from possible adverse reaction by fuzzing the source. Another danger is public confusion. I was once in a television control room at a moment when we could not see who was speaking although we could hear at least a dozen voices from the studio, and I thought at the time how bewildered newspaper readers must be when they read information from a plethora of unidentified sources. How can we expect to judge the reliability of a statement if it is attributed only to an "informed source?" Suppose, just to make a point, that instead of James Reston's by-line on his column, there only appeared these words: "By a high official of the *New York Times.*" . . .

All of this may appear hypocritical, coming as it does from someone who made his living by "backgrounding" the press. But I was troubled by the process, as were many of the reporters with whom I dealt, because while we knew the careful "backgrounder" to be useful and necessary, especially in the area of national security, we also felt it had become a habit of convenience, a rule rather than an exception. . . .

As Jules Frandsen, veteran head of the Washington bureau of United Press International, has said: "A lot of skullduggery in Government and in Congress would never come to light if everything had to be attributed. Employees often can't afford to risk their jobs by talking for attribution." Nonetheless, the practice is so consistently abused that some commonly accepted ground rules are in order.

A step in the right direction would be for representatives of the various press organizations to meet and try to agree among themselves on these ground rules. . . .

Having tried on several occasions to mediate between journalists and the government, I am not sanguine about the possibility of reaching agreement within or among either group on what the ground rules for "backgrounders" should be. As a point of departure for trying, here are eight principles which, in my opinion, would help to bring some order into a ritual that at the moment can only be as confusing to the public as Haitian voodoo.

ONE: "Backgrounders" should be designed to *explain* policy rather than *announce* policy. This rule would discourage the use of unattributed quotations which turn "soft news" into "hard news."

TWO: "Backgrounders" in subjects other than national security and foreign affairs should be the exception rather than the rule.

THREE: The contents of a group "backgrounder" should not be disclosed for at least one hour after the conclusion of the session. This would permit time for cross-checking. It would also reduce the possibility of a public official using a backgrounder strictly for self-serving purposes.

FOUR: The rules should be clearly stated before the "backgrounder" begins by the principal or by his press spokesman.

FIVE: There should be only two levels of concealment. Either the reporter uses the information on his own—a practice that should be reserved for the most sensitive issues of national security—or it should be attributed as stated in the following principle.

SIX: The source should be identified by his specific agency. The loose anonymity of "high U.S. official," "top government officials," "friends of the President," or "visitors who've talked to the President" would be replaced by "A Defense Department spokesman," or "A U.S. Army official," or "White House sources." The reader would still be in doubt as to the authenticity and the reliability of the information, but the burden of proof would not be on the press completely.

SEVEN: The reporters should refuse to deliberately increase the obfuscation through such tactics as withholding the information until the source has left town (as in the case of General Westmoreland's "backgrounder" last November), or by attributing the information to plural sources when it comes in fact from one source (as also happened when the correspondents changed General Westmoreland into "some U.S. officials").

EIGHT: When a public official in a "backgrounder" refuses to permit attribution material that is patently self-serving but reporters nonetheless feel obliged to carry the story, they should carry a sentence attributing the information to a Pentagon (or State or White House) official "whose name is withheld at his insistence."

These suggestions are only the starting point for serious discussions by journalists and public officials. Other men will have better proposals. The important task is for the press to make some effort to deal with the problem. A "backgrounder" is useful to a public official and to a reporter, helping the one to get his viewpoint across and the other to gain valuable insight or information that he could not get if the official were required to speak for attribution. But what is convenient to the government and to the press is confusing to the public. These ideas are put forward with the *public* in mind. . . .

Whatever rules are agreed upon, the problem will be in getting the government to respect them. But even that is not so formidable an obstacle as it appears. Government officials only call a "backgrounder" to brief a large press gathering when those officials have something to put out. If the newspapers and the media most read and watched by Washington officials—in particular, the three networks, the wire services, and the Washington and New York City press—insist that the rules by which they will transmit the information be followed, respect for rules will grow in time. And with it the credibility of the American press.

Now we come to the credibility of the Government—the "Credibility Gap." Time and time again these questions are asked: Do Presidents and press secretaries really lie? There is the obvious answer: Before there were Presidents and press secretaries, there were Adam and Eve, and there is a little of each of them in all of us.

The question, however, goes far beyond a simple affirmation that public officials are human. The press has an obligation to increase the public's understanding of the "Credibility Gap" since we have certainly increased the public's awareness of it. I have no question but that the Government overreacted to the charges of incredibility, partly because any man grows defensive when his integrity is assaulted. But if the Government has over-reacted, the press has under-explained. The "Credibility Gap" became an overworked catch phrase that many people took for granted because they heard it repeated so often. What was otherwise and imprecise and poorly defined term took on the familiarity of an established creed which people read without thinking and repeat without understanding.

There has always been a credibility problem; the term is no recent addition to our political nomenclature. Some people trace it back to the premise of Plato that "The rulers of the State are the only ones who should have the privilege of lying, either at home or abroad; they may be allowed to lie for the good of the State." Plato has his apostles to this day; but they are not legion—they do not even often wind up in high places, fortunately. We will not be able to locate enough pathological liars in official Washington to dig a very deep "Credibility Gap." . . .

No, we have to look elsewhere for a fuller understanding of the matter. I am familiar with all the charges and with the evidence: the erroneous predictions of military progress, the attempts to put the best face on every crisis, the fiscal confusion, the stories of peace feelers raised and peace feelers dashed, and so on. But it is not as simple as all that, and some things should be said to put the problem into perspective.

There were times when the Government was less than candid about important matters which were not related to national security. Never did it fool the press. The Washington press corps, by and large, is a persistent posse, and no administration will escape being called into account for its mistakes and sins.

But the problem of credibility is far more complicated. For the purpose of perspective rather than exoneration, a few observations should be made about some of the factors that make this a difficult issue.

First, some things are simply not suited for telling on the time schedule an inquisitive press prefers. At the risk of appearing to hide the facts, a President must often remain quiet. This is especially true when a President deals with a crisis over which he has little control, but for which he must assume great responsibility. . . .

I am not referring to the deep-seated propensity for clandestine conduct that led one official to put a sign on his desk which said: "The secrecy of my job does not permit me to know what I am doing." Instead I am referring to the necessity for a President to resist commenting on a situation until he can be certain his words will produce the intended result. President Harding learned this the hard way when he jeopardized the disarmament conference of 1921 by giving reporters an off-the-cuff interpretation of the treaty. What he did not know was that his Secretary of State had already given the press his own interpretation of the treaty— and the two interpretations were at odds.

. . . Nuclear overkill is a daily concern of a President; verbal overkill ought to be, too. Reporters should do their best to find out what is going on, but they must also recognize that the President has no obligation to spoonfeed them with a full disclosure of every facet of official thinking on every subject they see fit to probe.

Second, events make lies out of the best promises. Circumstances change, and so must a President's strategy. . . . Woodrow Wilson surely meant what he said about keeping us out of war; but circumstances overtook him, and he found it necessary to do what he did not intend to do. In 1964, Lyndon Johnson declared that he sought no wider war in Southeast Asia, that he would not send American boys to do the fighting for Asian boys. One year later he widened the war and American boys were sent to fight it. For these decisions the President has been accused of breaking faith with the American people, of lying, of deliberately doing what he had said he would not do, of creating the "Credibility Gap." If it were only that simple! Even when it leads him to be at odds with his former position, a President can ill afford to have a closed mind or to fail to do what *he believes* is best, no matter what *he said* or *believed* earlier.

Third, a President must sometimes reach conclusions from inconclusive evidence. There are times when a decision seems imperative before all the evidence is in. The choice may be between acting on the basis of information at hand—inconclusive though it be—or not to act at all. But Presidents know that each decision—to act or not to act—can have far-reaching consequences. No one could prove that the Marines were needed to save the lives of Americans at the Embajador Hotel in Santo Domingo, but his Ambassador was telling the President that those lives were endangered. Later the press and others, with the benediction of hindsight, would argue that they were not required.

Some of the claims of government are incredible. I used to make them —although I was gone last year when the Department of Transportation revealed how the Bureau of Public Roads was bringing God back to American life. One of the Department's press releases began:

"There are 36 churches alongside the 60-mile Interstate Beltway (I-495) which rings the Nation's capital. And half of them have been built since 1958 when the route of the circumferential highway first became known." This, according to spokesmen of the Department of Transportation's Federal Highway Administration, points up vividly "the importance of the highway transportation system to the country's community life." This is known as straining the obvious.

A more serious cause of incredibility has been raised by Ted Lewis of the *New York Daily News*. Last year he wrote a column in which he quoted the statement made in 1963 by Secretary of Defense Robert McNamara that American troops could begin to be withdrawn from South Vietnam by 1965. Lewis was reprimanded by a spokesman for the Pentagon for writing that there had definitely been a "deliberate effort by Defense Secretary McNamara . . . to make things look better than they were." In quoting from the White House statement of October 2, 1963, he was told, "you have overlooked the very important final paragraph of that statement. It reads: 'The political situation in South Vietnam remains deeply serious. The United States had made clear its continuing opposition to any repressive action in South Vietnam. While such actions have not yet significantly affected the military effort, they could do so in the future.' " Lewis did not bother to reply to the spokesman, even though, at Hickam Air Force Base, six weeks after the issuance of the statement in December, Secretary McNamara had again talked about some U.S. personnel being able to "return by the end of the year." Why did the newspapers at the time latch on to prediction about troop returns? Lewis answered, "Because people wanted to know how long our boys would be over there."

"My point is," he wrote me, "that there is a natural oversimplification in news handling due to limited space and public interest. Responsible government officials should know this. If a statement is distorted out of context, it is because it was susceptible to an honest oversimplification. Why don't people in Washington realize this is the heart of the credibility problem? McNamara's own case is only one of hundreds. He promised— in effect—when he should have expressed hope it would turn out that way."

Secretary McNamara unquestionably meant well as did the others in those "hundreds" of other cases. But Ted Lewis has a point. Many good intentions have gone awry in Washington because defuscation is susceptible to honest oversimplification. With each incident the confidence of Americans in the veracity of the government has diminished.

It is not possible to restore overnight what has been lost over the years, but a few steps can be taken at the top that will establish a climate of candor which is the minimum requirement for building trust between government, press, and people. If the new President elected in November wishes to work in such an environment, he will be advised to begin with four simple but essential elements:

First, regular press conferences—at least once each month—the purpose of which should not be to announce the news but to explain the news. The timing of press conferences must fit the convenience of the President. However, they should be scheduled, and they should be frequent. And for all the short comings, they should also be televised.

Second, access for the press to second- and third-level officials in the White House and in each Department—men below the President and the Cabinet Secretaries who know the details of what is happening and who can increase a reporter's understanding or knowledge without abusing his responsibility.

Third, minimum use of "backgrounders" and unattributed quotations. The indiscriminate practice smacks of the secretiveness that Americans resist as alien to an open society.

Fourth, a willingness to live and let live. Some Presidents have regarded the press as an instrument of government, not an independent arm of the people. Some have been eager to woo the press; others to criticize it. Some have wished to make cronies of reporters; others to make cheerleaders of them. Modern Presidents have realized that they can never effectively govern unless they learn to reach the people through the mass media, and the wise ones have discovered how to go through or over the press to the people.

What the press and government should seek from each other is a mutual no-poaching agreement, for the press and the government are not allies. They are adversaries. That should be repeated. They are adversaries. Each has a special place in our scheme of things. The President was created by the Constitution, and the press is protected by the Constitution—the one with the mandate to conduct the affairs of state, the other with the privilege of trying to find out all it can about what is going on.

How each performs is crucial to the workings of a system that is both free and open but fallible and fragile. For it is the nature of a democracy to thrive upon conflict between press and government without being consumed by it.

If neither the government nor the press can take for granted the confidence of the people, each of us must guard against poorly-formed judgments about the other and against an unperturbable sense of security about our own well being.

All of this is important because we are in quite difficult straits in this country. The deepest crises are not Vietnam and the cities, but cynicism about the political order and a corroded confidence in our ability to communicate with one another and to trust one another. For such crises the requirements are large—to revive the public spirit, to restore the political vigor, and to rouse the nation from her present querulous divisions to a new sense of purpose.

The government has quite a duty, for the issues must be made plain, the truth clear, if these things are to be done. But the role of the press is no less. As William Allan White said, "This nation will survive, this state will prosper, this orderly business of life will go forward if only men can speak in whatever way given them to utter what their hearts hold—by voice, by postal card, by letters, or by press."

SPIRO AGNEW

The Power of the Press

*Address before the Montgomery Chamber of
Commerce, Alabama, November 29, 1969.*

One week ago tonight I flew out to Des Moines, Iowa, and exercised my right to dissent.

There has been some criticism of what I had to say out there. Let me give you a sampling.

One Congressman charged me with, and I quote, "A creeping socialistic scheme against the free enterprise broadcast industry." That is the first time in my memory anybody ever accused Ted Agnew of entertaining socialist ideas.

On Monday, largely because of this address, Mr. Humphrey charged the Nixon Administration with a "calculated attack" on the right of dissent and on the media today. Yet, it is widely known that Mr. Humphrey himself believes deeply that unfair coverage of the Democratic Convention in Chicago, by the same media, contributed to his defeat in November. Now, his wounds are apparently healed, and he casts his lot with those who were questioning his own political courage a year ago. But let us leave Mr. Humphrey to his own conscience. America already has too many politicians who would rather switch than fight.

Others charged that my purpose was to stifle dissent in this country. Nonsense. The expression of my views has produced enough rugged dissent in the last week to wear out a whole covey of commentators and columnists.

One critic charged that the speech was "disgraceful, ignorant and base," that it "leads us as a nation into an ugly era of the most fearsome suppression and intimidation." One national commentator, whose name is known to everyone in this room, said "I hesitate to get into the gutter with

"The Power of the Press," by Vice-President Agnew is reprinted from *Frankly Speaking*, Public Affairs Press, Washington, D.C., 1970, with permission.

this guy." Another commentator charges that it was "one of the most sinister speeches I have ever heard made by a public official." The president of one network said it was an "unprecedented attempt to intimidate a news medium which depends for its existence upon government licenses." The president of another charged me with "an appeal to prejudice," and said it was evident that I would prefer the kind of television "that would be subservient to whatever political group happened to be in authority at the time."

And they say *I* have a thin skin.

Here are classic examples of overreaction. These attacks do not address themselves to the questions I have raised. In fairness, others—the majority of critics and commentators—did take up the main thrust of my address. And if the debate they have engaged in continues, our goal will surely be reached: a thorough self-examination by the networks of their own policies—and perhaps prejudices. That was my objective then; it is my objective now.

Now, let me repeat to you the thrust of my remarks the other night, and make some new points and raise some new issues.

I am opposed to censorship of television or the press in any form. I don't care whether censorship is imposed by government or whether it results from management in the choice and the presentation of the news by a little fraternity having similar social and political views. I am against censorship in all forms.

But a broader spectrum of national opinion *should* be represented among the commentators of the network news. Men who can articulate other points of view *should* be brought forward.

And a high wall of separation *should* be raised between what is news and what is commentary.

And the American people *should* be made aware of the trend toward the monopolization of the great public information vehicles and the concentration of more and more power over public opinion in fewer and fewer hands.

Should a conglomerate be formed that tied together a shoe company with a shirt company, some voice will rise up righteously to say that this is a great danger to the economy; and that the conglomerate ought to be broken up.

But a single company, in the nation's capital, holds control of the largest newspaper in Washington, D.C., *and* one of the four major television stations, *and* an all-news radio station, *and* one of the three major news magazines—all grinding out the same editorial line—and this is not a subject you have seen debated on the editorial pages of the *Washington Post* or the *New York Times*.

For the purpose of clarity, before my thoughts are obliterated in the smoking typewriters of my friends in Washington and New York, let me emphasize I am not recommending the dismemberment of the Washington Post Company. I am merely pointing out that the public should be aware that these four powerful voices hearken to the same master.

I am merely raising these questions so that the American people will become aware of—and think of the implications of—the growing monopolization of the voices of public opinion on which we all depend—for our knowledge and for the basis of our views.

When the *Washington Times-Herald* died in the nation's capital, that was a political tragedy; and when the *New York Journal-American,* the *New York World-Telegram and Sun,* the *New York Mirror* and the *New York Herald-Tribune* all collapsed within this decade, that was a great, great political tragedy for the people of New York. The *New York Times* was a better newspaper when they were alive than it is now that they are gone.

What has happened in the city of New York has happened in other great cities in America.

Many, many strong independent voices have been stilled in this country in recent years. Lacking the vigor of competition, some of those that have survived have, let us face it, grown fat and irresponsible.

I offer an example. When 300 Congressmen and 59 Senators signed a letter endorsing the President's policy in Vietnam it was news—big news. Even the *Washington Post* and the *Baltimore Sun*—scarcely house organs of the Nixon Administration—placed it prominently on the front page.

Yet the next morning the *New York Times,* which considers itself America's paper of record, did not carry a word. Why?

If a theology student in Iowa should get up at a PTA luncheon in Sioux City and attack the President's Vietnam policy, my guess is that you would probably find it reported somewhere the next morning in the *New York Times.* But when 300 Congressmen endorse the President's Vietnam policy, the next morning it is apparently not considered news fit to print.

Just this Tuesday, when the Pope, the Spiritual Leader of half a billion Roman Catholics applauded the President's efforts to end the war in Vietnam, and endorsed the way he was proceeding—that news was on page 11 of the *New York Times.* But the same day, a report about some burglars who broke into a souvenir shop at St. Peters and stole $9,000 worth of stamps and currency—that story made page 3. How's that for news judgment?

A few weeks ago here in the South, I expressed my views about street and campus demonstrations. Here is how the *New York Times* responded:

"He [that's me] lambasted the nation's youth in sweeping and ignorant generalizations, when it is clear to all perceptive observers that American youth today is far more imbued with idealism, a sense of service and a deep humanitarianism than any generation in recent history, including particularly Mr. Agnew's."

That seems a peculiar slur on a generation that brought America out of the Great Depression without resorting to the extremes of either fascism or Communism. That seems a strange thing to say about an entire generation that helped to provide greater material blessings and personal freedom—out of that Depression—for more people than any other nation in history. We are not finished with the task by any means—but we are still on the job.

Just as millions of young Americans in this generation have shown valor and courage and heroism in fighting the longest and least popular war in our history—so it was the young men of my generation who went ashore at Normandy under Eisenhower and with MacArthur into the Philippines.

Yes, my generation, like the current generation, made its own share of great mistakes and blunders. Among other things, we put too much confidence in Stalin and not enough in Winston Churchill.

But whatever freedom exists today in Western Europe and Japan exists because hundreds of thousands of young men in my generation are lying in graves in North Africa and France and Korea and a score of islands in the Western Pacific.

This might not be considered enough of a "sense of service" or a "deep humanitarianism" for the "*perceptive critics*" who write editorials for the *New York Times*, but it's good enough for me; and I am content to let history be the judge.

Now, let me talk about the younger generation.

I have not and do not condemn this generation of young Americans. Like Edmund Burke, I would not know how to "draw up an indictment against a whole people." They are our sons and daughters. They contain in their numbers many gifted, idealistic and courageous young men and women.

But they also list in their numbers an arrogant few who march under the flags and portraits of dictators, who intimidate and harass university professors, who use gutter obscenities to shout down speakers with whom they disagree, who openly profess their belief in the efficacy of violence in a democratic society.

The preceding generation had its own breed of losers—and our generation dealt with them through our courts, our laws and our system. The challenge now is for the new generation to put their own house in order.

Today, Dr. Sidney Hook writes of "storm troopers" on the campus; that "fanaticism seems to be in the saddle." Arnold Beichman writes of "young Jacobins" in our schools who "have cut down university administrators, forced curriculum changes, halted classes, closed campuses and set a nation-wide chill of fear through the university establishment." Walter

Laqueur writes in *Commentary* that "the cultural and political idiocies perpetrated with impunity in this permissive age have gone clearly beyond the borders of what is acceptable for any society, however liberally it may be constructed."

George Kennan has devoted a brief, cogent and alarming book to the inherent dangers of what is taking place in our society and in our universities. Irving Kristol writes that our "radical students . . . find it possible to be genuinely heartsick at the injustice and brutalities of American society, while blandly approving of injustice and brutality committed in the name of 'the revolution'."

These are not names drawn at random from the letterhead of an Agnew-for-Vice-President Committee.

These are men more eloquent and erudite than I. They raise questions that I have tried to raise.

For among this generation of Americans there are hundreds who have burned their draft cards and scores who have deserted to Canada and Sweden to sit out the war. To some Americans, a small minority, these are the true young men of conscience in the coming generation. Voices are and will be raised in the Congress and beyond, asking that amnesty should be provided for "these young and misguided American boys." And they will be coming home one day from Sweden and Canada, and from a small minority they will get a heroes' welcome.

They are not our heroes. Many of our heroes will not be coming home; some are coming back in hospital ships, without limbs or eyes, with scars they shall carry the rest of their lives.

Having witnessed firsthand the quiet courage of wives and parents receiving posthumously for their heroes Congressional Medals of Honor, how am I to react when people say, "Stop speaking out, Mr. Agnew, stop raising your voice."

Should I remain silent while what these heroes have done is vilified by some as "a dirty and immoral war" and criticized by others as no more than a war brought on by the chauvinistic, anti-communism of Presidents Kennedy, Johnson and Nixon?

These young men made heavy sacrifices so that a developing people on the rim of Asia might have a chance for freedom that they will not have if the ruthless men who rule in Hanoi should ever rule over Saigon. What is dirty or immoral about that?

One magazine this week said that I will go down as the "great polarizer" in American politics. Yet, when that large group of young Americans marched up Pennsylvania and Constitution Avenues last week—they sought to polarize the American people against the President's policy in Vietnam. And that was their right.

And so it is my right and my duty, to stand up and speak out for the values in which I believe. How can you ask the man in the street in this country to stand up for what he believes if his own elected leaders weasel and cringe?

It is not an easy thing to wake up each morning to learn that some prominent man or institution has implied that you are a bigot, a racist or a fool.

I am not asking any immunity from criticism. That is the lot of the man in politics; we would have it no other way in this democratic society.

But my political and journalistic adversaries sometimes seem to be asking something more—that I circumscribe my rhetorical freedom, while they place no restrictions on theirs.

As President Kennedy once observed in a far more serious matter, that is like offering an apple for an orchard.

We do not accept those terms for continuing the national dialogue. The day when the network commentators and even gentlemen of the *New York Times* enjoyed a form of diplomatic immunity from comment and criticism of what they said—that day is past.

Just as a politician's words—wise and foolish—are dutifully recorded by the press and television to be thrown up to him at the appropriate time, so their words should likewise be recorded and likewise recalled.

When they go beyond fair comment and criticism they will be called upon to defend their statements and their positions just as we must defend ours. And when their criticism becomes excessive or unjust, we shall invite them down from their ivory towers to enjoy the rough and tumble of public debate.

I do not seek to intimidate the press, the networks or anyone else from speaking out. But the time for blind acceptance of their opinions is past. And the time for naive belief in their neutrality is gone.

But, as to the future, all of us could do worse than take as our own the motto of William Lloyd Garrison who said: "I am in earnest. I will not equivocate. I will not excuse. I will not retreat a single inch. And I will be heard."

FRED W. FRIENDLY

Some Sober Second Thoughts
on Vice President Agnew

In defending Vice President Spiro Agnew, one of the most fair-minded men in the United States Senate said, "It is the pig that is caught under the fence that squeals." The analogy may be partly accurate, but the question is who is stuck under the fence—the broadcast journalist or the administration? Long ago, when broadcasting was fighting for its right to be responsible, Edward R. Murrow, then under attack, spoke words that might be paraphrased today: When the record is finally written it will answer the question, who helped the American people better understand the dilemma of Vietnam—the administration or the American journalist? History, of course, will decide that question. But I would suspect that in the struggle between the news media and the last two administrations, the record has been with the journalists.

The American people are worried about Vietnam, race, and youth, the three crucial stories of our time. What the Vice President of the United States is attempting to do is create doubts in the minds of the American public about the motivation and background of those charged with the responsibility of trying to understand and explain these complicated and sensitive controversies.

When Mr. Agnew asks, "Are we demanding enough of our television news presentations?" he is certainly asking a question that others, including many inside the profession, have asked for a generation. For some, the Vice President's question seemed to be about raised eyebrows, caustic

Fred W. Friendly is on the faculty of the Graduate School of Journalism of Columbia University. He is the former president of CBS News and author of the book, *Due to Circumstances Beyond Our Control.* "Some Sober Second Thoughts on Vice President Agnew," copyright 1969 Saturday Review, Inc., is reprinted from *Saturday Review,* December 13, 1969, with permission.

remarks, and too much news analysis. For me, his speech was really about too little analysis. In fact, the Vice President may have provided a most valuable service in his Des Moines speech. He sharpened an issue that has been diffuse for too long, inviting us all to consider once again the state of broadcast journalism.

Agnew and I share the view that television journalism leaves something to be desired. We both fear the concentration of great power in a few individuals in the broadcasting industry. But we are apparently in profound disagreement on not only the nature of the networks' coverage of President Nixon's Vietnam address, but even more importantly, on our crying need for more, not less, interpretive reporting. We require bolder, not blander illumination of the issues that divide men of reason.

Where Agnew went astray, in my view, was in his suggestion that the media ought somehow to be a conduit for the views of the government, or merely a reflector of public opinion. He was not the first nor the last high official to equate fairness and the possession of great power with the obligation of conformity.

The Vice President has forgotten history when he criticizes ABC's journalistic enterprise in arranging for Ambassador Averell Harriman to participate in the broadcast that followed Mr. Nixon's speech of November 3. I don't think President Kennedy rejoiced in having the Republican Senator from Indiana, Homer Capehart, critique his Berlin crisis speech of 1961 nor in having Ladd Plumley, president of the National Chamber of Commerce, pursue him after his controversial 1962 speech on the state of the economy. How many times after a major address did President Johnson have to listen to the cutting remarks of Minority Leaders Everett Dirksen and Gerald Ford? It was all part of the democratic process. After all, the President had had prime time on all three networks, and a small measure of counter-fire from the loyal opposition was hardly stacking the deck. In the end of the day, perhaps ABC might not be faulted for having invited Ambassador Harriman, an experienced negotiator with the Hanoi government, but rather for not having asked him enough hard questions.

The Vice President doubts that President Kennedy, during the Cuban missile crisis of 1962, had his words "chewed over by a round table of critics" immediately following his address to the nation. Would the Vice President believe Sander Vanocur, Ray Scherer, Frank McGee, David Schoenbrun, Roger Mudd, George Herman, Richard C. Hottelet, and Douglas Edwards? The date on that was October 22, 1962. The Vice President did not mention the Bay of Pigs, but certainly he must remember the news analyses and the GOP counter-briefings that followed. President Kennedy, who earlier had called upon broadcasters for self-censorship of the story in the national interest, later told the managing editor of *The New York Times* that revelation of the Bay of Pigs plan might have saved the nation "a colossal mistake."

A generation ago the most savage denouncements against news analysis involved Senator Joseph McCarthy. In an inflammatory speech in Wheeling, West Virginia, in 1950 he declared there were 205 Communists in the State Department. Good news analysis, in fact, good reporting, would have required that the journalist not just hold up his mirror to that startling event, but that he report that the Senator had not one scrap of evidence to substantiate so extravagant a claim. It took broadcasting several years during the McCarthy period to learn that merely holding up a mirror could be deceptive, as in fact holding up a mirror to a riot or a peace march today can be deceptive. It took the shame of the McCarthy period and the courage of an Ed Murrow to elevate broadcast journalism to a point where it could give responsible insights to issues such as those raised by the junior Senator from Wisconsin.

For generations, editors and students of journalism have tried to define news analysis and interpretive reporting. The late Ed Klauber, one of the architects of broadcast news standards, offered the most durable description. I have always kept it in my wallet, and I provide copies to all my students at the Columbia Graduate School of Journalism:

> What news analysts are entitled to do and should do is to elucidate and illuminate the news out of common knowledge, or special knowledge possessed by them or made available to them by this organization through its sources. They should point out the facts on both sides, show contradictions with the known record, and so on. They should bear in mind that in a democracy it is important that people not only should know but should understand, and it is the analysts' function to help the listener to understand, to weigh, and to judge, but not to do the judging for him.

If the Vice President would test the brief analyses of November 3 against Mr. Klauber's criteria, I think he might agree that the correspondents did not cross the line in any attempt to make up the viewer's mind on a course of action. Agnew felt that the response to the President on November 3 was instant analysis. But it seems fair to remind the Vice President that the administration had provided correspondents with advance copies of the speech for study earlier that evening, and there had been a persuasive White House briefing on the content. While the comments of the correspondents were clearly appropriate, my own personal opinion is that only those of Eric Sevareid and Marvin Kalb were probing and thoughtful. Kalb conceivably erred in not quoting pertinent paragraphs from the Ho Chi Minh letter that he believed were subject to different interpretation from that of the President.

Part of our Vietnam dilemma is that during the fateful August of 1964, when the Tonkin Gulf Resolution escalated the war, there was little senatorial debate worthy of the name, and there was a dramatic shortage of news analysis. If I am inclined to give the networks an A for effort and a B for performance the night of November 3, 1969, let me tell you that I give CBS News and myself a D for effort and performance on the night of August 4, 1964, when President Johnson, in his Tonkin Gulf speech, asked for a blank check on Vietnam. In spite of the pleas of our Washington bureau, I made the decision to leave the air two minutes after the President had concluded his remarks. I shall always believe that, if journalism had done its job properly that night and in the days following, America might have been spared some of the agony that followed the Tonkin Gulf Resolution. I am not saying that we should have, in any way, opposed the President's recommendations. But, to quote Klauber's doctrine of news analysis, if we had "out of common knowledge or special knowledge . . . [pointed] out the facts on both sides, [shown] contradictions with the known record," we might have explained that after bombers would come bases, and after bases, troops to protect those bases, and after that hundreds of thousands of more troops. Perhaps it is part of the record to note that Murrow, who understood the value of interpretive journalism from his years as a practitioner, and from his experience as director of the U.S. Information Agency, called minutes after the Johnson speech to castigate me and CBS for not having provided essential analysis of the meaning of the event.

One key aspect of the Vice President's speech did strike me as relating to the public interest as distinguished from the administration's political interest. This was his concern over the geographic and corporate concentration of power in broadcasting. Here he had the right target, but a misdirected aim. His criticism of broadcasters for centralization and conformity better describes the commercial system and its single-minded interest in maximum ratings and profits.

To some extent, it may be true that geography and working out of New York and Washington affect the views of Dan Rather of Wharton, Texas, Howard K. Smith of Ferriday, Louisiana, Chet Huntley of Cardwell, Montana, David Brinkley of Wilmington, North Carolina, Bill Lawrence of Lincoln, Nebraska, and Eric Sevareid of Velva, North Dakota. But I, for one, simply do not buy the Vice President's opinion that these responsible decision makers in news broadcasting and the professionals who work with them are single-minded in their views or unchecked in their performance. There is an independent, sometimes awkward complex of network executives, station managers, producers, and reporters whose joint production is the news we see. They represent a geographic, ethnic, and political profile nearly as far ranging as American society itself, with the tragic exception of blacks. The heads of the three major network news bureaus find their constituencies and their critics among the station managers they serve, the correspondents they employ, sponsors they lose, and in the wider public they please and occasionally disappoint. The news program emerges from a complicated system of argument, conflict, and compromise.

Beyond that, the record suggests that the best professionals recognize and acknowledge their limitations. Walter Cronkite was the first to admit that he erred in some of his reporting at the 1968 Democratic convention. It was David Brinkley, admitting that no reporter could always be objective but could only strive for fairness, who gave the Vice President a high visibility target. In his commentary of November 3, Eric Sevareid clearly noted that his views were "only the horseback opinion of one man and I could be wrong." Yet, if the Vice President's aim was wild, his target of concentrated power is valid and endures. The "truth" of commercial broadcasting is that it maximizes audiences by maximizing profits. This system minimizes the presentation of hard news and analysis, leading the broadcast journalists into occasional oversimplification in the interest of time, overdramatization in the interest of impact.

If such distorting tendencies do exist, and I believe they sometimes do, the proper measure is not to subject the performance of professional journalists to governmental direction nor to majority approval. Rather, the task for government is to apply its leadership and authority to expand and diversify the broadcasting system and environment in which professional journalists work.

I do not see these public actions as inconsistent with or disruptive of the protections of the First Amendment. When Congress passed the Communications Act enabling the FCC to restrict a limited number of frequencies and channels to a limited amount of license-holders, everyone's freedom was slightly qualified because everyone cannot simultaneously broadcast over the same television channel. The Communications Act insisted that license-holders operate their franchise "in the public interest, convenience, and necessity." By every definition I have ever heard, that includes responsible news coverage. Selling cancer-giving cigarettes and not providing enough news and public affairs programing is certainly ample reason to reconsider a station's license, and doing so has nothing to do with the First Amendment. The FCC would be fulfilling longstanding national policy by demanding more, not less, public service broadcasting from the commercial systems, as well as by accelerating development of a publicly supported noncommercial alternative.

The Vice President quotes Walter Lippmann to make a case that the networks have hidden behind the First Amendment. He does not add that Mr. Lippmann's point was that this demonstrated the necessity for just such a competitive, alternate system that most commercial broadcasters today support. Lippmann has also said that "the theory of a free press is that the truth will emerge from free reporting and free discussion, not that it will be presented perfectly and instantly in any one account." Public television, with national interconnection due in part to a new ruling by the FCC, now has a chance to make that "free reporting and free discussion" 25 percent more widespread and more effective.

In the days since the Vice President's speech, I have been jarred by the strange coalition of Americans who find an assortment of reasons for identifying with parts of the Vice President's remarks. The mobilizers for peace don't like the way the peace march was covered or, as they put it, left uncovered. My Democrat friends point to the Humphrey defeat, which they say happened at the hands of the television cameras in Chicago. My journalism students at Columbia feel that time after time broadcasters of my generation misjudge the youth movement and the black movement. In the end, I have had to plead with these students to believe in the integrity of a Cronkite, a Smith, a Brinkley, and in the professionalism of their producers—men such as Les Midgley of CBS, Av Westin of ABC, and Wally Westfeldt of NBC. My defense has been only partly successful, and this has been with an audience generally quite hostile to the main thrust of the Agnew attack. With sadness, I have painfully learned that the reservoir of good will that broadcast journalists could once rely on in time of crisis has now been partially dissipated.

Perhaps if the public knew that the broadcast newsman is fighting for longer news programs, fewer commercials, more investigative reporting, there might be a broader sense of identity.

The broadcast journalist knows how little news analysis appears on the air. Five or eight minutes after a major presidential address is not interpretive journalism as much as it is time to be filled to the nearest half hour, or to the nearest commercial. He also knows that a half hour minus six commercials is just not enough air time to present and analyze the news properly. Perhaps the broadcast newsman of today can no longer afford the luxury of abdicating his role in a decision-making process that now so clearly affects his profession and his standards. He is a far better newsman than the public ever sees and he has far more power to change the system than he and the public imagine.

For a long time the broadcasting companies have relied on the prestige of their news organizations to enhance their own corporate prestige, in fact, their very survival. The reputation of these newsmen is now at stake. They need to do their best, not their worst. They need to be seen at their most courageous, not to slip into timidity. This is not a time for public relations experts, although there will be a frantic search for a corporate line that will once again salvage the good name of broadcasting.

Television's battles will not be fought or won with the polemics of corporate handouts, First Amendment platitudes, or full-page ads. They will be won by what is on the air, and they will be lost by what is *not* on the air. It is later than many people think, and we all have Agnew to thank for reminding us.

Here we stand, with the image orthicon tube, the wired city, and the satellite the greatest tools of communication that civilization has ever known, while the second highest officeholder in the land implies that we use them less. Here we are in 1969, Mr. Vice President, with one leg on the moon and the other on earth, knee-deep in garbage. That's going to require some news analysis.

What the Vice President says is that he wants editorials (which network news divisions don't use) labeled for what they are. Certainly it is general custom to label news analysis and comment when it is taking place, and omission of that, even under the pressure of time, is a mistake.

But Agnew ought to have labeled his speech for what it was. Did he want to encourage responsible journalism, or did he wish to silence it?

The second salvo from the Agnew shotgun contained more buckshot and had even less precise aim. His facts were wobbly and subject to immediate rebuttal. He might have checked to see whether it was only the early out-of-town edition of *The New York Times* that missed the story of the 359 members of Congress who signed a letter endorsing the President's Vietnam policy. Making charges against the power of the *Times* and *The Washington Post* is the kind of anti-conglomerate philosophy usually identified with liberals. The Vice President jarred his own aim by being self-serving. His targets were only those organizations which he considered to be critical. The mighty complex that controls two of the largest newspapers in the nation—the New York *Daily News* and the Chicago *Tribune*, plus television and radio stations in those two cities and a lot more in other cities—was left unscathed, together with other media conglomerates that control huge circulations. Could the fact that hawks rather than doves fluttered atop those mastheads and transmitters have given them immunity?

Perhaps the journalist and the party in power are always destined to be on the outs. President Eisenhower was pretty sore with television news until he left office and became a big fan. President Kennedy was reading and watching more, and enjoying it less. President Johnson watched three sets and knew how to talk back to three talking heads at once, and the Nixon administration has let us know where it stands. It is my theory that, when the message from Des Moines or from the White House itself is always a valentine or a garland of flowers, television and radio will have failed their purpose.

RICHARD L. TOBIN

When Newspapers Do Their Thing

The unparalleled usefulness to the American public of a truly great newspaper, such as *The New York Times* or *The Washington Post* (and the disastrous loss to that public when a *Herald Tribune* dies), has seldom been as dramatically capsuled as in the recent matter of the Pentagon papers and their brackish revelation. Whatever the legislation—and the case is bound to go on for months, even years—we cannot but believe that the American public had a right to these historical documents, that the *Times* and the *Post* served an essential function as a free and uncensored medium of public information, and that not one soldier now in Vietnam will suffer the slightest inconvenience or hurt because Pentagon history before 1968 was published in an American newspaper.

Press and public were not the only segments of American society to find fascination in the case of the Pentagon papers. The U.S. Supreme Court postponed its normal summer recess to go more thoroughly into the vital arguments from both sides—whether valuable secrets had been given away, whether the Republic had been endangered by publication of the historical documents, whether the information bore in any way on current confidential diplomatic or military maneuvers, whether the First Amendment outweighed all other matters in this historic case.

Scotty Reston put it best of all when he wrote: "Great court cases are made by the clash of great principles, each formidable standing alone, but in conflict limited, 'all neither wholly false nor wholly true.'" The *Times* case is an example of the oldest of conflicts between freedom and security. It goes back to John Milton and his *Areopagitica*, which in the seventeenth century cried out against government censorship. In Milton's time the government claimed it had the right to decide, in effect, to li-

---

Richard L. Tobin is Communications Editor of the *Saturday Review*. "When Newspapers Do Their Thing" is reprinted from *Saturday Review*, July 10, 1971, with permission. Copyright 1971 Saturday Review, Inc.

cense what could or could not be published prior to publication. From Milton on, all advocates of freedom of the press have used the *Areopagitica* as a north star.

"*Come, dear. Head up, shoulders back, chest out. Show the world you don't give a toot what the 'Washington Post' said.*"
Drawing by Al Ross reprinted from *Saturday Review,* October 10, 1970, with permission. Copyright 1970 Saturday Review, Inc.

Reston goes on: "So a judgment has to be made when the government argues for security, even over historical documents, and the *Times* argues for freedom to publish. That is what is before the court. It is not a black and white case—as it was in the Cuban missile crisis when the Soviet ships were approaching President Kennedy's blockade in the Caribbean. It is a conflict between printing or suppressing, not military information affecting the lives of men on the battlefield, but historical documents about a tragic and controversial war; not between what is right and what is wrong, but between two honest but violently conflicting views about what best serves the national interest and the enduring principles of the First Amendment."

The inside story of the greatest news beat in modern times reads like something out of Hecht and MacArthur. The first inkling most *Times* staffers had that something extraordinary must be going on occurred when, one by one, top reporters began to disappear. Hedrick Smith, a first-rate diplomatic reporter about to be assigned to Moscow, departed quietly from the Washington Bureau newsroom. Soon after, Neil Sheehan, veteran Vietnam correspondent, was conspicuously absent. Then E. W. Kenworthy, an environmental expert, vanished. When staff members asked Robert Phelps, news editor of the Washington Bureau, where everybody had gone, he ducked the question, but bureau gossip had it that Sheehan was "on assignment," Kenworthy was "on vacation," and Smith was "off studying Russian."

In the New York office, three editors from the foreign news desk late this spring disappeared suddenly from 43rd Street and, unknown to the staff generally, holed up in the Hilton ten blocks away. Fox Butterfield, a top New Jersey suburban reporter, the son of Lyman H. Butterfield, the eminent historian, and grandson of industrialist Cyrus Eaton, dropped out from the metropolitan staff and also moved into the Hilton. Soon a mountain of reference books on the Vietnam War followed the reporters and editors into the hotel. A. M. Rosenthal, the managing editor, and Arthur Ochs Sulzberger, the publisher, of the *Times*, were in on "Project X" from the beginning. Rosenthal said later: "There was a hell of a lot of discussion at high level, but no voices were raised and nobody got mad at anybody else." From the first, Rosenthal was certain that the Pentagon material was authentic and that the *Times* would eventually publish it.

To make things even more mysterious for the rest of the staff, temporary walls were erected in one section of the composing room and a few selected typesetters were assigned to work within this secrecy, having been told to reveal nothing about the extraordinary material they were setting. Late in the afternoon of Saturday, June 12, makeup men who were laying out the Sunday paper were notified that a highly secret story would start on page 1 and jump to six full pages inside. By early evening "Project X" was in publication and the *Times* metropolitan and foreign news desks were swamped with phone calls, chiefly from broadcasters wanting to pursue the fantastic scoop. Managing Editor Rosenthal said of the *Times* staff that it was unified by "Project X" as never before, a common pride in a news beat of transcendental importance to the nation, the world, and, quite obviously, the journalistic fraternity. No one at the *Times* had to be told this was the prize story to end them all. And the gag around the newsroom all week was "All the news they let us print."

Years ago, *The New York Times* was condemned for not having published information it had about U-2 flights over the Soviet Union, classified information if ever there was such. Again, the *Times* was attacked vigorously for playing the government's game when it refused to publish a story ready for print that Cuban freedom fighters were about to land at the Bay of Pigs the following morning. Later, President Kennedy publicly stated that he wished the *Times* had published the story that day—it might have saved him and the whole United States a lot of grief. The *Times* withheld reports, by agreement with President Kennedy, on the Cuban missile crisis. The *Times* knew that Kennedy was deploying the Atlantic Fleet to blockade the Russians in case they refused to withdraw their nuclear armaments from Cuba after an eyeball-to-eyeball confrontation. Incidentally, the paper was roundly condemned for publishing the

Dumbarton Oaks papers on the organization of the United Nations and also for printing inside information on what had actually happened at Yalta. Because the nation's security was at stake, every good newspaper in this country from time to time has withheld vital news stories, usually reporting the details later.

How did the world press react to publication of the documents on the Vietnam War? In brief, it overwhelmingly supported both the *Times* and *Post*. The *Times* of London, perhaps the most influential and certainly one of the most carefully written newspapers in the world, put it succinctly: "All governments find that they have to be less than frank and all governments are divided by their own hopes, but to go to war on a lie is a different matter." In France, *Le Monde* said: "*The New York Times* has perhaps violated certain rules, but it will certainly have contributed to raising the prestige of the United States if, by its audacity, it provokes the citizens of the Union to demand respect for the Constitution, that is to say, better control over the Executive."

In our country, the New York *Daily News*, hardly a friend of the *Times* and about as hawklike as a mass-circulation newspaper can get, supported its cross-town rival to the hilt in thirteen beautifully chosen words: "In a free country, a newspaper is supposed to act like a newspaper." The Long Island daily *Newsday* said: "The *Times* has done a distinct public service in publishing this heretofore secret history," sentiments echoed by *The Wall Street Journal*, the St. Louis *Post-Dispatch*, the Los Angeles *Times*, and other top dailies across the country. *The Christian Science Monitor* felt that the legal judgments are of supreme importance historically and that the decisions would no doubt be a landmark.

The case of the Pentagon papers is intriguing because it marks the first time in American history that the federal government has gone to court to prevent a nationally known newspaper from printing material of vital importance to the country. It is all very well for wags like H. L. Mencken to say that government is the natural enemy of all well-disposed, decent, and industrious men. To those who have thought that Vietnam was a mistake from the beginning, the censorship battle is an open-and-shut case. The fact remains, however, that the White House and many on Capitol Hill firmly believe that *The New York Times* took stolen goods and distributed them. Many responsible people in Washington are of the opinion that if the *Times* and all the other newspapers that have followed suit get away with this one, there won't be much classified material safe at any point in the future. What makes the *Times* case more pertinent than any other in memory is that the greatest and most powerful newspaper in this country did not simply print a précis or summary of the Pentagon report but published classified memoranda verbatim. On the other hand, the *Times* felt it had no choice in terms of the national interest. Should the federal government's accusation ultimately stand, there is no telling what might happen to the First Amendment and the basic principles of press freedom. No President before Nixon has, even through amanuenses, taken a major newspaper to court to prevent publication of a major story, though Thomas Jefferson, Abraham Lincoln, Theodore Roosevelt, Woodrow Wilson, and Franklin D. Roosevelt were sorely tried at times and perhaps even tempted to let unfriendly newspapers have it right between the eyes.

What makes this case a classic, then, is that it is in fact neither black nor white; there is a good deal to be said on both sides, legally, ethically, and professionally. While it is true that the news media, including radio and television, must act responsibly when the national interest is involved, since a free press would vanish if democracy failed, it is equally true that when something desperately needs public airing, such as exposure of the highest echelons of government, there is simply no vehicle other than the press to bring it all to light and correction.

Longtime diplomat Averell Harriman once said: "If governments can't have private papers kept in confidence, I don't know how you can do business in government." Such an observation is valid when negotiations are in progress between countries and ideologies. But the publication of significant documents years later does not violate Mr. Harriman's premise, and, as the *Times* itself said editorially of its own now historic court case, it surely represents a milestone in the endless struggle of free men and free institutions against the unwarranted exercise of government authority. That's what being a newspaperman is all about.

KENNETH AUCHINCLOSS

Victory for the Press

In the Supreme Court of the United States, great constitutional collisions ordinarily occur in slow motion, and the sharpest legal disputes unfold with the stateliness of a minuet. But cases No. 1873 and 1885 were exceptions from the moment they were hastily inscribed on the Court's docket two weeks ago. The Justices agreed one day to review the cases and scheduled oral arguments for the very next. Lawyers toiled through the night on briefs that their opponents barely had time to scan; along with the Justices, they readily admitted that they had not had a chance to examine all the documents on which the controversy turned. For the first time in fourteen years, the Court's term was extended to permit a prompt ruling, and when it came, each of the nine Justices—for the first time in memory—turned out to have written a separate opinion of his own. But somehow, despite the rush to judgment and the discord of judicial views, cases No. 1873 and 1885 produced a dramatic reaffirmation of one of the fundamental American liberties. By a vote of 6 to 3, the Court last week blocked the government's attempt to suppress publication, in *The New York Times* and *The Washington Post,* of the secret Pentagon history of the Vietnam war.

The ruling against press censorship broke no new legal ground—the constitutional presumption against "prior restraint" of any publication springs from the First Amendment and has been articulated by the Court several times, including a landmark 1931 opinion barring the state of Minnesota from suspending a squalid journal of anti-Semitic bigotry. What made last week's decision momentous was the prestige of the litigants and the significance of the material whose publication was at issue. On one side was arrayed the executive branch of the United States Government:

Kenneth Auchincloss is General Editor of *Newsweek* magazine. "Victory for the Press" is reprinted from *Newsweek,* July 12, 1971, with permission. Copyright Newsweek, Inc.

on the other, two of the greatest newspapers in the land. The documents in question included top-secret records of a war in which the nation was still engaged, whose release, according to the government, would do "grave and irreparable" damage to the national interest. Few clearer gauges of the sanctity of the First Amendment freedoms, few plainer demonstrations of the openness of American society, could be imagined than the High Court's ruling in favor of the press.

Freed at last from restraint, the Times and the Post quickly resumed publishing their accounts of the Vietnam "secrets." The new disclosures documented the record of mounting U.S. involvement during the Kennedy years, from JFK's early authorization of covert intelligence operations in North Vietnam to heavy American connivance in the coup that toppled Ngo Dinh Diem in the fall of 1963. They also brought to light increasing unrest over the war—and particularly the bombing of the north —within the counsels of the Johnson Administration as early as 1965. Defense Secretary Robert McNamara, it turns out, urged the President in October 1966 to cut back the bombing and consider a coalition government including Communists in Saigon so the U.S. could get out.

And even before the Court's decision, other newspapers broke their own versions of the Pentagon war papers. The respected *Christian Science Monitor* became the fourteenth journal to print fresh revelations from the secret documents. Alaska's Sen. Mike Gravel conducted an emotional and finally teary series of readings from the 47-volume "history" in a midnight committee hearing. Pentagon papers seemed to be fluttering into the public domain through so many open windows that it was doubtful that the government, even if it had carried the day in court, could ever have shut them up again. The effort was probably never very popular; in a Gallup poll completed just before the ruling, a 58-to-30 majority of those familiar with the case thought the newspapers were right in printing the story.

The ultimate source of all the leaks, Daniel Ellsberg, finally emerged from almost two weeks in hiding to give himself up to Federal authorities —and to proclaim what he had done. "I am prepared for all the consequences," he said. That could be up to ten years in prison and a $10,000 fine under an indictment returned by a Federal grand jury the same day. The government, meanwhile, moved to repair the security system that had proved so deficient. An Air Force team moved into the Rand Corporation, the West Coast think tank where Ellsberg apparently obtained his copy of the report, and took over custody of its store of secret documents. The State Department began considering new procedures for automatic declassification of secrets after a period of years, and bills were introduced in Congress to give the law-makers a role in determining which materials would be declassified, and when.

NEWSPAPERS ON NOTICE

Attorney General John Mitchell, whose efforts at censorship had led to the Administration's embarrassing reversal in court over prior restraint, threatened to pursue an alternative course. He announced he would prosecute "all those who have violated Federal criminal laws in connection with this matter." Plainly, that included not only Ellsberg but any accomplices (he admitted he had some but refused to name them). Beyond that, the announcement put the newspapers on notice that they were also liable to prosecution for any violations in their past—or future —accounts of the purloined documents.

For the moment, however, the press was jubilant over what seemed a famous victory. *Times* publisher Arthur Ochs Sulzberger expressed "complete joy and delight" at the Court's decision. At the *Post,* publisher Katharine Graham said she was "extremely gratified." Echoed executive editor Benjamin Bradlee: "It's beautiful." Politicians were, if anything, even more expansive. Minnesota Sen. Hubert Humphrey (whose hopes for a Presidential nomination, many thought, had been all but smothered by the disclosures) declared that "the Court has performed its most valuable service for many a year," and doves on both sides of the aisle hailed the vindication of the public's "right to know." There were a few dissents. GOP Sen. Gordon Allott of Colorado, for one, thought the newspapers had set themselves above the law—"This," he said, "cannot be permitted."

Similar misgivings were sounded even among some of the Supreme Court Justices who voted with the majority in last week's ruling. Indeed, a close reading of the nine separate opinions made it clear that the press's apparent triumph was far from unqualified. The *Times* and the *Post* had won the main issue, which was the most immediate one: their right to publish the documents in their possession without prior censorship. But at least four of the nine Justices thought that criminal penalties, as opposed to prior restraint, might be imposed on the newspapers if they had published material gravely injurious to the U.S. And only two members of the Court believed that the First Amendment bars censorship in any circumstances. The Court, it seemed, had considerable qualms about the newspapers setting themselves above the law, but it had even more about the government setting itself above the First Amendment.

If the outcome did not represent total victory for the press, one reason was that neither the *Times* nor the *Post* had sought such a result. To win their cases, each realized, they did not need to wrest from the Court an ironclad guarantee of the freedom from prior censorship in all circumstances. Indeed, if they had rested their argument on such an absolute position, they would have courted defeat. For it is well known that the Court includes only two such First Amendment absolutists, Hugo Black and William Douglas. Two others, William Brennan and Thurgood Marshall, are generally found—with Black and Douglas—in the Court's liberal bloc on questions of civil liberties. And, as it turned out, these four had voted, when the Court considered whether even to hear arguments in the *Times* and *Post* cases, to dismiss the government's contention out of hand. So the newspapers needed only one more vote to win, but it would have to be found somewhere in the Court's middle or conservative wing.

Accordingly, they conceded at the outset—as the Court itself had observed in the 1931 Minnesota decision—that there might be some highly unusual instances in which the First Amendment guarantees could be overridden. But the burden of proof upon the government to demonstrate the need for such an exception, they argued, is very great, particularly since the government based its authority for censorship not on any specific act of Congress but on an unstated "inherent" power of the President as conductor of the nation's foreign policy or as Commander in Chief. And the government, they contended, had never supplied evidence that publication of the Pentagon papers would in fact produce the desperate damage that it alleged.

A BROAD LEGAL NET

This approach, it turned out, cast the legal net broadly enough to bring six Justices over to the newspapers' side, albeit for different reasons. Black and Douglas, true believers in the First Amendment's inviolability, indicated that even if Congress had enacted a law permitting prior restraints on the press, it would be unconstitutional. Marshall was willing to grant that Congress might validly pass such a law, but since it had not done so, he said, the Court had no business doing the job instead. Brennan conceded that even in the absence of a law, there might be a case for prior restraint if the government could prove, not just allege, that "publication must inevitably, directly and immediately cause" some serious harm to the nation in wartime—but that case had not been made.

The newspapers' two key catches were middle-of-the-roaders Potter Stewart and Byron White. "They were the swing votes," admitted one top Justice Department hand. "We knew we had to get them to win." But Stewart, even though he was persuaded that publication of the documents would do some of the harm the government suggested, could not agree that "disclosure of any of them will surely result in direct, immediate and irreparable damage to our nation or its people." And he joined White in an even broader opinion that questioned the government's contention that "inherent powers" offered grounds for prior restraint whenever publication would do "grave and irreparable" injury to the national interest. "To sustain the government in these cases," White declared, "would start the courts down a long and hazardous road that I am not willing to travel, at least without Congressional guidance and direction." He also pointed out that a test based on grave and irreparable injury to the Republic would be an invisible guideline; any time the Court found some disclosure would cause such injury, it would have to keep the specifics secret, thus making the case useless as precedent.*

"FRENZIED TRAIN OF EVENTS"

The minority took a different tack altogether. The three dissenters did not contend that the government had proved its case and that the restraining orders should permanently stand. Rather they complained bitterly of the frantic pace and slipshod manner in which the entire proceeding had been conducted. Chief Justice Warren Burger, noting wryly that the *Times* had seen fit to defer publication of the material for three to four months for its own purposes, wondered why it could not delay a few weeks more for the sake of orderly adjudication. Thanks to the unwarranted rush, the Chief Justice argued, "we literally don't know what we are acting on. As I see it, we have been forced to deal with litigation concerning rights of great magnitude without an adequate record, and surely without time for adequate treatment either in prior proceedings or in this Court." Justice John Harlan, who called the issues "as important as any that have arisen during my time on the Court" (sixteen years), ticked off a list of key questions that had been slighted or ignored in "this frenzied train of events." Along with Justice Harry Blackmun, they believed that the cases should be returned to lower courts for more orderly and thorough treatment.

But Justice Harlan went further. Like some of the majority Justices, he was troubled by the "grave and irreparable damage" criterion, but his qualms lay in a different direction. To him, this test would require the Court to enmesh itself in questions of foreign and defense policy to a degree wholly unwarranted by the constitutional doctrine of the separation of powers. He argued that the only proper functions of the courts

---

* In preparing their briefs, the Post's lawyers encountered some of the anomalies created by the use of secret material in the judicial process. Government security guards kept watch outside the door as they drew up their secret responses to the government's secret affidavits, then swept up both sets of documents to take to court; the paper's lawyers were not even allowed to keep a copy of the secret briefs they had themselves written.

were to ensure that the subject matter "does lie within the proper compass of the President's foreign relations power" and that the determination of secrecy had been made by an authorized official. Such firm judicial restraint stood at precisely the opposite pole from Justice Brennan's demand that if the executive branch wanted the judiciary to aid in preventing publication, "it must inevitably submit the basis upon which that aid is sought to scrutiny by the judiciary."

On another point, however, some members of the majority and minority found themselves in agreement. Stewart, Burger and Blackmun all aligned themselves with a pointed admonition to the press delivered by Justice White. The fact that the government had failed to justify prior restraints in these cases, he pointed out, did not mean that criminal convictions might not be in order. And if the press were shown to have revealed information in violation of criminal statutes, said White, "I would have no difficulty in sustaining convictions . . ."

This language encouraged some disappointed government lawyers to believe that the outcome would not be a total loss. "I would hope that the Court's opinions," said an Administration legal strategist, "will persuade the papers to put some restraint on themselves." And Secretary of State William Rogers called on the press to "recognize an obligation to refrain from the publication of information" damaging to the national security. He offered the government's assistance in identifying documents that might be harmful, but there were no known takers. "The series will continue just as we had intended before the interruption," declared *Times* managing editor A. M. Rosenthal. At the *Post*, lawyers and one reporter privy to the government's secret brief culled the forthcoming articles for disclosures that might do genuine damage. Only minor changes were made, according to managing editor Eugene Patterson.

IMPATIENCE FOR WITHDRAWAL

For the time being, at least, any injuries the Pentagon papers might cause the country seemed less apparent than the injuries the Administration itself had sustained from its futile effort to suppress them. It had drawn far more public attention to the documents than they would have otherwise received. It had linked itself to the past Administration's Vietnam policy. And it had reinforced an impression of governmental highhandedness in Vietnam policy that may well increase public impatience for withdrawal and reduce the Administration's flexibility.

As for the legal effects, the long-run influence of cases 1873 and 1885 were extremely hard to measure. "Great cases like hard cases make bad law," Justice Oliver Wendell Holmes once observed. And, indeed, with nine separate opinions on the record, none of them had the force of precedent for the future. Important questions had been left entirely unresolved. The Court had not been able to fashion any test of when prior restraint might be justified, although a majority of the Justices thought there might be such an occasion. The mysteries of what Harlan called "a singularly opaque statute," the Espionage Act, which might or might not outlaw publication of information harmful to the United States, remained unsolved.

But the overriding importance and value of the case seemed to be this: the First Amendment had been subjected to its most exacting challenge in many years and had emerged intact. The power to decide what news is fit to print remained outside the government's domain.

PART THREE

Advocates

Introduction

Separation of news from editorial comment is an American press tradition which flowered early in this century. The tradition has been idealized, perhaps romanticized, in the notion of "objective" reporting, difficult as that notion is to define. Critics of the news media have grumbled for years that the tradition has been violated more often than observed, not only in newspapers and newsmagazines, but also on radio and TV.

The New Journalists of the 1970s, who include Tom Wolfe, Gay Talese, Nicholas von Hoffman, Norman Mailer, and a growing number of young still-unknowns in city newsrooms across the land, agree that the old objectivity should be scrapped. Agreement seems to end here, however, for New Journalists have different words to describe both their means and their goals. Some speak of themselves as advocacy reporters, others as activists journalists; others say they belong to the "tell-it-as-I-see-it" school. Truman Capote has even come up with what he calls the "new non-fiction," pointing to *In Cold Blood* as an example. Quite apart from their views on stance and style of reporting, many New Journalists also say the reporter should have more to say about editorial policy, traditionally controlled entirely by management.

The debate between the activist-advocacy reporters and the older objectivity reporters is reminiscent of the argument that went on during the McCarthy period of twenty years ago between those who wanted more "interpretative" reporting and those who held fast to objectivity. Many of the same points were made then by both sides. Today's objectivity diehards seem to forget that the interpretation school had won the argument by the mid-50s. And the advocacy-activist reporters seem to ignore the similarities between interpretative and "tell-it-as-I-see-it" reporting.

The pressures for activist-advocacy reporting today spring from the media-public credibility gap, mounting demands for social change, and the conviction of many young journalists that news media are too bland, too superficial, and too conservative. Some European newspapers, the

American college press, and the underground press are providing models for change.

As the debate becomes more heated, both sides tend to move closer to agreement that "objectivity" and "advocacy" are code words serving chiefly to confuse issues. Both sides tend to agree that whether he is working on an interpretative or an activist story, the reporter needs to be an expert on the subject about which he is reporting; he must be fair and have a high regard for accuracy, and his account should be complete.

J. K. HVISTENDAHL

The Reporter as Activist:
Fourth Revolution in Journalism

American journalism is embroiled in its fourth revolution, introduced to the country in the belligerent tones of Vice President Spiro T. Agnew in his Des Moines speech of November 1969. This revolution, like most social revolutions, has even those who are most directly involved in complete chaos and confusion. The revolution is real, those who are involved are in earnest, but the goal is not necessarily the demise of American journalism.

The first revolution was the freeing of the American Press from the threat of control by government. The first and fourteenth amendments to the Constitution made it legal, and eighteenth-century rationalism made it philosophically desirable to criticize actions of the government. The editors of partisan newspapers after the revolution supplied somewhat more criticism than the government wanted.

The second revolution was the growth of the "objective press," brought about largely by the press associations which developed after the invention of the telegraph. Because they served many papers, with many and sometimes violently differing points of view, the press associations had to present the news as objectively as possible, without opinions or evaluations of the authors. The press association made a solid contribution to journalistic writing, and the objective style became the model for journalistic writing.

The third revolution was interpretive reporting, in which the reporter reported the facts objectively, but attempted to explain them or interpret them in a way that would make them meaningful to the reader and

Professor Hvistendahl is a member of the journalism faculty at Iowa State University. "The Reporter as Activist: Fourth Revolution in Journalism" is reprinted from *Quill*, February, 1970, with permission.

listener. Both World War I and World War II contributed to the growth of this type of reporting; readers and listeners wilted before a barrage of objective but totally confusing messages about the war. By interpreting the news to anxious audiences, H. V. Kaltenborn, Elmer Davis, Boake Carter and other "name" commentators commanded audiences of millions. Newspaper columnists like Raymond Clapper, Thomas L. Stokes, Marquis Childs, Walter Lippmann, and Ernest K. Lindley came on the scene for the same reasons.

Now the fourth revolution is upon us, and the revolutionists are activist reporters. The journalistic activist believes he has a right (indeed an obligation) to become personally and emotionally involved in the events of the day. He believes he should proclaim his beliefs if he wishes, and that it is not only permissible but desirable for him to cover the news from the viewpoint of his own intellectual commitment. He looks at traditional reporting as being sterile, and he considers reporters who refuse to commit themselves to a point of view as being cynical or hypocritical. The activist believes that attempting to describe the events of a complicated world objectively seldom results in the truth for anybody—the source, the reporter, or the reader or listener.

Some of the symptoms of the growing activism as reported in a recent *Wall Street Journal* article reprinted in the December *Quill:*

> Some 500 Time, Inc. employees attended anti-war discussions in the company auditorium on Moratorium Day.
>
> The *Chicago Journalism Review,* a publication by reporters dedicated to pointing out the lapses of the very papers for which they work, is now in its second year of publication.
>
> Reporters on at least a half dozen major papers in the country have asked their publishers for a more active role in their paper's policy decisions, as have the employees of *Time.*
>
> Two young women reporters on the New York *Post* were fired for refusing to have their bylines on stories which they thought demeaned women, but were rehired after other *Post* reporters eliminated their own bylines in sympathy.

Those of us who have been associated with university publications should have seen the fourth revolution coming. For surely the college and university press has provided the early warning system. College and university newspapers, some of the best in the country and some of the worst, have steadily de-emphasized "straight news." Opinion pieces abound, and not only on the editorial pages. The *Carltonian,* of Minnesota's prestigious Carleton College, has relegated all straight news to a daily bulletin, and has turned the entire college paper into a journal of "think" pieces, somewhere between a newspaper and a magazine in format.

"Truth-as-I-see it" reporting, rather than activist reporting, might be a more accurate description of the fourth revolution. The new reporters don't claim that they, or anybody else, have a corner on the truth. But they insist that the reporter, like the scientist, has an obligation to report the truth as he sees it. In the long run, they believe, the reporter who is seeking the truth will serve the reader and listener better than the traditional reporter who attempts to describe an event accurately, reduce it to symbols which fit the news conduits of the various media, and then pipe the product to the consumer who is to make of it what he will.

The activist believes the modern media "lie by sanitation" and sin by omission. The media omit important observations by the reporter because they are "editorial in nature." They clean up and homogenize the news to make it fit the orderly world of the establishment, of which the press is too much a part. Read this excerpt from a letter written by a young journalism graduate after his first job on a large Midwestern newspaper:

> In July I went on a walk through _____, the city's worst black ghetto, with the President of the American Public Health Association. We visited homes of five ghetto residents to talk with them about their health problems.
>
> My assignment was to pour out my heart in the story. I did. But by the time the copy desk got through with the material it was unrecognizable.
>
> Every reference to tenement was changed to "apartment" and all mention of rat tracks, month-old garbage, and abandoned buildings standing open to kids and arsonists (law requires all abandoned buildings in the city to be boarded up) was edited out.

The reporter thought that he'd been asked to "pour out his heart," but apparently not to the extent that he could describe a ghetto neighborhood in terms which showed his feelings, and might in turn convey similar feelings to his readers.

The truth-as-I-see-it newsman rejects the conduit, or common carrier, theory of the press. The amount that can flow through the conduits is miniscule compared to the totality of available news. The consumer can't possibly be given all the facts about a situation as complicated as, for example, Vietnam. The process of news selection is and always has been subjective; there are no reliable external criteria (first-year journalism books to the contrary) by which anyone can decide with any precision what is news and what isn't news.

If it is indeed true that a news story starts out as a subjective decision on the part of the press service, city editor, or television program director, the question then arises as to whether the story shall be released without further responsibility on the part of the media. Vice President Agnew would probably say yes. But for the activists there are several reasons why the newsman's responsibility should continue. Because only a small part of the totality of relevant information can be presented to the reader or viewer, the situation (as far as truth-as-I-see-it goes) is one-sided and is likely to mislead the reader or listener. The content of a news event, within the reporter's own knowledge, may be patently false, exaggerated or misleading but is offered to the reader without comment and with the implication that it is true. "Objectivity" may be served but the truth isn't.

The classic example of "common carrier" reporting, of course, was that of the late Senator Joseph McCarthy. McCarthy made charges on the floor of the Senate which reporters knew were false, but they were obliged to report the stories without comment or warning because the newspapers they worked for were "common carriers." The reporters had no obligation to truth-as-they-knew-it other than to quote the senator correctly, but it was a frustrating experience for those who knew they were spreading false information.

A second example is Nixon's speech on Vietnam, which was evaluated immediately after delivery by television commentators, and which led to strong condemnation of the media by Vice President Agnew in his Des Moines speech. Agnew was perturbed in part because the commentators seemed to be in general agreement that there was nothing substantially new in Nixon's speech, a judgment that can be supported by even a casual reading of the President's speech. It is possible that President Nixon, being a skilled politician, hoped that the *impression* would be left that he had a new policy on Vietnam. Would the truth have better been served if the television commentators had acted as common carriers only, when their experience with politics and news had told them that the public needed some additional information which might bring them somewhat closer to the truth?

From the viewpoint of communication theory, the "objective" reporter or writer expends most of his responsibility with the source. He is obliged to quote the sources correctly, and accurately describe the news event. Further, he must not in any way permit his own views to provide a warning to the reader if he perceives the information to be false or defective. The reader or listener must be the judge; the writer has no responsibility to the audience other than to deliver the message. The activist reporter with his emphasis on truth-as-I-see-it feels responsibility to the audience. He asks, "If I deliver an 'objective' message to the reader, but that message is likely to take the reader farther from the truth rather than bring him closer to it, who has been served?"

Another area in which the truth-as-I-see-it journalist demands more of the share of the action is in the news selection process. The women reporters on the New York *Post* refused to have their bylines on an interview of Mrs. Gil Hodges. According to their value system, women are people and should appear in the news on their own merit, not on the merit of their husbands. (If this value were widespread in American journalism, Jackie Kennedy Onassis would soon have complete privacy.)

The point is not that one point-of-view is necessarily more valid than another, but there are *multiple points of view* in a diverse society and more of these should surface in the press. For the most part, the "gatekeepers" who make the news decisions in the media are in the bifocal set, and they inevitably make news judgments that reflect their own training and backgrounds. Like all of us, they are victims as well as beneficiaries of all they have experienced. They have "learned" that the public will lap up columns of type on murder cases, so they have given the public columns of type on the Sam Sheppard cases while Lake Erie gets little attention until it is biologically dead. As one young reporter expresses it, "The American press is always last to recognize the disease, but is first to report the funeral."

The activist believes that the base of news judgment should be broadened to include more newsmen with contemporary social conscience, who are actively interested in solutions to social problems, and who might make the press an active partner, rather than a passive chronicler, of social change.

Truth-as-I-see-it reporting might not only help to eliminate some of the excesses of journalism but also the practice of making mountains out of trivial molehills. Astronaut "Buzz" Aldrin in a UPI story criticized news media for a practice that is so common that it is taught routinely in schools of journalism (it's called "getting the peg"). Aldrin says, "we were talking about the G (gravity) airplane, and simulations for one-sixth G and zero G and somebody happened to ask the question, did you ever get sick in the airplane?"

"I admitted it had happened—that I did once on one flight and this turned into 'Aldrin reveals lunar sickness' as a headline, and I think that's pretty misleading."

In another instance, Aldrin's uncle was talking to another passenger on an airplane, and happened to mention conversationally that some scientists had speculated that lunar rocks might burst into flame when exposed to oxygen. "Well, this turned into a headline, because the man was a reporter: 'Aldrin Fears Lunar Rocks.' " These stories may have had inconsequential effects, but the effect on George Romney's political future when newspapers chose to play up his famous remark that he'd been "brainwashed by American generals" in Vietnam probably ended his presidential hopes.

There are at least two other compelling reasons why it might be well to take a tolerant view of truth-as-I-see-it reporting. America faces tremendous environmental and political problems which can only be solved by concerted action. Outmoded forms of government must be changed. A new and saner view needs to be taken of the nation's defense. If the press is to act as a neutral bystander, waiting to report the symptoms of disaster as they appear, what social agency is to marshal the people and the institutions to the task at hand?

The second reason is that the institutions of our society are so vast that the truth about them may never emerge, or emerge so late as to be downright dangerous. It took twenty-one months for the "secret" to surface about the massacre of several hundred Vietnamese civilians by American troops. It took over a year to "discover" that the Air Force has spent an extra, unauthorized billion dollars on the development of a cargo plane. And whoever heard of Watts or Hough before the fire bombs started falling?

Like most revolutions, this one had its roots deep in the past. The libertarian tradition of the American press, as envisioned by Thomas Jefferson, assumed a free marketplace of ideas, from which the truth would emerge. The libertarian press did not encompass "objectivity," and it assumed that personal opinions would be expressed and the best of them would survive. (Jefferson couldn't possibly have contemplated the difficulty of the truth emerging into the marketplace from the Pentagon.) Being personally and emotionally involved in stories they are writing is nothing particularly new to American reporters. Almost every Pulitzer prize-winner has been an activist to the extent that he involved himself personally and emotionally in the story for which he won the prize. Clark Mollenhoff, reporter turned presidential assistant and press critic, was himself noted for his high personal involvement in the stories out of Washington which he wrote for the Des Moines *Register* and *Tribune,* and for which he won a Pulitzer prize. News magazines, *Time* especially, have bordered on this type of reporting for some time, although they have toned down the personal element by a cloak of anonymity. *Look* magazine owes at least a part of its postwar success to vigorous first-person reporting by concerned writers who were given their editorial head. The same week President Nixon delivered his policy speech on Vietnam, *Look* published a seven-page article by Foreign Editor J. Robert Moskin entitled "Vietnam: Get Out Now." The article was followed (not preceded by) a three-paragraph editorial supporting Moskin's stand.

Truth-as-I-see-it reporting is not editorializing. It is an honest attempt on the part of the reporter to bring together all the material that he can on a subject on which he has strong feelings. The article may be one-sided or it may be balanced. Perhaps his decision is to make no decision. But it is an honest attempt to seek the truth. If the reporter is honest, he will be accurate and he will be fair. But he'll follow the information he has to its logical conclusion, and make judgments, if judgment seems apparent to him.

Lest panic set in, it should be noted that not all reporting should or need be done by activists, and not all reporters may be dedicated to "truth-as-I-see-it." "Objective" news reporting did not entirely supplant the biased reporting of the partisan press. Partisan reporting is still present in labor publications, most of the underground press, and in the editorials of many a respected newspaper. Interpretive reporting did not replace objective reporting, and the need for interpretive reporting remains. And truth-as-I-see-it will no doubt supplement, rather than replace, other approaches to reporting.

For the most part, this type of reporting calls for specialists, highly trained in their specialty. Unlike editorials, it is by-line reporting representing the accumulated wisdom of one individual rather than of the newspaper or television station. Much of the necessary-but-routine reporting from obituaries to baseball scores could be done by high school or junior college graduates; the truth-as-I-see-it reporters should be university graduates, preferably with a Master's degree in a specialty field.

If the media are to function as catalysts for action in vital political and social institutions in America, as well as continue their functions as common carriers of information, the organization of the newsroom will have to change. Most newspapers are organized to process the news, not to originate it. A more realistic organization of daily papers would be along lines of special areas of knowledge—the economics editor, the environmental specialist, the political editor, the urban affairs editor, the transportation editor, the leisure time editor, the science editor. More responsibility would be thrust on editors and reporters to carve out their own stories.

The long-haired, mustachioed creatures from the colleges and universities beginning their apprenticeship on America's newspapers, magazines, radio and television stations represent what may be America's last chance for a vital and vigorous press. But if they are turned off by an establishment press while the garbage mounts, law enforcement deteriorates, the ghettos grow as fast as the military budget, the airports get ever more crowded while train service disappears, they will turn to other pursuits. For on the whole the activist-type college editors are the brightest, most talented of the current crop of young journalists.

The established press can harness the vitality and concern of this new breed of journalist to the nation's serious problems. Or the press can retain its traditional status as a common carrier of news and faithfully record the failures of America's social, political, religious, and economic institutions as they occur. Then, says the young activist, they can comment at length on just what went wrong and who is to blame. The comment would be on the editorial page, of course.

NORMAN A. CHERNISS

How to Handle the
New Breed of Activist Reporters

. . . I am at least as much concerned about inactive editors, naturally by my definition, as I am by activist reporters. I must say, too, I don't think you can discuss the activism of the young without keeping in mind the complacency of the old.

Okay. If the long-hair battle was ever worth fighting—and God and I combine to keep my own hair attractively short and sparse—the fight is lost. Look around you. And while I don't happen to like long hair on men, it is not *my* hair, it is *their* hair. Worst of all, it is probably true that if, say, Homer Bigart's hair fell below his shoulders and his trousers were belled and blatant 'til hell wouldn't have them, he would still do just as well as a reporter as he does now. Maybe better in certain obvious situations. . , . .

If there are editors actually playing around, so to speak, with this dire problem of bra-lessness, I can only conclude they fancy the prospect of daily personal inspection.

Hair and clothes ought to be of professional concern, when they adversely affect professional performance. . . .

Young reporters—all three sexes—and students are masses of contradictions. They are all-knowing and un-knowing, self-confident and insecure. They confuse certitude with certainty. They are idealistic and selfish, generous and greedy. They are arrogant and vulnerable. They are bright and boring. They are tolerant, sometimes to a fault, of their generation,

---

Norman A. Cherniss is associate editor of the Riverside (Calif.) *Press-Enterprise*. "How to Handle the New Breed of Activist Reporters," is slightly abridged from *The Bulletin* of the American Society of Newspaper Editors, May, 1970, and is reprinted with permission.

not so tolerant of yours. They are human and young, and, if you forget it, they will remind you at a time opportune to them. There can be about them something of the child who, having killed his parents, pleads for an orphan's mercy from the court.

"Ambivalent" is a favorite word with them right now, and, God knows, they are that.

They want the rights of age, whatever those are, and the privileges of youth. They want to prolong adolescence, having heard that what lies between it and the retirement community can be something of a drag. They fear being co-opted, even corrupted. They want your money, but they are afraid of what may go with it.

On the whole, remembering that they've got problems and pressures, they're not bad. The best of them are very good, in both the professional and personal sense. And most of them give a damn.

Because they do, they complain a lot. Those with great interest in newspapers—and that seems to be a disturbingly diminishing number—complain about them. They complain of their irrelevancy, their blandness, their lack of courage, their lack of compassion, their bad writing, resistance to change, crisis reporting, superficiality, preoccupation with trivia, failure to tell about people as distinct from institutions, failure to effect social change, failure sometimes even to recognize it. And salaries. And more.

Since these happen to include many of my own complaints, maybe I am hearing what I want to hear. But I have also been hearing most of the same complaints from my peers and elders at professional conferences at least as far back as when Norman Isaacs was at the *St. Louis Star-Times*.

A difference is that they are made now with greater fervor, and sometimes with greater sincerity, by the young than by the old. It seems to me they come with greater urgency now, too, from people just in or just coming into our profession. I mean people young enough to disclaim responsibility for a situation where even the Associated Press Managing Editors Association—never yet accused of radicalism or excessive self-criticism—acknowledges a serious credibility gap between newspapers and their readers.

And I suppose a credibility gap, a crisis of confidence, exists also between younger reporters and older editors. I would remind you that it wasn't simply the demand for a proper medium for dirty classifieds that brought the underground press into being or allows it to spread. . . .

[A] deservedly respected editor complained to me recently that younger newsmen tend to look upon the Black Panthers as archangels. I doubt the universality of that assessment. But when even violent revolutionaries have their lives shot out from under them with what seems to be less than proper pretext, or when the Eighth Amendment is bent badly against them, then concern is not limited to ghetto poolhalls and Leonard Bernstein's salon.

It is not enough to worry about handling "activism" in the newsroom. What creates protest, what creates activism? It is important to remember that many of the younger newsmen and journalism students look upon journalism as the extension, or communication, of social science. The eminent sociologist Robert Nibset wrote recently in *The New York Times* Book Review of the "most unbelievable" revolt among younger social scientists generally, "this revolt against objectivity, this scuttling of the idea of dispassionate reason is the study of man and society. . . ."

It's going on in newspaper journalism, too, and we have to deal with it because it's there. And the problem isn't as simple as appeals to Sweet Reason, reminders that editors are uncompromisingly interested in the Pursuit of Truth, or, failing such nobility, threats to surrender newsroom children to Mrs. Agnew and Mrs. Mitchell for spanking.

Having never been one automatically to impute wisdom to the old, I am certainly not going to assume it in the young automatically. But I think they ought to be listened to, and I think they can be talked to. And I think we're all going to have to adjust to doing these obvious things, with the old obligated to show as much candor as the young have, or think they have. And you're going to have to deal rationally with the sometimes irrational. If you don't bear the cross, you can't wear the crown.

Where newspapers *as* newspapers are concerned, despite the "generation gap," a term which ordinarily means simply "I don't want to discuss it," I'm not sure there is a great deal of difference between the complaints of the dedicated and enlightened young and the dedicated and enlightened old. Where there is disagreement, often it arises over proposed correctives.

It's going to have to be made clear that that which jeopardizes the integrity of the news columns, however nobly motivated, isn't worth it. It's going to have to be explained that turning the news columns into a series of personal editorials, without so much as an "on-the-other-hand," is hardly going to narrow the aforementioned credibility gap, not where a general audience is involved. I think it is often necessary to explain to young reporters the difference between a general audience and a college or a college-educated audience without downplaying the need to educate the general audience. I think it often necessary to explain that the French and British newspapers, famous for mixing reporter opinion and straight reporting, do not serve one-newspaper communities.

There is a curious contradiction in mixtures of straight reporting and reporter opinion: The reader is so dumb he can't form an opinion unless the reporter makes clear his own and what the reader's should therefore be; the reader is so smart he can readily sort fact from opinion in the advocacy or personal opinion report. And there is about advocacy journalism the erroneous presumption that it will always be in behalf of Noble Causes.

Yet, I also think we're going to have to get rid of the debate over "objectivity" by getting rid of the word. If it was ever universally understood by such subjective creatures as newspaper editors, it has of late been defined and redefined too much, to the end that it has been drained of meaning. The younger people I know, acutely conscious of human failings, ordinarily would substitute "honesty" and "fairness" and "accuracy" as criteria, terms with which editors in their better moments do not ordinarily quarrel.

We hear much of "involvement." I think there is plenty of room for a young reporter to get involved in a substantial story and to do it with feeling. I think he can get caught up in it, as good reporters always have, and can make a contribution which will satisfy his soul and that of an intelligent editor, without going ape. There is a difference between getting caught up and getting carried away. But too often involvement has come to mean not merely properly personal accounts, including live-ins and the like, nor even just preoccupation with a cause; too often it has come to mean preoccupation with self, even self-exaltation.

There is a limit to "involvement" and "participation," and I cannot imagine why an editor should be afraid to stand up and say, "This far and no farther." If conscience tells the reporter he must be an active participant in the demonstration he is supposed to report, we must not love him the less for responding to conscience, but to hell with him as a reporter.

I cannot imagine why a newspaperman at any level wants to run around with an advertisement on his lapel—whether he is bleeding publicly for social justice, so that he won't be suspect to his peers, or advertising his commitment to the Chamber of Commerce, so that he won't be suspect to his peers. I feel the same about the younger newsman who requires a lapel button to remind him of his politics at a given time as I do about the older editor who requires a monogram on his pajamas to remind him of his name as he departs the day or rises to greet it.

There are, too, those young "activists" who would transplant student government—regular or ad hoc—to the newsroom and subject the editorial process to Robert's Rules, or something less polite. And some of them are whizzes at it. My limited exposure to student government, particularly where it moves into areas historically the provinces of the faculty, leads me to doubt that it can be any significant part of the solution to the manifold problems of schools, whatever the demands for it. Rather, I am led to wonder if it isn't in fact a student joke; helping the faculty look foolish has got to be a greater lark than throwing underwear from a dormitory window or snagging it below ever could have been.

I think younger reporters, to say nothing of the older ones, ought to be counseled with and ought to expect to have their opinions respected. I don't think everybody in the newsroom should have an equal voice or vote in the editorial process. Decision by committee, especially at newspapers, doesn't bespeak activism, only inaction.

That counseling is very important. The better young newsmen want not only to give you their opinion, they want yours—and your interest and your help. These are sometimes remarkably hard for them to get. There are editors who deplore outside involvement while demonstrating their own by seldom being seen in the newsroom or available in their offices.

In the name of whatever you consider holy, when these younger people pose questions, give them straight answers and try to have answers you are at reasonable pains to make intelligent. "We've always done it this way" is not an intelligent answer. Nor is, "Because I say it's so." They know God made you editor; you have to make it clear why He chose as He did.

And in your discussions of how things used to be, and still should be, never forget the final arrow these young people hold in their little quivers: "If you're so damn smart and have been doing things so damn right, why are you and newspapers and society in general in so much trouble?"

There is a kind of activism by the young as yet undiscussed, the active insistence that high professional standards be demanded of them and their older colleagues and the companion insistence that editors maintain high standards for themselves. Give these younger people something in which they can take pride and in which they can get properly involved —a relevant, intelligently and purposefully edited newspaper. Inevitably there is some adaptation by the young to whatever scene they come upon; give them a scene worth adapting to.

I think that by and large the young complainants are trying to tell you what you should already know about your newspaper and about society. If what you're doing is wrong, it ought to be challenged; if what you're doing is right, it can withstand challenge. . . .

I still believe that in most situations the best, most effective, reporter is going to be the one who "sits in the house of life with his hat and coat on."

But all this takes some explaining to younger reporters, understandably caught up by the passions of these times. I think it is best done on a personal basis, by editors who also give a damn and who show it by handling the "new breed of activist reporters" as what they are: human beings.

And I would suggest that it will all come with greater grace and more effectiveness from editors who are not activists in every civic organization around, who are not businessmen before they are editors and who are not participating personally and directly in the other branches of government.

DAN ROTTENBERG

Words of Caution
for Rebellious Reporters

Reporters rejoice and push onward, editors hestitate, publishers cower behind their desks in fearful realization that the day of judgment has finally come. That, if we are to believe some reports, is the current state of affairs in the news industry since something called the "reporter power" movement began sweeping the country. In *Esquire,* in *Time,* in *Newsweek,* and, of course, in CJR, we read of numerous cases in which working newsmen are standing up to their bosses by publishing journalism reviews, demanding a say in editorial policy, insisting on a voice in the selection of their superiors, and even talking about taking control of their papers altogether.

All of this is well and good—up to a point. Editors need to be shaken out of the complacent notion that the affairs of their suburban neighbors and of their downtown club colleagues are the major concerns of the day. Publishers need to be put on notice that reporters' souls are not for sale. And to the extent that the new working press activism has accomplished these things and has helped produce better news media, it has been a valuable force, as any astute editor or publisher will readily admit.

But the flush of victory in the initial skirmishes has prompted talk among some reporters of "seizing control" of their newspapers. To be sure, much of this talk can be likened to that of the union leader who demands a fifteen-hour week but later settles for thirty-five. Nevertheless, much of it is intended seriously and sincerely, so it should be pointed out that a lot of the rhetoric now being tossed off by some leaders of the

---

"Words of Caution for Rebellious Reporters" is reprinted from *Chicago Journalism Review,* January, 1971, with permission. Dan Rottenberg is managing editor of the *Review.*

reporter movement may well be rendered invalid soon by technological changes in the industry—if indeed they ever were valid.

Consider a few current articles of faith in the movement:

1. A publisher can't put out a good newspaper if he's interested only in making money; the news shouldn't be viewed merely as a product, to be marketed like groceries.

2. Reporters have the right to participate in the determination of newspaper policies.

3. Newspapers should be required to open their pages to anyone who wishes to express himself.

4. If working newsmen were given control of their newspapers, they would necessarily do a better job than the present editors and publishers.

It is all well and good to talk about reporters' rights, a newspaper's obligation to the truth, and the need of a better informed public. But it should be kept in mind that within ten years, newspapers as we now know them may no longer exist. Thanks to the development of two-way cable television, people will be able to push a button on their TV set and receive instantly whatever news stories or features they would like to read. If, for example, a man's tastes are such that he wants to read Mike Royko and George Tagge but nothing else, he will be able to do so. Every reader will become his own editor, for better or for worse; the only newspapers to survive will be those which can convince readers that they can assemble a better package of news and features than the reader can.

In short, however we may deplore the thought of determining the news in the market place, the name of the game in future years will continue to be convincing readers that they should buy and read one publication or news service rather than another.

Much of the talk in the reporters' movement ignores this hard fact of life, assuming instead that since most daily newspapers are monopolies, they have captive audiences. Maybe they do for the time being, but they won't for long. That is why any idealistic takeover of a newspaper by reporters is bound to fail unless there is someone in the group crass enough to engage in the kind of hustling and salesmanship necessary to attract readers' attention . . . someone as crass, say, as some of the very publishers the reporters are now rebelling against.

So perhaps it's worth pointing out that an idealistic publisher isn't always an asset. I have run into many idealistic publishers, and I can only conclude that a newspaper could do worse than have a hard-headed businessman running the show.

I recall one publisher who was so idealistic that he used to print a large picture of George Washington on the front page of his paper about once a month. His idealism also included loyalty to his community—which he spared from unpleasant or controversial ideas—and loyalty to his friends, whom he protected from embarrassment in print. His paper was unprofitable, but he said he was willing to swallow the losses in order to protect and boost his community.

In time he sold out to a man who announced his intention to make the paper profitable. The new publisher took George Washington off the front page, put an end to favoritism in news coverage, and set out to report everything that would be of concern to local people. The idea, he said, was to give people a paper they couldn't do without. He wasn't an idealist, just a good businessman: in the ten years since the acquisition, circulation has shot up a full 50 percent, and the paper is now in the black. It's also, incidentally, very good. And I don't think it's a coincidence that the nation's best newspapers are also among the most profitable: the *New York Times,* the *Wall Street Journal,* the *Washington Post,* the *Los Angeles Times,* the Knight chain, for example.

It would be naive to suggest that quality is the sole factor in determining profits. But it certainly is *a* factor, and in the long run it may well be the major factor.

Similarly, publishers shouldn't be discouraged from treating the news as a "product." They should be encouraged. Any publisher who viewed the news strictly as a product would see that the best product is achieved when the news is handled by newsmen without outside interference. Columbia Broadcasting System may own the New York Yankees, but it doesn't keep a corporate executive in the dugout.

As for the notion that newspapers should somehow be required to throw open their pages to anyone who has something to say—one wonders how long people would go on reading a newspaper that made no attempt to separate the wheat from the chaff. There may be easier ways to kill the newspaper industry than to force editors to print every handout that comes across their desks, but I can't think of one offhand.

It's also worth mentioning that when a working newsman saddles himself with the responsibilities of ownership—as some newsmen apparently seem anxious to do—the newsman's judgment is inevitably colored. Instead of devoting himself single-mindedly to reporting the news, he worries also about what's good for the paper and how to help the community grow and prosper.

I'm reminded of the case of a friend of mine, a small-town Indiana editor who frequently clashed with his publisher on matters of news policy. Sometimes the editor would win his point, but on other occasions he'd be unable to bring the publisher around to his view. On such occasions, my friend would remark bitterly, "Some day I'll run my own paper; that's the only way to get complete editorial freedom."

In due course that friend of mine did indeed assume the dual titles of editor and publisher of his paper. Need I add that the paper under his dual leadership wasn't nearly as lively or meaningful as it had been previously? The sparkling paper produced by the give-and-take between editor and publisher had been replaced by a droning sheet run by one man ensnared by conflicting responsibilities.

In short, life—and the newspaper business—doesn't always turn out as you envision it. To those who recite the rhetoric of the reporters' revolt, I would submit my own list of rhetorical warnings for newsmen:

1. As publishers go, a self-styled community savior is a greater danger to honest reporting than a hard-hearted businessman.

2. The coming technological revolution will probably drive all mediocre newspapers out of business. You might mention this to your favorite editor or publisher the next time you get together.

3. You can demand ownership, but don't be so quick to accept it. It may corrupt you, just as it corrupted many of those whose thrones you now seek to overturn.

DAVID SANFORD

The Underground Press

There is nothing very underground about the underground press. The newspapers are hawked on street corners, sent to subscribers without incident through the U.S. mails, carefully culled and adored by the mass media. About three dozen of them belong to the Underground Press Syndicate [now called Liberation News Service] which is something like the AP on a small scale; through this network they spread the word about what is new in disruptive protest, drugs, sex. Their obsessive interest in things that the "straights" are embarrassed or offended by is perhaps what makes them underground. They are a place to find what is unfit to print in *The New York Times*.

The *Berkeley Barb, The East Village Other, The Fifth Estate, The LA Free Press* are among the more familiar and successful of the papers. They make the aging *Village Voice*—of which they are all derivative—seem very Establishment indeed. The hippie thing brought them to flower; but the death of hippie (the funeral was in early fall and the obit was in *Newsweek*) has apparently not diminished them. They are all the things their admirers think they are—exciting, informative, In, irreverent, refreshing, audacious, lively; they haven't sold out like everybody else. But they are also recklessly undisciplined, often badly written, yellow, and, taken in large doses, very very boring.

Nevertheless these papers have been said to provide the most exciting reading in America. At least they try—by saying what can't be said or isn't being said by the staid daily press, by staying on the cutting edge of "In" for an audience with the shortest of attention spans. There is nothing worse for an underground paper or its readers than to be the last to know.

David Sanford is managing editor of *The New Republic*. "The Underground Press," originally titled "The Seedier Media," is reprinted by permission of *The New Republic*, © 1967, Harrison-Blaine of New Jersey, Inc., from the issue of December 2, 1967.

It took months for the revelations about the psychedelic pleasures of smoking banana peels, for instance, to travel to the daily papers and news magazines. And by the time a few weeks ago that the daily press reported that scientists had concluded it was all a hoax on the hippies, nobody who reads the *East Village Other* particularly cared. They had gone on to other things. They could sneer and remember they had been at the source, at the beginning of that long trip through the media to obsolescence.

The underground press is a photographic negative of the bourgeois newspapers and magazines; it registers many of the same images but all the colors are reversed. Anyone who sat down a few years ago and asked himself what isn't being reported, what causes are without champions, what words can't be printed, then decided to put out a newspaper that did everything differently, would have invented the underground. What the *LA Times* is for, the *LA Free Press* is likely to be against. Daily papers report arrests, for example, but from the standpoint of the police. That is their mental set; they are in the law-and-order bag. The underground papers are prone to see arrested persons as *victims* of the cops: "On Friday between 8 a.m. and 8:30 a.m. Judy (an antiwar protester) was arrested at the intersection of 13th and Broadway. She was standing with a group of people in the intersection. A cop knocked her down and grabbed her. A group of protesters circled the cop and began arguing that she hadn't done anything. More cops arrived. The cop who had knocked Judy down then let go of her. She began to move down Broadway and was chased by the cop who knocked her down again and dragged her to a patrol car. She was charged with assault on an officer." Here the *Berkeley Barb* in simple, letter-to-a-friend didactic style leaves no doubt about its position on the police. Cops attack innocent girls, and charge *them* with assault. No phony balanced coverage. No on-the-one-hand-on-the-other-hand TV documentary stuff. Judy is *Barb's* friend. The negative is black and white—a corrective to all the news about unruly demonstrators and police officers trying to maintain order. Police brutality has become a shibboleth for the underground papers, serviceable and pat. The treatment people get at the hands of police is "rough," "completely unnecessary," "totally unprovoked." "Cops are dumber and less imaginative than we usually suppose."

Since alienation is their thing it is understandable that underground papers sometimes seem to reject bourgeois journalistic values of accuracy and balance. The recent Pentagon demonstration as reported by the *Washington Free Press*, for example, included bayonettings, demonstrators who were knocked unconscious, the Pentagon as an "isolated house of death" rather like a gas oven in Nazi Germany. Such flights into fancy are characteristic of this spontaneous freak-out journalism, the purest lode of which is to be found in the *Oracles,* colorful Los Angeles and San Francisco publications, which are all mind excursion.

The underground press often reads like some kind of Harvard *Lampoon* parody of the tabloid press complete with news stories, editorials, reviews, classified ads, and advice columns. But instead of Heloise there is Hip-pocrates (Dr. Eugene Schoenfeld)—the motorcycling, demonstrating MD, whose syndicated advice appears in several UPS papers. Sometimes he is really helpful since he answers questions you wouldn't dare ask the family doctor. Sample question: "I've never had any sexual experience but my friends tell me it's groovy. . . . Please give me some advice on how to have intercourse." Answer: "My favorite occupational therapist thinks your friends are right. I suggest you read. . . ." In the same column that the dialogue appeared Dr. Schoenfeld passed along tips on how to remove pubic hair, where to go for help if you suspect you're queer and don't like what you suspect, and a helpful anecdote on autoerotism: "There is a story about a little boy who was found masturbating and told that he would go blind unless he stopped. 'Well,' he pleaded, 'can I do it until I need eyeglasses?' " In another column Hip-pocrates was asked "Is there anything specially abnormal with having one breast slightly larger than the other? I find it inhibiting at times, though my lover says he doesn't even notice it. Is there any way to balance the situation?" Answer: "Breasts are rarely exactly alike in size and shape. Your lover probably enjoys the variation; perhaps he even has a favorite."

The underground press is predictable. Some papers are more political, others more psychedelic, others more aberrant, but for the most part they care about Dow, drugs, the draft, abortion, cops, rock, flicks, and sex, perhaps not in that order. They are as current as this week's pot bust and draft-card burning. They oppose the war and their most interesting features are their want ads, especially if you are a sadist looking for a masochist.

PART FOUR

Interpreters

Introduction

When radio news came of age in the thirties and forties, newspaper editors began to realize they could no longer rely on "scoops" or first-ness for their primary appeal to readers. Initially, they counted on their ability to give more detail and greater variety of news than was possible on radio.

Then television news came onto the scene in the fifties, and this sparked a debate among newspapermen on whether objectivity was possible in interpretative stories. By the time TV news had come of age in the sixties, newspapers had accepted the need for putting added effort into explanation of the meaning behind events—interpretation.

Meantime, newsmagazines had emerged as a sign that some audiences were hungry for more than unrelated fact stories. The success of *Time* magazine, launched in 1923, hinted that routine "what happened" news coverage was inadequate for millions of readers. Newsmagazines exploited the fact that while audiences were turning to radio and TV for spot news, they still wanted more explanation, even though they were unable, or unwilling, to give much time to it.

Media critics inside and outside the profession still find too little interpretation either in print or on television. Yet the audience for this more serious reading, or viewing, is limited. In TV the best interpretation is done on documentaries and magazine-style programs. But such programs rarely attract audiences as big as those viewing mass-appeal Westerns or situation comedies.

So the news media face a dilemma: the most expensive kind of reporting, requiring skilled, experienced reporters with time to dig and write thoughtfully, satisfies the smallest audiences.

Few newspapers have staff reporters who devote full time to interpretation. The tendency is to rely on wire services and syndicated columnists to handle backgrounding and interpretation. Often, this means that newspapers carry more interpretation of national and international news than of local developments.

Still, there is general agreement on the need for more and better interpretative reporting, costly as it is and limited as its audience may be.

ROBERT SHERRILL

The Happy Ending (Maybe)
of "The Selling of the Pentagon"

ACT I

COMBAT SCENE—
PLANES STRAFING, RIFLEMEN
ADVANCING ORDNANCE EXPLODING
TANK SWINGING INTO ACTION—

ROGER MUDD (VOICE OVER)

Last spring American soldiers fought a two
day battle that did not get into the newspapers
or onto the television news broadcasts. Very few
people even knew about it. The battle was
fought neither in Vietnam, nor in Cambodia,
nor anywhere else in Southeast Asia. All the
action took place in North Carolina. This was
a military exercise, but it was also an exercise
in salesmanship—the selling of the Pentagon.

Robert Sherrill is Washington editor of *The Nation*. "The Happy End-
ing (Maybe) of 'The Selling of the Pentagon' " is reprinted from *The New
York Times Magazine*, May 16, 1971. © 1971 by The New York Times
Company. Reprinted by permission.

The "happy ending" occurred in August, 1971, when the U.S. House of
Representatives rejected a motion, 226 to 181, to find Dr. Frank Stanton,
president of CBS, in contempt of Congress for refusing to disclose unused
film of the "Selling of the Pentagon" to the House Interstate and Foreign
Commerce Committee.

MARINES LINED UP
IN FRONT OF GRANDSTAND

MARINE SPEECH

Gentlemen, today we have shown you the individual Marine—the man who implements foreign policy. He comes from all walks of life, all over the USA. He's not much different from the young men we see on the street corners of America today, except he's been trained as a Marine.

He believes in what he is doing, and he's dedicated to his country and to the job at hand, whatever it may be. In short, we could say he has a lot of plain old, red-blooded American guts. Now this concludes our demonstration at this range. The escorts will now show you to your buses. Thank you very much.

APPLAUSE FROM CIVILIANS IN
GRANDSTAND, THEN TITLES:

"CBS REPORTS: The Selling of the Pentagon."

OPENING   ROGER MUDD ON CAMERA

Nothing is more essential to a democracy than the free flow of information. Misinformation, distortion, propaganda all interrupt that flow.
· · ·

From the reaction that was stirred by the rest of this C.B.S. documentary (the first two pages of the original script appear above), one would never have guessed its very ordinary editorial origins. Richard Salant, president of C.B.S. News, was watching the rival N.B.C.'s "First Tuesday" program a year or so ago, and was struck by one segment of it which had been made by the Atomic Energy Commission. He thought to himself (or so close associates relate the incident), "Well, my God, does the A.E.C make its own films? Who said they should do this, and how much of it is going on?"

Eventually—Salant was in no rush; these things are never done hurriedly by the networks—he assigned Peter Davis to look into the matter of Government public relations.

Davis, 34, whose first job after Harvard ('57, *magna cum laude*) was as copy boy on this Magazine, is one of the brighter producers in the television industry, a worthy offspring of Hollywood writer Frank Davis, among whose credits is the screenplay for "The Train," and of the late novelist, Tess Slesinger, who had joined her husband in doing the screenplay for "A Tree Grows in Brooklyn."

Davis spent ten weeks prowling around various cavernous portions of the bureaucracy in Washington before deciding—with Salant's approval—to use the Pentagon as his case study because "although all of the agencies do a lot of self-serving publicity, the one that has the most influence over the country's mind, and the one that is the most conspicuous is, of course, the Department of Defense."

Ten months later, after a production cost of about $100,000, "The Selling of the Pentagon" was aired over 165 of C.B.S.'s 204 affiliated television stations on Feb. 23.

Some of the livelier material was left out—no mention was made, for example, of either the major who kicked a soldier in the shins to keep him from talking to Davis or of the Army officer who tried to seduce one of the C.B.S. girl researchers to find out what the investigation was all about —but it was still an interesting and effective show.

When compared to the usual animated headlines that pass for in-depth reporting on TV, it certainly deserved the special Peabody Award it received. But it was hardly a revolutionary program, and, except in television, it broke no new turf. It told of how the Pentagon every year spends between $30 million and $190 million (there is, as you can see, a bit of duplicity in such matters as budget)—the latter figure being more than the three commercial television networks, C.B.S., N.B.C. and A.B.C., spend annually on their news programs—to persuade the American people that the military services are doing some mighty fine work. The Pentagon's P.R. minions were filmed at county fairs, in shopping centers and at staged "warfare clinics" demonstrating to youngsters and housewives and visiting V.I.P.'s that killing can be an exciting business.

Virtually all of the information in the show had been reported earlier, and much more fully in newspapers and magazines, or, most certainly, in books going back ten years to Fred Cook's "The Warfare State" and as recently as Senator J. William Fulbright's "The Pentagon Propaganda Machine."

But inasmuch as not many people read, and a great many people watch television, some of Washington's most powerful pro-Pentagon politicians felt that their interests had for the first time been attacked in a truly significant and dangerous way. And it made them very angry.

Congressman F. Edward Hébert, Chairman of the House Armed Services Committee, said he was going to find out how much the Pentagon spends with C.B.S. television each year (he found that it spends $1,238,350 in Army recruiting advertisements alone)—the implication seeming to be that he would try to cut it off. Surely, C.B.S. deserved to have its pocket picked, for it had turned out "one of the most un-American things I've ever seen . . . on the tube," he said, "the greatest disservice to the military I've ever seen on television, and I've seen some pretty bad stuff." It was filled with "vicious, devious innuendoes," and besides that, Hébert concluded with a flourish, C.B.S. had obtained part of its film footage by deceit.

Defense Secretary Melvin Laird, rather restrained, said it was an unprofessional job of reporting. And Vice President Spiro Agnew, having warmed up in half a dozen previous speeches condemning the documentary, reached his splenetic peak at the St. Patrick's Day banquet at Boston's Middlesex Club, where he damned the Davis production as "a subtle but vicious broadside against the nation's defense establishment." He went on to suggest that with Davis's hand in it, he wasn't a bit surprised to see C.B.S. turning out another faked documentary.

After all, hadn't Davis helped create "Hunger in America," which showed the shriveled baby that was supposed to have died from hunger and, some say, really died from something else? And wasn't C.B.S. the outfit that had played along with the gang that wanted to stage an invasion of Haiti? (Agnew neglected to mention that the Federal Communications Commission, after investigating both efforts, praised C.B.S. for the job it did on "Hunger" and cleared it of charges that it had tried to rig the invasion.)

Congressman Harley Staggers, the West Virginian who worked as a coach and sheriff before turning to politics, announced that his special investigating committee would look into the whole field of TV news reporting to see how much of it is staged, but made to appear spontaneous.

There were many other attacks, not all relating specifically to "Selling" but apparently encouraged by the furor developing around it. A number of Congressmen and Senators began dusting off some of their favorite anti-TV legislation; one bill would make it a felony to lie over the airwaves, but it does not specify who the judge of veracity is to be. And Senator Clifford P. Hansen, Republican of Wyoming, put on his own show in Room 457 of the Senate Office Building—a show of clips from C.B.S. and N.B.C. coverage of the Laos invasion—and invited the other 534 politicians on Capitol Hill to come by and watch what he hoped would prove that not only are documentaries not to be trusted, but neither are the nightly news shows. (The turnout for this wasn't too good; besides himself, only one Senator came to watch.)

In response to the intense political fire, C.B.S. ran "Selling" again on March 23, partly to let everyone who had missed the first showing know what the dispute was all about (170 C.B.S. affiliates, an increase of five,

ran the program the second time around) and partly to provide an excuse for airing a "postscript" program featuring the angry remarks of some
of the above-mentioned politicians.

Meanwhile, Peter Davis, already aware that there were things to cope
with, had flown off for a short vacation in Nassau. But that was dis-
rupted ominously on the morning after Agnew's Boston speech, when
C.B.S. rang up and told him, "Okay, it's happened. Agnew has attacked
not only your broadcast but you personally, because of 'Hunger in America,' and we've got to get ready. This is going to be a long siege."

Before going on to the second reel of our melodrama, we'll take a few
questions from the audience. Do people in the network news business
actually, seriously use words like "siege" when describing their relationship with Federal officials? Why don't they just ignore the critics or, even
more satisfying, respond to them in a patronizing way?

The answer to the first question is yes, absolutely, they feel they are
under a pestilential assault. Perhaps A.B.C. should be exempted from that
statement. Although Elmer W. Lower, president of A.B.C. News, has
talked of the "specter of censorship," A.B.C. vice president James Hagerty,
who was Eisenhower's press secretary, says that he feels no pressure from
the Nixon Administration and, even if he did, "we can live with it."

Officials of the two giant networks, C.B.S. and N.B.C., however, are
not so accommodating. Julian Goodman, president of N.B.C., and Frank
Stanton, president of C.B.S., agree that the kind of heavy-handed Government attempts to influence network news that has been visible during the
last two years is something new to their experience. Sometimes Lyndon
Johnson used to blister their ears on the phone. "You know Johnson's
style," said Stanton. "When he's exercised he isn't a very quiet persuader."
And sometimes he imperiously summoned the network brass to the White
House for an in-person dressing-down. But never before, say Goodman
and Stanton, has there been an Administration that publicly attempted to
humiliate and whip the networks into line.

Do network officials really feel that White House spokesmen have no
right to criticize publicly what the newscasters say? In moments of extreme irritation, some will take that position. Shortly after Vice President
Agnew's famous double-barreled blast at the networks in November, 1969,
C.B.S. News chief Salant told a meeting of the Arizona Broadcasters Association: "The important point I raise is whether the *source* of the criticism was, in the circumstances, proper. I hope I do not shock you if I
turn Voltaire around and suggest that even if I agreed with every word
the Vice President said, I question his right to say it. What I am saying is
that these issues should be debated and discussed—and I would be happy
to sit down and discuss them with Mr. Agnew—on the day he is no longer
Vice President of the United States." In calmer moments, however, most

network chieftains would more likely agree with Goodman, who proposes only that "when the Administration feels that facts have been given incorrectly, they should hold some kind of news conference where the people who reported the news can respond."

As for the question about why the networks don't just shrug it off, the beginning of an answer comes from N.B.C. executive vice president David Adams: "You haven't seen this sort of attack leveled at *The New York Times*, with this sort of drumfire, although I think *The Times* has reported the Indochina war in its own terms, print, much in the same way we have reported it with pictures and motion and sound. But there haven't been daily and weekly attacks on *The Times*, and *nobody* has cut out the stories and pasted them up and said, 'Look what they're doing,' and invited Congressmen to come and look. Now, that's a difference.

"And the reason there is that difference is, we're a licensed press." What he means is, nobody yet has figured out how to make licenses and freedom of the press compatible.

Although the networks themselves are not licensed by the Federal Government, each network owns five major television stations which are worth many millions of dollars in equity—it is almost impossible to put a long-term price tag on these stations—which are licensed by the Federal Communications Commission. And the supposed peril of these licenses, which must be renewed every three years, is something the network lawyers never, never allow their corporate masters to forget.

Actually, too much is made of this peril. To get a license from the F.C.C. a station has to submit a rough idea of how much it intends to feed the community in the way of entertainment, talk, news and that abstract blob called public service. So long as it lives up to its promises in a very general way, it will have no problem getting its license renewed. It can run the dullest talk shows, the most pathetically trivial entertainment, the same rerun movies week after week, and news that hardly skims the surface—and the F.C.C. won't care. The F.C.C. avoids all questions of quality. It is prohibited by law from censoring the news, and in recent rulings it has vowed to steer clear of all questions of the "truth" of events shown on TV (except where there seems to be evidence that the news was rigged or purposely slanted). Almost the only stricture on the coverage of current events is the "fairness doctrine," which requires that on controversial issues both sides be given a reasonable amount of time. But the regulation permits a station to blank out both sides of the issue if it wants to. In any event, the F.C.C. is very offhanded in its endorsement of the doctrine; President Nixon has had a record amount of TV for controversial topics, but the Democrats have had precious little rebuttal time. Maybe the best measure of the fairness doctrine's potency is in the fact that only one station has lost its license for being unfair.

If ever a fear was hypothetical, this one that hovers around television business offices certainly is. None of the hundreds of TV stations—neither those owned by networks, nor those owned by others—has ever lost its license because of its news coverage, yet the very thought of risking one of those golden licenses for something as transient as a hard-hitting news story turns the corporate heart to Jell-O.

So when Vice President Agnew says publicly that "the views of this fraternity [television network newsmen] do not represent the views of America" and "perhaps it is time that the networks were made more responsive to the views of the nation"—the corporate ear picks up that word "made," which automatically triggers the awareness that a majority of the members on the F.C.C. now belong to the same party that controls the White House, and the network men sit up a bit straighter.

Letters of protest from members of Congress are treated very courteously by network officials, who assign staff members to answer every point of inquiry, no matter how asinine. Heavy-duty "Congressional relations" offices are maintained by every network. And critical inquiries from powerful pressure groups that could swing weight with the White House and Congress are also answered with elaborate care, because, as Goodman says, "Our problem is not only with existing regulations but with what Congress might do in response to a feeling that it should clamp down."

Correctly or not, many in the industry feel that the Administration—as well as its allies in Congress—is using the license threat as a club to get more favorable news coverage. Salant says, "There is coercion and intimidation here, for Government intervention and coercion can take a multitude of sinister forms other than naked censorship."

From the networks' point of view, perhaps the most impressive techniques of intimidation have been these:

• Forcing the news departments into enormously costly and time-consuming defenses of their programs.

• Attempting to create a kind of civil war between the networks and their affiliates.

• Maintaining a constant war of nerves with both the networks and their affiliates, letting them know that somebody with the power to punish is watching from Washington.

Which brings us back to the siege Peter Davis was facing. The drill is well remembered by Fred Friendly, now a professor of journalism at Columbia University and a Ford Foundation official, but for many years a news director at C.B.S. With the late Edward R. Murrow, he practically invented the documentary. "You get an eight-page accusation about something controversial in the program, and you send back a twenty-page rebuttal. This inspires a new forty-page response from the lawyers and lobbyists for some outfit who have nothing else to do. And that takes you sixty-five pages to answer, and you get back a new seventy-three-page list of accusations. They know what they're doing—they know—it's a game with them."

But it's no game to the newsmen. Defending "Hunger in America"—another of the prize-winning documentaries Agnew denounced in Boston—cost C.B.S. an estimated six figures. Davis was associate producer of the show, Martin Carr the producer. "Hunger"—perhaps the most powerful documentary since the exposure of the abuse of migrant workers in "Harvest of Shame" more than a decade ago—revealed that the United States Department of Agriculture was scuttling its own food-for-the-poor programs, with the encouragement of the Congressional farm committees.

The farm bloc went out for revenge. Carr says House agriculture leaders got the F.B.I. to detach two agents for their use, and they sent them hounding down every person who had talked to or in any way assisted the producers of the show. The G-men accumulated an endless list of innuendoes, all of which Carr had to respond to.

San Antonio civic leaders, who were trying to lure tourists to Hemis-Fair that year, said they had been slandered. Some 100,000 hungry Mexican-Americans in town? Nonsense. As for the film of a baby who had died of malnutrition in a San Antonio hospital, that was quite a distortion, said Representative Henry Gonzalez of Texas, and for weeks thereafter he peppered the Congressional Record with speeches undercutting the credibility of the show.

That, too, Carr had to respond to. For more than a year he did nothing but answer inquiries, meet with lawyers and make trips to Washington to defend his production. In fact, he never again did a documentary for C.B.S. and, fourteen months after his ordeal began, tired of fencing with issues that had nothing to do with whether there is or is not hunger in America, he simply gave up and moved over to N.B.C. for a fresh start.

The dispute over "Selling" has plunged Davis into an identical routine. At the time I saw him, which was about three weeks after the Agnew speech in Boston, Davis had already turned out about seventy pages of rebuttal and responses to flak coming from the Pentagon and Congress and some newspapers and C.B.S.'s own attorneys. There is no letup in sight. Davis thinks he may still be working at his defense next spring.

"The Pentagon, now that we've told the truth about it, is telling lies about us, and they are telling them at a very rapid pace," he says. He's mad. "We have to answer each of these things. We can't keep up with this. They simply have too many foot soldiers over there. Jesus, they are doing this every single day."

One of the things the Pentagon has done is recruit some editorial support both from the trade press and the regular dailies. The Air Force/ Space Digest made some nasty cracks about shows that were "snipped" and "glued" together—but that could be expected from a magazine supported by the military-industrial establishment. What really rattled the network people was the series of editorials in *The Washington Post* that said maybe the Pentagon had a point—maybe a couple of the quotes used in the show had indeed been juggled to the point of distortion. Feeling skewered from behind, Davis raged: "Did you see The Post's yakking about our using doctored transcripts? And yet the so-called 'prepared text' the Pentagon gave *The Post* was itself incomplete. *The Post* did nothing but rewrite a Pentagon handout without even a lazy phone call to those of us who worked on the transcript to find out if the Pentagon's outline was an accurate transcription of what we filmed."

(Responding from *The Post,* editorial writer Meg Greenfield said that no handout had been rewritten, and that, in three telephone calls to C.B.S. to ask for its side of the argument, she did get as close to the program as narrator Roger Mudd, who said the Pentagon allegations weren't worth responding to.)

A dozen other top C.B.S. officials, including Salant, have been spending as much as three-fourths of their time in the same way, every day, preparing either for a congressional hearing or a fight with the F.C.C., or both. Final cost of the defense of "Selling" is expected to exceed $100,000 —as much as the show cost to produce in the first place.

Most irritating of all to the people involved is the quality of some of the questions they are forced to respond to.

One from Representative Hébert: Do you have any record that C.B.S., or any individual from C.B.S., ever asked for any free services from the military?

Answer: Yes. In 1969, when Roger Mudd was chairman of the dinner committee of the Radio/Television Correspondence Association, he signed a letter requesting the presence of the Marine Band.

From the Government's side the "war of nerves" is fought by letting the stations know they are being observed; Herbert G. Klein, White House director of communications, and his deputy, Al Snyder, are very adept at this. When a major Nixon speech is coming up, Klein and Snyder have been known to get on the phone to twenty or thirty stations and prod them a bit; and afterward, there might be another call to find out if the stations intend to editorialize, and if so, what they intend to say.

After Nixon's war policy speech on Nov. 3, 1969, Dean Burch, chairman of the F.C.C., telephoned network presidents to get transcripts of their commentaries. This was widely interpreted as a proxy action for Nixon himself; Burch, a former chairman of the Republican National Committee and a close friend of the President, is frequently consulted by the White House on matters relating to the broadcast industry, though the F.C.C. is supposed to be an independent agency and outwardly tries to maintain that air.

One of the more amusing efforts at over-the-shoulder influence is told by Salant: "Klein was up here at the Columbia Journalism School for some lecture a couple of months ago and he called me and said it was important. He wanted to see me. Well, he sat there and made small talk, and then he reached into his pocket and pulled out what seemed to be the back of an envelope with a lot of scribbling on it, and he said, 'the Vice President didn't see that '60 Minutes' segment you did on 'The Young Agnew' but Mrs. Agnew was very unhappy.' In that program we explained that Agnew wasn't a very good student; we tried to get his records from high school, but at Government request they had been withdrawn. I don't remember whether Klein said Mrs. Agnew had passed her unhappiness directly to him or whether she had passed it on to Mr. Agnew who had passed it on to Klein. Anyway, he was up to complain about it.

"So I said, 'We have a letters to the editor segment in '60 Minutes.' If you or Mrs. Agnew or the Vice President want to react to it, we would be glad to put that in the next broadcast.' We never heard from them again."

Last month radio station W.C.B.S. in New York did a series of editorials criticizing the Nixon war policy. Shortly thereafter, Joseph Dimbo, vice president of C.B.S. Radio and general manager of W.C.B.S., received this letter from Ronald Ziegler, White House press secretary:

"I was interested to read your editorial regarding the Vice President's remarks on the news media. One portion of the editorial aroused my curiosity. I would appreciate your outlining for me in more specific terms what you consider the Nixon Administration's 'embarrassing failures' at home and in Indochina."

A high C.B.S. official observed: "If you were a publisher or editor of a paper, you could laugh at that and throw it into the wastebasket. But when you are licensed by the F.C.C. and the F.C.C. is made up predominantly of Republicans and you get a letter like this from the White House press secretary, you're shaken by it."

Salant believes that "someday" a station is going to lose its license for ideological reasons. "The closest we ever came was after Agnew's first series of attacks on the press in Des Moines and Montgomery in 1969. The first speech just hit the networks, but he broadened the second speech to go beyond TV to denounce *The New York Times* and *The Washington Post*, and literally within five weeks after that speech the station that Post-Newsweek owns in Miami was shut down for a hearing because a group of six guys came in and said they should have the license because they could do a better job, and so on. Those six guys were all friends and former associates of the President's. Now, maybe it was just a coincidence. They finally abandoned their petition, but *The Post* had to spend a lot of money getting ready in the meantime. This sort of thing creates shock waves on stations all around the country. They say, hey! The one thing they fear more than anything else is getting into one of these comparative hearings on renewal.

"At least one of C.B.S.'s television licenses was held up on renewal pending the answering of complaints about 'Hunger in America.' I don't remember if more than one station was involved, but it was held up for more than a year. If you lost the station, it would be like losing $100-million. The stakes are huge. This is the only business I know of where there is capital punishment. You can fix prices, you can bribe, you can do all the naughty things that businessmen do and get fined, but never knocked out of business—unless you're in television. That's what the penalty is here. People are nervous."

Jittery industry men put a special interpretation on what Salant calls "Big Brother watching us with counters and stopwatches." Part of this is the daily news digest plunked on the President's desk at 8 A.M. sharp each day. Those who have seen the digests say they contain little comments like, "Mr. Brinkley, with his customary sarcasm, . . ." etc. Sometimes the attitude overflows the White House to intrude as it did recently upon the Dick Cavett evening talk show.

Apparently under pressure from Klein's deputy, Snyder, A.B.C. executives induced Cavett to let one of the Administration's pro-SST technicians go on the show and tout the wonders of the supersonic airplane before the issue of its funding came to a final vote in the Senate.

Snyder, in an interview with columnist Nicholas von Hoffman, admitted that he telephoned A.B.C. officials and "suggested" this change in the format of the show because the White House felt Cavett had had too many anti-SST guests. Snyder denied that the White House clocks all programs—including even entertainment shows—to see what public issues are mentioned, how long they are talked about, and what opinions are favored. No, he said, he just happened to be watching the Cavett show.

Perhaps the Nixon Administration's most successful gambit at the present moment is—if the network worriers interpret it correctly—the effort to conquer the industry by dividing it: the affiliates versus the networks. At the recent National Association of Broadcasters convention in Chicago, Herb Klein read a message from Nixon praising local stations "particularly in the area of news and public service programing."

Either out of paranoia or experienced insight, most of the top network men agree that this theme made it a divisive speech. Goodman, Adams, Stanton, Salant see it as one.

"I think right now they've come to the realization that this is where they can really get us," says Salant. "I've seen in the last few weeks a rather deliberate effort to drive a wedge. You saw the President's message to the N.A.B. in which he distinguished between network and affiliates, and Klein always does this, and so do the usual Senators—the Brocks and the Doles—Dole does this especially—the Hruskas and the Hansens. They keep on saying: now the *local* stations do a great job. They draw that distinction, and one sees uneasiness on the part of our affiliates. I think they are nervous about us. I think they [the Administration] are saying to the affiliates, we know that you guys can shut off the network any time you want. And indeed they can. It's against the law for us to require any affiliate to carry one of our broadcasts. And so the affiliates can ruin us—shut us off, if they want. They could just not clear for us. Some 30 stations don't take our news hour on Tuesday night, for example, out of 200 or so. I remember when we did a '60 Minutes' piece on the racial problems of our Army in Germany, one of our affiliates down South not only refused to carry that segment but canceled the news hour permanently from there on.

"I think the Administration and other people who want to get at us recognize that this can happen, so the affiliates do have a great leverage over us. They can't dictate content but they can express immense uneasiness, with all sorts of inherent or implicit threats."

Last May at their annual meeting in the Waldorf Astoria, N.B.C.'s affiliate representatives became somewhat passionate in their private session (that is, the session to which network officials aren't invited). Stanley Hubbard Jr. of KSTP-TV in St. Paul, Minn., who is reported to have thrown the first stone at network news coverage, says the affiliates didn't go so far as to take a vote of "no confidence" in N.B.C. objectivity—as Goodman heard had been done—but that many of the station representatives did agree that, as Hubbard says, "people who live in New York are subject to that kind of ingroup membership that reads *The New York Times*. They have a different slant on what's going on from people who live in the Midwest. The general tone of the meeting was, 'Goddamit, why doesn't the network take things from Chicago and the Twin Cities more often, and get other people's slant on what's going on internationally and nationally?" But both Goodman and Adams insist that what went on in the stormy group discussion was not a true reflection of how most of their affiliates feel in more rational moments.

But at C.B.S., Les Midgley, executive producer of the nightly news, says their affiliates probably do mean it. "It's no secret that many of our affiliates do not approve of what we do," he said. "A lot of the station managers who carry Eric Sevareid, for example, on our broadcast every night would rather not. They squawk to us all the time. They complain to me, they complain to Walter [Cronkite]. They say, 'Gee, why do you fellows have to keep running this kind of rough stuff?' And if they had control over it, they probably wouldn't run it. We certainly listen to them, but I don't think they influence the way we do things."

But turning off, and thereby having a most emphatic influence on the documentaries, is an easier matter than turning off the regular news. And, in the opinion of Fred Friendly, the Administration is right on target when it strikes at the soft underpocketbook of the affiliates in this way because "the affiliates are a very queasy lot. They don't want to be in the broadcast journalism business—with few exceptions. Most of them just want to turn on the faucet every morning and get their share of the revenue from the network. Some of them don't even carry Cronkite or Brinkley.

"The acceptance of documentaries is shameful. For several reasons. First of all, the affiliates would rather sell the time to a fifth rerun of a movie or 'I Love Lucy' or whatever they can get their hands on where they can keep 100 percent of the revenue. If they take something from the network, their share is less than half that. Secondly, the ad rate for documentaries, because they get a comparatively low audience, is far less than it is for the big commercial network projects. On a big entertainment show, a minute may sell for something like $60,000 to $70,000. On a documentary the minutes will sell for $12,000 to $15,000, if they sell them.

"So you can see what the local stations want. And with that as their *real* reason, they now have—and have had for some time, those who want it—the additional excuse of being urged by the White House to 'watch out for those sophisticated guys with their eyes too close together in New York and Washington.' "

Cooperation, says Friendly, comes easy to them. "If you've ever been to an affiliates meeting—again with some notable exceptions—you'd think you were with a coalition of Spiro Agnews. It isn't so much the big cities. You don't have these problems in New York, Chicago, Los Angeles, San Francisco. You have these problems in the comparatively small markets, but which make up half the affiliates. It's the same old battle between big cities and, as Jack Fischer of *Harper's* once called them, the country slickers.

"They don't want to change the balance which is stacked on the side of the rural. Between the lines, some pretty rough things were said about agriculture in 'Hunger in America,' and these affiliates don't want to have a close examination of agriculture. Then, when you get the Pentagon to working on these regions through contractors and subcontractors, it just spreads like, not wildfire but a whole lot of little brush fires. And the affiliates with this smoke screen and everything else say, 'Don't give us any more of these documentaries. We don't want to carry them in the first place, and you're going to put us out of business.'

"In a tug of war like that, I would hate to see what would happen and I don't know who would be the victor in the end. Salant is a very gutsy guy and my admiration for him is enormous. I'm sure he's not going to change at all. But it can become very, very hard to get good programs on the air."

The attempted manipulation of the affiliates was seen most clearly about a year and a half ago when a spokesman for the White House tried to get the C.B.S. affiliates advisory board to form a subcommittee and, as one recalls the advice, "go out to Vietnam and let the network know how unhappy you are and speak to the reporters about being too dovish and see whether you can't straighten them out." Salant nixed that one quick.

To many network officials, the worst thing about the current struggle with government is the discrediting of the news product, as a product.

Like everything else on television—soap operas, sex, song and dance, conversation—news in a nice way is also viewed as a product, to be sold both to advertisers and the public. N.B.C. executive vice president Adams puts it this way: "Broadcasters live by their acceptance by viewers. If an atmosphere is set in this country that persuades people not to believe in television news shows because they are all slanted and because television newsmen are by and large left of center and pink and anti-Administration, that atmosphere will grow and television will lose part of its credibility. If it loses some of that, it loses some of its whole operation. These things proceed, tiny step by tiny step, each one almost invisible." If people think the merchant's news has turned sour, they may get the idea other items on the shelf have spoiled, too.

The official "phony baby" dogma after the hunger show is a pretty good example of what rattles the networks, but an even better example was the Government's counter-offensive after the showing on Cronkite's evening news, Nov. 3, 1969, of a South Vietnamese soldier stabbing a prisoner to death while United States military advisers looked on.

The Pentagon was furious. So were some of the White House people, who began privately telling favored print journalists they thought the show was a hoax: Take our word for it, the prisoner being stabbed was already dead; or, if not that, then it was all just a training exercise, nothing for real; or, if not that, then instead of American advisers it was probably an Australian caper. These leaked suspicions were widely reported in such cooperative papers as The Des Moines Register.

After six months of this, C.B.S. decided to talk back on another newscast. Cronkite turned over seven minutes to correspondent Don Webster, who, having laboriously retraced his steps, had film on everything: an interview with the Vietnamese soldier who had done the stabbing, blowup shots of the insignia on the helicopter wings to prove that it was United States, not Aussie soldiers looking on, evidence that it was a very real mission, not a training exercise—quite enough to justify Cronkite's closing remarks, "We broadcast the original story in the belief it told something about the nature of the war in Vietnam. What has happened since then tells something about the Government and its relation with news media which carry stories the Government finds disagreeable."

But with only thirty minutes—minus deodorant and instant-coffee advertising time—to cover the news of the world each night, no network can afford to devote many seven-minute fragments to rehashing its old news to prove authenticity.

There is also a limit, some believe, to how much of a drubbing television newsmen and their bosses can take from the Government before they begin to give a little, to hold back the tough shots, to give even less depth to their coverage than is customary.

Without exception, the top executives and news directors of every network insist that the constant abrasion from the Government has not worn away any of their news-dispensing zeal.

Still, it is easy to find people who feel this *could* be a consequence.

N.B.C. News president Reuven Frank: "Every time you undertake something that is just not quite as bland as all the other things you do, you worry about—will I be cited by the F.C.C.? Will I have to testify to an examiner? Will I have to turn out my papers for them to look at? Will I be called by that House committee or that Senate committee?" But no, he says he doesn't know of anybody "who has collapsed in the face of this lately."

Adams: "If you are operating in the newsroom of a local broadcast station, and you are doing your job, and one day three lawyers from your company walk in with an F.C.C. inquiry about something you have treated, and you spend eighteen hours going through your files, maybe next time you have an issue you want to treat you'll think, 'Jesus Christ, do I have to go through all that?' and you may not do it the same way."

Stanton: "These things are bound to have an effect on your organization, no matter how much you try to protect your staff. After several experiences where they are pulled up short, where they have to testify, it's bound to have an erosive effect."

Salant: "I have to worry about guys out in the field getting unhappy about being taken off the job to answer these things, and saying 'Oh to hell with it, I'll do stuff on ecology from here on out.' And you have to worry about guys in the field trying to second guess you and thinking I don't want them to do the hard-hitting material."

Again, A.B.C. must be excepted from the survey. Tom Wolf, who is in charge of documentary production at that network, says, "I can't remember in the last five years that I've had this job getting a specific complaint. I would like to be able to say, after W. C. Fields, 'I fought my way through a wall of human flesh, dragging my goat and canoe behind me,' but it's not true, unfortunately."

There is no such levity at N.B.C. and C.B.S. Of the critical barrages he has been subjected to after such shows as "Hunger," Martin Carr reflects: "I believe in what I do and I feel very strongly about what I do and I get a great deal of pleasure out of hopefully making people's lives a little better to live. However, it is not exactly lost on you that after you make one of these films, when you are chained to your desk for months on end, with extra work and no extra sympathy and no extra pay, that maybe if you had done something less controversial you wouldn't have brought all of this down on your head to begin with. And I think it's why a lot of producers don't do more controversial shows. They feel finally that it isn't worth it."

Despite all of management's disclaimers about not giving in to the pressures at the top, some in the industry see things differently. F.C.C. Commissioner Nicholas Johnson says that about the time of Agnew's Des Moines speech, "I received confidential, personal reports that network management began taking a much more detailed interest in the attitudes and copy of its newsmen."

Though A.B.C. adamantly denies there is any substance to it, one of the most stubborn rumors is that Frank Reynolds, formerly a commentator on the evening news show, was dislodged from that position in response to demands from the White House, where, it is said, a most unfriendly dossier was kept on him.

C.B.S., in an unprecedented move, blanked out the face of Abbie Hoffman because he appeared on a talk show wearing a shirt made from the American flag; C.B.S. censored Carol Burnett's request that her audience send peace letters to Coretta King; Commissioner Johnson says A.B.C. refused to show one football half-time program with pro-peace overtones because it was "too political" but showed another football half-time program praising the military; shortly after Agnew's first blast at the networks, none of them assigned crews to cover the Peace Moratorium, one of the largest outpourings of human flesh ever to assemble in Washington, with estimates of the turnout ranging from a quarter- to a half-million persons. When the networks responded in these ways, some critics came to the conclusion that television management was going into hawkish contortions to please President Nixon and his spokesmen, such as Senator Robert Dole, Chairman of the Republican National Committee, who recently damned the networks as being not only too liberal but too "antiwar."

As the 1971 affiliates meeting approached, Hubbard, the booster of more Middle West-toned news at the 1970 convention, said, "Things have got much better. I don't know whether it was Agnew, or whether the networks changed on their own."

Of all the capitulations, however, none has made the networks seem more pitiful than their cooperation with the Justice Department or just about anybody else who approached with a subpoena. Things are a bit better now, but until about eight months ago, says Sam Suratt, C.B.S. archivist, "it was sort of everyone for himself in the Justice Department and everywhere else as to latching onto our material. For a time we were feeling terribly paranoid."

And well they might feel that way, though to some degree it was their own fault. Every time the Justice Department felt like going on a law-and-order fishing expedition, it would send a brigade of gumshoes parading through the network libraries, waving a subpoena and scooping up all the used and unused film, all the notes, documents and anything else they could carry away. Then they would spend months and months sifting through this material looking for some clue to a criminal or un-American act. Sometimes they returned the material to the networks, and sometimes they didn't. The networks offered between little and no resistance.

The most painful episode was when the Justice Department took away the film Mike Wallace had done in private sessions with Eldridge Cleaver and other Black Panthers in Algiers. To get the Panthers' permission to sit on their skull sessions, Wallace had guaranteed that no Government agent would get his hands on it. Then—in what C.B.S. executives now blushingly identify as "a terrific amount of confusion"—Attorney General John Mitchell's men simply walked in and walked away with the goods. Now that word of that has gotten around, network newsmen are reportedly finding it more difficult to get people to tell their secrets off the record.

However, in doing this, the Government may have done the networks their greatest favor. They might have gone on indefinitely taking all the other guff from the F.C.C., from congressional investigators, from irate pressure groups and from the White House. But when the Justice Department began looting their files of material no legitimate print journalist would think of surrendering to a court order, the network newsmen, prodded by embarrassment, decided to take a stand.

Or at least some of them seem to have decided to. When Congressman Staggers had a subpoena served on C.B.S., demanding all of its used and unused films, plus notes and a list of everyone its newsmen had talked to in preparing "The Selling of the Pentagon," he explained that he only wanted to see if C.B.S. had done a fair job editing its material.

And Stanton and Salant promptly announced that that was exactly what they had no intention of putting up with. "This," says Salant, "is the place to tell them that how we edit is none of their business. I suppose they could bring contempt against the witness who says that—I hope it's me." Stanton, too, who does not appear to be the jailbird type, says he is definitely willing to serve time if necessary to protect C.B.S.'s news material. N.B.C. officials have announced that they support C.B.S.'s position all the way. And the American Society of Newspaper Editors, meeting in Washington recently, voted a "Right On!" resolution—especially welcome to the networks, who feel that the free press has not been giving the licensed press enough moral support.

Bucking a Congressional committee, however, is trivial stuff compared to bucking the F.C.C. If the F.C.C. should demand that C.B.S. answer voluminous questions about its news-gathering and editing techniques in the making of this documentary (for a time, C.B.S. officials feared it might; the F.C.C. has said it won't), or any other documentary, would C.B.S. be daring enough to say no to that arbitrary body? Yes, said Salant, "If the F.C.C. asks us such questions, we might give them an answer, but that answer could be of the nature of, politely, "It's none of your business.' "

This may not sound like a terribly exciting eventuality. But to people in the television business it is revolutionary. It has never been done before.

So, television fans, you've got your happy ending after all. Maybe. This adversity and harassment that the networks are being subjected to may do the trick. Just as Christians had to be fed to lions for the sport of Romans in order to transform an obscure sect into worldwide religion, the martyring of a few producers and executives may, by a latter day miracle, inspire television to become a real journalistic medium.

PHILIP MEYER

The Risks of Interpretation

*Neither objective nor interpretative reporting is
adequate in covering today's fast-moving story of
the rise of the black man. We need more
intensive fact-finding efforts.*

In the beginning, the goal of the journalist was objectivity. I define "be-ginning" in purely subjective terms. My journalism training began in that carefree time between the end of World War II and the Korean War. The United States was the exclusive possessor of nuclear energy, there was no draft, and the world was stable and not too competitive.

It seemed so straightforward then. Our task was to record public events from a stance that was detached, impersonal and unprejudiced—much as a man from Mars might record them.

The journalist was never to be a part of events nor to affect their direc-tion or outcome. His role was merely to record what happened and let the chips fall where they might.

We were, of course, often accused of affecting events by what we put in the paper, and we had a stock repertory of denials. Were student panty-raiders abetted by our page-one reports of their activities in the student daily? Don't blame us for putting the story in the paper. Blame the panty-raiders. Was the university embarrassed by our report of an argument between the basketball coach and the athletic director? Blame them, not us who, detached and objective, merely reported the argument.

It was a good time, but it was too short. Just as we were learning that objectivity was the answer to the ambiguities that confront the journalist, a running national story was demonstrating the inadequacy of objectivity.

Philip Meyer is a journalist with the Washington bureau of Knight Newspapers. "The Risks of Interpretation" is reprinted from *The Bulletin* of the American Society of Newspaper Editors, April, 1969, with permis-sion.

The story was of Senator Joseph McCarthy and his spectacular charges of Communists in government.

Newspapers were covering it by the old rules, and McCarthy was capitalizing on the inadequacy of those rules. The rules said, report what happens; tell both sides; if the total picture is conflicting and ambiguous, it is for the reader, not the writer, to decide where truth lies. McCarthy was a U.S. Senator. When a senator says something startling, it is news, whether what he says is true or false. If it is false, someone will say so, and, true to our code of objectivity, we'll print that, too.

This kind of objectivity, we see now, is a cop-out. It is an excuse for failure to take the time, effort and expense needed to tell what is really happening.

When McCarthy was finally cut down, the most telling blows from the news media were struck by interpretive reporters who made no pretense of objectivity. The best example was the late Edward R. Murrow whose filmed summary of McCarthy's career was a masterpiece of subjective editing.

Murrow didn't have to tell the viewer anything; he merely showed him filmed excerpts from the McCarthy career. This is a classic technique of fiction writing. One of the basic rules that Prof. Theodore Morrison drills into his creative writing students at Harvard is, "Show, don't tell." But the selection of what to show is, of course, not objective.

In interpretive reporting, you begin with your own notion of what the events you are talking about mean. And then you invite the reader's attention to the selected facts that will bring that picture into clear focus.

Interpretive reporting makes it possible to explore complex events with more thoroughness and insight than a simple recitation of objective facts. In today's fast-moving and complicated world, this is a major advantage over simple objectivity. But the advantage of interpretive reporting is only as good as the insight of the reporter who is doing the interpreting. And we reporters tend to be conventional people with conventional ways of looking at things. So our interpretations seldom do more than reinforce the conventional wisdom.

It is still possible today to agree with John Milton that:

> though all the winds of doctrine were let loose to play upon the earth, so truth be in the field, we do ingloriously . . . to misdoubt her strength. Let her and falsehood grapple: who ever know truth put to the worse in a free and open encounter?

In the long run, truth will survive. The trouble today is we can't always afford to wait for the long run. The McCarthy era began in 1950 and lasted four years. Yet, the evidence of his fakery was available, for those who were willing to dig it out and call attention to it, from the beginning.

Today there is another fast-moving story for which traditional objective reporting simply is not adequate. Neither is the newer interpretive reporting, because so many of the interpretive reports start from the wrong assumptions. It is the story of the rise of the black man from a passive, repressed minority to an active, competing minority.

It is important for all of us, black and white, to know exactly what is going on here. We are not always finding out.

The objective approach focuses on the loudest and most flamboyant of the Negro extremists—the apostles of violence and separatism—and then balances it with statements from Roy Wilkins that most Negroes are still law-abiding believers in integration. The truth, it is implied, lies somewhere between. The space between, unfortunately, is far too wide to prevent the reader from getting lost.

Interpretive reporters then come to the rescue. The most common interpretations see the Negro mood in historical perspective. First, the black man strives for equality with nonviolent methods to achieve integration; then his feelings of black pride are awakened and he rebels against his former allies, the patronizing white liberals; finally the cycle is completed with the end of nonviolence and the new prevailing goal of a separate black "nation within a nation."

This picture of what has been happening in black America has the advantage of being clear, lucid, and internally consistent, as all good interpretive reporting is. Its disadvantage is that it is wrong.

The error is overinterpretation: Straying too far from the objective data in the otherwise praiseworthy effort to construct a coherent picture for the reader. In time, of course, we can expect truth to emerge victorious from this grappling of the winds of doctrine.

But there is reason to believe that we should not wait. It is important to find out now which way the Negro freedom movement is heading, which of the competing ideologies are taking hold and which are dying. There are a number of reasons why it is important to have this information now, but for the moment I will cite just one: There is in the new Administration a growing realization that our options in dealing with the problems of the inner-city ghettos are severely limited.

Even if the end of the war in Vietnam frees $15 billion a year for domestic improvement; even if the steady growth in the Gross National Product adds another $7 billion in proceeds from the expanding tax base, we shall still have to make difficult choices among strategies for using that money.

Basically, there are two important options, and I believe they are mutually exclusive: Dispersing the ghetto and destroying its self-perpetuating pathology; or gilding the ghetto and trying to treat its symptoms with more and more government services. There is not enough money to do both. Improving the ghetto could perpetuate its problems by reducing the incentive for getting out.

Nevertheless, if the prevailing mood of the inner-city Negro is for separatism in semiautonomous black enclaves in the central cities, then the ghetto-gilding strategy may be best. But if the prevailing sentiment is for integration, then spending money on preserving the ghetto would be a tragic mistake.

Charting the mood of any group in a situation of social conflict is not something best left to the traditional methods of either the objective or the interpretive reporters. The former will declare, "On the one hand this and on the other hand that," and leave us no wiser. The latter will generalize from the newest and most bizarre ideas. Eventually, some social scientist will come along and tell us what has been going on, but that will be several years later when the decisions from wrong information have already been made.

The answer, I think, is for us to abandon the old arguments about objective vs. interpretive reporting and concentrate on more intensive fact-finding efforts. In a way, this is a reactionary return to the old ideal of objectivity, but with this difference: Instead of reporting competing viewpoints for what they are worth, we would be making an effort to determine just what it is that they are worth. In developing more intensive fact-finding methods, we need not turn our back on interpretive reporting either. Instead, we can hope to reduce the distance of the leap from fact to interpretation and therefore produce more trustworthy interpretations.

How do we develop better fact-finding methods? The social and behavioral scientists have perfected some tools that we can use with profit. Without trying to turn journalists into social scientists, we can make the fact-finding procedures of journalism more disciplined and exacting. In probing racial attitudes, the most obvious such tool is survey research.

Two of the Knight Newspapers, the *Detroit Free Press* and the *Miami Herald,* have used it to test some of the conventional wisdom about trends in the black ghetto. Among the ideas tested were some which had been rather widely disseminated by both conventional objective reporting and conventional interpretive reporting:

1. The death of Martin Luther King caused a sudden gain for advocates of Negro violence and a corresponding loss of faith in nonviolent methods.

2. Negroes are turning away from the old goal of integration and embracing a new ideology of black separatism.

3. The ideas involved in the expressions, "black power," "black sepa-

ratism" and "burn, baby, burn," are all different degrees of the same phenomenon: a growing, anti-white militancy.

Each of these statements is demonstrably false in the cities where they were tested.

In Miami, an exploratory study of attitudes and grievances in three ghetto areas was conducted early in 1968. Besides helping to make up for a long history of neglect of the problems in the black community, this study provided a baseline for measuring future shifts.

When Dr. King was assassinated, Negro leaders, sociologists and editorial writers were quick to leap to the conclusion that nonviolence and the drive for integration had been struck down with him or at least suffered an immediate setback. We were able to test this proposition, because our survey had included measures of King-type militancy—we called it conventional militancy—and of attitudes toward violence. What we found in a resurvey was the exact opposite of the popular assumption: The number approving of violence had held steady while the proportion who believed in Dr. King's ideals had increased.

In Detroit, two surveys of the riot area were made thirteen months apart. There, where the nation's worst riot had politicized Negro grievances and given prominence to the more militant leaders, one would expect to find the most conspicuous gain in anti-white attitudes—if, indeed, the new militancy is characterized by anti-white attitudes.

The second survey showed growing impatience for redress of grievances, but it was not accompanied by a gain in anti-white feeling. Negro grievances, in Miami as well as Detroit, were often centered on housing problems. Therefore, a good measure of a person's attitude toward integration as a strategy for black improvement is his response to this question: "Would you rather live in a neighborhood with only Negro families or in a neighborhood that had both Negro and white families?"

In 1967, three weeks after the riot, 61 percent of Detroit inner-city blacks said they would prefer mixed housing. Thirteen months later, the question was put to another sample, drawn by identical methods in the same neighborhoods. This time the number preferring mixed housing had increased to 75 percent.

This does not mean that there are not people who are separatists now and were not separatists before. Since this was not a panel study (in which the same people are interviewed each time, as in Miami), we can measure only net shift and not turnover. It is possible, for example, that younger people are moving out of the integrationist ranks and being replaced by older, more conservative Negroes who had never before considered integration a meaningful goal. Nevertheless, the net shift was toward integration, and we would have failed in our job as newspapermen if we had

THE RISKS OF INTERPRETATION   163

let the noisy separatist element convince us and our readers that they were the advancing tide.

Finally, I think the Detroit project demonstrated that lumping black power advocates, the separatist or black nationalist element and the advocates of violence all under the heading of "militant" is a dangerous and misleading oversimplification. In fact, it is worse than an oversimplification. It's just plain wrong.

As journalists, we are in the business of creating oversimplifications. Without oversimplifying, we'd seldom communicate anything. But we have to be wary of going too far, and we need to be choosy about the oversimplified stereotypes we create. The stereotype of the dashiki-wearing, separatist, bomb-throwing black power advocate serves only to confuse and alarm our up-tight white readers. It does not illuminate.

Working with the Detroit data, we used factor analysis—a method of reducing a large number of interrelated variables to a smaller, manageable number of underlying influences—to produce some new oversimplifications that would be both useful and statistically valid.

The first two factors extracted proved to be clearly descriptive of black power and black nationalism as separate and unrelated attributes. Black power was expressed as a feeling that Negroes should organize politically and economically and exercise united effort through the existing system. Black nationalism was defined by attitudes in favor of avoiding whites, building a separate black society, and a sense that people of African descent are basically superior. It was also associated with approval of violence.

The key point here is that these two factors or attitude clusters—black power and black nationalism—are uncorrelated. Knowing a black man's position on the black power scale is no help in guessing where he stands on black nationalism—and vice versa.

Therefore, when we talk about militants, we should, in fairness and for the sake of complete reporting, explain what kind of militancy we are talking about.

In Detroit, far more follow black power than black nationalism. For example, 80 percent called it 'very important' for Negroes to get more political power by voting together to get officials who would look out for the Negro people. Only 5 percent say it is very important for Negroes to avoid having anything to do with white people as much as possible. We add needlessly to white fears and racial misunderstanding when we confuse the former group with the latter.

Unfortunately, the people who write for newspapers and the people who read them are often in too much of a hurry to consider such distinctions. Stereotyped thinking is a difficult habit to break, and the habits which we adopt as reporters quickly become the habits of our readers. It is therefore important to spot the important distinctions as early in the game as possible, and this requires some sophisticated, systematic techniques for gathering and processing information.

When newspapers print bad news, readers sometimes, with ill-formed logic, blame the paper which brought the message rather than the causes of the event itself. If we didn't know about it, these critics seem to say, it would be just as if it hadn't happened.

Our standard response—and I've said it a thousand times, taking crank calls at the city desk—is, "We don't make the news, Mister, we just print it." But such a response falls somewhere short of perfection because we don't stand on one side of a glass wall with the news events on the other. The old argument about whether a newspaper is a mirror or a molder of public opinion is a useless one. We interact with the public and with the news. A newspaper is an instrument of cultural diffusion.

When I was an undergraduate, college boys around the country competed with one another to see how many fraternity brothers could crowd into one phone booth. It was not by chance that this happened on campuses from California to Massachusetts in the same short period. A new cultural phenomenon was being diffused by the news media.

And if you don't believe this can be serious, consider a tentative finding from research for the National Commission on the Causes and Prevention of Violence: That political assassination threatens to be with us for the foreseeable future because the attention given to the assassins of the past six years has made assassination part of our national culture.

Moreover, there is evidence that public attention is a sufficient payoff to motivate some persons to violence. It is we of the media who provide that payoff. I have no easy answer to that problem. I do offer a difficult, partial answer to the related problem. We should be conscious of our role as disseminators of mass culture and think twice about what we disseminate.

We can't, of course, afford to ignore the Stokely Carmichaels or the Black Panthers. But neither can we afford to misunderstand what they do and say nor to give them importance beyond their actual place in the cross section of black attitudes. And we must work very hard to avoid stereotypes that lump the new separatists with the great majority of black activists who are constructive militants.

Otherwise, we risk diffusing cultural fiction and helping it to become cultural fact. If the world becomes what we say it is, we ought to be careful about what we say it is.

ROY E. LARSEN

The Thinking Man's Medium

During the fifty years of my career in publishing, the function of general interest and informational magazines in American society has been radically changed by the advent of new communications media, by the rise of millions to affluence, by the vastly increased formal education of our people, and by the growing complexities of our private, national, and international lives.

When I was in knee breeches, there was no radio. I was out of college for some years before Al Jolson sang "Mammy" in the first talking motion picture. I had lived through two world wars and the Great Depression before there was television. My contemporaries and I may not have realized it fully at the time, but we were witnessing forward strides in communications comparable to the giant stride of Gutenberg five centuries earlier.

Each of these new media, of course, offered alternative means for the public to get part of the information and entertainment it wanted, and each was therefore awarded a portion of the public's attention time, which before had been devoted mostly to print media. Each of the new media prospered as it deserved, and is continuing to prosper.

The arrivals of radio fifty years ago and television twenty-five years later were unquestionably blessings for mankind—but they were also traumatic experiences for all print media, and especially for the editors and publishers of general interest magazines. After all, for about 100 years magazines had been the principal bearers of entertainment and certain kinds of information into the home. The new media that invaded our nation's castles without bothering to ring twice were regarded by

Roy E. Larsen is vice chairman of the Board of Time, Inc., publisher of *Time, Life, Fortune, Sports Illustrated,* and *Time-Life Books*. "The Thinking Man's Medium" is reprinted from *Saturday Review*, November 14, 1970, with permission. Copyright 1970 Saturday Review, Inc.

some—not including myself—as interlopers and upsetters of apple carts. Our industry fought them tooth and nail as they came, but they refused to go away. It was years in each case before we admitted that they were here to stay and that each had virtues print media did not have. Try as we might, for instance, no magazine could rival the hilarious silences of a Jack Benny on radio or the sense of participation we all felt as TV showed us man's first step on the moon.

"Bob, do you have something I could read that won't make me think?"
Drawing by Ed Reed reprinted with permission of The Register and Tribune Syndicate, 1971.

If you will forgive what seems to be boasting—because it is—I was one of the first to use an electronic medium—radio—as a means of promoting a magazine. Some of you may remember "The March of Time"—on radio or in motion pictures—which dramatized some of the news to be found in the magazine and enticed some thousands of radio listeners to become subscribers to *Time*. As circulation manager of the magazine during that Depression period, my motto was: "If you can't beat 'em, use 'em."

Later on, as president of Time Inc., and in recognition of the great virtues of TV as a new communications medium, I recommended that our company get a piece of the new action by going into TV ourselves. We did, to the extent possible by law, and we have not been sorry. I might add that we have also invested quite heavily in the *next* generation of electronic communication, currently known as cable TV, and are seriously exploring video cartridges.

Although the competition between magazines and TV as advertising media is still going on, it seems to me that a lot of general interest magazines, including those in which I have been active, wasted a lot of effort and money during the late fifties and sixties in trying to meet TV head on in a battle for the advertising dollar. For a while there—too long a while, it now appears—we argued almost exclusively in terms of audience size and cost per thousand readers or viewers. We got into some pretty fancy arithmetic on that gambit, and wasted a lot of our energies in internecine warfare. Finally, it dawned on us—as it had twenty-five years before with radio—that numbers should not be the name of the game. It is true, of course, that TV is a fantastic mass medium, capable of reaching practically everyone with a set of eyes and ears. It is also true that several magazines regularly reach audiences far larger than do regular television offerings. The *significant* competitive fact, however, is not the mere size of the audience but the characteristics of that audience. It is not just the eyes and ears that count; what is between them is equally important.

Much to the joy of publishers, research has shown beyond question that the people who read significant magazines are the thinking men and women of our time. The magazine audience is a select audience, including a high percentage of people with the most resources, education, and influence. The magazine audience includes the generals and captains and lieutenants of the Command Generation—and the top revolutionaries as well. It includes a high percentage of the involved ones, the people who will lead other people wherever we are going.

We live, of course, in a participatory democracy, where all men are equal under the law and in their chances at heaven. But we also live in an Orwellian world where some animals are "more equal than others." Given the vagaries of the DNA molecule, some men seem born to lead and some to follow. Some are participators in the passing parade and some are spectators. It is to those whom chance has made more equal than others, to those who lead, and to those who participate that the better magazines particularly address themselves. No one is excluded, of course. Everyone who can stand the heat of the kitchen is welcome. But the selection of the audience for magazines is not really made by publishers; it is made by readers who voluntarily give their attention to editors because they hope to learn.

This elite audience for magazines—thinking men and women—are testifying with hard cash as to how important magazines are to them. The voluntary circulation of the better magazines, despite sharply increased costs to the reader and despite the temptations of more spectacular media, has increased steadily. Certain kinds of people want magazines because they need them, because they feel magazines can help them in their personal and professional lives.

The journalistic medium that offers the highest protein content, and to which readers bring their most serious attention, is the news-oriented magazine. Before they open such a magazine, readers know what they have a right to expect. They have the right to a hard, keen, skeptical, yet benign look at the world's performance, reported urbanely and illuminated by flashes from the past and blips from the future. They expect the correspondents, writers, researchers, and editors who have gathered and checked the facts, written them up, and pointed them up to have thrown out the fluff and the empty calories, and to have preserved the essence in its proper sweet or sour sauce. They expect these professionals to have argued among themselves about the significance and implications of what has happened, and to have had the courage at least to intimate what readers should make of it all and severally. In short, thinking people look to news-oriented magazines for the kinds of information and the sophistication of judgment they need for the strategic part of their personal planning—and often of their business thinking, too.

I do not have to enumerate the problems on which we all would probably appreciate some help and guidance. The cities. The environment. Drugs. The race problem. Poverty. The Indochina war. The war in the Middle East. The good life. The midi skirt. Boredom. Any one of us could list fifty problems of our time, each vying for the top of the list.

But events are not all that is happening. There is also occurring a kind of electrical phenomenon, something of the kind usually blamed on global fields of magnetic force, sunspots, or subtle emanations from moon rocks. Its name is polarization. In their attitudes on major questions, major groups of our people seem to have withdrawn as though by magnetism to the extremes of their positions so as not to be bothered with any such nonsense as finding a middle ground with anyone else. Parents have withdrawn to their pole and gaze frigidly out at their children raising hell at their pole, and at their own parents complaining of neglect in California. White people gather at the white pole, increasingly wrapped in snow, and black people gather at the black pole, wrapped in impatience. Other polarizations involve consumers and manufacturers, strictly private enterprisers and would-be socialists, Bible thumpers and the sons of Cain, women's liberationists and male chauvinists. I suppose the ultimate polarity is between dyed-in-the-wool conservatives and wild-eyed liberals, the one group crying for the imposition of order and the other for revolution.

Many polarized people believe they are the sole custodians of answers and that all the answers are simple. But today's problems are not simple, and they will not yield to shallow analysis and instant or emotional solutions. Whether we like it or not, life in the Seventies is unprecedentedly complicated. What seems simple is complex; what seems obvious is subtle. In fact, anything that seems to be, probably isn't.

There is considerable evidence that millions of people—especially many of our youth—have become inclined toward simplistic solutions to complicated problems, because for years they have seen problems dramatically presented and neatly solved on television within a thirty-minute period, minus commercials. Millions have been tempted to the fantasy that reality is something either black or white, good or bad, desirable or reprehensible—never anything in between. And millions are inclined to believe, on the evidence of Dan'l Boone or *Mission: Impossible,* that the good guy always beats the bad guy in the end.

Clearly, there is additional information to be provided if our society is to meet its sophisticated problems in a sophisticated way, if the people who pull levers in polling booths are to pull the right ones for the right reasons.

All media are addressing themselves to this need, and doing it well. The protein content of both radio and TV is higher than ever before; I've never seen more thoughtful beards and shining pates on the tube. The better newspapers are now concerned not only with hard news but with its soft implications. And magazines of an informational nature have become increasingly cerebral, as befits the most sophisticated medium of all.

Thought, of course, is the most sophisticated action of which man is capable. Deep thought is work, and it is done best when the mood is there, time is available, and distractions are absent. One trouble with the electronic world of Marshall McLuhan is that it does not stay put to await the convenience and the mood of the viewer; it puts on its show by the clock and goes away. Except in sports, McLuhan's world offers no instant replays, and the puzzled listener's "How's that again?" goes forever unanswered. A magazine, on the other hand, is a patient and thoughtful thing that will bide its time for the convenience of the reader. It can answer the "How's that again?" by offering replay at the flick of an eye or finger.

It would appear that our society's solution to current problems will be wise or willful, simplistic or knowing, largely in direct relation to the way in which magazines continue to help guide thinking people through the complexities of an ever-changing world.

OTTO FRIEDRICH

There Are 00 Trees in Russia:
The Function of Facts in Newsmagazines

The most careful checking by a platoon of researchers does not necessarily add up to the whole truth

Of course I'm sure—I read it in *Newsweek*." For several years, this slogan appeared in large advertisements all over the country. The advertisements usually showed no people, simply some scene of affluence and presumed influence, a board room or a golf club. From some unseen figure of authority came a huge white cartoon-style balloon filled with the crushing rejoinder, "Of course I'm sure—I read it in *Newsweek*."

The theory behind the advertisements was probably sound. Since *Newsweek* has fewer reporters, writers, and editors than its omniscient rival, *Time,* since it has a smaller circulation and less influence than *Time,* its chief claim to attention is that it makes a reasonable effort at fairness in summarizing the week's events. By boasting of its congeries of columnists, *Newsweek* manages to imply that everything else it publishes is the simple factual truth. Its recent ads promise a magazine "where you can always distinguish fact from opinion." One of them, portraying Walter Lippmann next to Washington bureau chief Benjamin Bradlee, emphasizes the special qualities of the latter: "The facts he gets are often 'firsts'—are always *facts*."

Time, of course, has never admitted the validity of these accusing insinuations from its smaller *Doppelgänger. Time* has always opposed the idea of mere objectivity, and it acknowledges a certain bias in favor of

Otto Friedrich is a journalist and novelist. "There Are 00 Trees in Russia" is reprinted from *Harper's Magazine,* October, 1964. Copyright © 1964 by Minneapolis Star and Tribune Co., Inc. Reprinted by permission of the author.

democracy, free enterprise, and the enlightened human spirit. But it insists that its experienced staff simply distills the facts of the news into the truth. Earlier this year, one weekly Publisher's "Letter," which normally serves as a medium of self-congratulation, sadly criticized the Soviet Union for expelling *Time*'s Moscow correspondent: "Soviet officials have never been able to understand or accept or even get accustomed to our kind of reporting." What the Soviets couldn't understand, *Time* went on, was that "our stories on the Soviet Union come from a wide array of sources available to our writers and editors in New York and to our correspondents elsewhere around the world." Thus *Time*'s kind of reporting doesn't depend primarily on having a reporter at the scene of the event. "From these many sources . . ." *Time* concluded, "we will continue to report frankly and deeply on the Soviets despite last week's reading-out of our correspondent." (There is still one other smaller and less interesting newsmagazine, but *Time* and *Newsweek* understandably ignore the Brobdingnagian claims of the *U.S. News & World Report*, which purports to be "America's Class newsmagazine.")*

Despite the competing claims of *Time* and *Newsweek*, they have a certain identity of both purpose and technique. Not only is the basic function of the two magazines almost the same, but the editor, national editor, and foreign editor of *Newsweek* are all alumni of *Time,* and there is a kind of all-purpose newsweekly office jargon that involves phrases like "the cosmic stuff" and "give it some global scope."

To anyone who has ever tried to work with these concepts and techniques, the newsmagazines' easy equation of facts, news, and truth can be rather disturbing. A reporter doesn't have to be a philosopher to know that "the facts" do not necessarily represent the truth, and that neither one of them necessarily represents the news. That men should live at peace with one another might be described as truth, but it is not a fact, nor is it news. That a certain number of children were born yesterday in Chicago is a fact, and the truth, but not news. Journalism involves an effort to discover, select, and assemble certain facts in a way that will be not only reasonably true but reasonably interesting—and therefore reasonably salable. Because of the eagerness with which an anxious and uninformed public buys anything which promises "the real story," it is easy for editors to forget these distinctions and boast about producing the facts and the truth in the name of freedom of the press and "an informed electorate."

* At the end of 1963, the ABC circulation figures were as follows: *Time*—2,958,590; *Newsweek*—1,664,563; *U.S. News & World Report*—1,293,836. [Editor's note: 1971 Ayer's Guide lists these circulations for the news magazines: *Time,* 4,268,091; *Newsweek,* 2,611,184; *U.S. News and World Report,* 1,878,321.]

THE FETISH OF THE FACTS

Behind this forgetfulness lies an enduring and endearing myth of American journalism, the myth of the police reporter and the city editor. Like all myths, it once had a certain reality. When I first went to work on the Des Moines *Register,* I was the police reporter, and I turned in my copy to a dour assistant city editor who spoke with a cutting Missouri accent and didn't believe in anything. No three-paragraph story about a minor burglary was immune to his questions about the number of floors in the burgled house, the denomination of the stolen bills, or the location of the shards of glass from the broken window. Of all possible answers, the least acceptable was "I guess so." "Let's not guess, let's know," he would retort. Sometimes I had to telephone him a half-dozen times from my bare, yellow-walled cubicle in the police station to verify trivial details in trivial stories. The copy that he finally sent to the composing room was, as nearly as possible, the facts.

Quite a few years have passed since then, and I no longer expect reporters to know the answers to questions about their stories. I have grown accustomed to their complaints that the facts in question can't be discovered, and to their further complaints about being questioned at all. They have some justification, for what happens in the U.S. Senate or the French cabinet simply can't be covered like a mugging on Sixth Street in Des Moines. The facts are more elusive, and, in a way, less important, for the physical details of who spoke to whom are relatively meaningless until they are put into perspective by an act of judgment and a point of view. In other words, the legendary police reporter and the legendary city editor no longer exist as criteria; their talents and techniques are irrelevant to most of the major news stories.

The newspapers and news agencies acknowledge this. Later editions of newspapers correct the factual mistakes and the misjudgments caused by the need for speed in getting out the first edition; a wire service revises a story with the euphemistic confession of error: "First lead and correct." It is among magazine editors, many of whom have never worked for newspapers or wire services, much less seen the inside of a police station, that the myth of "reporting the facts" remains strongest. Since a magazine must go to press several days, or even weeks, before it appears on the newsstands, and since it remains on display for at least a week, errors and all, magazine editors have developed a fetish about absolute accuracy on the most inconsequential facts, a fetish that even makes "the facts" a substitute for reality. To be sure that you can be sure because you read it in *Newsweek* (or *Time* or, for that matter, *The New Yorker* and a number of other magazines), there has come into existence an institution unknown to newspapers: the checker.

The checker, or researcher, is usually a girl in her twenties, usually from some Eastern college, pleasant-looking but not a *femme fatale*. She came from college unqualified for anything, but looking for an "interesting" job. After a few years, she usually feels, bitterly and rightly, that nobody appreciates her work. Her work consists of assembling newspaper clippings and other research material early in the week and then checking the writer's story at the end of the week. The beginning of the week is lackadaisical, and so is the research, but toward the end, when typewriters clack behind closed doors and editors snap at intruders, there are midnight hamburgers and tears in the ladies' room. For the checker gets no credit if the story is right, but she gets the blame if it is wrong. It doesn't matter if the story is slanted or meretricious, if it misinterprets or misses the point of the week's news. That is the responsibility of the editors. What matters—and what seems to attract most of the hostile letters to the editors—is whether a championship poodle stands thirty-six or forty inches high, whether the eyes of Prince Juan Carlos of Spain are blue or brown, whether the population of some city in Kansas is 15,000 or 18,000.

The first question about this fetish of facts, which no newsmagazine ever questions, is whether these facts, researched and verified at such enormous trouble and expense, really matter. Obviously, there is an important difference between saying that Charles de Gaulle accepts Britain's entry into the Common Market, which a number of prominent reporters used to report, and saying that de Gaulle opposes Britain's entering the Common Market, which mysteriously turned out to be the case. But how much does it really matter whether a newsmagazine reports that de Gaulle is sixty-seven or sixty-eight years old, six feet one or six feet two, that he smokes Gauloises or Chesterfields, that he eats a brioche or a melon for breakfast, that Madame de Gaulle puts fresh roses or does not put fresh roses on his desk every day? Judging by the legend of the police reporter and the city editor, and judging by the amount of space the newsmagazines devote to such minutiae, it matters very much to provide "the facts" and "provide them straight." Despite the public statements of principle, however, the men who usually care the least about such details are the men who actually write and edit the newsmagazines.

HAWKS WHEEL OVER CYPRUS

There is an essential difference between a news story, as understood by a newspaperman or a wire-service writer, and the newsmagazine story. The chief purpose of the conventional news story is to tell what happened. It starts with the most important information and continues into increasingly inconsequential details, not only because the reader may not read beyond the first paragraph but because an editor working on galley proofs a few minutes before press time likes to be able to cut freely from the end of the story. A newsmagazine is very different. It is written and edited to be read consecutively from beginning to end, and each of its stories is designed, following the critical theories of Edgar Allan Poe, to create one emotional effect. The news, what happened that week, may be told in the beginning, the middle, or the end; for the purpose is not to throw information at the reader but to seduce him into reading the whole story, and into accepting the dramatic (and often political) point being made.

In beginning a story, the newsmagazine writer often relies on certain traditional procedures of his special craft. They change little from year to year, but, for purposes of examination, we might select the first three issues of *Time* and *Newsweek* last May.

"Flowers were in bloom on the crumbling towers of St. Hilarion, and hawks turned soundlessly high above Kyrenia." This is *Time*'s beginning for a story on civil strife in Cyprus. The "weather lead" is always a favorite because it creates a dramatic tone; because, by so obviously avoiding the news, it implicitly promises the reader more important things to come.

Then there is the "moving-vehicle lead," most often a description of a plane landing. In one of these May issues, *Time* began a story this way: "One foggy morning in Berlin, a yellow Mercedes from the Soviet zone drew up at the tollgate at the Heerstrasse crossing point." *Newsweek*'s beginning was almost identical: "Shortly after 5 o'clock in the morning a heavily shrouded black Mercedes bearing license tags issued by the Allied Control Commission in Germany rolled quietly into the no man's land between the Western and Russian sectors of Berlin." (There is no real contradiction between the black Mercedes and the yellow Mercedes, for the magazines were focusing on two different vehicles involved in an exchange of spies.)

Another favorite is the "narrative" opening involving an unidentified person: "The hooded, gambler eyes tracked the jurors as they filed into the courtroom" (*Newsweek*, on the trial of Roy Cohn); or the provocative quote involving an unidentified object: " 'She's in there,' pointed one proud Pinkerton. 'She's the most magnificent thing I've ever seen' " (*Time*, on the appearance of Michelangelo's Pietà at the New York World's Fair). Occasionally, the newsmagazine writer just gets bored with it all: "There was a sense of *déjà vu* about the whole affair—an uncanny paramnesic feeling that all of this had happened before" (*Time*, on the May Day Parade in Moscow).

The writer had some reason to be bored. Presumably assigned to write a full-page lead story on the week's events in Eastern Europe, he had only two things to say—that nothing much had happened at the May Day Parade, and that the Romanians were playing off the Russians against the Chinese for their own benefit. In elaborating on this, he engaged in some characteristic newsmagazine equivocation: "Dej is playing a double game in the Sino-Soviet conflict, one that could lead to plenty of trouble—or perhaps to a certain amount of freedom." But though the story has nothing much to say, it absolutely bristles with the facts that newsmagazines use as a substitute for reality. It tells us what Khrushchev was wearing (a Homburg) and what had been eating lately (cabbage rather than meat). It tells us how to pronounce the name of Romania's Galati steel combine (Galatz) and what its rolling mill cost ($42 million). It gives us a figure for Romanian industrial growth (15 percent) and a translation for the name of the Romanian Communist newspaper *Scînteia* (*Spark*). And to persuade us that the activity in Romania is important, the story reports as alphabetical fact that "every Communist from Auckland to Zanzibar took note of it."

As a rule, facts are not scattered around so indiscriminately, like sequins ornamenting some drab material, for their main function in a newsmagazine story is to illustrate a dramatic thesis. When *Newsweek* begins a story on an African "summit conference," for example, it is apt to open with a variation of the moving-vehicle lead, which might be called the crowd-gathering lead: "Some came in sleek Italian suits from the Via Condotti . . ." Did any African premier really wear clothing from the Via Condotti? The problem would never arise on an ordinary newspaper, since it doesn't particularly matter where the African statesmen buy their clothes. But since the newsmagazine writer starts with a dramatic concept —the African leaders are a self-indulgent lot—he needs a dramatic concept to illustrate it.

An even more characteristic opening dramatized *Time*'s cover story on Henry Cabot Lodge:

> In the early-morning gloom of Saigon's muggy pre-monsoon season, an alarm clock shrills in the stillness of a second-floor bedroom at 38 Phung Khac Khoan Street. The Brahmin from Boston arises, breakfasts on mango or papaya, sticks a snub-nosed .38-cal. Smith & Wesson revolver into a shoulder holster, and leaves for the office.

This is a fine example of the well-trained virtuoso at work, not only disguising the subject of the story but combining a series of insignificant facts into a cadenza of exotic weather, breakfast food, strange street names, and gunplay. The author was so pleased with the results that he went on repeating himself for three paragraphs, which disclosed that the temperature that day was ninety degrees, with 90 percent humidity, that Lodge's moving vehicle was a Checker Marathon sedan, that the U.S.

Embassy building is located at 39 Nam Nghi Boulevard, and that Lodge's office desk contains yet another gun, a .357 Smith & Wesson Magnum. There are two reasons for this inundation of minutiae. The first—based on the theory that knowledge of lesser facts implies knowledge of major facts—is to prove that *Time* knows everything there is to know about Lodge. The second—based on the theory that a man who carries a gun is tough and aggressive—is to dramatize the basic thesis, that Lodge would be a good Republican candidate for President.

IN SEARCH OF THE ZIP

But what does the specific fact itself matter? Does it matter whether Lodge carries a .38-cal. Smith & Wesson or a Luger or a pearl-handled derringer? Does it make any difference whether he lives on the second floor of 38 Phung Khac Khoan Street or the third floor of some other building? The newsmagazines have provided their own answer by evolving a unique system which makes it theoretically possible to write an entire news story without any facts at all. This is the technique of the "zip." It takes various forms: Kuming (a deliberate misspelling of "coming" to warn copy editors, proofreaders, and printers not to use the word itself), or TK, meaning To Kum, or, in the case of statistics, 00 (the number of zeros is purely optional). This technique enables the writer to ignore all facts and concentrate on the drama. If he is describing some backward country, for example, he can safely write that 00 percent of its people are ravaged by TK diseases. It obviously doesn't matter too much whether the rate of illiteracy is 80 percent or 90 percent. Any statistic will sound equally authoritative. It is the checker who is responsible for facts, and she will fill in any gaps.

Filling in the "zips" is sometimes costly. One former newsmagazine writer, for example, recalls some problems that arose when he was writing a cover story on General Naguib, then the President of Egypt. Naguib, he wrote, was such a modest man that his name did not appear among the 000 people listed in *Who's Who in the Middle East*. Moreover, Naguib disliked luxury and had refused to live in the royal palace, surrounded by an 00-foot-high wall. A cable—as the writer tells the story—duly went to the Cairo stringer. There was no answer. Indignant at the stringer's feck-lessness, the editors changed the copy so that neither of the missing facts was needed. A week later, came a cable saying something like this:

AM IN JAIL AND ALLOWED SEND ONLY ONE CABLE SINCE WAS ARRESTED WHILE MEASURING FIFTEEN FOOT WALL OUTSIDE FAROUKS PALACE AND HAVE JUST FINISHED COUNTING THIRTYEIGHT THOUSAND FIVE HUNDRED TWENTYTWO NAMES WHOS WHO IN MIDEAST

When both the writer and the researcher accept this as a game, the search for the key fact can become pure fantasy. On one occasion, for example, a newsmagazine editor wrote into a piece of copy: "There are 00 trees in Russia." The researcher took a creative delight in such an impossible problem. From the Soviet government, she ascertained the number of acres officially listed as forests; from some Washington agency she ascertained the average number of trees per acre of forests. The result was a wholly improbable but wholly unchallengeable statistic for the number of trees in Russia.

In the normal case of the 00, however, someone calls a government agency to get the official answer. The results are sometimes equally strange. One *Newsweek* researcher recalls the story of the Sudanese army, which a writer had described as "the 00-man Sudanese army." No newspaper clippings could fill in the figure, and telephone calls to the Sudanese Embassy in Washington indicated that nobody there could either. The Sudanese may well have been surprised that anybody should want to know such a figure. As the weekly deadline approached, an editor finally instructed the checker to make "an educated guess," and the story appeared with a reference to something like "the 17,000-man Sudanese army." There were no complaints. The *Newsweek* story duly reached Khartoum, where the press complaisantly reprinted it and commented on it. Digests of the Khartoum press returned to Washington, and one day a Sudanese Embassy official happily telephoned the *Newsweek* researcher to report that he finally was able to tell her the exact number of men in the Sudanese army: seventeen thousand.

DOCUMENTING THE DREAM

Once you go beyond the Des Moines police station, you find yourself dealing more and more with some equivalent of the Sudanese Embassy. The "facts," which are supposed to form the basis of the news, are often simply unknown. Yet in any week's issue of any magazine of journalism, you can find the most impressive statistics—00 percent of the people of Brazil are illiterate, or the per capita income of the Burmese is $00.00.

Newsmagazine writers are very skilled in the popular sport of statistics. With the cooperation of various partisan sources, they make comparative projections of the American and Russian gross national product in 1970—when nobody has more than a vague estimate of what these figures will be even in 1965. The birth-control lobby issues horrendous statistics about the number of human beings who will be living on every cubic yard of earth in the year 2000, and yet all such projections are based heavily on the estimated future populations of China and India, estimates that vary even today by hundreds of millions. All over the world, in fact, most estimates of population, illiteracy, illness, idustrial growth, or per capita income are little more than wild guesses. "Let's not guess, let's know," the assistant city editor in Des Moines used to say, expressing a characteristically American desire for certainty. At one point during one of the periodic crises in Laos, however, an American correspondent bitterly complained to a Laotian government spokesman that he had spoken to sixteen government officials and got sixteen different versions of the facts. The Laotian was bewildered. It seemed perfectly natural to him, he said, that if you spoke to sixteen different officials you would get sixteen different answers.

The Laotian was wise in acknowledging and answering the first fundamental question about the fetish of facts: Does it really matter which "fact" is to be officially certified as "true"? He was equally wise in acknowledging and answering a second question: Does anyone really know which "fact" is "true"? He was equally wise in raising a third question, and implying an answer: Every man sees the "facts" according to his own interests.

Governments and business corporations have long acknowledged this by employing public-relations men and "information officers" to make sure that any facts make them look virtuous. *Time* once quoted a French spokesman's poetic definition of his job: "*Mentir et dementir*" (to lie and to deny). And in the world of newsmagazines, seeking the certainty of unascertainable facts, official government statistics carry a surprising weight. On one occasion, for instance, I was writing a story about the economic problems of Sicily, and I wrote that approximately 30 percent of the inhabitants were unemployed, which I believed to be roughly true. When I saw the story in print, I read that something like 8 percent of the Sicilians were unemployed. In other words, one of Europe's poorest areas was scarcely worse off than the United States—but this was the official statistic that the Italian government had given to the researcher. "After all," as one of the researchers once said, "we have to protect ourselves."

The basic purpose of the newsmagazines' facts, however, is not to report the unemployment statistics in Sicily, or the shopping habits of African statesmen, but to provide an *appearance* of documentation for what are essentially essays. The *Time* cover story on Lodge, for example, with its fact-choked lead, eventually arrives at the question of whether the Republicans might nominate Goldwater because no Republican can defeat President Johnson anyway. "This defeatist attitude is pretty silly," comments *Time, The Weekly Newsmagazine*. "Sure as his political moves have been, Johnson could still stumble politically. And healthy as the President may seem, there is always that dread possibility of disablement or worse. The Republican nomination is therefore nothing to give away for the mere asking." After that Olympian declaration, the *Time* story goes on to

outline the Lodge supporters' hope for their candidate's triumphant return to the United States. "A foolish fantasy?" *Time* wonders. "Perhaps.
But that is one of the most enchanting things about U.S. politics: dreams
can and do come true."

Unfortunately, the perils of prophecy are high. The week after the
Lodge story, which assumed that the Ambassador would sweep onward
from a victory in the Oregon primary, *Time* had a rush out with a cover
story that began, a little hysterically: "Battling Nelson did it! Battered,
bloodied, beaten, taunted, hooted, and laughed at during bitter, frustrating months, Republican Nelson Rockefeller never gave up, never stopped
swinging." This story, too, concluded with a warning to Republicans not
to accept defeat: "Nelson Rockefeller doesn't think like that—and in Oregon he demonstrated that perhaps it is a pretty poor way of thinking." No
man waits for *Time*, however, and when Barry Goldwater finally won the
Republican nomination, the editors declared that it had been inevitable:
"Goldwater won the presidential nomination by arduously cultivating support at the precinct and county levels . . . What helped clinch it for
Goldwater was the fact that a strong conservative tide was running in the
U.S., fed by a deep disquiet at the grass roots over the role of an ever-
expanding Government. Goldwater and the tide came together, and the
one could not have succeeded without the other."

On a less exalted plane, the typical newsmagazine story almost invariably reaches a point where the writer drops the factual ballast and summarizes his views on the importance of the week's events. And there is
nothing wrong about this. In view of the general inadequacy of American
newspapers and the ignorance of the American public, an informed evaluation of the week's news is something to be commended. Yet if the reality
were candidly admitted, it would antagonize the newsmagazine readers.
The English, who read newspapers on a scale that should shame most
Americans, appreciate magazines that frankly comment on a body of presumed knowledge, such as *The Economist, The New Statesman,* or *The
Spectator*. Most Americans, however, taught to believe that they should
assimilate the "facts" for themselves, reject such American counterparts as
The New Republic and *The Nation*. They accept the newsmagazines not
as magazines of commentary or interpretation but as magazines which
will tell them yet more facts, "the real story."

NEWS BREAK OR NEWS LEAK?

Here is the flaw in the newsmagazines' equation of fact and truth. For
if you assume that nobody really knows or cares how many men there are
in the Sudanese army, as newsmagazine editors do every time they use

the term "00," you acknowledge the hypocrisy of your claim to be simply reporting the facts; then you take on the sacerdotal role of providing not the facts but "the truth." (It is worth noting that newsmagazine reporters chronically complain that their "files"—the reports they send in—are ignored when the final story is written.) Apart from the size of the Sudanese army, what is really going on in the Sudan? Apart from the number of trees growing on the steppes, what is really going on in Russia? Or in London and Paris and Washington?

It is in the major political capitals, where the major news is made, that the myth of the police reporter in pursuit of the facts has become particularly irrelevant. A skillful police reporter turned loose in the Pentagon not only wouldn't be able to get the right answer, he wouldn't even be able to find the person who knew the answer. The officials of the State Department or the Quai d'Orsay speak only to people they know well. And the reporter who persuades himself that he represents the so-called "Fourth Estate" very often becomes an unofficial and perhaps unconscious spokesman for the government he is assigned to cover. At the very least, the capital correspondent thinks he is the intermediary divinely chosen to interpret the activities of politicians to the electorate; quite often, he acquires a vocation to educate and inspire the politicians themselves; rarely does he realize that in representing a "Fourth Estate" he serves the government as an instrument for leaks, propaganda, and outright lies. After all, if you're having a candlelit dinner with a Secretary of State, isn't it the better part of valor to assume that anything he tells you is "the truth"?

The situation remains much the same from one Administration to another, but one incident that still seems most illustrative occurred a few years ago. At a time when no Berlin crisis was visible in the daily press, the Washington bureau manager of a newsmagazine telephoned his superiors to say that a major Berlin crisis was imminent. Having had access to the President, he reported that "the only thing on the President's desk" was a melodramatic plan to evacuate U.S. dependents from Berlin, to mobilize reserves, and to behave as though war were imminent. This was a little puzzling since the Russians apparently hadn't done anything about Berlin recently, but the newsmagazine was so impressed by the President's supposed anxiety that it printed a major story about the supposed "emergency plan." When that issue appeared, the President was reported to have telephoned an executive of the magazine and asked how he could jeopardize the national interest with such an article. He even announced publicly that he was calling in the FBI to investigate the Pentagon to see who had leaked such a dangerous story to the magazine. The editors, who had thought they were acting for rather than against the national interest, were very much embarrassed. But the FBI somehow never suceeded in finding or punishing the culprit who had leaked the story.

It remained for the *New York Times*, one of the last redoubts of independent journalism in Washington, to suggest that the President had called in the FBI to investigate the leaking of a highly tentative "emergency plan" so that the Russians would think it was a real emergency plan. Not long after this, the President was on the air, urging Americans to build bomb shelters because of the impending Berlin crisis. And the newsmagazine, which spends tens of thousands of dollars every year to verify the per capita income of nonexistent peasants in Thailand, was left wiping the pie off its face. It could only wipe in dignified silence. For unlike the daily newspaper, which can publish a political "leak" one day and the official denial the next, the newsmagazine purports to tell not just the facts but the inside, authoritative, "real" story, and thus it remains peculiarly vulnerable to inside, authoritative, real propaganda. It cannot deny what it has authoritatively told as the truth without denying itself.

MY OWN DE GAULLE

And yet the myth survives—we must report the facts. Every statement must be checked and double-checked. One day in March of 1958, when it seemed that France was drifting toward chaos, a newsmagazine editor assigned me to write a generally sympathetic story about Charles de Gaulle and his views on France's future. Our Paris bureau chief was an ardent Gaullist and sent a long file to explain de Gaulle's policies. And since I had long been an admirer of de Gaulle, I felt no misgivings about writing an article outlining the hopeful prospects for a Gaullist France. But there was nothing in the Paris file and nothing in de Gaulle's own writing that seemed to provide an adequate summary of the Gaullist contempt for the Fourth Republic. And so I ended with a note of typical newsmagazine rhetoric, that France's main problem was to remake itself. This, I concluded, "involves a change in outlook and atmosphere, an end to the meanness, corruption, and squabbling that have darkened the past decade." When I saw the published version, I saw to my surprise that my own rhetoric had somehow become de Gaulle's rhetoric. "This, he adds," it said, referring to de Gaulle, " 'involves a change in outlook and atmosphere . . .' " And so on. When I asked the researcher how my words had become de Gaulle's words, she said that the quotation marks had been added by an editor, who had answered her protests by saying, "Well, that's his idea, isn't it? He *could* have said it."

So the matter rested, for a few weeks, and then I went on vacation. During my vacation, the army and the mob seized control of Algiers, and France shook, and de Gaulle announced his readiness to return to power, and the researcher sent me a page torn from the New York *Herald Tri-*

bune, quoting de Gaulle on every known issue. And what was his view on the basic condition of France? France must remake itself, he said, and this "involves a change in outlook and atmosphere, an end to the meanness, corruption, and squabbling that have darkened the past decade."

By now, I can only assume that this statement is a documented "fact," like the "fact" that there are 00 men in the Sudanese army and 00 trees in Russia. Until some Laotian, who never met a Des Moines police reporter, suggests that neither facts nor news is necessarily the truth.

NICHOLAS JOHNSON

The Silent Screen

Julian Goodman, president of NBC, believes that television "is now under threat of restriction and control." Frank Stanton, president of CBS, says that "attempts are being made to block us." Elmer Lower, President of ABC News, thinks he may "face the prospect of some form of censorship."

I agree. Censorship is a serious problem in our country. My only dispute with these network officials involves just *who* is doing the censoring. They apparently believe it's the Government. I disagree.

NBC recently cut Robert Montgomery's statements off the air when, during the Johnny Carson show, he mentioned a CBS station being investigated by the Federal Communications Commission. Folk singer Joan Baez was silenced by CBS when she wished to express her views about the Selective Service System on the Smothers Brothers show. Now, of course, the entire show has been canceled—notwithstanding the high ratings and its writers' recent Emmy. Sure there's censorship. But let's not be fooled into mistaking its source.

For at the same time that network officials are keeping off your television screens anything they find inconsistent with their corporate profits or personal philosophies, the FCC has been repeatedly defending their First Amendment rights against Government censorship. Just recently, for example, the FCC ruled—over strong protests—that the networks' coverage of the Chicago Democratic convention was protected by the Constitution's "freedom of the press clause." In other decisions, the commission refused to penalize radio station WBAI in New York for broadcasting an

Nicholas Johnson is a Commissioner of the Federal Communications Commission. "The Silent Screen: An Outspoken FCC Commissioner Speaks Out" is reprinted from *TV Guide* ® Magazine, July 5, 1969, with permission. Copyright © 1969 by Triangle Publications, Inc., Radnor, Pennsylvania.

allegedly anti-Semitic poem or a CBS-owned station for televising a "pot party."

Many broadcasters are fighting, not for *free* speech, but for profitable speech. In the WBAI case, for example, one of the industry's leading spokesman, *Broadcasting* magazine, actually urged that WBAI be *punished* by the FCC—and on the same editorial page professed outrage that stations might not have an unlimited right to broadcast profitable commercials for cigarettes which may result in illness or death.

This country is a great experiment. For close to 200 years we have been testing whether it is possible for an educated and informed people to govern themselves. All considered, the experiment has worked pretty well. We've had our frustrations and disappointments as a Nation, but no one has been able to come up with a better system. . . .

Central to our system, however, is the concept of an educated and informed people. As Thomas Jefferson said, "The way to prevent error is to give the people full information of their affairs." Our founding fathers were familiar with censorship by the King of England. They were going to replace a king with a representative Congress. But they were concerned lest any American institution become powerful enough to impede the flow of information to the people. So they provided in the First Amendment that "Congress shall make no law . . . abridging the freedom of speech . . ." Why "Congress"? I believe they assumed Congress would be the only body powerful enough to abridge free speech. They were wrong.

A lot has happened to the creation and control of information in this country since 1789. That was an age of town meetings and handbills. Today most information comes from the three broadcasting networks, ABC, CBS, and NBC, and the two wire services, Associated Press and United Press International. As Professor John Kenneth Galbraith has reminded us in *The New Industrial State,* seventy years ago the large corporation confined itself to mass production in heavy industry. "Now," he writes, "it also sells groceries, mills grain, publishes newspapers, and provides public entertainment, all activities that were once the province of the individual proprietor or the insignificant firm."

It is easy for us to forget how large, profitable, and politically powerful some corporations have become. In 1948 about half of all manufacturing assets in the United States were controlled by 200 corporations; today a mere 100 corporations hold that power. A single corporation such as American Telephone & Telegraph (one of the FCC's many regulated companies) controls the wages and working conditions of 870,000 employees, purchases each year some $3.5 billion in goods and services, has assets of $37 billion, and has annual gross revenues in excess of $1.4 billion. . . .

I am not suggesting that large corporations are inherently evil. Not at all. They have created much of our wealth. I am merely urging that we be aware of the fact that large corporations have both the incentive and the power to control the information reaching the citizens of our free society.

Sometimes corporate pressures to control what you see on television are just plain silly. For example, in his book, *TV—The Big Picture*, Stan Opotowsky reports that "Ford deleted a shot of the New York skyline because it showed the Chrysler building . . . A breakfast-food sponsor deleted the line 'She eats too much' from a play because, as far as the breakfast-food company was concerned, nobody could ever eat too much." Often, however, corporate tampering with the product of honest and capable journalists and creative writers and performers can be quite serious. Sometimes there is a deliberate alteration of content; sometimes needed information is squeezed out by more profitable "entertainment" programming.

On Feb. 10, 1966, the Senate was conducting hearings on the Vietnam war. Fred Friendly, who was president of CBS News at the time, wanted you to be able to watch those hearings. His network management did not permit you to watch. If you were watching CBS that day you saw, instead of George Kennan's views opposing the Vietnam war, the fifth CBS rerun of *I Love Lucy*. Fred Friendly quit CBS because of this decision, and subsequently wrote *Due to Circumstances Beyond Our Control* to tell the story. He began his book with the quotation, "What the American people don't know can kill them." Indeed it can. In Vietnam, about 35,000 so far. We have been shown miles of film from Vietnam, it's true. But how much has television told you about the multibillion-dollar corporate profits from that war? . . .

The FCC has ruled that broadcasters can't present one point of view on a controversial issue and censor all others just to serve their own beliefs and profits. The "Fairness Doctrine" requires that all viewpoints be presented. The FCC applied this doctrine to cigarette commercials. And what was the response of the broadcasting industry? It fought the decision with all the economic and political strength at its command. It has finally gone all the way to the Supreme Court to argue that a doctrine which limits its power to keep *all* information about the health hazards of cigarette smoking from the American people is a violation of broadcasters' First Amendment rights!

Or how about the 50,000 people who die each year on our highways? . . . How many television stations told you—either before or after Ralph Nader came along—that most auto-safety engineers agree virtually *all* those lives could be saved if our cars were designed properly? Nader, in *Unsafe at Any Speed*, speculates about "the impact which the massive sums spent ($361,006,000 in 1964 on auto advertising alone) have on the communication media's attention to vehicle safety design."

Television certainly didn't take the lead in telling us about unfit meat, fish, and poultry. (Chet Huntley was found to have been editorializing *against* the Wholesome Meat Act at a time when he and his business partners were heavy investors in the cattle and meat business!) Bryce Rucker, in *The First Freedom,* notes that:

> Networks generally have underplayed or ignored events and statements unfavorable to food processors and soap manufacturers. Recent examples are the short shrift given Senate subcommittee hearings on, and comments favorable to, the 1966 "truth in packaging" bill and the high cost of food processing. Could it be that such behavior reflects concern for the best interests of, say, the top fifty grocery-products advertisers, who spent $1,314,893,000 in TV in 1965, 52.3 percent of TV's total advertising income?

All Americans are concerned about "the crime problem." Have you ever stopped to wonder why the only crimes most of us hear about are, in the words of the Presidential Commission on Law Enforcement and Administration of Justice, "the crimes that are the easiest for the poor and the disadvantaged to commit . . ."? What we haven't been told is that much of the crime in the United States is "white-collar" crime; that the rich steal as much or more than the poor. . . .

Did you ever find out from television, for example, that a *single* recent price-fixing case involved a "robbery" from the American people of more money than was taken in *all* the country's robberies, burglaries and larcenies during the years of that criminal price fixing? The crime commission declared that "it is essential that the public becomes aware of the seriousness of business crime." Why is it the news media do not tell you about *these* threats to "law and order"? . . .

One could go on and on. . . . Most of the Nation's 160,000 coal miners have "black lung" disease (the disintegration of the lung from coal dust) in one form or another. Mine operators may refuse to pay for fresh-air masks—or support workmen's compensation legislation. Some television stations in coal-mining areas have, until recently, refused to televise programs offered them by doctors about this serious health hazard. . . . One current sampling showed that 20 percent of the color TV sets studied were emitting excess X-ray radiation. Natural gas pipelines are exploding as predicted. And did you know that the life expectancy of the average American adult male has been *declining* in recent years?

Note what each of these items has in common: (1) human death, disease, dismemberment, or degradation, (2) great profit for manufacturers, advertisers, and broadcasters, and (3) the deliberate withholding of needed information from the public.

Many pressures produce such censorship. Some are deliberate, some come about through default. But all have come, not from Government, but from private corporations with something to sell. Charles Tower, chairman of the National Association of Broadcasters Television Board, recently wrote a letter to the *New York Times,* criticizing its attack on CBS for "censoring" the social commentary on the Smothers Brothers show. He said,

> There is a world of difference between the deletion of program material by Government command and the deletion by a private party (such as a broadcaster) . . . Deletion by Government command is censorship . . . Deletion of material by private parties . . . is not censorship.

Another *Times* reader wrote in answer to Mr. Tower:

> Mr. Tower's distinction . . . is spurious. The essence of censorship is the suppression of a particular point of view . . . over the channels of the mass media, and the question of who does the censoring is one of form only. . . .

He's right. The results are the same. You and I are equally kept in ignorance, ill-prepared to "prevent error," and to engage in the process of self-governing which Thomas Jefferson envisioned—regardless of who does the censoring.

A number of talented people *within* the broadcasting industry recognize its failings. One of the Nation's leading black announcers told me of his first job as a disc jockey. He was handed a stack of records, but forbidden to read any news over the air. Said his boss: "You're not going to educate the Negroes of this community at my expense." A high ABC network executive was recently quoted in the pages of *TV Guide* as saying, "There are many vital issues that we won't go near. We censor ourselves." Eric Sevareid has said of the pressures involved in putting together a network news show: "The ultimate sensation is that of being bitten to death by ducks." And the executive editor of the *San Francisco Chronicle* has warned: "The press is in danger. Not the exciting kind of Hollywood danger, but of dissolving into a gray mass of nonideas." For it is also a form of censorship to so completely clog the public's airwaves with tasteless gruel that there is no time left for quality entertainment and social commentary, no time "to give the people full information of their affairs." Mason Williams, the multitalented one-time writer for the Smothers Brothers, has left television in disgust and written a poem about his experiences with "The Censor," who, he says in conclusion,

> Snips out
> The rough talk
> The unpopular opinion
> Or anything with teeth

> And renders
> A pattern of ideas
> Full of holes
> A doily
> For your mind

Your mind. My mind. The mind of America.

Many Americans are trying to say something to each other. But the media haven't been listening. And you haven't been told. So some have turned to violence as a means of being heard. All you've been shown are the dramatic pictures; you know there's "something happening." But, like the Every-man of Bob Dylan's song, "You don't know what it is, do you, Mr. Jones?" The "Silent Screen" of television has left you in ignorance as to what it's all about.

The time may soon come when the media will have to listen. From many directions come suggestions for change. Law professor Jerome Barron says the courts should recognize a "public right of access to the mass media."

Free speech in this age of television, he believes, requires that citizens with something to say be permitted to say it over radio and television. Suppose you approach a television station with a "commercial" you have prepared either supporting or protesting the President's conduct of the Vietnamese war. It may no longer be sufficient for the station to say to you, "Sorry, we don't like your views, so we won't broadcast your announcement"—as a San Francisco station did last year to those trying to express their point of view regarding a *ballot proposition!* As the U.S. Supreme Court said a few days ago in the Red Lion case, upholding the constitutionality of the FCC's Fairness Doctrine:

> There is no sanctuary in the First Amendment for unlimited private censorship operating in a medium not open to all. Freedom of the press from governmental interference under the First Amendment does not sanction repression of that freedom by private interests.

In Holland, any group that can get 15,000 persons to support its list of proposed programs is awarded free time on the Dutch Television Network for a monthly program. There is even an organization for tiny and often eccentric splinter groups without 15,000 supporters. If a similar experiment were conducted in this country, groups interested in electronic music, drag racing, handicrafts, camping, as well as the league of Women Voters, the National Association for the Advancement of Colored People, local school boards, theater and drama associations, the Young Republicans (and, who knows, even the Smothers Brothers), could obtain television time to broadcast programs prepared under their supervision.

Or each network might devote a full one-third of its prime time (6 P.M. to 11 P.M.) programming to something other than entertainment or sports. It could be nonsponsored cultural, educational, and public-affairs programming. If the networks were required to stagger such fare, then at any given time during the 6 P.M. to 11 P.M. period of greatest audiences the American viewer would have an alternative, a choice. There would still be at all times two networks with the commercial-laden, lowest-common-denominator mass entertainment of situation comedies, Westerns, quiz shows, and old movies. The third, however, would have something else. . . .

The television-station owner, not the network, has ultimate responsibility for his programming. But somebody has to select his programs, you say; nobody's perfect. You're right. And all I'm urging is that, when in doubt, all of us—audience, networks, and Government—ought to listen a little more carefully to the talented voices of those who are crying out to be heard. In short, I would rather leave the heady responsibility for the inventory in America's "marketplace of ideas" to talented and uncensored individuals—creative writers, performers, and journalists from all sections of this great country—than to the committees of frightened financiers in New York City. Wouldn't you? I think so.

I am delighted the networks have raised the issue of censorship in America. I hope they will permit us to discuss it fully.

RICHARD S. SALANT

Equal Time:
A TV Executive Replies

Federal Communications Commissioner Nicholas Johnson's article in *TV Guide* ("The Silent Screen," July 5, 1969) is shocking, if true. It is just as shocking if it is not true. And as it relates to CBS News, it most certainly is *not* true.

Commissioner Johnson claims that, for economic reasons, broadcasters withhold information and suppress discussion of issues vital to Americans. Therefore, he concludes, broadcasters are hypocritically concerned about Government censorship, since the real evil is self-censorship arising out of broadcaster timidity and economic self-protection.

Much of Commissioner Johnson's article relates to broadcast journalism. To the extent that Commissioner Johnson deals with entertainment, I will leave to those responsible for that programming the task of examining Commissioner Johnson's accuracy, although the inaccuracy of his charges against television journalism raises serious questions about the rest of his charges.

But I can speak only in respect of broadcast journalism—and only for CBS News. And for CBS News, I state flatly that Commissioner Johnson is totally, completely, 100 percent wrong—on all counts.

Let me start with the most general aspect of Commissioner Johnson's frightening world of fantasy.

In the eleven years I was a CBS corporate officer and in the six years that I have been president of CBS News, to my knowledge there is no issue, no topic, no story which CBS News has ever been forbidden, or in-

Richard S. Salant is president of CBS News. "Equal Time: A TV Executive Replies" is reprinted from *TV Guide* ® Magazine, September 20, 1969 with permission. Copyright © 1969 by Triangle Publications, Inc. Radnor, Pennsylvania.

structed directly or indirectly, to cover or not to cover, by corporate management. Corporate management at CBS has scrupulously observed that vital doctrine of separation of powers without which honest journalism cannot thrive—the separation between the corporation and an autonomous news organization.

Second, the separation between CBS News and the sales department of the CBS radio and television networks and their advertisers has been complete. CBS News has no sales department. Its function is to choose the topics and stories and to prepare the broadcasts; the sales departments and the advertisers play no part in that process. No topic has ever been selected or omitted, and no treatment has ever been affected, by the imagined or expressed wishes of an advertiser. Long since, the policy has been established that CBS News makes the broadcasts, and the advertiser makes and sells his products, and never the twain shall meet.

Third, there has been no *self*-censorship: I—and, to the best of my knowledge, my associates at CBS News—have never avoided a topic or altered treatment to protect, or to avoid displeasing, corporate management or any advertiser. As I have stated, anybody in the organization who avoided a topic or distorted his normal judgments in the treatment of a topic in order to avoid offending the economic interests of any advertisers, or to please CBS management, would thereby betray his professional heritage and would disqualify himself from working with CBS News.

So much for the general principles. As far as I have gone to this point, the issue between Commissioner Johnson and me is, to the outsider, bound to be inconclusive: it is his word against mine, and I would not blame any third party who knows neither of us for giving the nod to the Commissioner, since I have a personal stake in my own reputation and the reputation of my CBS News associates and he at least appears to be a responsible, neutral Government official with the public interest at heart. So let us turn to each of the specific charges of suppression and avoidance which Commissioner Johnson advances to prove his general thesis. Taking them one at a time, the record shows he is wrong all along the line. His batting average turns out to be .000. At most, he proves himself to be a pitcher with more speed than control, rather than a hitter.

Item: Commissioner Johnson writes that "We have been shown miles of film from Vietnam, it is true. But how much has television told you about the multibillion-dollar corporate profits from that war?"

Plenty. We have included in our broadcasts the stories of Vietnamese corruption, of the operations of American business firms in Vietnam, and of war contractor costs. Example: Congressman Pike's disclosure of the sale to the Defense Department of $210 worth of generator knobs for $33,000. Example: a two-part report in June 1969 on Pentagon waste and overruns.

Item: Commissioner Johnson, stating that cigarette advertising "provides the largest single source of television's revenue," asks, "Would it really surprise you to learn that the broadcasting industry has been less than eager to tell you about the health hazards of cigarette smoking?"

Well, if it did surprise you, it would only be because you have not been watching CBS News. We have dealt continuously and in depth with the health hazards of cigarette smoking, long before the Surgeon General got around to his report and long before Commissioner Johnson publicly decided to become concerned about the problem. We started fourteen years ago, in 1955, in a two-part *See It Now* report. We broadcast a *CBS Reports:* "The Teen-Age Smoker" in 1962 and a special on Jan. 11, 1964, "On Smoking and Health," the day the Surgeon General's report was issued. On April 15, 1964, we broadcast *CBS Reports:* "A Collision of Interests," a detailed review of the issues raised by cigarette smoking. In our national health tests broadcast early in 1966, we again dealt with the hazards of smoking. We did another special hour-long broadcast in the beginning of 1968, "National Smoking Test" (about which *Newsday's* television critic commented: "It took courage on CBS's part to show the way. Especially since, as the program mentioned, the cigarette manufacturers are TV's largest advertisers. Viewers are in the network's debt"). We came back to the subject in *The 21st Century* series, in a broadcast entitled "The Wild Cell" (Feb. 2, 1969). We included stories in many of our other regularly scheduled broadcasts—for example, in *Calendar* on lung cancer and smoking in April 1962—and repeatedly we have covered in our regular news broadcasts all the developments—up to and including an interview on Thursday, July 3, with the current Surgeon General on cigarette advertising and the hazards of smoking. Since June 1963, our regularly scheduled news broadcasts have included eighty-four special film stories on cigarettes (including the showing of the American Cancer Society's antismoking film—in January 1967; and the attack by E. William Henry, then Chairman of the FCC, on television cigarette advertising—in March 1966).

Item: Commissioner Johnson refers to the "50,000 people who die each year on our highways" and then asks ". . . how many television stations told you—either before or after Ralph Nader came along—that most auto-safety engineers agree virtually *all* those lives could be saved if our cars were designed properly?"

I do not have a nose count of the number of stations. But, again, before the issue became very fashionable to discuss, CBS News did a one-hour pre-emptive, prime-time special May 13, 1966, "Crash Project—The Search for a Safer Car"—featuring Ralph Nader. If Commissioner Johnson's extremely selective perception has excluded that broadcast from his mind, I call to his attention this excerpt from a review in *Variety*, May 18, 1966:

Of more significance, however, than the arguments pro and con on car design was CBS's lack of inhibition in confronting one of the giants of advertising and letting the chips fall where they may. Thus a direct comparison of two competitive makes was shown with a tester from Consumers Union detailing the faults in one car and extolling the virtues of another while identifying both by name. This is indeed strong stuff and certainly more than most of the newspapers of the country would do under similar circumstances.

And on auto safety, CBS News did not hit and run: we have gone back to the subject not only in our "National Drivers' Test" broadcasts but in forty-four different reports in the *Morning News* and the *Evening News* since April 1965—dealing with the charges against the automobile industry and with the call-backs, including a demonstration of exactly what some of the defects leading to the callbacks were.

Item: Commissioner Johnson quotes Bryce Rucker as stating that "Networks generally have underplayed or ignored events and statements unfavorable to food processors and soap manufacturers. Recent examples are the short shrift given Senate subcommittee hearings on, and comments favorable to, the 1966 'truth in packaging' bill and the high cost of food processing."

Wrong again—in our news broadcasts, we covered those hearings and included statements of consumer representatives and witnesses in support of the bill. We have reported stories relating to alleged abuses in food processing. Just a few examples: On March 24, 1969, in the *Evening News with Walter Cronkite*, we reported the FTC allegation that the Campbell Soup Company had been putting clear glass marbles in bowls to make its soup look thicker in television commercials. And we reported the story of the dangers involved in pesticides contaminating cranberry sauce; the story about the dangers of botulism in canned tuna fish and the mass recall of canned tuna; the unfit meat story as it developed; Ralph Nader's testimony attacking the standards of intrastate meat packers; and the Government action against the Colgate-Palmolive sandpaper commercial.

Item: Commissioner Johnson asks, "What could be more essential than information about potentially harmful . . . drugs?"

He just asks, he doesn't say that we didn't cover it. He was lucky because if he had said it, he would have been wrong. Time and time again, we have reported such stories as the thalidomide story, the FTC allegations relating to aspirin and Bufferin, the Government action against drug price fixing, the hearings on the excessive cost of drugs, including Italian cut-rating and American profiteering in Latin America, the charges relating to dangerous side effects of the birth-control pill, the FTC action against Geritol and Tums—both heavy advertisers with CBS. On July 9,

1969 (after Commissioner Johnson's article), we reported briefly on the recent reports of the National Academy of Sciences on the ineffectiveness of drugs and pharmaceuticals; we dealt with the subject in more detail two days later, on July 11.

Item: Commissioner Johnson states that television fails to report on corporate crimes, and he makes specific reference, although not by name, to an important case of price fixing.

If I can guess what price-fixing case Commissioner Johnson is talking about, we most certainly reported it.

Item: Commissioner Johnson writes about "the inherent dangers in cyclamates (the artificial sweeteners in soft drinks)" and implies that television's failure to cover that story results in the danger being "scarcely known to the average America."

Wrong again. On the *Morning News* of April 11, 1969, we did a piece, running 7½ minutes, concerning cyclamates, and we also reported the story in the *Evening News.*

Item: Commissioner Johnson *seems* to say (sometimes his pen is quicker than the eye) that we ignored the "black lung" disease story—the dangers to miners' lungs resulting from coal dust.

The pattern is familiar: he is wrong; we did not ignore the story. We covered it in reporting the hearings in Washington and in West Virginia on the issue, and in a special broadcast on Feb. 11, 1969, entitled "Danger! Mines."

Item: Commissioner Johnson refers to the fact that "one current sampling showed that 20 percent of the color-TV sets studied were emitting excess X-ray radiation." Again, he doesn't say so, but the implication is that we didn't cover it.

Wrong again: we did—as long ago as August 1967, when we reported that the Surgeon General called for action on such radiation.

Item: Commissioner Johnson states broadly that we avoid stories of "human death, disease, dismemberment or degradation."

Let him drop into my office some time and see the viewers' mail that comes across my desk complaining that that is *all* we ever talk about, and criticizing us bitterly for not emphasizing more good news. Was Commissioner Johnson otherwise occupied during our almost nightly Vietnam coverage, or when we broadcast such documentaries as "Harvest of Shame," "The Silent Spring of Rachel Carson," "The Tenement," "Christmas in El Barrio," "The Poisoned Air," "Men in Cages," "Hunger in America"? And our continuing series on one street in a Washington, D.C., ghetto, Columbia Road, on the *CBS Morning News?*

Commissioner Johnson finds it easy to make out a case by simply ignoring what we have done. His implication is that, in deference to advertisers, we stay away from any news unfavorable to consumer products.

As we have just seen, he is wrong on every one of his specifics; we have covered each of the cases he mentions. And we have done other consumer stories as well which involved industry and network advertisers: for example, the housewives' boycott of supermarkets, protesting high prices; the gas-station game-and-prize practices; the dangers of flammable toys and clothing; toy guns and other war-like toys; the trading-stamp story; lumber-industry activities in the forests; the dangers of pesticides; automobile-insurance practices involving racial discrimination and arbitrary cancellation of policies; retail-credit abuses; automobile-warranty abuses; the dangers of cholesterol as a cause of heart and other diseases, caused by meat fats, butter fat, margarines, and other shortenings and vegetable spreads.

And, of course, implicit in Commissioner Johnson's thesis is the charge that about the last thing we would ever do is report stories unfavorable to CBS or CBS News itself. But again, the facts are to the contrary: for example, we have reported the charges against television for its alleged violence and effect on juvenile delinquency. We reported the charges that CBS "staged" a pot party. We reported former Secretary of Agriculture Freeman's attack on the accuracy of the CBS News documentary "Hunger in America." And as to Commissioner Johnson's favorite subject, the Smothers Brothers, it was CBS News which, last fall, even before the storm broke, did a segment of *60 Minutes* with the Smothers Brothers expressing their viewpoints about their role in television and their relationship to CBS; and it was CBS News which, on the day after their contract was canceled, included the only network interview with Tommy Smothers reacting to the CBS action.

As Commissioner Johnson says in his article, "One could go on and on." And the *facts*—about which one could go on and on—destroy the fantasy about which he goes on and on.

Others—perhaps more scholarly and careful than Commissioner Johnson—have examined the question of television news' integrity and independence, and have come to quite different conclusions. Thus, Herbert J. Gans, a sociologist who is making a long-range study of the mass media, stated (*New Yorker*, Aug. 3, 1968, page 55):

> Despite the old stereotype that media employees report the news as their owners and advertisers see fit, this is not true of national television and magazines, however true it may be of the local press. People who work in the media I have studied so far are surprisingly free from outside interference on the part of nonprofessionals and business executives, and can decide on their own what to cover and how to cover it.

It may well be that the Commissioner is too busy attending to his official duties, and making speeches, and writing articles, to permit him to know what really goes over the air. But Commissioner Johnson shows signs not only that he has no time to *look*, but he also has not time or inclination to *read*. For one of his lowest—and most mistaken blows—comes in his invocation of Eric Sevareid as a witness to support his thesis. In a paragraph explicitly devoted to management and advertising interference and pressures, Commissioner Johnson states that Eric Sevareid "has said of the pressures involved in putting together a network news show: 'The ultimate sensation is that of being bitten to death by ducks.' "

Never underestimate the carelessness or the disingenuity of Commissioner Johnson. Eric Sevareid indeed said exactly that several years ago. But Commissioner Johnson could have seen from the Sevareid statement itself, or from checking with Eric directly, that Eric (see his letter to *TV Guide*, July 19) simply was not talking about management or advertising interference or pressures. Eric *was* talking about what plagues us all in television journalism and for which not even Commissioner Johnson can supply a solution: the cumbersome apparatus of television journalism, with all its cameras and lights and technicians and layers of personnel which are inherent in the complex nature of our method of transmission. Eric was contrasting this with the simplicity of a reporter or a writer for print who can sit in a corner by himself, type out his story and send it in. All Commissioner Johnson had to do was to read Eric's statement.

The ultimate issues which Commissioner Johnson raises are important indeed. They involve the independence and integrity of broadcast journalism, free of management interference and advertising pressures—and free too from Government dictation or coercive suggestion. I happen to think that Commissioner Johnson has some esoteric and erroneous notions about the First Amendment. (Incidentally, the credit he bestows upon himself and his associates as the champions of the First Amendment in the Commission's handling of the complaints concerning our political-convention coverage is not quite justified. The Commission's *actions* in that case were rather less noble and rather less sensitive to the First Amendment than its belated words. After all, the Commission transmitted *every* complaint that it received and required us to address ourselves to them—including hundreds that, only months later, it announced were not within its permissible authority.)

I also happen to think that the spirit, if not the letter, of the First Amendment would, at the very least, compel a man in his position—a Government agent who, through his licensing power, has the power of life and death over broadcasters—to be exceedingly careful and accurate when he undertakes public statements about what broadcast news does and does not do and what it ought and ought not to do.

But, as I have stated elsewhere, the First Amendment includes the right to be wrong. Commissioner Johnson has certainly exercised that right.

PART FIVE

Advisers and Forecasters

Introduction

Journalists like to think of their media as providing society and its members with an "early warning system" to foretell changes—both good and bad—just beginning to appear on the horizon. When the media perform this function, they often combine the job of describing and interpreting the nascent change with advice on how to greet it.

Some New Journalists have criticized the media for being slow to recognize danger signals. Part of the explanation for this slowness may be that editors and reporters are event-oriented, and environmental and social changes do not always cause obvious news events—at least in the early stages. Thus, almost a decade passed after Rachel Carson's *Silent Spring* before the press began to take the ecology crisis seriously. Indeed, Miss Carson's book was widely attacked in the press when it was published, and *Time* called it "an emotional and inaccurate outburst." It was not until several years after the publication of *Unsafe at Any Speed* by lawyer Ralph Nader that the news media began to consider auto safety a valid editorial issue.

"Early warning" news is most often based on investigative or depth reporting, the most expensive kind in which any medium can invest. Such reporting *sometimes* leads to legislative or Congressional investigations, grand jury indictments, new trials for convicts long imprisoned, and Presidential commission studies. Great skill and enormous amounts of time are required to dig out information for such stories.

In television, this kind of journalism is done best by the documentary. Two of the most famous were Edward R. Murrow's program on Senator Joe McCarthy in 1953 and CBS's "The Selling of the Pentagon" in 1971.

Because both TV and radio programs are so transitory in character, the print media—newspapers, magazines, and books—seem best qualified for early warning reportage. Newspapers, wire services, and many magazines are turning more and more attention to such depth stories. For several years, the Associated Press has had a special assignment team of ten reporters, created specifically for investigative reporting.

The early warning reporters are, by extension, advisers. If enough Americans had been made aware of the implications of *Silent Spring* when it was published, legislation to outlaw manufacture and use of DDT would probably have come far sooner. On events and movements that matter, every report—fair or dishonest, good or bad—is a suggestion to the viewers, listeners, or readers that they take some type of action.

Understandably, then, there has been a growing tendency for journalists to look for criteria by which to judge how well they are doing their jobs of advising and forecasting. This helps explain the large number of press-bar codes for handling pretrial and trial publicity. After the ghetto riots of the late sixties, news media in many cities worked out codes with local police and other officials to make sure their procedures in moments of crisis were truly professional.

TERRY ANN KNOPF

Reporting News About Race

*A study of media performance reveals
improvements and a healthy willingness to
experiment with new procedures. But certain
shortcomings persist.*

Several years ago a resident of a small Northern town kept insisting to a local newspaper reporter that a policeman had been shot and killed during a racial disturbance there. The reporter checked and rechecked but was unable to substantiate the story. In fact a policeman had been killed, but in another city. The man simply had heard a garbled version of the story—not an unusual occurrence in the confusion that prevails during crises.

Crisis situations increase the need for news. During most serious disturbances, news media are bombarded with calls from anxious citizens wanting information, clarification, verification of what they have heard. So important is the flow of news through established channels that its continued absence can help precipitate a crisis. In 1968 in Detroit the absence of newspapers during a protracted strike helped create a panic: there were rumors in the white community that blacks were planning to blow up freeways, kill suburban white children, and destroy public buildings; in the black community, that white vigilantes were coming into the area to attack the residents. Gun clubs sprang up in the suburbs; black leaders urged preparation of survival kits. On March 7—nearly four months after the strike began—Mayor Cavanagh had to go on TV to plead for calm.

As racial disorders have become a familiar part of the national scene

Terry Ann Knopf is a research associate at the Lemberg Center for the Study of Violence, Brandeis University. "Reporting News About Race," originally titled "Media Myths on Violence," is reprinted from *Columbia Journalism Review*, Spring, 1970, with permission.

the media have demonstrated a growing awareness of their responsibilities and a healthy willingness to experiment with new policies and procedures. Technical improvements also have been made. The City of Detroit, for example, has built a press room large enough for 150 people, with independent telephone lines. Operational techniques have been modernized—the Pittsburgh police, among others, have on occasion provided a helicopter for the press. And central headquarters or "press centrals" have been established to help eliminate conflicting reports. Moreover, a number of cities have adopted or revised guidelines for reporting. These guidelines—sometimes formal, sometimes informal—urge that unnecessary interpretation be minimized, rumors be eliminated, unverified statements be avoided, and superlatives and adjectives in "scare" headlines be excluded. One set of guidelines put the matter simply: "Honest and dispassionate reporting is the best reporting."

In accordance with these guidelines, newspapers have tended to move away from the "shotgun" approach—the front-page buildup, complete with splashy pictures and boxscores of the latest "riot" news. Dramatic but meaningless predictions have also largely disappeared. In May, 1967, *U.S. News & World Report* declared that Newark was "not expecting trouble," while Cleveland was voted the city "most likely to explode—again." Cleveland failed to erupt in 1967, but Newark experienced one of the most massive outbursts in our country's history. This kind of journalism is much less common today.

There is also evidence of greater sympathy and sensitivity toward blacks. How far have we come? Consider the following comment from the *New York Times* on July 23, 1919, concerning the violent disorder in Washington, D. C.:

> The majority of the negroes (sic) in Washington before the great war were well behaved. . . . More of them admitted the superiority of the white race, and troubles between the two races were undreamed of. Now and then a negro intent on enforcing a civil rights law would force his way into a saloon or a theatre and demand to be treated the same as whites were, but if the manager objected he usually gave in without more than a protest.

These changes represent considerable improvement. But serious problems remain. Glaring instances of inaccuracy, exaggeration, distortion, misinterpretation, and bias have continued at every level—in newspapers and newsmagazines large and small, Northern and Southern, liberal and conservative.

The wire services are probably the most underexamined segment of the media, although as much as 90 percent of the news in some newspapers on a given day may come from the wires. One error in a wire service report from one city may be repeated in hundreds of newspapers and newscasts. In York, Pa., in mid-July, 1968, for instance, incidents of rock-and bottle-throwing were reported. Toward the end of the disturbance UPI in Harrisburg asked a stringer to get something on the situation. A photographer took a picture of a motorcyclist with an ammunition belt around his waist and a rifle strapped across his back. A small object dangled from the rifle. On July 18, the picture reached the nation's press. The *Washington Post* said:

> ARMED RIDER—Unidentified motorcyclist drives through heart of York, Pa., Negro district, which was quiet for the first time in six days of sporadic disorders.

The Baltimore *Sun* used the same picture and a similar caption:

> QUIET, BUT . . . An unidentified motorcycle rider, armed with a rifle and carrying a belt of ammunition, was among those in the heart of York, Pa., Negro district last night. The area was quiet for the first time in six days.

The implication of this photograph was clear: The "armed rider" was a sniper. But since when do snipers travel openly in daylight completely armed? Also, isn't there something incongruous about photographing a sniper, presumably "on his way to work," when according to the caption the city "was quiet"? Actually the "armed rider" was a sixteen-year-old boy who happened to be fond of hunting groundhogs—a skill he had learned as a small boy from his father. On July 16, as was his custom, the young man had put on his ammo belt and strapped a rifle across his back, letting a hunting license dangle so that all would know he was hunting animals, not people. Off he went on his motorcycle headed for the woods, the fields, the groundhogs—and the place reserved for him in the nation's press.

More recently, an AP man in Dallas filed a story on a student takeover at Southern Methodist University. The *Fort Worth Star-Telegram* in its evening edition last May 2 put the story on the front page and gave it a banner headline:

BLACKS SEIZE OFFICE OF S.M.U.'S PRESIDENT

Police Are Called to Stand By

> DALLAS (AP)—Black students with some support from whites took over the office of the president of Southern Methodist University today and swore to remain until their demands are met. . . .
> Reports from the scene said from thirty to thirty-five students were in control of [President] Tate's office.
> The takeover occurred during a meeting of Tate and a campus organization, the Black League of Afro-American and African College Students.

The story had one major flaw—it wasn't true. While about thirty-five students had met with the university president, they were not "in control" of his office; nor had they "swore to remain" until their demands were met. No such "takeover" had occurred. Glen Dromgoole, a staff writer for the *Star-Telegram*, later reported what really happened. The black students had met with the president for more than five hours discussing recent demands. The talks were more friendly than hostile. (At one point hamburgers were brought in.) By the end of the meeting, agreement had been reached on most of the issues. Apparently the wire service reporter had accepted the many rumors of a student takeover.

Martin Hayden of the Detroit *News* has suggested "an almost mathematical relationship between the level of exaggeration and the distance of news transmission." Edwin Guthman of the *Los Angeles Times* maintains that the early wire service report "is at the crux of the news media's problem." However, it is more likely that instances of misreporting remain a problem at *every* media level. The Lemberg Center for the Study of Violence, in investigating twenty-five incidents in which the news media had alleged sniping, found that, along with the wire services, local and nationally known newspapers bore a heavy responsibility for imprecise, distorted, and inaccurate reporting.

While treatment of racial disorders is generally more restrained today, the news media continue to overplay the more violent or sensational aspects of a story. The central media concern during the disorder at Cornell University last April, for example, was the emergence of the blacks from the student union. A picture of the students carrying rifles and shotguns, splashed across the nation, had a distorting effect on public opinion. The *New York Times* put the picture on page 1, and *Newsweek* used it on its cover the following week. Certain facts were largely ignored: prior to the disorder a cross had been burned in front of a black women's dormitory; the students had heard radio reports that carloads of armed whites were moving toward the campus; when the students emerged from the building their guns weren't loaded. What was basically a defensive response by a group of frightened students came across in the media as a terrorist act by student guerrillas.

Aspects of the disorders are dramatic and do merit extensive coverage. But the media still tend to equate bad news with big news and to confuse the obvious with the relevant. Thus when sixty-five students at Brandeis University took over a building last year it rated a story on the front page of the *New York Times*—despite that fact that there was no violence, that classes continued, and that the university suffered only minor inconvenience. I was on campus then. My only recollection of anything unusual was that on the first day or two an attendent asked to see my identification, and for the next week and a half I noticed large numbers of reporters, press cars, cameras, and other equipment. I sometimes wondered if there weren't more reporters outside than students inside the building. The *Times*, along with most newspapers, missed the unusual climax at Brandeis. In a war of nerves with the students, President Morris Abram showed consummate skill in handling the situation, remaining flexible on the issues, mobilizing the support of the student body and faculty, and, above all, refusing to call in police. Eleven days after the crisis had begun the students quietly left the building—a dramatic victory for the Brandeis community, a dramatic example of how to handle a university crisis in contrast to fiascoes at Columbia and San Francisco State. Yet the students' departure merely merited a *Times* story about three inches long, well off the front page.

Disparities between the headlines and news stories are another problem. Often much less occurs in the story than the headline would indicate. Last year, for example, some concerned parents in Jacksonville, Florida, removed their children from Kirby Smith Junior High School after a local radio station had broadcast an exaggerated report of a fight between black and white students. The school principal later indicated that "classes continued and there was no panic." Nevertheless the *Miami Herald* headlined its story last April 25: MOMS MOB SCHOOL AFTER RIOT 'NEWS.' Sometimes no violence occurs in the story, dramatic headlines to the contrary. A story appearing in the Boston *Globe* last May 10 told of a peaceful rally by a small group of students at a local theological seminary. According to the *Globe*, the rally was "brief and orderly." But the headline above the story read NEWTON CAMPUS ERUPTS.

The use of the word "riot" presents another problem because it has no precise meaning in terms of current disorders. *Webster's* defines a "riot" as a "tumultuous disturbance of the public peace by three or more persons assembled together and acting with a common intent." The difficulty is that "riots" have become so frequent and come in so many sizes and shapes as to render the word meaningless. There is something ludicrous about lumping together as "riots" Detroit, with forty-three deaths, 7,000 arrests, and $45 million in property damage, and an incident in which three people break a few store windows. Yet this is precisely what the news media still do. The continued media use of the term contributes to an emotionally charged climate in which the public tends to view every event as an "incident," every incident as a "disturbance," and every disturbance as a "riot." Journalists would do well to drop the word from their vocabulary altogether.

No law says the media have to interpret and not simply report the news, but having assumed this responsibility they have an obligation to make reasonable judgments based on careful analysis. Unfortunately, journalistic attempts in the direction of social science research have been rather amateurish, particularly where new trends and patterns are concerned. The case of the Cleveland "shoot-out" is a good example. On July 23, 1968, an intense gun battle broke out between the police and a group of black nationalists led by Ahmed Evans. Before the disorder was over 16,400 National Guardsmen had been mobilized, nine persons had been killed, and there was property damage estimated at $2.6 million. The Cleveland *Press* on July 24, 1968, compared the violence to guerrilla activity in Vietnam:

> . . . it didn't seem to be a Watts, or a Detroit, or a Newark. Or even a Hough of two years ago. No, this tragic night seemed to be part of a plan.

A reporter writing in the *New York Times* of July 28, 1968, stated:

> It marks perhaps the first documented case in recent history of black, armed, and organized violence against the police.

More recent reports have revealed that the "shoot-out" was something less than a planned uprising and that the situation was considerably more complicated than indicated initially. Unfortunately, following the events in Cleveland, disorders in which shots may have been fired were immediately suspected by the press of being part of a "wave." A series of errors involving a handful of cities became the basis of a myth—that the pattern of violence in 1968 had changed from spontaneous to premeditated outbreaks. Few of the nationally known newspapers and newsmagazines attempted to verify sniping reports coming out of the cities and over the wire services; few were willing to undertake independent investigations; and far too many were overly zealous in their assertions of a new "trend" based on limited and unconfirmed evidence. Unwittingly or not, the national media had constructed a scenario on armed uprisings.

Although having more time to check and verify reports than daily newspapers, the newsmagazines were even more vocal in their assertions of a "new pattern." On September 13, 1968, *Time* took note of an "ominous trend" and declared that the violence "appears to be changing from spontaneous combustion of a mob to the premeditated shoot-outs of a far-out few." The story went on to indicate that "many battles" had begun with "well planned sniping at police." Nearly a year later, on June 27, 1969—long after investigation by a task force of the National Commission on the Causes and Prevention of Violence, by the Lemberg Center, and by the *New York Times* (which reversed itself on the Cleveland question) had cast serious doubt about premeditated outbreaks in Cleveland and elsewhere—*Time* still was talking about the possibilities of a "guerrilla summer" and reminding its readers of the time in Cleveland when "police were lured into an ambush." Once started, myths are difficult to extinguish.

The most recent myth created by the media involves an alleged "shift" in racial disturbances from large to small cities. Last July 25 a syndicated reporter for the News Enterprise Association (NEA) noted:

> The socially sizzling summer has begun—but unlike recent history, it seems to be the minor, not the major, cities which are sweltering.

In an article entitled "Riots, 1969 Style," *Newsweek* declared on August 11:

> . . . the traditional riot scenario is still being played out this summer—with one major difference. This season the stage has shifted from the major population centers to such small and disparate communities as Kokomo, Ind., Santa Ana, Calif., Cairo, Ill., Middletown, Conn., and Farrell, Pa.

Last September 9 the *New York Times* captioned a picture:

> NEW RIOT PATTERN: Rioting in Hartford, Conn., last week . . . underscored the fact that smaller cities this summer have had more racial trouble than the big ones.

Similar stories appeared about the same time in scores of other newspapers, including the *Wall Street Journal,* the *Baltimore News American,* the *Woburn, Mass., Times,* and the *Pittsburgh Press.*

In fact, racial disorders occurring over the past few years—not just this past summer—have been concentrated in smaller cities. About 75 percent of all outbreaks recorded in 1968 by the Lemberg Center's Civil Disorder Clearinghouse occurred outside the 100 largest cities. For the first six months of 1969 and also for the summer no appreciable change in the percentage was noted. Furthermore, many of the cities cited as prototypes of this latest "new pattern"—Hartford and Middletown, Conn., Cairo, Ill.—have had disorders in previous years. The difference is that such outbreaks were completely overshadowed by a few enormous outbreaks in large cities such as Newark and Detroit.

Discovering the origin of these and other myths would be useful—a faulty wire service report, an inept reporter, an unreliable source. But aside from the fact that such a task would be almost impossible, it would miss a central point—that the system of reporting ensures that errors of fact and interpretation may be repeated, compounded, and reformulated as myths. In recent years the various components of the media have become extremely intertwined and dependent upon one another. The wire services, the nationally known newspapers, and the newsmagazines feed one another news and information. While the system undoubtedly speeds the flow of news to the public, it has encouraged a parrot-like character in which the various media segments tend to reproduce rather than examine one another's views.

In this respect the *New York Times'* caption proclaiming a NEW PATTERN assumes greater significance. Prior to its appearance in the *Times,* I talked with Jack Rosenthal, who had been working on a story on the relatively cool summer. When the subject of a new "shift" in violence came up I indicated that such allegations were false and misleading. Rosenthal wrote a thoughtful story, dwelling on police-community relations, civic programs, and the new community spirit among blacks. His story made no mention of a "new riot pattern." Apparently the caption writer had paid more attention to what *Newsweek* and the *Wall Street Journal* were saying than to his colleague at the *Times.*

The failure of the media to tell the complete story in the case of Cornell or the right story in the case of Cleveland goes beyond a lack of initiative or an inclination to sensationalize. It also indicates a bias—one which, notwithstanding Vice President Agnew's declarations, cuts *across* political and geographical lines. The media are no more aware of this bias than is the general public aware of its own. In part, we could call it a class bias in that those who comprise media staffs—reporters, editors, headline writers, etc.—are part of the vast American middle class and, as such, express its views, values, and standards.

Both the general public and the media share the same dislike of protestors; both are unable to understand violence as an expression of protest against oppressive conditions; both prefer the myth of orderly, peaceful change, extrolling the virtues of private property and public decorum. People are expected to behave in a certain way; they just don't go around yelling and cursing or throwing rocks. Both will grant that it took a revolution to secure our independence and a civil war to end slavery (at least officially), but that was all long ago and somehow different. The bias also has elements of racism in that color is never far from the surface. It is difficult to say where the class bias begins and racist bias ends. These elements are inseparable and reinforce each other, and both manifest themselves in the thinking of the public and media alike.

A growing body of research shows that racial disorders are a part of the social process. The process includes an accumulation of grievances, a series of tension-heightening incidents such as police harassment, and a precipitating event such as an arrest which crystallizes the tensions and grievances that have mounted—the "last straw" that triggers the violence. The "typical rioter" is young, better educated than the average inner-city black, and more dissatisfied. He wants a better job but feels that prospective employers will discriminate against him. He is likely to be a long-term resident of the city. (In a survey in Detroit, 90 percent of those arrested were from Detroit, 78 percent lived in the state, and only 1 percent lived outside the state.) He is extremely proud of his race and is politically conscious. He is more interested in and informed about politics than blacks who are not involved in a disorder. He is also more inclined toward political activism. (In one survey, nearly 40 percent of the participants in the disorder—as compared to only about 25 percent of the nonparticipants—reported having been involved in civil rights activity.) Finally, he receives substantial support from the rest of his community, which does not participate but regards the violence as necessary and beneficial.

As important as the findings in these studies are, they have made virtually no impact on the vast majority of the public. Most Americans continue to believe that violence is caused by a tiny and insignificant minority, that "outside agitators" and "criminal elements" are mainly responsible for isolated outbursts that have little or no social significance. Intellectuals must share a portion of the blame for this situation. Having completed their studies, they have been notoriously reluctant to roll up their academic shirtsleeves and assume leadership in presenting their ideas to the public. There is a trace of condescension in their assumption that good ideas from above will somehow trickle down to the "masses of asses," as one academic I know calls them.

Greater responsibility for the failure to confront the public's resistance rests with the news media. They have failed to commit their power and prestige on behalf of such studies. They have failed to place the ideas before the public and push for reform in an aggressive, effective manner—settling for a splash of headlines and stories initially, and little followup. Instead the media have opted for the status quo, reflecting, sustaining, and perpetuating outworn beliefs of their predominantly white audience.

Historically the notion of plots and conspiracies has always had great currency in this country—and in other countries, too. Prior to the Civil War, Southerners frequently viewed abolitionists as "outside agitators" trying to stir up the happy slaves. Violent interracial clashes during World War I were said to have been instigated by the Bolsheviks, and the outbreak in Detroit in 1913 was attributed to an "Axis plot." The current wave of disorders has been blamed on individuals such as Stokely Carmichael and H. Rap Brown or, for those who like a more international flavor, "Communist infiltrators." In a survey of six Northern cities by the Lemberg Center, 77 percent of all whites interviewed believed that "outside agitators" were a major contributing cause of disorders. When Los Angeles Mayor Sam Yorty recently blamed a rash of school disorders on a conspiracy of the Black Student Union, the Students for a Democratic Society, Communist sympathizers, and the National Council of Churches, he was following a long—though not very honorable—tradition.

Such allegations are usually made without a shred of evidence, except for an occasional "someone told me so." Nevertheless the media have frequently taken their cues from the public in formulating and circulating such reports. Misinterpretations of the events in Cleveland, along with assertions of a "new pattern" of premeditated violence, are blatant examples of this form of bias. But more often the bias is expressed in more subtle ways. For example, when rumors circulated that "outside agitators" were involved in a disturbance in Omaha, Neb., a news story appearing in the Arkansas *Gazette* last June 27 made reference to the rumors but also mentioned that the mayor had no evidence to support such reports. Yet, the headline above the story read: 'OUTSIDERS' LINKED TO OMAHA RIOTING.

A look at the way in which the disorders are written up reveals, tragically, that the majority of the media and the public share essentially the same view of the violence—as meaningless, purposeless, senseless, irrational. Media treatment of the disorders following the assassination of Rev. Martin Luther King, Jr., illustrates the point. The sense of loss and injury among blacks at the time of the assassination was extremely great —far greater than among whites. The unprecedented wave of disorders— approximately 200—was expressive of the anger, bitterness, resentment, frustration that black people everywhere felt.

How did the media handle the disorders? Stories in just two newspapers analyzed—the *Buffalo News* of April 9, 1968 (the day of Dr. King's funeral), and the *Trenton Times-Advertiser* one day later—are fairly typical. No attempt is made to place the violence in a social context. The reference to the assassination of Dr. King is perfunctory, with only a passing mention of his funeral and a few shouts about his death. Value-laden words receive unusual emphasis. The participants are "marauders," not men; they "rove" instead of run; they move in "gangs," not groups; they engage in "vandalism," not simply violence.

We have all grown so used to viewing blacks as stereotyped criminals that it is difficult to picture them in any other role; hence such frequent press concoctions as "roving gangs," "roving vandals," "roving gangs of rampaging teenagers," or, for variety, "a window-smashing rampage of roving gangs of Negro youths." The *New York Times* assertion last July 1 that "roving bands of ruffians" were involved in a disturbance in Middletown, Conn., seems somewhat feeble by comparison. The effect of such treatment by the media is to pander to the public's prejudice, reinforcing stereotypes, myths, and other outmoded beliefs. The media not only frighten the public but confuse it as well.

And let us not forget the effects on the news media. The proliferation of underground newspapers, radical publications, black journals, as well as underground radio stations on FM bands held by churches and universities, indicates that the media are failing to reach certain groups, and that they still lack sensitivity, sophistication, and skepticism commensurate with their important and strategic position.

EDWARD P. MORGAN

Who Forgot Radio?

I'm not very hopeful but I'd like to live to see the day when the public, its ears aching from the drumbeat of banality, would demand a marketable Dick Tracy two-way wrist radio in order to answer back at the awful stuff on the air waves. Maybe people don't care, but as far as I'm concerned, the broadcasting industry has littered my street of dreams with garbage. I am, I confess, something of a romantic about the medium of radio. Long before I ever worked in it, I was bewitched by its magic. Sometime in the middle twenties my father brought home one of the early DeForest sets, a big black box with a console as complicated as the instrument panel of a jetliner, a combination tube and crystal job with "cat's whisker" tuning and a revolving diamond-shaped aerial in whose wires I, figuratively, became hopelessly entangled. My night sounds had been the sharp, haunting bark of coyotes but now the boundaries of my world suddenly dilated far beyond the sagebrush hills of Idaho, and through the hissing swish of static, like a bell pealing in a snowstorm, came the sweet, wavering voices of KHJ, Los Angeles, KDKA, Pittsburgh, and, one enchanted evening, Havana, Cuba.

Radio has not lost but technically refined its magic. . . . Today, you can take the pulse and temperature of Boston or Bangkok through an instrument no bigger than a diamond brooch, a tiny collection of transistors lost in the palm of your hand.

But turn it on and what do you really get? A medicine man's pitch to

---

Edward P. Morgan is a well-known Washington broadcasting commentator. "Who Forgot Radio?" is part of a speech delivered in the lecture series "The Press in Washington" at the American University in Washington, D.C., on March 30, 1965. The essay also appears as part of a collection in the book *The Press in Washington,* published by American University. It is reprinted by permission of the author and the Washington Journalism Center, who hold copyright, 1965.

swallow a pill that will end backache by producing a mild diarrhetic action through the kidneys; a promise that some sugar-coated physic will regularize junior's bowels; a doom-cracking bulletin on the latest East-West crisis calculated to paralyze any adult intestinal tract; a report on the flow of traffic in the approaches to Main Street (it too is paralyzed), and then the loud rolling whang of the latest assault on folk music, to be followed in machine gun tempo by more commercials. . . . Now and then, as if he were extracting a pebble from the profitable shoe of commercialism, the announcer will toss out a public service message urging blood donations to the Red Cross, cash contributions to the Community Chest, and reverent attendance at the church of your choice.

Through the nineteen-twenties, the thirties, and most of the forties, radio reigned supreme as a medium of communications—though by no means supremely undeserving of criticism. There was Graham McNamee and the Rose Bowl games; FDR and his fireside chats; Bill Shirer reporting from Berlin the rise of the Third Reich and the beginning of Hitler's war; Ed Murrow from London bringing home to us nightly the agony and the heroism of the blitz; Elmer Davis twanging out his clean, cool five minutes of wisdom each evening from New York; Howard K. Smith with his incredibly sharp and informative Sunday half-hours from Europe; Eric Sevareid and his penetrating analyses from Washington and elsewhere. There was good drama along with the soap operas; *Information Please* along with the amateur hours; the *Town Hall of the Air* as well as dull harangues; not only vapid foolishness but dimensional documentaries and such wonderful recaptures of history as *You Can Hear It Now*. Fifteen-minute newscasts, if you can believe it, were not the exception but the rule, and Father Coughlin was not the only controversial commentator on the air.

Then the networks, national advertisers and, presumably, the public eloped with a brazen but seductive hussy called television and radio suddenly became an abandoned orphan. Like many a neglected juvenile it developed alarming symptoms of delinquency. It is against this tawdry background that the operation of radio coverage of the news from Washington must be examined.

In a puzzling but provocative recent book entitled *Understanding Media*, the director of the Centre for Culture and Technology at the University of Toronto, Professor Marshall McLuhan, writes "one of the many effects of television on radio has been to shift radio from an entertainment medium into a kind of nervous information system. News bulletins, time signals, traffic data, and, above all, weather reports now serve to enhance the native power of radio to involve people in one another." The frustrated broadcast journalist in Washington would like to involve people more perceptively with the news, to make radio, for example, an information nervous system rather than a nervous information system. Instead, with exceptions that only tend to prove the rule, he is forced to squeeze his report on the national scene into a breathless two-minute package that often is shrunk to the ridiculous capsule of thirty seconds.

In just fifteen years the membership of the House and Senate Radio and TV galleries has more than doubled. In 1950 the total was 218 active and associate accreditations. (Associate members are based out of town, have gallery privileges when they come to Washington.) In 1964 the total was 491 accredited broadcast correspondents. Both the House and Senate galleries, ably presided over by Robert Menaugh and Robert Hough respectively, are proverbial beehives of activity. According to the most recent available count, they registered, for an eleven-month period 1225 radio interviews; 188 radio panel shows; 1175 news "spots" from the Capitol, broadcast live, on tape, or by telephone "beeper." There were 877 TV interviews during the same interval. Members of Congress, both Senators and Representatives, have come increasingly to use the broadcast facilities provided for them in the bowels of the Capitol building. Some 335 Representatives, for example, regularly utilize the radio or TV studios (most of them use both) for weekly or bi-weekly recording and films cut for five or fifteen-minute progamming on the stations in their constituencies. Congressmen frequently participate in special shows on such issues as poverty, medicare, immigration, et cetera. These specials average two a day.

Quantity-wise this all sounds very impressive. Quality-wise it is too often lacking in informative wisdom though there have been some excellent reporting and excellent programs emanating from Capitol Hill. CBS correspondent Roger Mudd's marathon daily progress report on the 1964 Civil Rights Bill was a unique if sometimes repetitive experiment. When he was New York's junior senator, Kenneth Keating's weekly interview and comment stint was a frequent must as a source of news, and colleagues—Republican and Democrats—considered their guest appearances with him almost as important (and often more comfortable) than the standard Sunday panel shows of the networks.

By and large, I suggest, radio reporting from Washington—and from almost everywhere else, for that matter—suffers most from what might be called instant spasms. Pour hot water over a dehydrated concentrate and you get instant coffee. Bring a processed cereal to a boil and you have instant oatmeal. Grind a news story down to a palmful of facts, pour on the audio for forty seconds, and serve. The quality of this journalistic spasm does not compare with instant food and is likely to cause mental indigestion. I am not arguing that you cannot impart a lot of information in intervals of a minute or less. Sentences such as "I love you" or "drop dead" can transmit a world of meaning in less than two seconds. I am arguing that the frenetic framework into which most broadcast news is now compressed produces a dangerously superficial picture.

There are at least a couple of other abominations. One comes under the heading of "actualities." The other could be labeled the compulsive monster of microphone-itis. Radio is sound but to justify itself in a broadcast, sound must have meaning. That includes the sound of voices. A tape recorder is a marvelous electronic butterfly net in which to capture the noises of the news but too often the process is carried to lengths that are utterly absurd. A stunned victim's halting phrases may give an on-the-scene sense to the report of an accident. There may be a legitimate measure of disaster in the noise of a hurricane, a mark of authority to the warden's description of a prison break in his own words and accent. But too often these actualities, while audible, are unintelligible. I would rather get my facts on a story from a trained newsman than have the information impeded by the mumbling voice of a so-called eye-witness butchering the English language. . . .

I'm not talking about documentaries or interviews in which there is time to turn around with questions and answers, but about these quick and interruptive splices of strange voices to establish the mobility of datelines: Radio has a portability that TV may never be able to match. I have had the good fortune to cover Richard Nixon's vice-presidential trips to Africa and the Soviet Union, President Eisenhower's extraordinary journey to India, and President Kennedy's historic visit to Berlin. Thanks to patient engineers who applied their special talents to unusual circumstances and were able to put the right circuit jacks in the right holes on the right wavelengths I was able to maintain my nightly quarter-hour program with hardly a hitch. I was even able to get through from such unlikely places as Monrovia, Liberia; Tripoli, Libya; and Sverdlovsk in Siberia.

The so-called "actualities" could indeed embellish a newscast far more than they do if we Americans on the whole didn't have such abominable diction or enunciation and could speak a simple sentence. While we're on the subject, interviews and panel shows could be far more lively and "listenable" if the protagonists could articulate more lucidly their thoughts, if any. What is there about the American way of life, upbringing, and education that makes so many men speak in monotones and so many women squeak like shrill shrews? We could learn a thing or two from our British cousins in the art of speech and expression and I'm neither demanding nor expecting a nation of Winston Churchills or Laurence Oliviers when I say this. . . .

This brings us to, in some respects, the more urgent matter of compulsivitis of the microphone. On stepping down from his lofty role as Secretary of State, Dean Acheson once told James Reston of the *New York*

Times, in effect, that there was a basic incompatibility between the press and the government, that reporters were constantly trying to find out what officials were trying to conceal, with the implication being that the higher the involvement of the story at hand with national security, the more intense the incompatibility. There is a basic truth here but in an open society like ours there are two honest interpretations of it, one by a responsible press and one by responsible officials and out of the tension between them flows, erratically sometimes, a current of information vital to an informed public opinion. That is the theory at least. Sometimes it does not work. Paradoxically the addition of radio and television to the media of communications has often made it harder rather than easier to make this system work. The reason is the ubiquitous microphone and its companion tool the TV camera.

An important caucus breaks up at a political convention and some hapless official is waylaid in the corridor to say something, at gunpoint, in a manner of speaking, with the heavy artillery of radio and television zeroed in on him. Out comes banality or evasion. What else is the victim likely to say under such circumstances? The Secretary of State flies off to a crucial conference. Before his plane leaves he has to run the bristling gamut of the thrusted microphones. He says he is confident that the conference will produce a useful exchange of views. After his plane lands he goes through the same ritual all over again. He has high hopes that the conference will produce a useful exchange of views. After the conference is over a communique is issued and a spokesman assures the microphones that there *has* been a useful exchange of views.

This dubious travelogue is news? It is an exercise in the thinnest and most synthetic kind of journalism. The interviewee, a past master of the art of manipulation of the meaningless expression by now, has long since ceased to become the victim. The public is the dupe and broadcast journalism is an accessory before, during, and after the crime. When the tense three-hour confrontation between President Johnson and Alabama's Governor Wallace ended on that sunny but chilly Saturday afternoon of March 13th, the President guided the governor through a writhing waiting-room full of reportorial flesh to a cluster of microphones outside the executive west wing of the White House not for a news conference but for a statement for the electronic gear, deployed and waiting. They had an exchange of views, the governor said, not with notable agreement but the President, he added, behaved, as he always does, like a gentleman and the governor hoped that his deportment had been gentlemanly. . . .

Questions can be as ridiculous as answers—another liability of the actualities and ubiquitous microphone techniques. I caught one broadcast from Travis Air Force Base in California of interviews with some of the first service families to be evacuated from South Vietnam after President Johnson had expanded American counter-strikes against the Communists. Obviously desperate to get *something* on tape, one reporter asked a returning Army wife, "and do you feel your husband will be ok there, now that you've gone?" While we're attacking the clumsy query and the cliché I soberly suggest that we working broadcasters all sign a pledge of abstinence and never again ask a candidate's wife how it feels to have her husband nominated. I'd be willing to break the pledge, naturally, if there was reason to believe the lady would reply, "what a stupid question," or "this is the last straw. I've been trying to get Horace to quit politics for years. Now I'm leaving him."

These perhaps slightly ulcerated criticisms should not be taken as justifying the free and untrammeled transit of men and women who make the news to and from their appointments without any attempt by the press to find out the score but there is a distinction, or should be, between news and nonsense. The old-fashioned shoe-leather approach of the reporter patrolling his beat is still valid and for the most part is still the best way to dig out the facts. On the other hand, "live" coverage of certain events can be unbeatable, not just for immediacy but for dimension. If the principals and broadcasters can train themselves—restrain themselves, it might be better said—to concentrate on substance, not just the sensational, then Congressional committee hearings will be even more newsworthy and instructive to the public. It is possible that "live" coverage of the sessions of House and Senate themselves would be a benefit to the country and maybe even improve the quality of Congress, or at least its debate. Let us not go overboard with optimism on these prospects however, for if we are candid with ourselves, live radio and television coverage of national political conventions has not improved the function of those cumbersome events at all.

The thoughtful, conscientious broadcast reporter is probably the most frustrated member of the Washington press corps. He makes his rounds, as do his colleagues of the newspapers and magazines. He goes to hearings, background briefings, filibuster sieges, news conferences at the White House, the State Department, and the Pentagon. He goes endlessly to lunches and dinners with people in or behind the news. He seeks key officials out in their bureaucratic lairs for interviews. He reads mountains of material, from handouts to the *New York Times*. And when he has his story he has to squirt it through a tiny hole of time in a five-minute or a fifteen-minute news roundup on the air.

The *CBS World News Roundup*, at eight o'clock every morning on radio, used to be one of the most vital sources of intelligence in Washington. The government, especially the executive branch, listened for news that might beat—or set in clearer perspective—the diplomatic dispatches from our embassies abroad. It wasn't nationally sponsored however and the local ad spots sold by affiliates on a "co-op" basis were not profitable. So at one point, when I happened to be director of news for CBS, the network brass decided to take that fifteen-minute journalistic gem off the air. I sounded the alarm in Washington and thanks in large part to James Hagerty, then White House news secretary for President Eisenhower, we got some high-level testimonials, some of which were almost threatening in their emphasis on the program's value. It stayed (and that is the only accomplishment I can think of worth remembering in my brief tenure as a junior broadcasting executive). The *World News Roundup* continues and so do counterparts on ABC and NBC but they are all so loaded with disconcerting commercials now that it is hard to separate the news from plugs for liver pills, laxatives, [and] body deodorants. . . .

New York Herald Tribune columnist John Crosby once wrote that I had "one of the more enviable jobs around." He was talking about my five-nights-a-week assignment of fifteen minutes of news and comment, sponsored by ABC radio and the AFL-CIO. I am well into my eleventh year at that same job and as far as I am concerned, Crosby's words are truer than ever. I wish, in a way, that they weren't so. That is to say, I wish there were more competition. Not just in the fifteen-minute time segment. The eclipse of the quarter hour by these five-minute bursts that are called newscasts is bad enough. (They are nearer to three minutes when you subtract the commercial time.) But I am free to voice opinion and critical comment, even including criticism of broadcasting and organized labor. I wish that journalistic phenomenon were not so unique. If the trade union movement, with all its warts, dares encourage it, why can't General Motors, or the National Association of Manufacturers, or the American Medical Association, or the organized groups of the radical right sponsor broadcasts that report the news and in addition paint arrows of responsible criticism that point inward as well as outward? The sinews of our society would be stronger and Washington would be a livelier place for the electronic journalist to ply his trade, if they did.

Some people are shocked by the little-known fact that approximately seven identifiable right-wing extremist groups sponsor, by conservative estimate, some 7,000 radio and TV (mostly radio) broadcasts a week in 50 states. I am also shocked. But I am more shocked by the fact that so many broadcasting stations seem to welcome and encourage this sulphurous stuff, which might be called yellow journalism of the air (though I would not ban it if it does not violate the law), while at the same time powerful elements of the radio-TV industry and, it must be added, their advertisers, tremble with apoplectic opposition to the airing of progressive or moderately liberal points of view. These are condemned as "controversial."

I indicated earlier that everybody abandoned radio in the scramble to television. This is not quite true. There are almost as many radio sets in the country today as there are people and the number, like the population, is increasing. The Electronic Industries Association counted 179,476,000 radio sets in the United States at the end of 1964, including more than 51 million car radios. . . . Indeed radio broadcasting remains a richly prosperous industry especially on an individual station basis. (Networks perennially have a hard time in radio profit-wise.)

In an angry and valuable speech at an Ohio State University seminar in Columbus just four years ago, Morris S. Novik, a radio consultant who helped Fiorello LaGuardia open and run New York City's station WNYC, sharply condemned commercial radio for its irresponsibility. "Radio today," Novik said, "is making more money, and has more listeners and more commercials and it also has less public service programming, less community action programs—and less standing in the community." Novik also revealed the depressing fact that while a relatively small number of independent and network-affiliated TV stations did not carry the Kennedy-Nixon presidential campaign debates in 1960, as many as 300 affiliates and more than 2,400 nonaffiliated radio stations failed to broadcast this unprecedented series.

Timidly, tenuously, radio stations are moving a little farther into the field of journalistic crusade and editorial comment. At first they dared do little more than back the United Givers Fund and condemn the toll of traffic deaths. There are some 26 radio stations in operation in the Greater Washington area. Some of them have boldly committed themselves to valuable public service. Station WAVA in Arlington, Virginia, for example, backs up an editorial campaign against smoking by refusing to accept cigarette ads. The editorials of WWDC are broadcast personally by the owner of the station, Ben Strose. The 50,000-watt voice of WTOP engages itself responsibly with community problems and WMAL has carried on such a sharp campaign against child abuse that corrective legislation has been introduced in Congress. I don't know of any station, however, in the nation's capital or elsewhere (and I would be happy to stand corrected) that has come near to the courageous aggressiveness of owner R. Peter Straus over his station WMCA in New York City. The station has produced breathtakingly factual documentaries about the scandal of housing in such slums as Harlem, has relentlessly criticized politicians, and demanded political action. Careful to honor the FCC's equal-time proviso, the station takes sides in election campaigns. WMCA and Straus through the courts and on the air led the fight to demand redistricting of the New York State legislature. The Supreme Court's "one-man, one-vote" decision included specifically an opinion supporting the suit that Straus had initiated.

Bernie Harrison, the careful radio-TV critic of the *Washington Evening Star*, says radio in and around the national capital "isn't yet doing the job it should be doing." In news, whether local, national, or international, too many stations are "headline hunters" and concentrate on the "rip and read" technique—the news is ripped off the AP or UPI tickers and read, not by experienced journalists, but by announcers. Harrison sees too much quantity saturation—weather forecasts, the time of day, police helicopter traffic reports, and the like—and not enough quality selection. Let nobody be fooled (and who is really?), the techniques of echo chambers, bell ringing, Morse code-signaling, and machine-gun delivery are no substitute for news on a newscast. . . .

Who forgot radio and its tremendous potential to inform and promote understanding? All of us, I'm afraid, in varying degrees. We are faced, it appears, with a growing dilemma. Instant communication, more or less, to virtually all parts of the planet is confronting us with an increasing volume of datelines and data from strange places, but the bigger the stream of information about everything the less we seem to know about anything. Here the dilemma mockingly tosses us on its horns: for the more spare time our still rising standard of living gives us to pause and reflect thoughtfully about the world and our problems in it, the less inclined we seem to be to put this leisure to good use.

Indubitably, we minions of the mass media, and especially our masters, the station and network owners, must assume much of the responsibility for our predicament. We do not purvey information, we merchandise it—especially in broadcasting. We do not provoke intelligent controversy, an exercise so vital to the health of an open society; we mesmerize, we sensationalize, we scandalize, and we temporize. Given a cataclysm, we can rouse ourselves to serious dedication, as the broadcasting industry did on the nation's black weekend of November, 1963. But as the *New York Herald Tribune*'s television critic, John Horn, has so aptly pointed out, in order to rise to such heights in journalistic excellence and public responsibility, broadcasting had to reject almost completely its daily code of operational ethics with its endless commercials and idiotic entertainment—to which it cozily returned almost immediately after John F. Kennedy was buried.

As for the newspapers, it isn't as if they didn't carry more than a whisper of meaningful information, it's that what informative dispatches they do publish are so thoroughly buried under the groaning poundage of supermarket, real estate, and used car ads that the reader is virtually exhausted after turning the pages before he can find what he is looking for —if he is looking.

Which brings up the startling question—if you'll pardon a few final variations from my assigned theme—are newspapers already dead, information-wise, and don't know it? After I, among others, mourned the demise of the Western edition of the *New York Times* in January, 1964, I received a communication from a high school history teacher near Los Angeles who said that while he was sad to see the edition die, he had become indifferent to newspapers, dull and ponderous as they were. He relies for his "instant information" on radio and television, backs it up with weekly magazines and his own general knowledge.

Another listener, who happens to be a teacher too, a professor of English at Los Angeles State College, had, perhaps, a more penetrating reaction: that our basic fault lies in education. Our schools are failing to produce the kind of citizens who would demand and support superior newspapers—and presumably, superior radio and television news and public affairs programs. Author of a textbook himself, the professor said his editor had informed him that "there seems to be a growing disposition among the school officials who buy textbooks to lump together analysis of the mass media with those really extraneous items which crept into the English curriculum during the past two decades and to dismiss them all as 'frills.'" . . .

The most shattering observation of all on our intellectual grasp came from a long-time friend of mine from Pasadena, who also happens to be in the teaching profession. "The Greeks and Romans didn't make it with their civilizations," he said, "and after two thousand years I don't think we are any smarter than they were." More knowledgeable, yes, in science, in medicine, in some of the mysteries of the mind, but more intelligent and wise? No. And in this age of marvels in communication, have the forces of the information media—especially radio and television—done their best to change that negative to a positive? You, I hope, already know the answer. . . .

NOEL PERRIN

The Poll of 1774

An age that is prepared to make serious decisions on the basis that 71 percent of Americans in some survey would rather be dead than Red, or that
42 percent in some other distrust Mr. Kennedy, or that 14 percent think
Walt Disney should be President—such an age is bound to be interested
in the group thinking of its ancestors. In particular, it should be interested in a curious document that came to light last spring. A friend of
mine who works for the Census Bureau found it in an old brass-bound
chest. He was down in a storeroom helping to pack records for shipment
to an atomic shelter when he stumbled across this old chest in a back corner. Naturally he put his work down and opened it. Inside he found a
thick folder tied up with crumbling string. Across the front was a title
written in confident black script:

"A Trustie and Reliable Survey of Publick Response to the Proposed
War with England. Prepared by Ben Franklin Associates and the Adams
Polling Company, by Order of the First Continental Congress, 1774."

My friend is not a scholar, and I don't guarantee that what follows is
letter-perfect. But allowing for minor mistakes (and correcting *ye* to
the after the first phrase or two), this is how the report read:

. . .

On ye fifth of September, 1774, ye delegates to ye Continental Congress
commissioned a study of Publick Opinion in ye thirteen colonies, that
they might better know the will of the People. For no great Operation on
the Body Politick should be approved, unless first there be a taking of the
Pulse. To this end, forty able men were hired, each a trained questioner,

Noel Perrin teaches English at Dartmouth College. Copyright © 1961,
by Minneapolis Star and Tribune Co., Inc. "The Poll of 1774," originally
titled "You Tell Them, Pop—You've Got the Vox," is reprinted from the
December, 1961 issue of *Harper's Magazine* by permission of the author.

such as a Barber, Newspaperman, or Common Gossip. These forty did each interrogate one hundred others, the most of the Common Sort, but some also of the Gentry. To every man were put four questions. First, Are you content with the present System of Government, that we be ruled from London? Second, Do you resent having British Troops quartered in your Colony? Third, What other Grievances have you again England? Fourth, Suppose the Colonies should declare their Independence from the British Crown. Would you take arms to preserve that Independence?

The Survey hath been completed this sixteenth of October. Here followeth a Summation of the Findings, together with an Appendix composed of complete Tables of Statisticks for each Colony.

To the first question, 1,116 people did say they were satisfied with the present System, and that we should not change; 983 were not satisfied, and said we should; and 422 did ask, What System? (These last included many Frontiersmen.) One thousand, four hundred and seventy-nine did say they had not thought on the matter.

To the second question, concerning the Quartering Act, the response was in no wise expected. Thirty-one of thirty-two men questioned in Augusta, Georgia, did say they wished there were more British Troops among us. All of eight maid-servants in New-York City felt the same way. It was even so throughout the Colonies, save only among Nests of Eggheads in Boston, among Tutors in Colleges, and among those on whom the troops are actually Quartered. For example:

"Someone's got to fight those ding-blasted Indians," said a Connecticut Merchant.

"Best customers I've got," spake an Albany Tavern-keeper. "Let's not kick out the chaps now."

"Their officers make the only civil Escorts for Quadrilles," a Young Lady of Quality told our interrogator in Philadelphia, while her Hairdresser did giggle and add, "Nay, who can resist a Red Coat?"

In sum, it appeareth that only an Informed Minority have the least understanding of the Trouble (let alone the Expense) brought on us by the presence of this Tyrannizing Army.

Of smaller Grievances the interrogators found a many. Almost 1,700 of those questioned do much condemn the tax on Tea. Several leading Clergymen wished there might be a Bishop in America, to the end that we should be spared our degrading dependence on the Lord Bishop of London. Many in Towns complain fiercely of the Stamp Tax (though many more do not seem to understand what it is). One hundred and sixty-three persons objected in principle to Taxation without Representation. Most Merchants oppose the Restrictions on foreign trade and manufacture.

But it must be admitted that a majority do not hold even one Grievance strongly. And while hundreds were filled with Intelligent Anger, it was discouraging to find that those who gave Frippery Answers were numbered in the Thousands. A few examples will suffice. A New-York apprentice, questioned on Tea, said, "Beat it, Dad. I frequent the Coffee House." A New-Hampshire politician (much fuddled with rum, and speaking his Mind) extolled monarchy openly. "The British, God bless them, they're making baronets by the bushel. Look at Sir William Pepperell and Sir John Bernard in Massachusetts-Bay. There's Sir William Johnson in New-York, Sir Nathaniel Duckinfield in North-Carolina, Sir James Wright in Georgia. I aim to be Sir Silos myself. Begone with your damned treason." A Scottish blacksmith in Virginia said King George had an Honest Face, the which was enough for him. Seven brothers who own a rich farm in Pennsylvania admitted they had never even heard of the Stamp Tax, and when it was explained to them, they said they wouldn't care if it was doubled. "None of us reads, none of us stidies law, and none of us aims to do either," the eldest brother explained.

To our final question, "Would you take up arms for Independence?", the replies were equally discouraging. Nine hundred and sixty-two men either said flatly, Nay, or threatened to report our Interrogator to the Governor. Seven hundred and three, mostly in New-England, said flatly, Yea. Another 839 said they might, "be that I get riled up," or if the pay is to be good. Twelve hundred and thirty-seven would not say, and generally demanded to know who would look after their farms and keep off the Indians if they came East to fight. The remaining 259 were Females, and they were not asked the last question.

When the entire Survey is considered, the Interrogators are of the opinion that there doth not exist Publick Support for the proposed War. Our people are ill-informed, scantly concerned, and sadly Muddy in their Thinking. Opinion, what there be of it, lieth more against the War than for it. No cause can hope to succeed with so little Backing. We therefore recommend to the honourable Delegates that the Continental Congress be disbanded, and that plans for Independence be laid on the Shelf. If conditions warrant, another and larger Survey might perhaps be profitably made in ten years.

(signed) Ira Beadle
Director of the Survey
October 16, 1774

. . .

It was late afternoon when my friend finished deciphering all this. Despite the obviously epochal nature of his find, he decided to save the tables of statistics for the next day and get on home. Then, as he was closing the folder and preparing to put it back in the chest, he noticed something written under the title. Closer examination showed it to be a dozen lines of script, in a handwriting he swears he has seen before. It was a note running thus:

"Barber Beadle's report was read to the assembled Delegates this seventeenth day of October. When 'twas finished, a Poltroon among us rose. 'Gentlemen,' said he, 'four thousand Colonials can't be wrong. We had better give up all thought of Independence.' An hubbub followed.

"Then stood up one of our greatest men. 'No Statesman,' he began 'was ever moved by the Casual Opinions of a few thousand Idlers. What the People do is like to be sound, but their Chance Answers are so much Moonshine.

" 'Gentlemen, we know our cause is just. We know that Independence must come. The flow of History can be stopped neither by a lunatick King nor an ignorant Populace. Let us get on with plans for the war.'

"When the Cheering had died, 'twas Voted that the Survey be put aside. 'Twas further Voted that as it was the First of its kind, so let it be the last. God grant that in our future no just call to Arms shall be stilled —nor no foolish one made louder—through such Trumpery as this."

My friend has still not learned from his subconscious which of our founding fathers wrote that note. He refuses to give the original to me, or to anyone else. But he has made me a copy, and I have thought it well, without further delay, to submit it to a candid world.

HARRY S. ASHMORE

A Case for Professionalism

In this Age of Journalists, newsmen are assumed to exert profound influence on public affairs, and to have the power to confer or withhold celebrity or notoriety; thus they are courted, and condemned, as never before. . . .

Journalists have done well in material terms, too. Their compensation in money, prestige and expense-account emoluments now at least equals that of any other professional with whom they would willingly compare themselves. . . .

Yet it appears that there is as much discontent among journalists as there ever has been. I intend some respect for my old trade when I suggest that this may be because, professionally and personally, they are peculiarly vulnerable to the dislocations that have virtually destroyed domestic tranquillity in the United States. In the nature of their calling they are positioned somewhere near what John Chancellor calls "the extreme center," and in an increasingly polarized society this involves maximum exposure.

. . . The mass media everywhere are organs of The Establishment. In a Communist country it is their function to defend and propagate the official faith; in a capitalist society they enjoy guarantees against state control and are expected to perform a critical role, but their economic dependence upon the prevailing system fixes limits to the range of dissent. Journalists can be stringently reformist and, in my view, they must be if they and the society they serve are to survive, but they cannot be revolutionary. . . .

The press . . . is included in the radical indictment of all the major in-

Harry S. Ashmore, a Pulitzer Prize Winner and former editor of the *Arkansas Gazette*, is president of the Center for the Study of Democratic Institutions in Santa Barbara, California. "A Case for Professionalism" is reprinted from *The Bulletin* of the American Society of Newspaper Editors, November-December, 1970, with permission.

stitutions of American society—the executive and parliamentary agencies of government, the courts, the church, the university, the market system, the political parties, even the family. A generation has arisen which regards none of these as sacrosanct, or even worthy of respect. The media, by serving as the principal instrument for recording this phenomenon, may be largely responsible for it, but the proprietors and most of the practitioners are no less appalled by the result.

There is some truth in the contention that the press is bound to suffer unpopularity when it adequately performs its function; if the media mirror the horrors and depredations of contemporary society, they may be greeted with the combination of disbelief and wrath commonly accorded the bearer of bad tidings. But this, surely, is a minor aspect of the credibility gap that is now alleged to separate the media from the disaffected young, the racial minorities, virtually the whole of the intellectual community *and* President Nixon's silent majority.

The usual reaction to this painful fact of life in the communications industry is a sanctimonious resort to the First Amendment, as though the issue were still the protection of John Peter Zenger against the king's bailiffs. It is an act of heresy for anyone in the business to admit that public affairs journalism, which once dominated the mass media and justified their privileged constitutional status, now rides piggyback on a massive popular entertainment enterprise.

Under the circumstances it is not surprising that there is little public awareness that the size, the composition and the character of the institutions that embrace and sustain contemporary journalism have been so altered in the middle years of this century they clearly raise issues beyond the ken of the eighteen-century establishmentarians who drafted the Bill of Rights.

Years ago Walter Lippmann wrote that it is the function of journalism to present a picture of the world upon which men can act. That picture now reaches most of the people as part of a package of broadcast images designed primarily for the senses and only incidentally for the mind. The initial result of this radical departure in mass communication may be measured in the fact that many of the young no longer draw a clear line between reality and romantic fancy—or at least no longer locate it according to the norms of their elders.

The American society finds itself quite literally confronted by the first generation weaned on television—a body of restive young people subjected from earliest imprinting to a torrent of fantasy and violence in which dramatic conflict is neatly resolved by the good-and-evil simplicities of a medieval morality play. From their secondary position the print media now must shoulder the primary burden for providing an offsetting antidote of perspective. I cannot find much evidence that they are succeeding.

The poet, Karl Shapiro, warned in a recent issue of the *Library Journal:*

> . . . this generation cannot and does not read. I am speaking of university students in what are supposed to be our best universities. Their illiteracy is staggering.
>
> We are experiencing a literary breakdown which is unlike anything I know of in the history of letters. It is something new and something to be reckoned with. We have reached the level of mindlessness at which students and the literate public can no longer distinguish between poetry and gibberish.
>
> Arrogance and ignorance always go hand in hand and now we are having both shoved at us from all sides. The greed and cynicism of even the best publishers appalls me; the wild exploitation of primitivism by the media has rendered us insensible and made us a party to every disease of esthetic decadence which the lower reaches of the imagination can concoct.

This indictment rightly goes beyond the presumed deficiencies of journalism and deals with the total cultural impact of the media; if broadcasting is the principal villain in this regard, the print media are not absolved, nor should they be. Yet such self-criticism as the media indulge in rarely embraces an overview of the communications system, but usually lapses into a self-serving exchange of stones between the glass houses in which publishers and broadcasters count up their profits. In the face of a presumed threat to the common domain, the ranks close and the apologists run the First Amendment up the Madison Avenue flagpole on behalf of practices that range from irrelevant to scurrilous.

. . . Perhaps the most conspicuous aspect of the contemporary media is their massive redundancy. In print and on the air reporters and commentators march in lockstep to overblow each issue as it arises, and the stylistic demands of the new journalism require that they treat the most complex matters in terms of a personality cult.

Although they are more gentlemanly in their techniques than were the yellow journalists of old, editors and news directors still consider themselves bound to come up with new and arresting material if they are to hold the circulation or the ratings. This leaves them vulnerable to the increasing company of highly skilled public and private manipulators of the news who are ready and willing to supply the demand and, in the process, underwrite a substantial, if not a majority, proportion of the total newsgathering cost.

Ben Bagdikian, national affairs editor of *The Washington Post,* has described how this works out in practice:

> . . . there are two main entrances to the news. One is reserved for conventional established voices. The other is for melodrama. Groups denied access through the front door come in through the back door of spectacular physical acts. . . . It is not just the crazies and the radicals who

stage pseudo-events. Every press conference is a pseudo-event. We live in a system of great centralized networks of communication and not in primary communities where we talk face-to-face or depend on word-of-mouth. So what has come to be called a pseudo-event is, in fact, the usual way of entering the news net.

Mr. Bagdikian accepts the practice as a sort of self-balancing adversary proceeding and contends that it represents no particular peril so long as journalists are left free to deal with it according to their own standards of discrimination. But it seems to me this assumes not only an extraordinary capacity and integrity on the part of newsmen, but a freedom of action the communications system no longer affords—not primarily because of policy limitations but because of the very nature of the matter with which they must deal and the relative contraction of the physical and temporal resources at their disposal.

Mr. Bagdikian's observations are particularly pertinent, since he functions these days in close proximity to the premier entrance to the news reserved for The Establishment. Washington has always been an arena of contending political forces, but since the advent of television the contest is no longer merely reported, it is projected in living color. Anyone who has observed this process at first hand can hardly doubt that inherent advantage lies with the incumbent officeholder and becomes insuperable at the level of the White House.

Chairman J. William Fulbright of the Senate Foreign Relations Committee, the principal foreign policy adversary of both Lyndon Johnson and Richard Nixon, testifies to the unevenness of the contest. "Whenever he wishes, (the President) can command a national television audience to hear his views on controversial matters at prime time, on short notice, at whatever length he chooses and at no expense to the Federal Government or his party," Fulbright says. By contrast the usual opportunity for rebuttal is limited to the low-rated Sunday afternoon network interview programs. . . .

While there are some signs of awareness that these institutional changes in the communications system demand attention, there remains the virtually universal assumption among journalists that any change will have to come from the top down, consciously brought about by owners and managers who recognize the necessity of protecting their independence from governmental intervention by responding intelligently to serious public criticism of their manifest shortcomings.

Not much serious thought seems to be given to the individual obligations of journalists in the changing milieu in which they now must work. The rumblings of rebellion among younger staff members in a few newsrooms have been in the New Left style—not so much a protest against slanted news as an insistence that it be slanted to conform to their own prejudices. At *Newsweek* the demand of young staffers for a voice in policy included insistence that the magazine run an antiwar ad on behalf of the employes, engage a columnist with strong antiwar views, approve a one-day symbolic strike, and take a stronger editorial line against the war.

This kind of agitation runs counter to the truculent independence that characterizes journalistic tradition. Most older practitioners cling to an ideal of intellectual autonomy, and it is this, rather than response to a collective social ideal, that prompts them to resist copyreaders who challenge their facts and change their style, and fight with editors who impose limitations of policy. But in fact there simply is no possibility of attaining the modern equivalent of what Marse Henry Watterson of the *Louisville Courier-Journal* once defined as the minimum requirements of journalistic success: Great wisdom, great courage, great energy and 51 percent of the newspaper's stock.

For better or worse, group journalism is the order of the day. Only a small, and I suspect diminishing, proportion of news or commentary originates in one man's idea, executed by him alone, presented in his own words, in the context of his choosing. This is manifestly impossible in the case of TV, which now transmits an estimated 80 percent of the news received by the American public. An hour TV news show contains fewer words than a single newspaper page. The main impact is visual, and this is provided by cameramen, directors, and film editors who, of necessity, work outside the control of the man who wrote the script—who may, but probably will not, be the man who presents the words on the air.

Under these circumstances it is not surprising that not much is heard of the old debate as to whether journalism might be truly constituted as a profession. The self-employment that has made professional status possible for doctors, lawyers, architects, and some other specialists is clearly out of the question for the journalist. He has got to work for somebody in order to obtain access to the tools of his trade; information is not news until it is printed or broadcast, and no one effectively manages that alone.

Yet I find myself wondering if the amorphous quality of the new corporate management of communication should not prompt re-examination of the possibility of professionalization at the working level. The old-time, highly individual proprietors rejected the notion on the ground that responsibility for the editorial product was indivisible and must rest ultimately with ownership.

But there is no longer much connection between ownership and management in communications, and the diffusion of responsibility is a leading characteristic of bureaucracy everywhere. I often amuse myself by visualizing an outraged citizen arriving with a horsewhip to seek satisfaction for a public insult perpetrated by NBC. I see him as a kind of Flying Dutchman of the RCA Building, passing in perpetuity from vice president to vice president. . . .

To even consider the possibilities of professionalization (or some equivalent protection for both practitioner and public) it is necessary to begin with a more satisfactory and comprehensive definition of journalism than any in common usage. Webster tells us a journalist is "a writer who aims or is felt to aim chiefly at a mass audience or strives for immediate popular appeal in his writings." There is, I would contend, a good deal more to it than that. It has been my observation that the public tends to expect too much from the media and, in frustration, to settle for too little. It might be useful, then, at least to establish what the journalist is not.

He is not a scientist, social or otherwise. The pressures of time and space rarely permit him to begin his examination of phenomena with a hypothesis; the data he collects are transient and fragmentary; the conclusions with which he ends his endeavor are tentative. His mission is to present the facts as they are available, but he rarely has reason to confuse their sum with the truth.

He is not an artist. He has no claim to poetic license, and it is fatal to his enterprise if he attempts to employ his imagination to construct a larger view than the facts at hand will support.

He is not a polemicist. The limit of argumentation for the journalist is advocacy, and this he must undertake with a decent respect for the opinions of mankind. He has to assume that his adversary has a right to challenge his view and that he has an obligation to treat the challenge seriously. His most resounding pronouncement must be studded with qualifiers, for it is a requirement of his calling that he put his opinion on record before all the returns are in—often before he has himself had the advantage of detached reflection upon what he has seen and heard and thinks he knows. Elemental honesty requires that he be long on tolerance and short on moral certitude.

Some of the most severe of these limitations result simply from the pressure of time. . . . The journalist has no control over the matters that occupy him, and he lives by deadlines as arbitrary as the clock on the wall.

There are also limitations of temperament. . . . And, I would add, it takes a special kind of integrity to hold to standards of honesty and fairness when pressures are so great, time is so short, and so many shortcuts and unassailable alibis are available to those who want to shade the news to promote a personal advantage or nurture a prejudice.

At the level of analytic reporting, the journalist must function in the manner described by John Fischer as that adopted by the occupants of Harper's "Easy Chair":

No sensible reader, it seems to me, will be interested in a writer's opinions on any subject unless he knows the facts on which it is based and the line of reasoning by which the judgment is reached. . . . (This) calls for something more than responsible reporting. It requires taking a position. It is not enough for a writer to say "There is a bunch of facts. Make what you can out of them." He is obligated to go a step further and say, "I have examined these facts as best I can, discussed them with other knowledgeable people and arranged them in some kind of order. Here, then, is a conclusion which commonsense might draw from them, and a course of action which a reasonable man might follow."

I would say that this is a fair definition of journalism. It extends into advocacy, but it stops short of a commitment to action. As Fischer says, . . . "The real function of such analytic reporting is to help readers arrive at conclusions of their own."

. . . What we now know about the impact of television news—and we don't know nearly enough—indicates that it has an intensely personal quality unlike anything journalists have encountered before.

This condition must be seen as posing grave new problems for those concerned with the ethics of journalism. But if it can be said to make the concept of professional responsibility more difficult to apply, it also makes it more urgent. While the complex supporting organization required to put the TV journalist in touch with his audience is beyond his own control, he is himself functioning at a point beyond the reach of the backstage executives who theoretically are responsible for the end product of all this effort. This leaves the typical recipient of the typical newscast—and his name has been certified by Nielson to be legion—dependent for his view of the great world upon a commentator who enters his living room with the manner of a confidant. As the Murrows and Sevareids and Huntleys who crossed the Great Divide from Gutenberg to Sarnoff pass on to their assorted rewards, this is almost certain to be a man chosen for charm rather than perspicacity.

While the special sensory quality of television may limit the kind of information that can be transmitted, it is possible that the new media hold vast potentials that have not yet been tested because we have locked them almost exclusively into the marketplace. One result is that in politics television has turned out to provide a new source of wholesale corruption, adding greatly to the influence of money in election campaigns and providing candidates a means of bypassing independent journalists with the direct merchandising appeal of paid advertising. Yet I can see how, for example, television holds the promise of opening up the political campaign process to illuminate political issues, provide for real dialogue rather than contrived confrontation and thereby restore the lost sense of citizen participation in their governance.

The question may be whether the rising generation will have the will and the patience to test and develop these possibilities. I have spent some time lately with student journalists, and they seem no more adept than their elders in coming to terms with the life-style of their contemporaries. It is not easy under any circumstances to take a detached view of rebellion, the casting out of old values, the breaking of icons. On the campuses, where the generational style is set, the revolt is characterized by the cult of the sensory, pushed to the extreme of denouncing the rational as irrelevant. The young journalists must deal with this exaltation of the emotional by contemporaries who make up the most conformist generation we have yet seen—one that declares the wisdom and morality of the elders open to challenge, but applies no similar test to its own leadership. So long as the vibes are good, a substantial number of students appear willing to follow the most extreme among them down the dead-end paths of violence, while the rest stand intimidated and silent.

If journalism is to survive—and I cannot imagine that a civilized community can exist without the near-focus perspective it alone provides—dealing with this phenomenon is going to require practitioners with 360-degree skepticism. They will find it necessary to challenge their own peers, question any proposition offered on faith and endure the peculiar loneliness that comes of marching alongside a movement and not being of it. Such are not in long supply on either side of the generation gap.

As I read the signs and portents, we are well past the time when practicing newsmen can afford to dismiss professionalism as a lofty but unattainable ideal. In the stormy times ahead some such concept may well prove essential as a standard to which the journalist can repair.

DISCUSSION AND ESSAY QUESTIONS

1. Author Max Ways deplores the "scoop . . . the gee-whiz" syndrome afflicting most American newspapers. Do you think newspapers would lose many readers if they devoted much more space to in-depth, interpretative stories and less to sensational reports?

2. Suggest two or three major trends in our society that you do not believe are being covered adequately by the news media. What do you suggest, specifically, that they do to improve their coverage? Is it likely that the newspaper, the magazine, and television could each make a special contribution to better understanding of these trends?

3. If you believed that a *local* press council was needed in your community, what steps would you take to try to start one?

4. Some publishers are accused of opposing press councils because they fear public scrutiny of their newspapers. Discuss this argument and its implications as far as publishers' motives and goals are concerned.

5. What would you suggest that daily newspapers do to improve their credibility, which is lagging behind that of TV and radio, according to several surveys?

6. Writer John Tebbel contends that the newspaper is "keeper of society's values." Do you think the newspaper is that important? In what ways does it keep—or fail to keep—society's values?

7. What rules do you think news media, including newspapers and television, should adopt in order to make sure that the presence of reporters, photographers, and cameramen does not influence the event being covered?

8. If you were a reporter covering a local murder case, what kinds of information, if any, might you try to withhold from publication?

9. Can you think of two or three kinds of situations in which a reporter and his editor should deliberately withhold a story about an important new development in government? If so, should the story be withheld for a short time, or indefinitely?

10. Vice President Agnew insists that he is not attacking the free enterprise broadcast system or the right to dissent. Discuss your reaction to his assertion. Is a threat to free press implied by his attack, as some critics have said?

11. Do you think networks should discontinue the practice of presenting comment and analysis immediately after Presidential television speeches? How do you react to the charge that network commentators have engaged in "instant analysis"?

12. Do you think the individual reporter should be given more oppor-

tunity to seek out his own assignments? If so, should any criteria of newsworthiness be established for him?

13. In what ways do you think a reporter's *participation* in a protest demonstration would make it possible for him to write a better report than he would if he had simply been an observer? In what ways would his participation reduce the credibility of his story?

14. Can you suggest reasons why some young people today find newspapers irrelevant, bland, cowardly, resistant to change, and superficial? Do you think these criticisms are valid? What should be done about the fact that so many youths are hostile to the daily press?

15. What do you think are the most important criteria for a good newspaper?

16. Do you think the aboveground press should do anything to respond to the need apparently being filled by underground papers? Has the underground press had any influence on the aboveground press, to your knowledge? If so, what examples of influence can you mention?

17. Make a list of four or five kinds of news stories that have been reported in the underground press but not in the aboveground press. Make another list of stories that were reported by both underground and aboveground papers, but in different ways, and discuss the differences.

18. Suggest four or five stereotypes often used by newspapers as a result of the habit of oversimplification. Are there any methods by which the reporter can steer around stereotypes?

19. Author Philip Meyer uses attitude surveys to illustrate his argument that more fact-finding is needed in order to strengthen interpretative reporting. Can you suggest any other kinds of tools from the kit of the political scientist or sociologist that might be used by the interpretative reporter?

20. Newsmagazines are less than 50 years old, while newspapers have been around more than 350 years. Does the success of the newsmagazines reflect on the job being done by newspapers? If so, how? Is there anything done by newsmagazines that newspapers ought to do?

21. The English public favors the personally flavored reporting of their journalists, a style that is comparable to that of American newsmagazines. Do you think U.S. newspapers would be more readable if they were written in such personal, dramatic styles?

22. Commissioner Nicholas Johnson of the Federal Communications Commission charges that a number of important stories were underplayed or ignored by TV, including truth in packaging, cyclamate

danger, black lung disease among coal miners, X-ray hazard in TV sets, and white-collar crime. Can you add to the list? Do you think Johnson is accurate? Or do you agree with Richard Salant of CBS News that he is not?

23. Assume that you are a TV news reporter. An advertiser comes up to you at a party and suggests that you withhold a forthcoming story that is expected to be unfavorable to his company. How would you respond? If you rejected the suggestion, how would you explain your reasons?

24. If you were making up a list of rules for all news media on coverage of news about violence, what would you include?

25. What arguments would you use to convince a big company that it should sponsor a regular program by a low-key, high quality news analyst on one of the radio networks?

26. Do you think politicians and government officials should base their decisions entirely on the results of public opinion polls? If so, would voters be less likely to elect candidates with strong convictions?

27. What are the hazards of team or "group" journalism, especially on television? Can you see any advantages?

28. Many news editors contend, "We don't make the news; we just report it." Do the news media, by their choices of news items and methods of reporting, act as a mirror of events, or do they—deliberately or unconsciously—influence the ways in which their audiences react to those events? Whatever your answer, give examples.

The
Entertainment
Media

PART ONE

Popular Art
As Entertainer for Millions

Introduction

All six of the major media—newspapers, magazines, books, television, radio, and movies—provide *both* information and entertainment. But we usually think of the print media as sources of information, while the "fun" media—radio, television, and film—are regarded as providers of entertainment.

When we discuss the entertainment side of the media—even print—we move quickly into the arena variously called popular or public art or mass culture. When the words "popular," "mass," or "public" are attached to "art" or "culture," a distinction is made between entertainment designed for a large, general group of people and that geared toward a specific audience. The term "specialized" is used by critics of mass culture to mean well-educated, sophisticated, sensitive, and critical. This select group enjoys a "high" culture of enduring value, as opposed to "middle" or "low" culture, which can be appreciated by anyone and is likely to last no longer than a single evening's entertainment.

Perhaps the most important single fact about the entertainment media —especially movies and television—is their commercial character. No matter how many other lofty aims he may have, the movie director or TV producer knows that his product must attract an audience of millions.

This fact leads to endless, and in some ways circular, arguments about whether any movie or any television program that appeals to a mass audience can possibly have artistic value. "Impossible!" shout most culture critics. Yet we know it is often possible for movies, television programs, books, and radio programs to achieve, by design or accident, both artistic and financial success.

There is no simple explanation for this anomaly. Most generalizations about popular art point to the conclusion that it all has to be "kitsch"— low culture. One generalization is that it is produced by teams, rather than by individuals, and that each team member is a highly skilled spe-

241

cialist. Another is that popular culture products are ephemeral by intention, created solely for an evening's fun.

A third generalization is that backers of mass culture exert pressure on team members to assure that the contents please as many as possible and anger no one. If the ingredients have the proper mix, they will titillate the Southerner, New Englander, and Westerner equally well. They will please audiences in cities and on farms; the wealthy and the white- or blue-collar workers; whites, blacks, and chicanos; college graduates and high school dropouts.

Popular art is also manufactured by an anonymous producer, not created by a recognized individual. The audience members are also anonymous, so far as the media producers are concerned; they register likes and dislikes largely through rating scores or box office figures.

Still, it is just as difficult to be rigid and final about these generalizations as it is to produce an unassailable definition of literature. Occasionally a mass medium offers a program of classical art, such as the TV network production of *Hamlet* several years ago, which reached more millions in a single performance than had been reached in all the thousands of performances since Shakespeare wrote the play in 1602. There have been countless instances of movies produced for the largest possible box office which turned out also to be artistically fine.

While we emphasize the commercial character of mass culture, we must also bear in mind that entertainment is its primary purpose. And each of us is entertained in many ways. The best educated man may enjoy the same movies or TV plays as the most illiterate.

Entertainment has many forms. Some find escape into fantasy a kind of entertainment. Others can relax and enjoy a probing exploration into human relationships or societal problems. There's a huge new audience for science fiction films that use fantasy to throw light on serious contemporary questions.

Many moviegoers who enjoy high art films also find occasional diversion in kitsch features. No one would claim that a filmgoer's moral or intellectual worth is either measured or determined by the type of film he chooses to see.

In the end, each of us defines entertainment in his own way, depending on a variety of shifting factors. Whatever standards of taste we have set for ourselves may be tempered by the need or mood of the moment, by the degree of physical fatigue or emotional lethargy, by the kind of activity or work we have just finished, or simply by the recommendation of a friend or neighbor.

Mrs. Homer Moore
to TV Guide

Dear Sirs:

I am a Midwestern farm wife, middle-aged and not well educated. I try to get to bed by 10:30 because we are usually up by 6, or earlier. I *love* television and, although I do have strong preferences, I can be tolerant about most of the shows and actors.

All of this makes me a perfect example of the favorite target of all TV critics' scorn: a square, a citizen of the Corn Belt, a part of the moronic masses! If I have a saving grace it's that I have a voracious appetite for printed words and, therefore, read many of the things TV critics have to say. I think I understand what they write, but if they are really saying what they believe, I don't understand why they believe as they do. I am not at all qualified to argue with any of them and I'm not just trying to be cute. I would like to have these questions answered by a TV critic:

What makes fantasy?

Critics scorn the idea used in *My Mother, the Car* as ridiculous, yet in "Peter Pan" we have the idea that people can fly without wings and refuse to grow up, and, what's more, we must see this young boy played by a middle-aged woman with a voice to match. At least *My Mother, the Car* is better cast. But it is called silly and "Peter Pan" is praised as a classic of fantasy. Why?

What is escapism?

I know what the word means, but why is it used so often for TV entertainment and not for, say, Shakespearean plays? Didn't the critics of his day think his plays were for the ignorant masses?

Reprinted with permission from *TV Guide* ® Magazine. Copyright © 1966 by Triangle Publications, Inc. Radnor, Pennsylvania.

Why not escapism?

I have supposed a little escapism helps keep me mentally stable and is a cheerful aid to my family. If I'm wrong, why?

What makes a soap opera?

I rarely have time to watch the daytime serials but surely they are as true to life as Shakespeare's Portia passing as a man and, without training, winning a law case. Yet one is considered moladramatic trash, and the other culture. Why?

What is good music?

Surely even critics agree that music is only for enjoyment, entertainment, or inspiration. Why, then, isn't it good or bad according to how it affects the listener? If I, an uneducated person, get deep pleasure from listening to Jimmy Dean and his Chuck Cassey singers, does that make their talent less worthy? It seems music is often rated lower if it *can* be appreciated by the masses. Why?

What is artistic freedom?

I often read that writers think they are hampered by the narrow-mindedness of the Corn Belt. Yet most of us accept *Peyton Place* as showing things that really do happen, over and over, in any size city or town, while the critics cry "smut." Why?

What is realism?

Writers or producers seem to think realism can only be tragic or brutal, and concern only the dark, seamy side of life. Doesn't it take even more talent to include the light, happy things of life in good drama?

These are some of the whys I wonder about, and if they are reasonably answered, I'll bet I won't be the only interested reader.

Sincerely,

Iveta Moore
Piedmont, Kansas

Marya Mannes' Reply
for TV Guide

Dear Mrs. Moore:

You deserve to be answered, not only because your questions go to the heart of television's functions but because you belong to the great majority of viewers who, by turning on their sets for hours each day, have far more power over the nature of TV than we—the tiny minority of TV critics—have ever had. Most viewers, in fact, don't even read us: They don't share your "voracious appetite" for print which has led you to question our values as we have questioned yours.

So here goes, one by one, for better or worse:

What makes fantasy? Fantasy is made by imagination: we imagine things we know are not real, but which we would like to believe. And the test of successful fantasy is whether for even fleeting moments we do believe it.

Now the reason "Peter Pan" has captured the imagination of four generations of children (and grownups) is because the play embodies two great human yearnings: to fly (all by oneself), and never to grow old. And whether Peter Pan was played by not-so-young women or by boys, most people chose to believe in him. It was due to the talents of Sir James M. Barrie that they could. (I was one of thousands of children who fell off the end of my bed trying to take wing.)

Now, I doubt that *My Mother, the Car*, will last beyond the end of one season. The idea behind it is not so much fantasy as a gag, or gimmick— good for some laughs, maybe, but hardly likely to stir the imagination. After you've said to yourself, "That's a funny idea, his mother being

---

Marya Mannes is an author and critic. Miss Mannes' reply to Mrs. Moore's letter is reprinted with permission from *TV Guide* ® Magazine. Copyright © 1966 by Triangle Publications, Inc. Radnor, Pennsylvania.

turned into an old car," what have you got? Another formula comedy to pass the time. But—fantasy?

What is escapism? Just that. To escape. To get away from the real world of worries, of tensions or problems, of daily boredom, of suffering, Some escape through drink or gambling or pills, some look at television entertainment. Everybody needs a break from reality once in a while. But is there any reason why this break has to be silly or cheap or poorly written stuff, with a phony laugh track tacked on? Danny Kaye's program, for instance, is a form of escape—but it has taste and wit and charm along with the fun.

As for Shakespeare, he managed to combine the most beautiful language in all literature with blood-and-thunder plots that have kept people enthralled for centuries. In other words, he gave both the mass and the minority what they looked for, and if his plays are not called "escapist" it's because they are so much more than that: They are mirrors of enduring human passions.

What makes a soap opera? Well, I have seen quite a lot of them, because I admire the acting and find them truly "escapist." Some of them seem true to a certain type of life, give or take extra murders and crises. That is, they're true to stereotypes of American middle-class suburbia and therefore not true of the millions of Americans who are neither middle-class nor white, nor of the many American wives who are too busy working to worry about all the things soap-opera housewives moan about.

As for Portia being "culture" and soap opera being "trash," here we are again at the difference between the imagination of a great writer and the slick formulas of Hollywood writing teams. If a woman in a Soap ever said the kind of things Portia does, I'd spend my day at the set.

What is good music? Music can be good or bad whether it is classical or popular, for the few or for the many. There is a great difference, for instance, between the Beatles, who do what they do extremely well, and the Animals, who are sick exhibitionists. There are superb folksingers and very bad ones. The difference depends on a lot of things, from the quality and range of their voices to the songs they use or the orchestrations they arrange.

In any case, it's no more true that something is good because it's popular than that something is *un*popular because it's *no* good. A lot of teenagers go squealing-crazy about some pop-singer who is all wail and no talent. A lot of adults are bored by Bach because they haven't got the faintest idea of what music is about. Nobody is going to stop you from enjoying any singer you like: It's your privilege. The only point here is that your enjoyment doesn't necessarily mean that he's good.

What is artistic freedom? Simply, the freedom of the artist (in the case of TV, the writer) to determine without interference what he writes about and how he writes it. It isn't only "Bible Belt" mentality or the hypocrisy of our middle-class "morality" that stops him from doing so. It's a television system that depends on getting the greatest possible audience to buy the products advertised. Since the sponsors can't risk offending certain groups of viewers, the writer can't really deal with anything controversial or unpopular, and many of the most important human problems are both. *Peyton Place*, on the other hand, has no point of view: It's merely a nighttime soap opera full of people in trouble.

What is realism? Realism isn't just seeing that the characters of a drama are dressed correctly in period, although that is desirable. Realism is the reflection of life as it is lived—really lived. This can be tragic or brutal, tender or violent, comic or corrupt. A light comedy is just as valuable as a dark tragedy, provided it is the product of talent and keen observation. If the "seamy side" of life seems to attract more writers than the "happy things," it's because we live in an age of change and violence which no artist can ignore, but which, unfortunately, too many mediocre writers use to exploit the public appetite for shock and sensationalism, particularly in the areas of crime and sex.

Taken as a whole, your questions really boil down to the one crucial question: "What is Good—or Bad? And who are you, the critics, to tell us which is which?"

Well, there is nothing harder to define than standards. Some standards are ageless, some are modified by time, all are subject to individual interpretation or prejudice. But I think it can be fairly said that a critic on a responsible newspaper or magazine has, in the pursuit of his profession, read more books, seen more plays, heard more music, looked at more art than the average television viewer. His judgment is based on years of experience and deliberation, from the vantage of which he expresses his opinion on the value—or worthlessness—of a given work in his field. He may not always be right, but he has earned his right to judge.

If he often seems unduly harsh on television fare, it is because he thinks the medium can do much better and the viewers deserve much better. We're all for entertainment—but why must it be silly and cheap? We're all for excitement—but why is a gun the only way to get it? We're all for popular music—but why must it all be for kids?

If you are happy with what you see on television, we can only envy you. If we, in turn, strike you as being too critical of the medium, you can ignore us. Yet it is a sign of your intelligence that you choose not to, and that you have asked questions which, although these answers may not satisfy you, need asking. Thank you, Mrs. Moore.

Marya Mannes

PART TWO

The Film
As High and Low Art

Introduction

The film is today enjoying a renaissance in America. Millions are discovering new insights and enjoying new experiences, even though the cost of moviegoing has far outstripped the inflation of most other living cost items. This is especially true for young people, but it is also true for those older persons, from thirty-five or forty on, who are able to pull themselves away from the "tube" long enough to visit their neighborhood movie house.

When television took over as "lowest common denominator culture" during the fifties, the movie was freed to seek new ways of finding audiences. Some now argue that film has become "high culture," yet nobody believes that *all* movies coming either from Hollywood or Europe are high culture. John Wayne and Clint Eastwood films chalk up huge box office figures regularly. Nor is there a sure relationship between the artistic value of a film and the fact that it was produced either on a shoestring or with a giant budget.

Since the producer's purpose is to make money, he—or the financial group behind him—will seek the widest possible audience. While all moviemakers today are aware that the majority of their audiences are youths under thirty-five, and while they seek to guarantee satisfaction to that age range, they are also eager to reach out for older persons.

Stanley Kauffmann points out that "only" fifty years passed between Edison's camera and *Citizen Kane*. But it's now more than thirty years since *Citizen Kane*, and more has happened to the film in the last 30 years than in its first fifty. Apart from enormous technical changes introduced in response to television competition, movies have matured in content. The new maturity goes beyond frankness about sex. It includes a willingness to explore far more honestly and freely the ambiguities and ironies of life than most movies did in the thirties and forties.

A flood of foreign films in the fifties and sixties influenced both moviegoers and movie-makers. At one time in the mid-sixties, more foreign-made films were showing in New York than American-made. Now the influence seems to go in both directions, with American directors, writers, and actors influencing foreign films at least as much as their directors, writers, and actors influenced ours a decade ago.

Because of the large amounts of money invested in every movie, those who work in films are under constant pressure to play it safe. Thus, a plot or theme that has been successful in the recent past is often used again and again in the hopes of producing another such success. This accounts for the tendency toward sameness which creative writers and producers fight constantly. An example was *The Sound of Music*, a big money-maker, which was followed by a series of sentimental costume musicals, all box office losers. Some movies based on great literary classics have been highly profitable; others, like *Anthony and Cleopatra*, have lost millions for their backers.

RICHARD SCHICKEL

The Movies
Are Now High Art

CULTURAL CLICHÉ: "Movies are the central art of our time." Or the most
relevant of the arts. Or the one that most efficiently reveals ourselves to
ourselves. Or, more simply, the one we like best.

All rise . . .

Be seated.

This Sunday's sermon attempts to analyze this particular tidbit of the
conventional wisdom, and it begins, as all good sermons should, with a
mea culpa. Like everyone who makes his living around movies, I have
indulged in this particular form of egocentricity; we all like to feel that
we're operating at the red-hot center of things. Indeed, together with the
New Leader's John Simon, I recently edited a little symposium in which
a dozen film critics addressed themselves to the question of film's centrality to modern experience and, not surprisingly, the majority of us more
or less unquestioningly agreed that film was The Thing. To be sure,
Newsweek's Joseph Morgenstern suggested that it would probably continue to take second place to "the mother art of weaponry." And the
redoubtable Andrew Sarris of *The Village Voice* raised some good ca-
veats, pointing out the pot scene was better reflected in pop music
than in pop movies, that a cinematic equivalent of "Pale Fire" is an im-
possibility, that TV has taken over many of the social functions the
movies used to perform. But most of us went along with the proposition,
and it is probably right that we did. It would be a poor lot of critics who
believed the art with which they perforce live is an insignificant or mean-

---

Richard Schickel is a New York critic of popular culture, especially
film. He is a film columnist for *Life* magazine. "The Movies Are Now
High Art" is reprinted from *The New Times Magazine,* January 5, 1969,
with permission. © 1969 by The New York Times Company.

ingless thing. Only the masochist—or a Dwight MacDonald—engages himself critically and regularly with an art for which he has no fundamental affection or at least respect.

Still, we are obviously prejudiced witnesses, and I am beginning to wonder if this prejudice—necessary to us if we are to maintain our sanity as we trudge from one screening room to another in midtown Manhattan —is necessary or sensible or desirable for the audience. I am beginning to think that the movies now bear a heavier weight of cultural ambition —and anxiety—than they were intended to bear. The very notion that they are as important to us as the centrality doctrine implies raises our expectations as we approach each film, to heights unprecedented even a decade ago, which means that the letdown, when the film fails to live up to those expectations—as inevitably most will—is all the greater.

Why, one wonders, have movies—humble, once-despised movies—become so important to us? The beginning of the answer lies, I think, in carefully defining that little word, "us." Who are we, those of us who care so much about the movies? Well, a recent survey taken at the behest of the Motion Picture Association of America discovered that some 50 percent of the movie audience is under twenty-four and that 75 percent of it is under forty. The moguls also discovered that the regulars, the people who go to the movies once a month or more, tend to be college students and college graduates. And it is reasonable to guess that, had they pressed their inquiry a little further, they would have found that among high school kids it is the ones who plan to go on to college who most regularly flick out.

Now, of course, from the vantage point of a writer for this magazine, or one of its readers, that means that everybody who is anybody is going to the movies—our friends, our co-workers, our kids. But really it only seems that way. The fact is that for the majority of Americans moviegoing is not even a peripheral, let alone a central, concern. Back before that great watershed date in our cultural history, 1948 (when television networking began), that was probably not the case. In that year some 3.4 billion admissions to the movies were sold. Since 1963 the number of tickets sold annually has stabilized around 1.1 billion—and this in a period of population growth. The industry's prosperity, thanks to increased ticket prices and the sale and production of films for TV, is now booming, but the fact is that it sells only 21 million tickets a week, meaning that all the movies on view in such a period attract an audience no greater than that of the weekly episode of a television show that is close to the peril point in the ratings.

So it turns out that Mr. Nixon's army of silent citizens—the factory worker and the farmer, the aged and the middle-aged, the people whose incomes range from poor to middle-middle class—besides grousing about taxes, worrying about law and order and flirting with the Wallace fantasy complete their misery by generally shunning such solace as the movies might provide them. Typically, however, John Q. Silent takes a dim view of what he hears is going on these days down at the old Bijou, which a few years ago was renamed The Art—about the time they ripped out the popcorn counter and replaced it with an espresso bar. Sex and Violence, sex and violence, that is what is going on down there. And they call it culture.

"The feature begins at 7:20 and the orgy scenes occur at 8:10, 8:47 and 9:05."
Drawing by Donald Reilly in *Look*, November 3, 1970. Reprinted with permission.

LOOK 11-3-70

O.K. Movies aren't movies any more. They are the playthings of The New Class, those who are custodians (or, perhaps, prisoners) of the technostructure. This is, I think, no small point, for it means there has been a fundamental reordering of film's place and function in our society. In the beginning, in the days of the nickelodeon, movies—because of their brevity, their cheapness and their silence—were truly an art of the masses and, as experience if not art, truly central to the lives of many people. They imposed no language barrier, no intellectual hurdles not easily surmountable by the illiterate (or the merely uncultivated), whether he was child, immigrant or rube. Even the addition of sound did not fundamentally change that basic relationship between film and audience.

As we have seen, it required television—free, damnably convenient, even less challenging than the typical pre-1948 film—to break up the longstanding love affair between the movie medium and its traditional audience. To put it simply, the new medium freed the older one from its thrall to the twelve- or thirteen-year-old mentality for which, in the past, the moguls cheerfully admitted they aimed. Though it seems, on the face of it, preposterous to regard any form of art or entertainment that attracts over a billion customers a year as anything less than a mass medium, that is precisely what movies have become: Something Less than a Mass Medium. Indeed, it seems to me that everything that is not television is, given that medium's potency, Something Less than a Mass Medium today.

What, then, are the movies? Is there some positive definition of them? I think they are best defined in terms of a process rather than in a single word or phrase. Film is a form that is now about halfway toward creating a conscious definition of itself as an art. It has yet to sever completely its ties to its folkish past. It has yet to fasten firmly to its future, which is, alas, as a high art, a thing to be savored more or less exclusively by what will pass as an élite—a new class—in the quite radically different society we are, willy-nilly and without malice aforethought, building in this country.

Now, two quick explanations must be appended to the foregoing. First, there is nothing unique about the development of movies in the direction I have outlined. All the arts—poetry, prose fiction, the graphic arts, music, the dance—had popular roots and developed, finally, into élite affairs over fairly long historical spans. The only difference between them and the movies is that the latter are an industrial art born in an age of rapidly accelerating industrial change, which means that they are going to complete this evolution much more quickly than the other arts did. It has taken them only a little more than a half-century to reach the mid-point in this development; it should take them no more than another twenty-five years to complete it.

Second, the élite to which films will soon be more or less exclusively directed will, obviously, be much larger, much less homogeneous, than any previous cultural élite the world has ever known. It will be an élite less sure of itself, less intensely educated, more panicky about its status than any we have ever known. But an élite it will be, for as journalist William A. McWhirter has put it, "The world is not so much divided between classes, races and religions as it is between those who know and those who don't; between Them and Us."

That little word again. For "us" the movies are, comparatively speaking, an easy art to appreciate. Even the very greatest films require only a couple of hours to consume, to get yourself in a position where you can claim to have "seen" them. The great novels, in contrast, demand far greater commitments of time in order merely to claim that one has "read" them. They also demand, as do the other traditional arts, a heavy investment in effortful study, not only of the texts themselves but of the vast body of critical literature that surrounds them. Filmic literacy is much more easily and pleasurably acquired; indeed, a fairly good grasp of film techniques is to be obtained more easily than is a good technical understanding of music, dance, or even painting. In short, movies are an almost ideal medium for half-baked intellectuals and, the population and educational explosions being what they are, we are very shortly going to have more of them than any other class of people. If the notion that the film is the central art of our time has any validity, it lies simply in the fact that this New Class is the most significant socioeconomic group of our time. They are the great consumers, not only of culture but of all the other doodads of affluence—notably such items as foreign food, foreign cars, foreign travel.

And foreign movies. In this, they recapitulate the special kind of provincialism of the wives and daughters of the industrial statesmen (or robber barons, as we used to know them) who established the institutions of our formal culture in the late nineteenth and early twentieth centuries and who would not buy a painting or go to a concert unless the artist were European, or at least, European-trained. The value of the Continental cachet has largely disappeared in the traditional arts, but, for the moment, it is very potent in film.

There is no question that much of the interest in foreign films is esthetically justifiable. Those that have been released here have generally been more interesting, more liberated and librating, than the best American products. It should, however, be remembered that we have seen only the crest of sundry new waves; we are rarely allowed to sport in the troughs, except, of course, when it comes to exploitable sex films, which are to our time what French postcards were to other epochs.

On the other hand, one observes a lack of critical spirit in our approach to many of these films, a certain faddishness—even cultishness—in the enthusiasm for them. Moreover, there is a great lack of historical perspective in our appreciation of the European film. The directors who created the French New Wave and the young Czech directors who have lately so excited us have been quite careful to note their debt to the great American directors whose work has profoundly influenced them; but, excepting the *auteur* critics, who hold that the director is the author of a film, few in this country have responded by taking a serious interest in these men or in the younger American directors who might, in time, achieve a comparable status in world cinema. In fact, it generally remains for the critics associated with the Parisian magazine, Cahiers du Cinéma, to point out to us the merits of people like Nicholas Ray, Don Siegel, and Sam Peckinpah, which does not seem to help them get work.

Of course, these three, along with many other equally underrated

American directors, are more or less committed to genre films, and Hollywood, though it continues to turn out Westerns and crime films and musicals, no longer has its heart in these matters. The *New Yorker's* Pauline Kael recently and rightly observed that since blacklisting and the breakup of the big studios (whose B pictures were the training ground for young directors) we have lost several generations of young moviemaking talent, men who were not perhaps destined for greatness, but for the kind of professional competence that is the bedrock on which a vital film industry is built. Unable or unwilling to tell good from bad among the European directors, afraid of entrusting large investments to young American directors, the industry has turned to what Miss Kael calls "the mediocrities and the bunglers of England"—a nation whose culture has always seemed very classy to us, but whose filmmakers (although they may not quite be "the sad joke" she says they have always been) are certainly joyless, imitative squares and have been (with a few great exceptions) since the earliest days of the movies. To hire these people to superintend the production of films on classic *American* themes is preposterous on the face of it, especially when someone like Peckinpah has not made a theatrical film in almost four years.

Miss Kael attributes this state of affairs to the "classic acumen" of our producers and that is certainly a factor. But there is, I think, more to it than that. The people now in charge in Hollywood are, like their basic audience, members of the New Class. As such, they are bright, bright, bright in their shallow little ways. They sense that they—that we—have lost something, some set of commonly held, virtually unconscious beliefs that helped the individual to define himself, that prevented the society from flying apart at the seams.

That something was recently defined by psychoanalyst Rollo May as "the myth of the mythless society." Like all the nations of the Western world since the eighteenth century, the United States has been energized by a belief in progress, both personal and social, through rationalism and individualism. However, as May is by no means the first to observe, both of these beliefs are, today, in a state of crisis, and nowhere is that crisis more deeply felt than among the New Class, which, of course, prides itself on getting news of this kind first. As a result all of our culture is in a state of anxiety that borders on the frantic. There is a legitimate feeling that none of the traditional cultural forms—including the traditional film genres—truly reflects the unpleasant day-to-day psychological reality that all of us experience. It is for this reason that we have turned, rather desperately, to Warhol and McLuhan, to "Futz" and "Hair," to Happenings and light shows. Never in history—at least in American history—has each sneeze, cough and burp of the avant-garde been so earnestly and intensively studied by so many for (*a*) clues to cultural salvation and (*b*) portents of a happier future and (c) escape. It is for this reason that we are presently putting such heavy pressure on the movies to grow up, to get serious, to be art.

But, as social critic David T. Bazelon pointed out some years ago, serious moviegoing has always involved a conflict "between one's desire to dream and one's desire to have a firmer relationship with high culture." In other words, there is a part of us that remains a child before the larger-than-life figures on the screen, figures that, in the darkness, inevitably have a magical, mythical quality about them. There is also a part of us that resents this reversion, that sternly calls us back to duty, "to relevance."

Now, back in the days when we really believed in the myth of the mythless society, there actually were, according to Dr. May, two integrating myths that had a peculiar hold on us—the one which dealt with the frontiersman and the one which dealt with the Horatio Alger figure. They were, if you will, a country myth and a city myth, and each figure, in his way, embodied those qualities of individualism and rationalism in which all of us held an implicit, unspoken faith. Much has been written, of course, about the movie Westerner and the movie gangster (who was merely Alger's boy grown up and grown rancid because no one else believed, as he still did, in really free enterprise). When these two characters were very well done, as they so often (indeed, routinely) were in the films of the nineteen-thirties and forties, conflict between the desire to dream and the desire for relevance was elegantly resolved by the simple expedient of satisfying both. These were "the good old-fashioned *movie* movies" that sentimental critics are always mourning for these days (and which, thank God, they still occasionally find). These were, as Bazelon said, "the heart of movies as cultural events [and] as release of dreams."

And now. I think, the heart has gone out of them—and out of our comedies and musicals which also revolved around familiar archetypes. Some producers try desperately to revivify the old forms, mostly by adding strong doses of very explicit sex and violence to them. (I am convinced that the outcry against S-and-V is an expression of cultural shock, not genuine moral outrage, by people who just don't expect to find such material in genre films where, not long ago, even a discreet kiss between cowpoke and schoolmarm was frowned upon and where death, when it came, was a bloodless "drilling.") Occasionally, we get an attempt at self-conscious purification of these forms, the sort of arty reactionaryism that made "Shane" and "High Noon" middle-brow bywords in the postwar years, when, in fact, anybody who really cares about the Western could name a half-dozen films (including, currently, "The Stalking Moon") that were considerably more interesting variations on the standard themes. Most often these days, one sees campy parodies of all the genres because, very simply, most of us simply can't believe in them anymore or, at the very least, don't want to be caught seeming to believe in them. The desperation of movie people confronted by this cultural phenomenon is beautifully exemplified by the new Kirk Douglas gangster film, "The Brotherhood," which the star caused to be produced under the direction of the heavy-handed Martin Ritt. Its ineptitude would do credit to perfidious Albion, but there is a special kind of moral blindness about it that I found intriguing. Douglas plays an old-style Mafia hood, running an assortment of labor and, one assumes, vice and protection rackets in the crude, small-timey way of his forefathers. He is still content to have his gunmen take care of stool pigeons in the old, vulgar fashion—they are seen taking one for a ride to the city dump and, when he is bumped off, stuffing the corpse's mouth with a symbolic canary. "No, no, no, Kirk." cry the leaders of his gangland family, "you don't understand. Times have changed. We're going into electronics, defense contracts, the big time." He turns out to be stubborn, unable to shift with the times and, ultimately, he must receive, from his own brother, the kiss of death.

Clearly, there is little to choose morally between the old-style and the new-style mobster. But the movie does choose. It actually gets very sentimental, almost lyrical, about the type Douglas portrays. In effect, it is a last hurrah for the *little* Caesars of our movie past, nostalgia for the small-scale, free-enterprise crook of our movie childhoods now invoked (simple-mindedly, to be sure) to divert us from his true nature, a diversion that no maker of the much more humble progenitors of "The Brotherhood" would have thought necessary or wise.

What it comes to is this: we have run out of myths. In the early forties, Albert Camus wrote: "The whole effort of Western art is to provide our imagination with types. . . . In desperation, it has invented the movie hero." But now the movies are full of antiheroes, and the institution of movie stardom, which was based on a system of heroic typology, is in total decline. Dr. May tells us, as many have, that the preferred life-style of our new age emphasizes cooperation, subjectivity, and collectivism, and who can doubt that he is right. And who is genius enough to make a satisfactory mythical hero out of a cooperative, subjective central figure whose aim is a harmonious collective society? Perhaps it can be done, and surely there will continue to be an atavistic place for the old stories and characters in television, which is aimed at those primitive souls who still think that we live in a highly competitive, individualistic, and more or less rational society, poor dears.

There are, of course, citizens of our world who might make very suitable mythic heroes for movies—revolutionary leaders, for example, foreign and domestic, black and white, young and old, though it is possible that they represent threats to the *status quo* too potent for comfortable assimilation into fiction. In any case, it is certain—as films like Jules Dassin's "Up-Tight" prove—that there is very little intelligent understanding of the type among professional filmmakers and thus small hope of their soon becoming the source of a new mythic richness in film. It is also possible that over a longish period of time an interaction between the underground and the aboveground moviemakers will produce a style of filmmaking so radically different from any we have known up to now that none of what we have been discussing will be germane. That, however, seems unlikely. The avant-garde produces a very abstract form of film, a thing of lovely surfaces, and stylistically exciting, but with none of the psychological resonance of either truly great art or, oddly, of the best popular movies.

For the moment, one imagines, the balance in our films will remain tipped in favor of our yearning for a firmer relation with high culture, away from the desire to dream—although Bazelon argues persuasively that the desire to dream at the movies remains very much alive. The audience that snobbishly refuses to attend American movies but goes religiously "to every lousy French film" is, he says, also looking for a dream— "It's just that you're not dreaming about this country." The implication —that we can no longer live psychologically in the United States—is interesting and more than a little frightening, and although this makes it very difficult for an excellent movie like the recent "Pretty Poison" to find its audience here, I do think that over the long run this, too, shall pass.

Meantime, if the new, more or less restricted film audience has yet to achieve the connection with high culture that they want and seem to need on a more than intermittent basis, there nevertheless has been one substantial gain in the content of our movies. They are, finally, beginning to examine, with an unprecedented degree of truthfulness, with a fine eye for accuracy of detail in setting and decor, a fine ear for language, some of the common issues of middle-class life. This year "Pretty Poison," "Petulia," "Rachel, Rachel" and, most notable of all, John Cassavetes's "Faces," have all, one way and another, plunged exploratory scalpels into the quivering flesh of the very culture that now supports the movies. All are about bourgeois yearnings—for love, for existential meaning—in the midst of affluence. All deal with various attempts to trick shallow life into making some sort of satisfying sense.

It seems to me, too, that since postindustrial societies are so much alike, we are not always escaping America when we go to see a foreign film. "Blow-Up," for instance, was a profound metaphorical examination of how technology as art fails us when we confront the timeless, universal mysteries of existence. Ingmar Bergman, whose stubborn insistence on making very difficult movies has rendered him unfashionable with the in-crowd lately, deals brilliantly in his latest films with the silencing effect of modern life on the humanistically oriented artist. Godard keeps probing in his infuriating, fascinating way at the half-formed revolutionary spirit of middle-class youth the world over.

In short, though we may have lost something quite valuable since movies became the "central art" of the "central people" of our time, we have also gained something. Or, more properly, we have gained a potential (still too often unrealized) for a greater, more direct understanding of the quality of our inner lives and the external world of both things and ideas which we inhabit.

That is—to re-emphasize my basic point—some of us have made a gain. There is a part of me that dislikes and distrusts this business of taking over what was once an art (or was it, then, merely a medium?) that belonged to everyone and making it into a semiprivate preserve. To put it very simply, the movies have their historical roots in the mass, and anything that is cut off from its roots is in danger. The experience of such a detachment may be exhilarating, but the risk should not be minimized.

To take just one example, whole generations learned to love movies in their preteen years, when they represented a very special kind of escape, when they were among the first, and the few, experiences one was allowed to engage in alone, free of parental supervision. In those days, when all movies were allegedly made for that conventionalized twelve-year-old mentality, that was perfectly feasible. Now, people find it impossible to allow their young children such freedom, and the kids are condemned to the generally wretched films made expressly for them and to a handful of more expensive—but generally no better—pictures that are advertised for family consumption. Worse, the movies have now formalized this style of censorship and, under the new classification system, theater managers will become moral cops, barring kids under seventeen from "X" category films. It is hard to see how, under these ground rules, a new generation will regard films as a "central" experience; absence may make the heart grow fonder, but one must first experience the presence for that cliché really to work.

What it all comes to is this: the first art (or quasi-art or presumptive art or whatever it is) that was entirely the creation of modern industrial society, the only art in living memory that operated, however crudely, on the basis of a kind of participatory democracy (with tickets the equivalent of ballots) is in the process of exchanging its broad-based democratic status for a more prestigious social and intellectual status, and one must measure the obvious gains that are accruing to it against the less obvious but no less real losses implicit in its new role. No one who believed, however fleetingly, however warily, in the movies' potential as a genuine art of the masses, one which appealed to all classes, one which could serve an

invaluable function as a kind of social cement, can be anything but sad-
dened by the alienation that very large numbers of people now feel about
the movies, an alienation that is imperfectly expressed by the protests
against sex and violence now so common. This shrinkage in the audience,
this slippage in the general interest in movies, the indignant, hurt, and
puzzled tone that pervades the letters any critic with a large audience receives, are all cause for alarm.

One is tempted to fear for the future of theatrical film, especially
with cable television, pay TV, and the possibility of home film libraries
which can be played through a television set now technologically feasible
and therefore inevitable. Movies truly will not be movies anymore if we
do not share them in public, in large groups before a large screen in
theaters. We do not need more socially fragmenting experiences; we do
need more integrative ones.

And yet the fear is controllable. There is—at least for a sizable number
of people—something mysteriously fascinating and basically resistant to
analysis about the attraction of film. Andrew Sarris put it very nicely in
that symposium of ours: "I happen to derive more pleasure from film than
from any other art, but that is *my* sensibility speaking, not necessarily
modern sensibility. I enjoyed movies before they were intellectually fashionable, and I shall enjoy them long after they have gone out of fashion.
I can no more renounce movies than literary men can renounce books."

Precisely. As he says, there is no way of knowing how history will regard the role of films in the shaping of our century's culture. All one
knows, finally, is that for some of us, no matter what our general views
about the broad trends in film and filmmaking, the movies are the only
game in town; and if all they were showing in the theaters was Warhol's
"Sleep," we would probably drag ourselves to see it, mourning the while
for the good old days and wondering whatever became of Randolph
Scott. I suspect—no, I am absolutely certain—that there will always be a
few million of us around. Enough to form some kind of audience for some
kind of movies. For us, they will always be the central art of our time.

PAULINE KAEL

Trash, Art,
and the Movies

*"Does trash corrupt? A nutty Puritanism still
flourishes in the arts, not just in the
schoolteachers' approach in wanting art to be
'worthwhile,' but in the higher reaches of
academic life with those ideologues who
denounce us for enjoying trash. . . . Do even
Disney and Doris Day movies do us lasting
harm? I've never known a person I thought had
been harmed by them . . ."*

Like those cynical heroes who were idealists before they discovered that
the world was more rotten than they had been led to expect, we're just
about all of us displaced persons, "a long way from home." When we feel
defeated, when we imagine we could now perhaps settle for home and
what it represents, that home no longer exists. But there are movie houses.
In whatever city we find ourselves we can duck into a theater and see on
the screen our familiars—our old "ideals" aging as we are and no longer
looking so ideal. Where could we better stoke the fires of our masochism

Pauline Kael's movie criticism is widely known through her books, *I
Lost It at the Movies, Kiss Kiss Bang Bang,* and *Going Steady,* in which
the full version of "Trash, Art, and the Movies" appears. She majored in
philosophy at the University of California, managed the first of the twin
art houses in this country, and now lives in Manhattan and reviews for
The New Yorker. Her long essay "Raising Kane," which appeared in *The
New Yorker* in early 1971, is available in *The Citizen Kane Book.* "Trash,
Art, and the Movies," excerpted here, is reprinted from *Harper's Magazine,*
February, 1969. Copyright © 1968, 1969, 1970 by Pauline Kael. Reprinted
by permission of Atlantic-Little, Brown and Co. and the author.

than at rotten movies in gaudy seedy picture palaces in cities that run together, movies and anonymity a common denominator. Movies—a tawdry art for a tawdry corrupt world—fit the way we feel. The world doesn't work the way the schoolbooks said it did and we are different from what our parents and teachers expected us to be. Movies are our cheap and easy expression, the sullen art of displaced persons. Because we feel low we sink in the boredom, relax in the irresponsibility, and maybe grin for a minute when the gunman lines up three men and kills them with a single bullet, which is no more "real" to us than the nursery-school story of the brave little tailor.

We don't have to be told those are photographs of actors impersonating characters. We know, and we often know much more about both the actors and the characters they're impersonating and about how and why the movie has been made than is consistent with theatrical illusion. Hitchcock teased us by killing off the one marquee-name star early in *Psycho*, a gambit which startled us not just because of the suddenness of the murder or how it was committed but because it broke a box-office convention and so it was a joke played on what audiences have learned to expect. He broke the rules of the movies game and our response demonstrated how aware we are of commercial considerations. When movies are bad (and in the bad parts of good movies) our awareness of the mechanics and our cynicism about the aims and values are peculiarly alienating. The audience talks right back to the phony "outspoken" condescending *The Detective;* there are groans of dejection at *The Legend of Lylah Clare*, with, now and then, a desperate little titter. How well we all know that cheap depression that settles on us when our hopes and expectations are disappointed *again*. Alienation is the most common state of the knowledgeable movie audience, and though it has the peculiar rewards of low connoisseurship, a miser's delight in small favors, we long to be surprised out of it—not to suspension of disbelief nor to a Brechtian kind of alienation, but to pleasure, something a man can call good without self-disgust.

A good movie can take you out of your dull funk and the hopelessness that so often goes with slipping into a theater; a good movie can make you feel alive again, in contact, not just lost in another city. Good movies make you care, make you believe in possibilities again. If somewhere in the Hollywood-entertainment world someone has managed to break through with something that speaks to you, then it isn't *all* corruption. The movie doesn't have to be great; it can be stupid and empty and you can still have the joy of a good performance, or the joy in just a good line. An actor's scowl, a small subversive gesture, a dirty remark that someone tosses off with a mock-innocent face, and the world makes a little bit of sense. Sitting there alone or painfully alone because those with you do not react as you do, you know there must be others perhaps in this very theater or in this city, surely in other theaters in other cities, now, in the past or future, who react as you do. And because movies are the most total and encompassing art form we have, these reactions can seem the most personal and, maybe the most important, imaginable. The romance of movies is not just in those stories and those people on the screen but in the adolescent dream of meeting others who feel as you do about what you've seen. You do meet them, of course, and you know each other at once because you talk less about good movies than about what you love in bad movies.

II

There is so much talk now about the art of the film that we may be in danger of forgetting that most of the movies we enjoy are not works of of art. *The Scalphunters,* for example, was one of the few entertaining American movies this past year, but skillful though it was, one could hardly call it a work of art—if such terms are to have any useful meaning. Or, to take a really gross example, a movie that is as crudely made as *Wild in the Streets*—slammed together with spit and hysteria and opportunism—can nevertheless be enjoyable, though it is almost a classic example of an unartistic movie. What makes these movies—that are not works of art—enjoyable? *The Scalphunters* was more entertaining than most Westerns largely because Burt Lancaster and Ossie Davis were peculiarly funny together; part of the pleasure of the movie was trying to figure out what made them so funny. Burt Lancaster is an odd kind of comedian: what's distinctive about him is that his comedy seems to come out of his physicality. In serious roles an undistinguished and too obviously hardworking actor, he has an apparently effortless flair for comedy and nothing is more infectious than an actor who can relax in front of the camera as if he were having a good time. (George Segal sometimes seems to have this gift of a wonderful amiability, and Brigitte Bardot was radiant with it in *Viva Maria!*) Somehow the alchemy of personality in the pairing of Lancaster and Ossie Davis—another powerfully funny actor of tremendous physical presence—worked, and the director Sydney Pollack kept tight control so that it wasn't overdone.

And *Wild in the Streets?* It's a blatantly crummy-looking picture, but that somehow works for it instead of against it because it's smart in a lot of ways that better-made pictures aren't. It looks like other recent products from American International Pictures but it's as if one were reading a comic strip that looked just like the strip of the day before, and yet on this new one there are surprising expressions on the faces and some of the balloons are really witty. There's not a trace of sensitivity in the drawing or in the ideas, and there's something rather specially funny about wit without *any* grace at all; it can be enjoyed in a particularly crude way—as Pop wit. The basic idea is corny—*It Can't Happen Here* with the freaked-out young as a new breed of fascists—but it's treated in the paranoid style of editorials about youth (it even begins by blaming everything on the parents). And a cheap idea that is this current and widespread has an almost lunatic charm, a nightmare gaiety. There's a relish that people have for the idea of drug-taking kids as monsters threatening them—the daily papers merging into *Village of the Damned*. Tapping and exploiting this kind of hysteria for a satirical fantasy, the writer Robert Thom has used what is available and obvious but he's done it with just enough mockery and style to make it funny. He throws in touches of characterization and occasional lines that are not there just to further the plot, and these throwaways make odd connections so that the movie becomes almost frolicsome in its paranoia (and in its delight in its own cleverness). . . .

Wild in the Streets is a fluke—a borderline, special case of a movie that is entertaining because some talented people got a chance to do something at American International that the more respectable companies were too nervous to try. But though I don't enjoy a movie so obvious and badly done as the big American International hit, *The Wild Angels*, it's easy to see why kids do and why many people in other countries do. Their reasons are basically why we all started going to the movies. After a time, we may want more, but audiences who have been forced to wade through the thick middle-class padding of more expensively made movies to get to the action enjoy the nose-thumbing at "good taste" of cheap movies that stick to the raw materials. At some basic level they *like* the pictures to be cheaply done, they enjoy the crudeness; it's a breather, a vacation from proper behavior and good taste and required responses. Patrons of burlesque applaud politely for the graceful erotic dancer but go wild for the lewd lummox who bangs her big hips around. That's what they go to burlesque for. Personally, I hope for a reasonable minimum of finesse, and movies like *Planet of the Apes* or *The Scalphunters* or *The Thomas Crown Affair* seem to me minimal entertainment for a relaxed evening's pleasure. These are, to use traditional common-sense language, "good movies" or "good bad movies"—slick, reasonably inventive, well-crafted. They are not art. But they are almost the maximum of what we're now getting from American movies, and not only these but much worse movies are talked about as "art"—and are beginning to be taken seriously in our schools.

It's preposterously egocentric to call anything we enjoy art—as if we could not be entertained by it if it were not; it's just as preposterous to let prestigious, expensive advertising snow us into thinking we're getting art for our money when we haven't even had a good time. I did have a good time at *Wild in the Streets*, which is more than I can say for *Petulia* or *2001* or a lot of other highly praised pictures. *Wild in the Streets* is not a work of art, but then I don't think *Petulia* or *2001* is either, though *Petulia* has that kaleidoscopic hip look and *2001* that new-techniques look which combined with "swinging" or "serious" ideas often pass for motion picture art.

III

Let's clear away a few misconceptions. Movies make hash of the schoolmarm's approach of how well the artist fulfilled his intentions. Whatever the original intention of the writers and director, it is usually supplanted, as the production gets under way, by the intention to make money—and the industry judges the film by how well it fulfills that intention. But if you could see the "artist's intentions" you'd probably wish you couldn't anyway. Nothing is so deathly to enjoyment as the relentless march of a movie to fulfill its obvious purpose. This is, indeed, almost a defining characteristic of the hack director, as distinguished from an artist.

The intention to make money is generally all too obvious. One of the excruciating comedies of our time is attending the new classes in cinema at the high schools where the students may quite shrewdly and accurately interpret the plot developments in a mediocre movie in terms of manipulation for a desired response while the teacher tries to explain everything in terms of the creative artist working out his theme—as if the conditions under which a movie is made and the market for which it is designed were irrelevant, as if the latest product from Warners or Universal should be analyzed like a lyric poem.

People who are just getting "seriously interested" in film always ask a critic, "Why don't you talk about technique and 'the visuals' more?" The answer is that American movie technique is generally more like technology and it usually isn't very interesting. Hollywood movies often have the look of the studio that produced them—they have a studio style. Many current Warner films are noisy and have a bright look of cheerful ugliness, Universal films the cheap blur of money-saving processes, and so forth. Sometimes there is a *spirit* that seems to belong to the studio. We can speak of the Paramount comedies of the Thirties or the Twentieth-Century Fox family entertainment of the Forties and Cinema-Scope comedies of the Fifties or the old MGM gloss, pretty much as we speak of Chevvies or Studebakers. These movies look alike, they move the same way, they have just about the same engines because of the studio policies and the *kind* of material the studio heads bought, the ideas they imposed, the way they had the films written, directed, photographed, and the labs where the prints were processed, and, of course, because of the presence of the studio stable of stars for whom the material was often purchased and shaped and who dominated the output of the studio. In some cases, as at Paramount in the Thirties, studio style was plain and rather tacky and the output—those comedies with Mary Boland and Mae West and Alison Skipworth and W. C. Fields—looks the better for it now. Those economical comedies weren't slowed down by a lot of fancy lighting or the adornments of "production values." Simply to be enjoyable, movies don't need a very high level of craftsmanship: wit, imagination, fresh subject matter, skillful performers, a good idea—either alone or in any combination—can more than compensate for lack of technical knowledge or a big budget.

The craftsmanship that Hollywood has always used as a selling point not only doesn't have much to do with art—the expressive use of techniques—it probably doesn't have very much to do with actual box-office appeal, either. A dull movie like Sidney Furie's *The Naked Runner* is technically competent. The appalling *Half a Sixpence* is technically astonishing. Though the large popular audience has generally been respectful of expenditure (so much so that a critic who wasn't impressed by the money and effort that went into a *Dr. Zhivago* might be sharply reprimanded by readers), people who like *The President's Analyst* or *The Producers* or *The Odd Couple* don't seem to be bothered by their technical ineptitude and visual ugliness. And on the other hand, the expensive slick techniques of ornately empty movies like *A Dandy in Aspic* can actually work against one's enjoyment, because such extravagance and waste are morally ugly. If one compares movies one likes to movies one doesn't like, craftsmanship of the big-studio variety is hardly a decisive factor. And if one compares a movie one likes by a competent director such as John Sturges or Franklin Schaffner or John Frankenheimer to a movie one doesn't much like by the same director, his technique is probably not the decisive factor. After directing *The Manchurian Candidate* Frankenheimer directed another political thriller, *Seven Days in May*, which, considered just as a piece of direction, was considerably more confident. While seeing it, one could take pleasure in Frankenheimer's smooth showmanship. But the material (Rod Serling out of Fletcher Knebel and Charles W. Bailey II) was like a straight (*i.e.*, square) version of *The Manchurian Candidate*. I have to chase around the corridors of memory to summon up images from *Seven Days in May*; despite the brilliant technique, all that is clear to mind is the touchingly, desperately anxious face of Ava Gardner—how when she smiled you couldn't be sure if you were seeing dimples or tics. But *The Manchurian Candidate*, despite Frankenheimer's uneven, often barely adequate, staging, is still vivid because of the script. It took off from a political double entendre that everybody had been thinking of ("Why, if Joe McCarthy were working for the Communists, he couldn't be doing them more good!") and carried it to startling absurdity, and the extravagances and conceits and conversational non sequiturs (by George Axelrod out of Richard Condon) were ambivalent and funny in a way that was trashy yet liberating.

Technique is hardly worth talking about unless it's used for something worth doing: that's why most of the theorizing about the new art of television commercials is such nonsense. The effects are impersonal—dexterous, sometimes clever, but empty of art. It's because of their emptiness that commercials call so much attention to their camera angles and quick cutting—which is why people get impressed by "the art" of it. Movies are now often made in terms of what television viewers have learned to settle for. Despite a great deal that is spoken and written about young people responding visually, the influence of TV is to make movies visually less imaginative and complex. Television is a very noisy medium and viewers listen, while getting used to a poor quality of visual reproduction, to the absence of visual detail, to visual obviousness and overemphasis on simple compositions, and to atrociously simplified and distorted color systems. The shifting camera styles, the movement, and the fast cutting of a film like *Finian's Rainbow*—one of the better big productions—are like the "visuals" of TV commercials, a disguise for static material, expressive of nothing so much as the need to keep you from getting bored and leaving. Men are now beginning their careers as directors by working on commercials—which, if one cares to speculate on it, may be almost a one-sentence résumé of the future of American motion pictures.

I don't mean to suggest that there is not such a thing as movie technique or that craftsmanship doesn't contribute to the pleasures of movies, but simply that most audiences, if they enjoy the acting and the "story" or the theme or the funny lines, don't notice or care about how well or how badly the movie is made, and because they don't care, a hit makes a director a "genius" and everybody talks about his brilliant technique (i.e., the technique of grabbing an audience). . . . Taking it apart is far less important than trying to see it whole. The critic shouldn't need to tear a work apart to demonstrate that he knows how it was put together. The important thing is to convey what is new and beautiful in the work, not how it was made—which is more or less implicit.

Just as there are good actors—possibly potentially great actors—who have never become big stars because they've just never been lucky enough to get the roles they needed (Brian Keith is a striking example) there are good directors who never got the scripts and the casts that could make their reputations. The question people ask when they consider going to a movie is not "How's it made?" but "What's it about?" and that's a perfectly legitimate question. (The next question—sometimes the first—is generally, "Who's in it?" and that's a good, honest question, too.) When you're at a movie, you don't have to believe in it to enjoy it but you do have to be interested. (Just as you have to be interested in the human material, too. Why should you go see *another* picture with James Stewart?) I don't want to see another samurai epic in exactly the same way I never want to read *Kristin Lavransdatter*. Though it's conceivable that a truly great movie director could make any subject interesting, there are few such artists working in movies and if they did work on unpromising subjects I'm not sure we'd really enjoy the results even if we did *admire* their artistry. (I recognize the greatness of sequences in several films by Eisenstein but it's a rather cold admiration.) The many brilliant Italian directors who are working within a commercial framework on crime and action movies are obviously not going to be of any great interest unless they get a chance to work on a subject we care about. Ironically the Czech successes here (*The Shop on Main Street, Loves of a Blonde, Closely Watched Trains*) are acclaimed for their techniques, which are fairly simple and rather limited, when it's obviously their human concerns and the basic modesty and decency of their attitudes plus a little barnyard humor which audiences respond to. They may even respond partly because of the *simplicity* of the techniques.

IV

When we are children, though there are categories of films we don't like—documentaries generally (they're too much like education) and, of course, movies especially designed for children—by the time we can go on our own we have learned to avoid them. Children are often put down by adults when the children say they enjoyed a particular movie; adults who are short on empathy are quick to point out aspects of the plot or theme that the child didn't understand, and it's easy to humiliate a child in this way. But it is one of the glories of eclectic arts like opera and movies that they include so many possible kinds and combinations of pleasure. One may be enthralled by Leontyne Price in *La Forza del Destino* even if one hasn't boned up on the libretto, or entranced by *The Magic Flute* even if one has boned up on the libretto, and a movie may be enjoyed for many reasons that have little to do with the story or the subtleties (if any) of theme or character. Unlike "pure" arts which are often defined in terms of what only they can do, movies are open and unlimited. Probably everything that can be done in movies can be done some other way, but—and this is what's so miraculous and so expedient about them—they can do almost anything any other art can do (alone or in combination) and they can take on some of the functions of exploration, of journalism, of anthropology, of almost any branch of knowledge as well. We go to the movies for the variety of what they can provide, and for their marvelous ability to give us easily and inexpensively (and usually painlessly) what we can get from other arts also. They are a wonderfully *convenient* art.

Movies are used by cultures where they are foreign films in a much more primitive way than in their own; they may be enjoyed as travelogues or as initiations into how others live or in ways we might not even guess. . . .

Every once in a while I see an anthropologist's report on how some preliterate tribe reacts to movies; they may, for example, be disturbed about where the actor has gone when he leaves the movie frame, or they may respond with enthusiasm to the noise and congestion of big-city life which in the film story are meant to show the depths of depersonalization to which we are sinking, but which they find funny or very jolly indeed. Different people and different cultures enjoy movies in very different ways. A few years ago the new "tribalists" here responded to the gaudy fantasies of *Juliet of the Spirits* by using the movie to turn on. A few had already made a trip of 8½, but *Juliet*, which was, conveniently and perhaps not entirely accidentally, in electric, psychedelic color, caught on because of it. (The color was awful, like in bad MGM musicals—so one may wonder about the quality of the trips.)

The new tribalism in the age of the media is not necessarily the enemy of commercialism; it is a direct outgrowth of commercialism and its ally, perhaps even its instrument. If a movie has enough clout, reviewers and columnists who were bored are likely to give it another chance, until on the second or third viewing, they discover that it affects them "viscerally" —and a big expensive movie is likely to do just that. *2001* is said to have caught on with youth (which can make it happen); and it's said that the movie will stone you—which is meant to be a recommendation. Despite a few dissident voices—I've heard it said, for example, that *2001* "gives you a bad trip because the visuals don't go with the music"—the promotion has been remarkably effective with students. "The tribes" tune in so fast that college students thousands of miles apart "have heard" what a great trip *2001* is before it has even reached their city.

Using movies to go on a trip has about as much connection with the art of the film as using one of those Doris Day-Rock Hudson jobs for ideas on how to redecorate your home—an earlier way of stoning yourself. But it is relevant to an understanding of movies to try to separate out, for purposes of discussion at least, how we may personally *use* a film—to learn how to dress or how to speak more elegantly or how to make a grand entrance or even what kind of coffee maker we wish to purchase, or to take off from the movie into a romantic fantasy or a trip—from what makes it a good movie or a poor one, because, of course, we can *use* poor films as easily as good ones, perhaps *more* easily for such nonaesthetic purposes as shopping guides or aids to tripping.

V

We generally become interested in movies because we *enjoy* them and what we enjoy them for has little to do with what we think of as art. The movies we respond to, even in childhood, don't have the same values as the official culture supported at school and in the middle-class home. At the movies we get low life and high life, while David Susskind and the moralistic reviewers chastise us for not patronizing what they think we should, "realistic" movies that would be good for us—like *A Raisin in the Sun,* where we could learn the lesson that a Negro family can be as dreary as a white family. Movie audiences will take a lot of garbage, but it's pretty hard to make us queue up for pedagogy. At the movies we want a different kind of truth, something that surprises us and registers with us as funny or accurate or maybe amazing, maybe even amazingly beautiful. We get little things even in mediocre and terrible movies— José Ferrer sipping his booze through a straw in *Enter Laughing,* Scott Wilson's hard scary all-American-boy-you-can't-reach face cutting through the pretensions of *In Cold Blood* with all its fancy bleak cinematography. We got, and still have embedded in memory, Tony Randall's surprising depth of feeling in *The Seven Faces of Dr. Lao,* Keenan Wynn and Moyna Macgill in the lunch-counter sequence of *The Clock,* John W. Bubbles on the dance floor in *Cabin in the Sky,* the inflection Gene Kelly gave to the line, "I'm a rising young man" in *DuBarry was a Lady.* Tony Curtis saying "avidly" in *Sweet Smell of Success.* Though the director may have been responsible for releasing it, it's the human material we react to most and remember longest. The art of the performers stays fresh for us, their beauty as beautiful as ever. There are so many kinds of things we get—the hangover sequence wittily designed for the Cinema-Scope screen in *The Tender Trap,* the atmosphere of the newspaper offices in *The Luck of Ginger Coffey,* the automat gone mad in *Easy Living.* Do we need to lie and shift things to false terms—like those who have to say Sophia Loren is a great actress as if her *acting* had made her a star? Wouldn't we rather watch her than better actresses because she's so incredibly charming and because she's probably the greatest model the world has ever known? There are great moments—Angela Lansbury singing "Little Yellow Bird" in *Dorian Gray.* (I don't think I've ever had a friend who didn't also treasure that girl and that song.) And there are absurdly right little moments—in *Saratoga Trunk* when Curt Bois says to Ingrid Bergman, "You're very beautiful," and she says, "Yes, isn't it lucky?" And those things have closer relationships to art than what the schoolteachers told us was true and beautiful. Not that the works we studied in school weren't often great (as we discovered *later*) but that what the teachers told us to admire them for (and if current texts are any indication, are still telling students to admire them for) was generally so false and prettified and moralistic that what might have been moments of pleasure in them, and what might have been cleansing in them, and subversive, too, had been coated over.

Because of the photographic nature of the medium and the cheap admission prices, movies took their impetus not from the desiccated imitation European high culture, but from the peep show, the Wild West show, the music hall, the comic strip—from what was coarse and common. The early Chaplin two-reelers still look surprisingly lewd, with bathroom jokes and drunkenness and hatred of work and proprieties. And the Western shoot-'em-ups certainly weren't the schoolteachers' notions of art—which in my school days, ran more to didactic poetry and "perfectly proportioned" statues and which over the years have progressed through nice stories to "good taste" and "excellence"—which may be more poisonous than homilies and dainty figurines because then you had a clearer idea of what you were up against and it was easier to fight. And this, of course, is what we were running away from when we went to the movies. All week we longed for Saturday afternoon and sanctuary—the anonymity and impersonality of sitting in a theater, just enjoying ourselves, not having to be responsible, not having to be "good." Maybe you just want to look at people on the screen and know they're not looking back at you, that they're not going to turn on you and criticize you.

Perhaps the single most intense pleasure of moviegoing is this nonaesthetic one of escaping from the responsibilities of having the proper responses required of us in our official (school) culture. And yet this is probably the best and most common basis for developing an aesthetic sense because responsibility to pay attention and to appreciate is anti-art, it makes us too anxious for pleasure, too bored for response. Far from supervision and official culture, in the darkness at the movies where nothing is asked of us and we are left alone, the liberation from duty and constraint allows us to develop our own aesthetic responses. Unsupervised enjoyment is probably not the only kind there is but it may feel like the only kind. Irresponsibility is part of the pleasure of all art; it is the part the schools cannot recognize. I don't like to buy "hard tickets" for a "road show" movie because I hate treating a movie as an occasion. I don't want to be pinned down days in advance; I enjoy the casualness of moviegoing —of going in when I feel like it, when I'm in the mood for a movie. It's the feeling of freedom from respectability we have always enjoyed at the movies that is carried to an extreme by American International Pictures and the Clint Eastwood Italian Westerns; they are stripped of cultural values. We may want more from movies than this negative virtue but we know the feeling from childhood moviegoing when we loved the gamblers and pimps and the cons' suggestions of muttered obscenities as the guards walked by. The appeal of movies was in the details of crime and high living and wicked cities and in the language of toughs and urchins; it was in the dirty smile of the city girl who lured the hero away from Janet Gaynor. What draws us to movies in the first place, the opening into other, forbidden or surprising, kinds of experience, and the vitality and corruption and irreverence of that experience are so direct and immediate and have so little connection with what we have been taught is art that many people feel more secure, feel that their tastes are becoming more cultivated when they begin to *appreciate* foreign films. One foundation executive told me that he was quite upset that his teen-agers had chosen to go to *Bonnie and Clyde* rather than with him to *Closely Watched Trains*. He took it as a sign of lack of maturity. I think his kids made an honest choice, and not only because *Bonnie and Clyde* is the better movie, but because it is closer to us, it has some of the qualities of direct involvement that make us care about movies. But it's understandable that it's easier for us, as Americans, to see *art* in foreign films than in our own, because of how we, as Americans, think of art. Art is still what teachers and ladies and foundations believe in, it's civilized and refined, cultivated and serious, cultural, beautiful, European, Oriental: it's what America isn't, and it's especially what American movies are not. Still, if those kids had chosen *Wild in the Streets* over *Closely Watched Trains* I would think that was a sound and honest choice, too, even though *Wild in the Streets* is in most ways a terrible picture. It connects with their lives in an immediate even if a grossly frivolous way, and if we don't go to movies for excitement, if, even as children, we accept the cultural standards of refined adults, if we have so little drive that we accept "good taste," then we will probably never really begin to care about movies at all. We will become like those people who "may go to American movies sometimes to relax" but when they want "a little more" from a movie, are delighted by how colorful and artistic Franco Zeffirelli's *The Taming of the Shrew* is, just as a couple of decades ago they were impressed by *The Red Shoes,* made by Powell and Pressburger, the Zeffirellis of their day. Or, if they like the cozy feeling of uplift to be had from mildly whimsical movies about timid people, there's generally a *Hot Millions* or something musty and faintly boring from Eastern Europe—one of those movies set in World War II but so remote from our ways of thinking that it seems to be set in World War I. Afterward, the moviegoer can feel as decent and virtuous as if he'd spent an evening visiting a deaf old friend of the family. It's a way of taking movies back into the approved culture of the schoolroom—into gentility—and the voices of schoolteachers and reviewers rise up to ask why America can't make such movies.

VI

Movie art is not the opposite of what we have always enjoyed in movies, it is not to be found in a return to that official high culture, it is what we have always found good in movies only more so. It's the subversive gesture carried further, the moments of excitement sustained longer and extended into new meanings. . . .

If we go back and think over the movies we've enjoyed—even the ones we knew were terrible movies while we enjoyed them—what we enjoyed in them, the little part that was good, had, in some rudimentary way, some freshness, some hint of style, some trace of beauty, some audacity, some craziness. It's there in the interplay between Burt Lancaster and Ossie Davis, or, in *Wild in the Streets*, in Diane Varsi rattling her tambourine, in Hal Holbrook's faint twitch when he smells trouble, in a few of Robert Thom's lines; and they have some relation to art though they don't look like what we've been taught is "quality." They have the joy of playfulness. In a mediocre or rotten movie, the good things may give the impression that they come out of nowhere; the better the movie, the more they seem to belong to the world of the movie. Without this kind of playfulness and the pleasure we take from it, art isn't art at all, it's something punishing, as it so often is in school where even artists' little *jokes* become leaden from explanation.

Keeping in mind that simple, good distinction that all art is entertainment but not all entertainment is art, it might be a good idea to keep in mind also that if a movie is said to be a work of art and you don't enjoy it, the fault may be in you, but it's probably in the movie. Because of the money and advertising pressures involved, many reviewers discover a fresh masterpiece every week, and there's that cultural snobbery, that hunger for respectability that determines the selection of the even bigger annual masterpieces. In foreign movies what is most often mistaken for "quality" is an imitation of earlier movie art or a derivation from respectable, approved work in the other arts—like the demented, suffering painter-hero of *Hour of the Wolf* smearing his lipstick in a facsimile of expressionist anguish. Kicked in the ribs, the press says "art" when "ouch" would be more appropriate. When a director is said to be an artist (generally on the basis of earlier work which the press failed to recognize) and especially when he picks artistic subjects like the pain of creation, there is a tendency to acclaim his new bad work. This way the press, in trying to make up for its past mistakes, manages to be wrong all the time. And so a revenge-of-a-sour-virgin movie like Truffaut's *The Bride Wore Black* is treated respectfully as if it somehow revealed an artist's sensibility in every frame. Reviewers who would laugh at Lana Turner going through her *femme fatale* act in another Ross Hunter movie swoon when Jeanne Moreau casts significant blank looks for Truffaut.

In American movies what is most often mistaken for artistic quality is box-office success, especially if it's combined with a genuflection to importance; then you have "a movie the industry can be proud of" like *To Kill a Mockingbird* or such Academy Award winners as *West Side Story, My Fair Lady,* or *A Man for All Seasons.* Fred Zinnemann made a fine modern variant of a Western, *The Sundowners,* and hardly anybody saw it until it got on television; but *A Man for All Seasons* had the look of prestige and the press felt honored to praise it. I'm not sure most movie reviewers consider what they honestly enjoy as being central to criticism. Some at least appear to think that that would be relying too much on their own tastes, being too personal instead of being "objective"—relying on the readymade terms of cultural respectability and on consensus judgment (which, to a rather shocking degree, can be arranged by publicists creating a climate of importance around a movie). Just as movie directors, as they age, hunger for what was meant by respectability in their youth, and aspire to prestigious cultural properties, so, too, the movie press longs to be elevated in terms of the cultural values of their old high schools. And so they, along with the industry, applaud ghastly "tour-de-force" performances, movies based on "distinguished" stage successes or prize-winning novels, or movies that are "worthwhile," that make a "contribution" —"serious" message movies. This often involves praise of bad movies, of dull movies, or even the praise in good movies of what was worst in them.

This last mechanism can be seen in the honors bestowed on *In the Heat of the Night.* The best thing in the movie is that high comic moment when Poitier says, "I'm a police officer," because it's a reversal of audience expectations and we laugh in delighted relief that the movie is not going to be another self-righteous, self-congratulatory exercise in the gloomy old Stanley Kramer tradition. At that point the audience sparks to life. The movie is fun largely because of the amusing central idea of a black Sherlock Holmes in a Tom and Jerry cartoon of reversals. Poitier's color is used for comedy instead of for that extra dimension of irony and pathos that made movies like *To Sir with Love* unbearably sentimental. He doesn't really play the super sleuth very well: he's much too straight even when spouting the kind of higher scientific nonsense about right-handedness and left-handedness that would have kept Basil Rathbone in an ecstasy of clipped diction, blinking eyes, and raised eyebrows. Like Bogart in *Beat the Devil* Poitier doesn't seem to be in on the joke. But Rod Steiger compensated with a comic performance that was even funnier for being so unexpected—not only from Steiger's career which had been going in other directions, but after the apparently serious opening of the film. The movie was, however, praised by the press as if it had been exactly the kind of picture that the audience was so relieved to discover it wasn't going to be (except in its routine melodramatic sequences full of fake courage and the climaxes such as Poitier slapping a rich white South- erner or being attacked by white thugs; except that is, in its worst parts). When I saw it, the audience, both black and white, enjoyed the joke of the fast-witted, hyper-educated black detective explaining matters to the backward, blundering Southern-chief-of-police slob. This racial joke is far more open and inoffensive than the usual "irony" of Poitier being so good and so black. For once it's *funny* (instead of embarrassing) that he's so superior to everybody.

In the Heat of the Night isn't in itself a particularly important movie; amazingly alive photographically, it's an entertaining, somewhat messed- up comedy-thriller. . . . What makes it interesting for my purposes here is that the audience enjoyed the movie for the vitality of its surprising playfulness, while the industry congratulated itself because the film was "hard-hitting"—that is to say, it flirted with seriousness and spouted warm, worthwhile ideas.

Those who can accept *In the Heat of the Night* as the socially con- scious movie that the industry pointed to with pride can probably also go along with the way the press attacked Jewison's subsequent film, *The Thomas Crown Affair*, as trash and a failure. One could even play the same game that was played on *In the Heat of the Night* and convert the *Crown* trifle into a sub-fascist exercise because, of course, Crown, the superman, who turns to crime out of boredom, is the crooked son of *The Fountainhead*, out of Raffles. But that's taking glossy summer-evening fan- tasies much too seriously: we haven't had a junior executive's fantasy-life movie for a long time and to attack this return of the worldly gentlemen- thieves genre of Ronald Colman and William Powell *politically* is to fail to have a sense of humor about the little romantic-adolescent fascist lurk- ing in most of us. Part of the fun of movies is that they allow us to see how silly many of our fantasies are and how widely they're shared. A light romantic entertainment like *The Thomas Crown Affair*, trash undis- guised, is the kind of chic crappy movie which (one would have thought) nobody could be fooled into thinking was art. Seeing it is like lying in the sun flicking through fashion magazines and, as we used to say, feeling rich and beautiful beyond your wildest dreams.

But it isn't easy to come to terms with what one enjoys in films, and if an older generation was persuaded to *dismiss* trash, now a younger gen- eration, with the press and the schools in hot pursuit, has begun to talk about trash as if it were really very serious art. College newspapers and the new press all across the country are full of a hilarious new form of scholasticism, with students using their education to cook up impressive reasons for enjoying very simple, traditional dishes. Here is a communication from Cambridge to a Boston paper:

To the Editor:
The Thomas Crown Affair is fundamentally a film about faith between people. In many ways, it reminds me of a kind of updated old fable, or tale, about an ultimate test of faith. It is a film about a love affair (note the title), with a subplot of a bank robbery, rather than the reverse. The subtlety of the film is in the way the external plot is used as a matrix to develop serious motifs, much in the same way that the *Heat of the Night* functioned.

Although Thomas Crown is an attractive and fascinating character, Vicki is the protagonist. Crown is consistent, predictable: he courts personal danger to feel superior to the system of which he is a part, and to make his otherwise overly comfortable life more interesting. Vicki is caught between two opposing elements within her, which, for convenience, I would call masculine and feminine. In spite of her glamour, at the outset she is basically masculine, in a man's type of job, ruthless, after prestige and wealth. But Crown looses the female in her. His test is a test of her femininity. The masculine responds to the challenge. Therein lies the pathos of her final revelation. Her egocentrism had not yielded to his.

In this psychic context, the possibility of establishing faith is explored. The movement of the film is towards Vicki's final enigma. Her ambivalence is commensurate with the increasing danger to Crown. The suspense lies in how she will respond to her dilemma, rather than whether Crown will escape.

I find *The Thomas Crown Affair* to be a unique and haunting film, superb in its visual and technical design, and fascinating for the allegorical problem of human faith.

The Thomas Crown Affair is pretty good trash, but we shouldn't convert what we enjoy it for into false terms derived from our study of the other arts. That's being false to what we enjoy. If it was priggish for an older generation of reviewers to be ashamed of what they enjoyed and to feel they had to be contemptuous of popular entertainment, it's even more priggish for a new movie generation to be so proud of what they enjoy that they use their education to try to place trash within the acceptable academic tradition. What the Cambridge boy is doing is a more devious form of that elevating and falsifying of people who talk about Loren as a great actress instead of as a gorgeous, funny woman. Trash doesn't belong to the academic tradition, and that's part of the *fun* of trash—that you know (or *should* know) that you don't have to take it seriously, that it was never meant to be any more than frivolous and trifling and entertaining. It's appalling to read solemn academic studies of Hitchcock or von Sternberg by people who seem to have lost sight of the primary reason for seeing films like *Notorious* or *Morocco*—which is that they were not intended solemnly, that they were playful and inventive and faintly (often deliberately) absurd. And what's good in them, what relates them to art, is that playfulness and absence of solemnity. There is talk now about von Sternberg's technique—his use of light and decor and detail—and he is, of course, a kitsch master in these areas, a master of studied artfulness and pretty excess. Unfortunately, some students take this technique as proof that his films are works of art, once again, I think, falsifying what they really respond to—the satisfying romantic glamour of his very pretty trash. *Morocco* is great trash, and movies are so rarely great art, that if we cannot appreciate great *trash*, we have very little reason to be interested in them. The kitsch of an earlier era—even the best kitsch—does not become art, though it may become camp. . . .

If we don't deny the pleasures to be had from certain kinds of trash and accept *The Thomas Crown Affair* as a pretty fair example of entertaining trash, then we may ask if a piece of trash like this has any relationship to art. And I think it does. Steve McQueen gives probably his most glamorous, fashionable performance yet, but even enjoying him as much as I do, I wouldn't call his performance art. It's artful, though, which is exactly what is required in this kind of vehicle—and if he had been luckier, if the script had provided what it so embarrassingly lacks, the kind of sophisticated dialogue—the sexy shoptalk—that writers like Jules Furthman and William Faulkner provided for Bogart, if the director Norman Jewison had Lubitsch's lightness of touch, McQueen might be acclaimed as a suave, "polished" artist. Even in this flawed setting, there's a self-awareness in his performance that makes his elegance funny. And Haskell Wexler, the cinematographer, lets go with a whole bag of tricks, flooding the screen with his delight in beauty, shooting all over the place, and sending up the material. And Pablo Ferro's games with the split screen at the beginning are such conscious, clever games designed to draw us in to watch intently what is of no great interest. What gives this trash a lift, what makes it entertaining is clearly that some of those involved, knowing of course that they were working on a silly shallow script and a movie that wasn't about anything of consequence, used the chance to have a good time with it. If the director. Norman Jewison, could have built a movie instead of putting together a patchwork of sequences, *Crown* might have had a chance to be considered a movie in the class and genre of Lubitsch's *Trouble in Paradise*. It doesn't come near that because to transform this kind of kitsch, to make art of it, one needs that unifying grace, that formality and charm that a Lubitsch could sometimes provide. Still, even in this movie we get a few grace notes in McQueen's playfulness, and from Wexler and Ferro. Working on trash, feeling free to play, can loosen up the actors and craftsmen just as seeing trash can liberate the spectator. And as we don't get this playful quality of art much in movies except in trash, we might as well relax and enjoy it freely for what it is. I don't trust anyone who doesn't admit having at some time in his life enjoyed trashy American movies; I don't trust *any* of the tastes of people who were born with such good taste that they didn't need to find their way through trash.

. . . We don't ask much from movies, just a little something that we can call our own. Who at some point hasn't set out dutifully for that fine foreign film and then ducked into the nearest piece of American trash? We're not only educated people of taste, we're also common people with common feelings. And our common feelings are not all *bad*. You hoped for some aliveness in that trash you were pretty sure you wouldn't get from the respected "art film." You had long since discovered that you wouldn't get it from certain kinds of American movies, either. The industry now is taking a neo-Victorian tone, priding itself on its (few) "good, clean" movies—which are always its worst movies because almost nothing can break through the smug surfaces, and even performers' talents become cute and cloying. The lowest action trash is preferable to wholesome family entertainment. When you clean them up, when you make movies respectable, you kill them. The wellspring of their *art,* their greatness, is in not being respectable.

VII

Does trash corrupt? A nutty Puritanism still flourishes in the arts, not just in the schoolteachers' approach of wanting art to be "worthwhile," but in the higher reaches of the academic life with those ideologues who denounce us for enjoying trash as if this enjoyment took us away from the really disturbing, angry new art of our time and somehow destroyed us. If we had to *justify* our trivial silly pleasures, we'd have a hard time. How could we possibly *justify* the fun of getting to know some people in movie after movie, like Joan Blondell, the brassy girl with the heart of gold, or waiting for the virtuous, tiny, tiny-featured heroine to say her line so we could hear the riposte of her tough, wisecracking girlfriend (Iris Adrian was my favorite). Or, when the picture got too monotonous, there would be the song interlude, introduced "atmospherically" when the cops and crooks were both in the same never-neverland nightclub and everything stopped while a girl sang. Sometimes it would be the most charming thing in the movie, like Dolores Del Rio singing "You Make Me That Way" in *International Settlement;* sometimes it would drip with maudlin meaning, like "Oh Give Me Time for Tenderness" in *Dark Victory* with the dying Bette Davis singing along with the chanteuse. The pleasures of this kind of trash are not intellectually defensible. But why should pleasure need justification? Can one demonstrate that trash desensitizes us, that it prevents people from enjoying something better, that it limits our range of aesthetic response? Nobody I know of has provided such a demonstration. Do even Disney movies or Doris Day movies do us lasting harm? I've never known a person I thought had been harmed by them, though it does seem to me that they affect the tone of a culture, that perhaps—and I don't mean to be facetious—they may poison us collectively though they don't injure us individually. There are women who want to see a world in which everything is pretty and cheerful and in which romance triumphs (*Barefoot in the Park, Any Wednesday*); families who want movies to be an innocuous inspiration, a good example for the children (*The Sound of Music, The Singing Nun*); couples who want the kind of folksy blue humor (*A Guide for the Married Man*) that they still go to Broadway shows for. These people are the reason slick, stale, rotting pictures make money; they're the reason so few pictures are any good. And in that way, this terrible conformist culture does affect us all. It certainly cramps and limits opportunities for artists. But that isn't what generally gets attacked as trash, anyway. I've avoided using the term "harmless trash" for movies like *The Thomas Crown Affair* because that would put me on the side of the angels—against "harmful trash," and I don't honestly know what that is. It's common for the press to call cheaply made, violent action movies "brutalizing" but that tells us less about any actual demonstrable effects than about the finicky tastes of the reviewers—who are often highly appreciative of violence in more expensive and "artistic" settings such as *Petulia*. It's almost a class prejudice, this assumption that crudely made movies, movies without the look of art, are bad for people.

If there's a little art in good trash and sometimes even in poor trash, there may be more trash than is generally recognized in some of the most acclaimed "art" movies. Such movies as *Petulia* and *2001* may be no more than trash in the latest, up-to-the-minute guises, using "artistic techniques" to give trash the look of art. The serious art look may be the latest fashion in *expensive* trash. All that "art" may be what prevents pictures like these from being *enjoyable* trash; they're not honestly crummy, they're very fancy and they take their crummy ideas seriously. . . .

VIII

2001 is a movie that might have been made by the hero of *Blow-Up*, and it's fun to think about Kubrick really doing every dumb thing he wanted to do, building enormous science-fiction sets and equipment, never even bothering to figure out what he was going to do with them. Fellini, too, had gotten carried away with the Erector Set approach to moviemaking, but his big science-fiction construction, exposed to view at the end of 8½, was abandoned. Kubrick never really made his movie either but he doesn't seem to know it. Some people like the American International Pictures stuff because it's rather idiotic and maybe some people love *2001* just because Kubrick did all that stupid stuff, acted out a kind of super sci-fi nut's fantasy. In some ways it's the biggest amateur movie of them all, complete even to the amateur-movie obligatory scene—the director's little daughter (in curls) telling daddy what kind of present she wants.

There was a little pre-title sequence in *You Only Live Twice* with an astronaut out in space that was in a looser, more free style than *2001*—a daring little moment that I think was more fun than all of *2001*. It had an element of the unexpected, of the shock of finding death in space lyrical. Kubrick is carried away by the idea. The secondary title of *Dr. Strangelove*, which we took to be satiric, "*How I learned to stop worrying and love the bomb*," was not, it now appears, altogether satiric for Kubrick. *2001* celebrates the invention of tools of death, as an evolutionary route to a higher order of *nonhuman* life. Kubrick literally learned to stop worrying and love the bomb; he's become his own butt—the Herman Kahn of extraterrestrial games theory. The ponderous blurry appeal of the picture may be that it takes its stoned audience out of this world to a consoling vision of a graceful world of space, controlled by superior godlike minds, where the hero is reborn as an angelic baby. It has the dreamy somewhere-over-the-rainbow appeal of a new vision of heaven. *2001* is a celebration of cop-out. It says man is just a tiny nothing on the stairway to paradise, something better is coming, and it's all out of your hands anyway. There's an intelligence out there in space controlling your destiny from ape to angel, so just follow the slab. Drop up.

It's a bad, bad sign when a movie director begins to think of himself as a myth-maker, and this limp myth of a grand plan that justifies slaughter and ends with resurrection has been around before. Kubrick's story line—accounting for evolution by an extraterrestrial intelligence—is probably the most gloriously redundant plot of all time. And although his intentions may have been different, *2001* celebrates the *end of man;* those beautiful mushroom clouds at the end of *Strangelove* were no accident. In *2001, A Space Odyssey* death and life are all the same: no point is made in the movie of Gary Lockwood's death—the moment isn't even defined—and the hero doesn't discover that the hibernating scientists have become corpses. That's unimportant in a movie about the beauties of resurrection. Trip off to join the cosmic intelligence and come back a better mind. And as the trip in the movie is the usual psychedelic light show, the audience doesn't even have to worry about getting to Jupiter. They can go to heaven in Cinerama. . . .

IX

Part of the fun of movies is in seeing "what everybody's talking about," and if people are flocking to a movie, or if the press can con us into thinking that they are, then ironically, there is a sense in which we want to see it, even if we suspect we won't enjoy it, because we want to know what's going on. Even if it's the worst inflated pompous trash that is the most talked about (and it usually is) and even if that talk is manufactured, we want to see the movies because so many people fall for whatever is talked about that they make the advertisers' lies true. Movies absorb material from the culture and the other arts so fast that some films that have been widely *sold* become culturally and sociologically important whether they are good movies or not. Movies like *Morgan!* or *Georgy Girl* or *The Graduate*—aesthetically trivial movies which, however, because of the ways some people react to them, enter into the national bloodstream—become cultural and psychological equivalents of watching a political convention —to observe what's going on. And though this has little to do with the art of movies, it has a great deal to do with the appeal of movies. . . .

X

When you're young the odds are very good that you'll find something to enjoy in almost any movie. But as you grow more experienced, the odds change. I saw a picture a few years ago that was the sixth version of material that wasn't much to start with. Unless you're feebleminded, the odds get worse and worse. We don't go on reading the same kind of manufactured novels—pulp Westerns or detective thrillers, say—all of our lives, and we don't want to go on and on looking at movies about cute heists by comically assorted gangs. The problem with a popular art form is that those who want something more are in a hopeless minority compared with the millions who are always seeing it for the first time, or for the reassurance and gratification of seeing the conventions fulfilled again. Probably a large part of the older audience gives up movies for this reason—simply that they've seen it before. And probably this is why so many of the best movie critics quit. They're wrong when they blame it on the movies going bad; it's the odds becoming so bad, and they can no longer bear the many tedious movies for the few good moments and the tiny shocks of recognition. Some become too tired, too frozen in fatigue, to respond to what *is* new. Others who *do* stay awake may become too demanding for the young who are seeing it all for the first hundred times. The critical task is necessarily comparative, and younger people do not truly know what is new. And despite all the chatter about the media and how smart the young are, they're incredibly naïve about mass culture—

perhaps *more* naïve than earlier generations (though I don't know why). Maybe watching all that television hasn't done so much for them as they seem to think; and when I read a young intellectual's appreciation of *Rachel, Rachel* and come to "the mother's passion for chocolate bars is a superb symbol for the second coming of childhood" I know the writer is still in his first childhood, and I wonder if he's going to come out of it.

One's moviegoing tastes and habits change—I still like in movies what I always liked but now, for example, I really want documentaries. After all the years of stale stupid acted-out stories, with less and less for me in them, I am desperate to know something, desperate for facts, for information, for faces of non-actors and for knowledge of how people live—for revelations, not for the little bits of show-business detail worked up for us by show-business minds who got them from the same movies we're tired of.

But the big change is in our *habits*. If we make any kind of decent, useful life for ourselves we have less need to run from it to those diminishing pleasures of the movies. When we go to the movies we want something good, something sustained, we don't want to settle just for a bit of something, because we have other things to do. If life at home is more interesting, why go to the movies? And the theaters frequented by true moviegoers—those perennial displaced persons in each city, the loners and the losers—depress us. Listening to them—and they are often more audible than the sound track—as they cheer the cons and jeer the cops, we may still share their disaffection, but it's not enough to keep us interested in cops and robbers. A little nose-thumbing isn't enough. If we've grown up at the movies we know that good work is continuous not with the academic, respectable tradition but with the glimpses of something good in trash, but we want the subversive gesture carried to the domain of discovery. Trash has given us an appetite for art.

PART THREE

Television: Mass Culture

Introduction

Network TV captures the attention of almost 75 million viewers almost every night, which makes it the obvious favorite of the masses. During each evening's three hours of prime time, sets are turned on in two-thirds of all American homes.

The very size of its audience probably helps explain the bland, forgettable character of much TV entertainment. Advertisers like the giant size of the market and the captive audience that must listen to their messages night after night. To hold audiences of that size for their advertisers, broadcasters believe they must not offend anyone.

As the country turned into the seventies, there were rumblings of trouble for the television industry. Cable television, public broadcasting, and video cassettes were the actual and potential intruders threatening to erode the base of network TV, and thereby cut its commercial revenue. The FCC was also encouraging more local program origination and had stopped all cigarette commercials.

The bland and soporific mass culture that dominated network television through the sixties appeared likely to remain a staple diet through the current decade. But there were signs that its quantity might be cut somewhat as the networks tried to woo minority audiences back with larger servings of stimulating fare.

GARY A. STEINER

The Question of "Balance"

To what extent . . . should television be pre-empted in the public service, like land for highways or the school system? To what extent should
it be left entirely free to try to please its audience, like the movies or magazines? That is a policy matter based on value judgments not open to
empirical discussion. Sir Robert Fraser has clearly stated the logical alternatives:

> If, like Plato, we believe in Golden Men who know best and if we get our
> way, we will not be troubled by problems of quantity and quality in
> television, not if we have the luck, that is, to be Golden Men ourselves, for
> we will provide ordinary people with the amount and kind of television we
> think is good for them. But if we agree not with Plato but with Moll about
> the great social problem of human happiness, then we must face the logic
> of our preference. The television that is produced will reflect what people
> do like, not what we think they ought to like, and it is not of great rele-
> vance to criticize television.[1]

It is often pointed out that TV is not comparable to films or magazines
because of the limited number of channels available. This, the argument
runs, makes it necessary to regulate and license TV broadcasters in the
public interest. But that coin has two sides. The Mill democrats might
counter that the government has even less business pre-empting a limited

---

[1] Sir Robert Fraser, in an address given at Scarborough, England.

Gary A. Steiner, who died recently, was professor of psychology at the
Graduate School of Business of the University of Chicago. "The Question
of 'Balance' " is from his book The People Look at Television: A Study
of Audience Attitudes, pp. 240–46, Alfred A. Knopf, Inc., New York, 1963.
Copyright © 1963 by the Bureau of Applied Social Research. Reprinted
by permission of Alfred A. Knopf, Inc.

resource. If one or two newspapers are regulated "in the public interest," the public can reject the regulator's decision by turning to others. But if *all* available television is geared to an authority's conception of what the public needs, the latter is left no choice but to take it that way or not at all. Why, counter the Platonists, should the network bosses' control of content be more acceptable? Because, return the Millites, they are under pressure to maximize the audience (and therefore to please it); and the government agency is not.

What television *should* do is not, then, an empirical matter. But what television *could* do, is—and that is the main reason for raising the issue. It seems to me that the weak, or at least the questionable, link in the Platonic position is the absence of a truant officer. We can and do force children into the classroom, but can we force adults to attend the necessary or beneficial programs?

In principle, we can certainly prevent them from seeing those we consider harmful, by censorship—but no one is really in favor of that. The real question is to what extent, or how often, people would choose to watch the *better*, more enlightening, less escape-filled schedule. Both the ratings and our limited data suggest that the answer is "not often," at least under conditions where a choice exists.

If all channels were simultaneously elevated, at least during some hours, some attendance would undoubtedly be forced—but how much, or for how long, no one really knows. . . .

The program distinctions implicit in these considerations usually take the form of two general dichotomies: information or public service vs. entertainment; and within the second, "class culture" vs. "mass culture." Let me pursue each of these in a little more detail.

"PUBLIC SERVICE" VS. "ENTERTAINMENT"

To date, our national answer to this value issue has been a compromise. The Government in effect tithes the industry: for 10 percent devoted to Caesar, it allows 90 percent to be devoted to Circus. The industry *may* entertain most of the time so long as it also provides a share of "public service."

Now, I think it worthwhile to question the consequences of this dichotomy, especially the rather narrow and specific definition of "public service" or "public affairs" programming invoked by the FCC and thus by the industry. In effect, the consideration of "public service" is restricted to news coverage, informational programming, and religious or secular editorializing. Each station is charged with fulfilling a limited quota—as much as it has "promised" in its license application. In turn, it is apt to consider its "service" obligations fulfilled if and when it can point to *x* hours, regardless of quality or intrinsic interest.

It seems to me that the FCC and other evaluators of broadcaster performance must recognize entertainment as a legitimate and perhaps most significant "public service." Even *within* the civic objectives presently implicit in the "public service" category, there can be serious question as to which program form really does the most good—especially if the size of the audience is included in the comparison. If the objective is spiritual "uplift," are five unwatched minutes of incantation by a local preacher really worth more than *Martin Luther* or some equivalent on *The Late Show?* Is the serious consideration of civic issues more often aroused by three aldermen or professors around a table, or by dramatic presentation in an entertainment context—e.g., "message" film (*Snake Pit, Blackboard Jungle, Pinky, Gentlemen's Agreement,* etc.), or social drama (Ibsen, Williams, O'Neill, Chayevsky), and so on?

And beyond the present civic objectives of "public service," there is the matter of enriching, provoking, stimulating, even soothing the emotional or aesthetic sensitivities. In short, entertainment and recreation *per se,* when really good, certainly contribute a valuable public service. That under the present system a station might well feel more pressure to present sectarian religion or the water commissioner than an opera or serious drama,[2] strikes me as a curious misapplication of a communications resource, and certainly raises questions about the underlying value judgment.

In short, *if* broadcasters are to be evaluated on how well they serve the public, the consideration might be expanded—at least conceptually— to the total schedule. Entertainment shows do many of the things the present "public service" shows are supposed to do: often better, certainly for more people. Secondly, good, enriching entertainment should be recognized *as* public service, perhaps the most important public service performed by TV.

Now, clearly this cuts two ways, and perhaps that is why the industry has not made this obvious point long ago and defended it vigorously. If there is to be a public service credit for the moral lessons contained in a serious drama, there will be debits for programs that appear to subvert American values; if broadcasters can claim civic benefits in a dramatic presentation, or personal tragic-catharsis in a good western, they will be held responsible for the juvenile delinquency or emotional disturbance that someone else sees as an obvious consequence of other (or even the same) programs.

So this line of reasoning tends to open a Pandora's box of questions to which there are no real answers—some, because there is not enough evi-

---

[2] And this is perhaps the most realistic alternative. Broadcasters are far less likely to displace a highly rated western or comedy show with such classic presentations than they are to consider substituting them for the required "public service," which gets still lower ratings.

dence (do crime shows really induce crime?); others, because they are normative and entirely outside the realm of scientific inquiry (*should* the public be stimulated or provoked by television programming that may disturb some immature or susceptible minds? *What* values should drama reinforce? Nihilism? Middle-class? Integration or segregation? Pacifism? Patriotism? Etc.). Once entertainment is examined in the light of service or disservice, we have to face such issues and their related consequences, censorship or control of content, which nobody wants and nobody can implement.

But, if not formally, then at least informally, there should be a mutual awareness that great good and harm to the community probably rest in the type of entertainment a station presents. Station operators should not sleep soundly just because they have exceeded their quota of "public service"; neither should the critics continue to talk almost entirely in such easy dichotomies of program classification.[3]

ENTERTAINMENT LEVEL — VAST WASTELAND OR MASS TASTELAND?

It is clear that most of today's entertainment programs are designed to please most of the people—and our study indicates that they usually succeed. It is equally clear that most of the programs do not please all of the people—at least not equally; that significant differences in taste exist, especially between audience segments with different levels of cultural attainment.

By definition, the better-educated, more sophisticated viewers will have tastes different from (and in their opinion, better than) those with less exposure to the finer things. So long as differential education and cultural levels exist in the population, so will different capacities to appreciate and enjoy various forms of diversion and recreation. That is inevitable. So it is probably inevitable that programs catering to the "mass taste" are, for the intellectual, synonymous with "vast waste"—though he may not always take explicit account of that fact and its consequences:

> If you decide to have a system of people's television, then people's television you must expect it to be . . . and it will reflect their likes and dislikes, what they can comprehend and what is beyond them. Every person of common sense knows that people of superior mental constitutions are bound to find much of television intellectually beneath them. If such

[3] All discussants, of course, should give up clichés in favor of specific evaluations. *The Untouchables* can't touch Shakespeare or the Greeks when it comes to real (audience-experienced) "violence"; *Alice in Wonderland* and Gulliver "escape from reality" as few canned comedies do; and religion, as I am not the first to point out, may be an even more effective soporific or opiate than *The Late Show*.

innately fortunate people cannot realize this gently and with good manners, if in their hearts they despise popular pleasures and interests, then, of course, they will be angrily dissatisfied with television. But it is not really television with which they are dissatisfied. It is with people.[4]

"BALANCE" — THE ANSWER, OR THE QUESTION?

These and other taste distinctions within the total audience raise questions about what the general level and nature of TV entertainment *should* be, and most important, about the range of its coverage and the relative proportions at various points. Should television "cater to" or should it "elevate"? *Whom* should television serve, and how often?

From the democratic point of view,[5] an appealing answer is "balance." These are not issues to be decided one way or the other; the obvious resolution is to spread the medium across the diversity of tastes and interests represented in the audience. The air waves belong to the people—everyone should have his fair share:

> Let me make clear that what I am talking about is balance. I believe that the public interest is made up of many interests. There are many people in this great country and you must serve all of us.

But that, of course, simply states the problem. The issue lies not in the principle of "balance," but in its practical translation. What does "fair share" mean? Who is, and who is not, getting his at present?

This is the locus of the debate, and the question is not just one of information. Suppose we *really* knew what every viewer *really* wanted to see, how much of it, and during what hours. How would that information, complete and final as it would be, translate into a balanced schedule that takes these conflicting interests into account, each in its fair measure?

Here are some of the issues in vastly oversimplified form. Suppose there are only *two* audience segments, A and B; and only two types of programs, "a" and "b." Assume, further, that tastes are obligingly differentiated in the simplest possible manner—A will watch only "a," and B, only "b." Finally, let us say that A's outnumber B's by three to one, and that A's, on the average, presently watch twice as much TV.

Now, what would a perfectly balanced schedule look like? Should there be equal amounts of "a" and "b," so that every individual audience member has an equal chance of having his interests served? Should there be three times as much "a" material because it has three times the potential

---

[4] Sir Robert Fraser, at the Manchester Lunch Club, May 17, 1960.

[5] The Platonic alternative, of course, removes all issues other than who will decide, and who will decide *that*.

audience? Or twice as much, on the grounds that each "a" consumer has twice the appetite? Or should it be sixfold over "b," to take both of these differences into account?

In real life, of course, the picture is not nearly so "simple," and the conceptual problems (unsolved in the simple case) multiply unbelievably. In the first place, we need at least all the letters in the alphabet, and some of their combinations, to describe the possible taste and program categories. Next, the audience groupings are not really mutually exclusive, and what is worse, they have differential taste flexibility. A's will watch some "b," and vice versa; but the chances are not the same: for example, the college-educated watch comedy or adventure far more frequently than the barely literate will tune to heavy information. In some case, then, the first choice for one segment is a close second choice for another; while the preferred fare of the second may be entirely uninteresting or incomprehensible to the first. That, too, should get into the equation.

In real life, also, the different segments make differential use of the total medium. Some depend almost entirely upon TV for entertainment and information, while others have many other sources that cater to their special tastes. Should that be a factor; if so, how much weight should it get?

In the economic sphere, we ordinarily leave such problems to the "invisible hand," or free market. That giant computer assumes that willingness to pay is a good indicator of need or want, puts all the facts together, adds the appropriate weights, and decides what shall be produced, and in what quantities. It makes both Chevrolets and Cadillacs, rock-and-roll records and stereophonic tapes of organ recitals. And it makes each in about the quantities that people want (and, incidentally, at appropriate differential costs).

But some argue that that model is largely unworkable or inapplicable here, where a limited resource is allocated to a limited number of licensed "producers" or distributors, under certain constraints, who sell not directly to the public but to advertisers.[6]

According to them, "balance" cannot be defined as what happens of itself when you simply leave the present system alone. And so it seems to me to rest with those employing the concept—whether to argue that television is or is not balanced—to state precisely what they mean, and how they know. If "balance" is to be a real and not just a rhetorical goal, we have to know how far away we are, and especially how we know when we get there.

---

[6] Most free-market economists consider the licensing procedure the *only* relevant constraint.

ROBERT ECK

The Real Masters

of Television

As the television network librarians begin to tally and rack this season's last cans of film and tape, it is possible to predict with sad certainty what next year will bring.

Except for more old movies, next year's commercial television will be the same as this has been. The same green tendrils of hope will grow into the same weedy crop of formula-written, formula-directed shows, ranging from pseudo-Westerns through cast-iron fantasies, to what *Variety* once called hix pix. This prediction is also valid for 1968, and the year after that, and the year after that, ad infinitum.

Why can't commercial television be improved? After all, its diseases seem to be no mystery. Everyone knows it is infested by evil advertising men who befoul the programs with their greedy touch. Their dupes, the sponsors, are for the most part a group of well-meaning, affluent bumblers —misguided souls who need instruction in cultural responsibility from you, me, Goodman Ace, and David Susskind. The networks they deal with are stupid bureaucracies, dominated by frightened vice-presidents, natural enemies of everything that is fresh and intelligent. To make matters worse, all three idiot species are being bamboozled by a fourth: the audience researcher, a charlatan who has persuaded them he can take a continuous count of the nation's many millions of television viewers, either by telephoning the homes or bugging the sets of a thousand or two families whose identities are shrouded in mystery. By contrast to these fools

Robert Eck is an associate copy director of one of the country's busiest advertising agencies, based in Chicago. "The Real Masters of Television" is reprinted from the March, 1967 issue of *Harper's Magazine* by permission of the author. Copyright © 1967 by Minneapolis Star and Tribune Co., Inc.

and villains, there are a few exemplary sponsors who, out of the sheer goodness of their enlightened hearts, pay for the programs you and I like. And waiting in the wings is a benevolent government, needing only stronger prompting to move onstage and straighten out the mess.

If these familiar figures of cocktail-party folklore even came close to representing the actualities of commercial television, there might be some hope for improvement. But they do not. They are a collection of wishes, falsehoods, and semitruths, embodied in explanatory myths. As we shall see, it is not because of these myths but because of the more complex realities underlying them that commercial television is as amenable to reform as the adult Bengal tiger.

THE MYTH OF
THE EVIL ADMAN'S INFLUENCE

While it has become fashionable among intellectual liberals to lay the sins of our materialism at the doorstep of the advertising agent, today's television programming is one sin he can rightly disclaim. He has virtually nothing to say about it. There was a time when he was a grand panjandrum of programming, but that was thirty years ago, in the heyday of radio, when advertising agencies literally produced the programs their clients sponsored. In 1940, for example, A. D. Lasker, the head of Pepsodent's advertising agency, could decide whether Bob Hope, popular star of Pepsodent's radio show, would get the thousand-dollar weekly raise he was asking for. In 1967, Johnny Carson, popular star of *The Tonight Show*, who earns over $200,000 a year, need not even say hello to an advertising agent.

Although the business patterns of radio carried over into the early days of television, by the mid-1950s the television networks succeeded in taking away from the advertising men the controls they had historically exercised over program material. In this, the networks had no choice. Not only were television shows far more difficult to produce than radio shows, but television itself was rapidly growing into a business far more vast and risky—a business in which the profits (and the eventual existence) of a network depended not on its ability to cozen sponsors but to deliver measurable audience. Programming—the means of doing this—could not be left in the hands of outsiders, semi-professionals, men to whom entertainment was only a sideline.

For the same reasons, production of television shows shifted from Chicago and New York to the foothills of the Santa Monica mountains. The moviemakers out there were not only the most expert producers of mass entertainment but also the most efficient. The money put into a live production is gone the moment the floodlights die, but films can be sold and resold, again and again, both here and abroad. A filmed TV series can be profitable even if it loses money on its first run.

Nowadays, the networks make a practice of inviting advertisers and their agencies to preview the prototype films of such series (the pilots), but that's about as far as it goes. Admen do not put programs on the air, don't materially change them once they're on, and don't take them off.

THE MYTH OF
THE AUDIENCE-COUNTING CHARLATANS

Nothing about television has been the subject of so much childish pique and wishful thinking as the rating servies which undertake to measure television audiences. Inside the business, they are hated and feared, because their tabulations can make a man a potential millionaire or a failure in a matter of weeks. Outside, they are distrusted by many egocentric citizens who refuse to believe that the viewing habits of a small group of strangers could possibly reflect their own and, by the same token, the nation's. These are the people who, in the words of a disgusted research director, "think you have to drink the whole quart of milk to discover it is sour."

The plain truth about audience counting is that nobody in his right mind would spend millions out of a private, corporate, political, or charitable purse to propel images into an uncharted void. Even the BBC uses random samples of its audience for guidance. And while random sampling can always be attacked because it only approaches perfection, so can a literal head-count. The more heads that must be counted, the more chances there are for human error in interviewing and arithmetic. This is why the Bureau of the Census sometimes prefers random sampling to a total count.

The standard, though far from the only audience sample in the television business is that of the Nielsen Audimeter survey, which measures audience continuously by means of a recording device attached to television sets in some 1,400 homes. There are a few drawbacks to this ingenious system. First, it assumes that whenever a set is turned on, so are its owners, which is usually, but not always, true. Second, families who are *not* keenly interested in television generally refuse to let the Nielsen people install Audimeters in their sets. Third, not all Audimeter recordings reach Nielsen headquarters in Evanston, Illinois, in time for inclusion in the tabulations. Fourth, the Nielsen sample has an admitted statistical error of three points.

Of course, the networks, the advertisers, the agencies, all of whom employ statistical experts, are fully aware of the weaknesses of the Nielsen figures; but they also know that these figures are considerably better than none at all, so they use them in a fairly uninhibited fashion.

The two most important aspects of this use seem to have escaped public notice:

(1) Both the men who run the networks and the men who run the companies that use network advertising know that everyone uses the same audience figures and that, therefore, their competitors are subject to the same errors and inadequacies as are they. For competitive business purposes, the inadequacies of the ratings tend to wash out over a period of time, just as would the inadequacies of a short deck in a poker game.

(2) The audience count is not a popularity contest or even primarily a guide to the judgment of network executives. It is part of a financial measurement.

For each dollar a businessman spends, he wants a comparative measure of what it has bought. In the case of advertising audience, his measure is cost per thousand people reached. He started using this measure long before network television, or even network radio, existed. To find which of several newspapers or magazines gave him the most for his money, he divided the cost of putting an ad in each of them by the number of thousands of people who bought copies. Now he does the same for television, dividing the cost of a minute commercial (about $40,000 in prime evening time) by the number of thousands of viewers who were tuned in.

"How much do I pay for every thousand people my commercial reaches —a dollar-and-a-half, a dollar-seventy-five, two dollars, two-twenty-five?" It is on the answer to this question that television shows succeed or fail, far more than on the gross figures of the Nielsen or Trendex ratings. The BBC, of course, would never use its audience figures in this way, but the BBC has no stockholders and requires no profits.

THE MYTH OF
THE BUMBLING, UNENLIGHTENED SPONSORS

A shocking thing has happened to most old-fashioned television sponsors. They have disappeared. In their place is a heartless scheme called a scatter plan. Except in moments of extreme frustration, nobody in the business ever wanted a sponsor to vanish. A few years ago, in fact, the networks would only sell the commercial use of a weekly show to a regular weekly sponsor or, at most, to two alternating sponsors. However, the supply of companies with enough advertising money to buy television time this way is limited. NBC and CBS, then the undisputed leaders of the field, were able to attract such large advertisers without undue difficulty. But it was a different matter for ABC. Lacking the programming, the audience, and the stations to get all the large sponsors it needed, ABC began selling off its unsponsored time *à la carte*, offering smaller advertisers the chance to buy a minute here and a minute there.

What began as pure expedient has since grown to be the dominant trade practice, transformed into the scatter plan, a sophisticated purchasing device that permits the advertiser to purposefully scatter his commercials among different shows on the same network. Most television advertisers, including the biggest, are delighted with the scatter plan because it permits them to reach a wider number of viewers; it offers them more likelihood of reaching the kind of viewers they want to reach; it lets them suit their expenditures to the season (as the barrage before Christmas or June graduation indicates); and it averages their risks. Sponsored shows may turn out to be unwatched turkeys; scatter plans do not.

That's why probably three-quarters of all national television—amounting to around a billion dollars annually—is now paid for by scatter plans. It's not unusual for Procter & Gamble, one of the country's three or four heaviest television advertisers, to have commercials for its products on thirty to forty shows. A booming pharmaceutical firm such as Miles Laboratories may have commercials on half that number.

A scatter plan is born when an advertising agency tells the networks that one of its clients is in the market for television time, and describes the nature of the desired audience. If a client is a breakfast-food maker, he will usually want a family audience, which he can get by scattering his commercials among . . . early evening shows. . . . If he makes floor wax, he will pick daytime shows that appeal more to women than to children. The businesses that make stickum for false teeth and mine gold out of tired blood want to talk to older people, which means they prefer such shows as *Candid Camera*, *What's My Line?*, and *The Lawrence Welk Show*.

The scatter plans submitted by the networks are almost never bought before being subjected to a process of juggling and horse trading: "Look, the way it is now, the price is all wrong. A dollar-fifty-four a thousand. And you've given us four minutes on *Make a Bet*, which we all know is a dog. Tell you what, though, we'll take two of those four minutes on *Make a Bet*, if you'll give us the other two minutes on a *Lucy* re-run." If the suggested changes are made and the plan bought, a housewife in Houston will see a new commercial while watching a re-run of *I Love Lucy*. She will never know or care that somewhere up North, an agency man is telling his client, "On the basis of the Nielsens, we are getting daytime women for a dollar-forty-seven a thousand," and that she is a .147-cent daytime woman.

For all his arrogant foibles, the old-time sponsor usually took a proprietary pride in his show. It was more apt to be a manifestation of his vanity than an accurate reflection of the show's intrinsic worth, but it did exist and it could be appealed to. It has been replaced by the depersonalized processes of an audience market, in which viewers by the millions are counted, sorted, graded, and sold to specification at so much a thousand head. There is not much to be gained by writing a letter of praise—or disgust—to a scatter plan.

THE MYTH OF
THE EXEMPLARY, ENLIGHTENED SPONSORS

Most of the fast-vanishing breed of real sponsors remaining on television are distinguished by their benignity. They sponsor fine programs and regularly receive Good Boy Medals in the form of various trophies, plaques, and journalistic commendations, accompanied by the wistfully spoken hope that other advertisers will take the hint and become good boys, too.

This, alas, will never be. The good sponsor is a rare bird not only in its sponsoring habits but also in its generally peculiar business characteristics. Unlike the bulk of television advertisers, the sponsor of the *Bell Telephone Hour* is a huge natural monopoly whose profits will not be even slightly affected by the way it uses television. The *Hallmark Hall of Fame* is the darling of one of the last of the old school of owner-managers, a rough-hewn multimillionaire named Joyce Hall, who can do pretty much what he likes. What he likes is to sponsor inoffensive plays of proven worth, elegantly produced. The extent to which this has helped Hallmark sales will never be known since greeting-card sales do not respond to television advertising in the directly traceable way sales of many household products do.

Other "cultural" sponsors are often companies with small advertising budgets who use the opportunity afforded by public-affairs or cultural-uplift shows to buy television time cheap. Prior to each season, the networks plan for and underwrite the costs of a number of thoughtful pieces of reportage and a few well-intended dramatic shows, knowing even as they do it, that low audience forecasts will make it necessary to sell them off to commercial sponsors at a loss.

A startling insight into the strange economics of such programs is provided by the case of the Arthur Miller play, *Death of a Salesman,* one of the most impressive shows of 1966. It was produced by David Susskind and sponsored by Xerox Coropration, a company that in May 1966, received a trustees' award from the Academy of Television Arts and Sciences for its contributions to the betterment of television programming.

However, Susskind was not paid to produce *Salesman* by this exemplary sponsor, but by CBS, in whose vaults the completed tape reposed for some months while CBS vainly sought sponsors—and while the asking price kept dropping. When Xerox at last bought the telecast of the play, they got it for what can be described in today's market as a song. The financial realities behind *Death of a Salesman* are:

Production cost (with no profit for the network)	$580,000
Network time charges	300,000
Total cost to CBS	$880,000
Price to Xerox	250,000
Net loss to CBS	$630,000

In other words, the real sponsor of *Death of a Salesman* was the network, which cut its losses by selling the ostensible sponsorship to Xerox, a company whose enormous profits and lack of need for broad television audience eminently qualify it for the role of patron of the arts.

As time goes by, we shall probably see fewer rather than more good sponsors in television. In the case of the authentically benevolent sponsors, the by-guess-and-by-God judgment of old-line management will give way to the facts-and-figures quantification of Harvard Business School graduates. The rest of the good sponsors are dependent on the willingness of the networks to produce and sell good shows at fire-sale prices. Since the networks' recent profits have been phenomenal, we can assume their current willingness to absorb losses for the sake of prestige is about as high as it is ever going to be. Any reverses in profit will probably be reflected by the departure of some of those good sponsors who are only good when the network helps them be.

THE MYTH OF
THE STUPID BUREAUCRATIC NETWORKS
AND THEIR FRIGHTENED VICE-PRESIDENTS

"Television is a triumph of equipment over people and the minds that control it are so small you could put them in the navel of a flea and still have room beside them for a network vice-president's heart."

When Fred Allen said that in 1952, he was suffering from an illusion still shared by millions who assume from the nature of most television programming that the networks are in the communications and entertainment business.

They are not.

It is true they deal in communications and entertainment. It is true that millions of words are annually printed to describe television programming. It is also true that from time to time, a network president will strike a Belasco pose. But the fact is that, unlike a Belasco, a Merrick, or a Bing, he collects no subscriptions and has no box office. He gets every cent of his money from advertisers. The network he operates is a gigantic, electronic medicine wagon with a Hollywood cast, whose entire reason for being lies in its ability to gather millions of men, women, and children to see and hear the advertiser's pitch.

The networks' business is the audience-delivery business, and if their vice-presidents are frightened men, they have good reason to be. They are involved in a unique and frightening enterprise. Their customer, the typical television advertiser, is a maker of package goods. His products (soda pop, soap, prepared foods, etc.) cost little, are bought often, and are used in every home. His audience requirements are limitless and unrelated to cultural or socioeconomic levels. He wants as much audience as he can get as cheap as he can get it.

This customer's principal audience supplier, the network, knows that for its part, the more scatter-plan audience it can deliver per dollar of production and telecasting charges, the lower the advertiser's true cost will be, the more he will tend to use the network for his advertising, and the more money the network will make. What this has led to is unparalleled in the history of publication, radio, theater, or motion pictures—a quest for audience which, carried to its logical end, is impossible and absurd. The mechanical rabbit each network is chasing is no less than total share of total audience: all the television viewers in the United States. No network will ever catch the rabbit, but they cannot stop themselves from trying.

The consequences of the chase revealed themselves drastically for the first time during the 1959–60 season, a year that gave the lie to the irreparable optimists who thought, and still may think, that television, properly used, can slowly lift the tastes of the masses, shaw by shaw, until 25 million American families commonly spend evenings of Shakespeare in their living rooms.

In 1959, NBC and CBS were sufficiently rich and successful to try to inaugurate a process of cultural uplift and were, in fact, presenting a fairly wide spectrum of regular programming which ranged from *Playhouse 90* to the equally well-rehearsed *$64,000 Question*. ABC, unfortunately, was poor, insecure, and ambitious. In the fall of 1959, under the guidance of a shrewd, personable sales executive, Oliver Treyz, ABC launched a group of new shows distinguished by stylized violence and unstylized gore. Its many new cops-and-robbers shows included the renowned *Untouchables* series, as well as *Hawaiian Eye* and *The Detec-*

tives, while five new Westerns brought its total number of Westerns to a total of ten a week.

This move was righteously criticized in press and pulpit but, in terms of the multitudes of viewers it could deliver to advertisers, the 1959–60 season proved the turning point in the fortunes of ABC. As an audience-delivery system, it suddenly moved up from a low third place to a close second, forcing NBC and CBS to compromise their programming standards so rapidly and completely that by spring of 1961, Olie Treyz had what must have been the extreme pleasure of salting his competitors' wounds. In a speech delivered in April of that year, he accused NBC and CBS of slavishly copying ABC's grand new program ideas and coolly suggested they stick to their own lasts.

Of course they weren't about to follow Treyz's advice. He had taught them a lesson of the most unforgettable kind: an expensive one. In the audience-delivery business, you do not have the luxury of setting either your standards or those of your audience. Instead, they are set for you by the relative success of your competitors.

Since then, the pursuit of total audience has been conducted with tactics not always successful but usually pragmatic and cunning. In general, the networks have learned how to deftly mass-produce the predictable novelties and uncomplicated heroes, clowns, and villains that have always delighted the mass of humanity. . . . Zane Grey, Gene Porter, Conan Doyle, and most of the other turn-of-the-century popular novelists could have been highly successful television writers. Moreover, if you bother to examine such popular home entertainment devices of the thirties as *The Saturday Evening Post* and *Collier's,* you will find a blueprint for most of today's nighttime programming in the form of serial episodes built around a few continuing characters: the Mr. Glencannon sea stories, the Ephraim Tutt law stories, the Perry Mason and Nero Wolfe detective stories. Westerns were an editorial habit. Other program materials can be traced to the once-popular, now vanished, pulp magazines that specialized in war, Western, crime, and science fiction.

In the circumstances, it is inaccurate to complain that the audience-delivery systems are subverting the popular taste. What they are doing is accommodating it better than it has ever been accommodated before. A prime example is the TV version of the Western. Western films have been a foolproof staple of the entertainment field ever since Blace Tracey silently gunned down Silk Miller in *Hell's Hinges,* fifty years ago, because they can be filmed with cost-cutting speed and almost invariably make money. So it is hardly surprising to find a lot of television time given over to the horse opera. What comes as a slight shock is to realize that many of television's so-called Westerns—including the most popular—aren't real Westerns at all. From time to time, a posse may still pursue the villains up the draw, a stage may be held up, there may be gunfights; but for the most part television's Western heroes are concerned with Human Problems. The badman is as frequently reformed as killed. Often he is completely missing from the script.

For purposes of audience delivery, the trouble with the authentic Western is that its appeal is restricted to grown men and small boys; so a bastard form has begun to replace it, the sagebrush soap opera: Marshall Dillon of *Gunsmoke* is Dodge City's resident sociologist and Ben Cartwright, the patriarch of *Bonanza*, is kindly, wise, old Father Barbour in chaps. Underneath the outward semblance of the violent morality play that men and boys find relieving and pleasurable, the sagebrush soap opera presents the emotionally manipulative, self-conscious interplay of communal and family personalities women enjoy. The hero may, in fact, be an entire family, because the show is intended to attract entire families.

The immense popularity of *Bonanza*, champion of this new breed, testifies to the fact that the constant attempt to deliver larger audiences has made American commercial television the most awesome mechanism of mass entertainment ever devised. Week in and week out, *Bonanza* draws audiences far larger than the total population of most European countries. A number of other shows draw almost as strongly; and during the prime evening hours, the average number of viewers attracted by the combined offerings of the three networks can be estimated at around 70 million.

That is quite a house.

To suggest in the face of such monumental achievement that the networks have failed is to spit into the wind. In their own terms, at least, they have been a resounding success. Today, as they settle into their mature business practice, we can confidently expect them to continue chasing the uncatchable rabbit with the sharpened skills and elastic agility born of bitter but rewarding experience. Theirs is an infinite pursuit which has in it small room for cultural dabblings.

THE MYTH OF
THE BENEVOLENT GOVERNMENTAL POWER

During his tenure as crusading chairman of the Federal Communications Commission, Newton Minow, with strong support from the press, managed to badger the networks into carrying slightly more public-service programming. He also managed to convey to the public the impression that the federal government was capable of improving the quality of commercial television.

That is mostly a false impression. Not only is the power to regulate program content specifically denied the Commission under section 326 of the Federal Communications Act; it is doubtful that any such power could exist because of the practical difficulties that lie in the way of defining it. To put up a stop sign at a traffic intersection, and require everyone to come to a full stop before crossing, is a perfectly workable arrangement. But to put up a sign saying "good judgment," and to pass a law requiring everyone to use good judgment before crossing, verges on nonsense. Yet the problem of defining good judgment at an intersection is trivial beside the problem of defining good judgment in the construction of the 7,000 hours of programming each station broadcasts in the course of a year.

What the government can do—and has done very little—is encourage alternatives to commercial network television. . . .

The common denominator of these alternatives is that all of them— UHF, satellite communications, pay-TV—are products of advances in a sophisticated and rapidly accelerating technology. This technology itself eventually may supply the most flexible and practical alternative to commercial television in the form of a simple, low-cost video recorder-player for home use. There now exists a small recorder which uses ordinary quarter-inch audio tape to record and play back both color and black-and-white television programs. Invented by Marvin Camras of the Illinois Institute of Technology's Research Institute, it is capable of recording or playing two hours of unbroken material and could be made to sell for less than $300. In essence, the video recorder (and someday there will be even easier and cheaper forms of it) is an alternative not only to commercial television, but also to pay-TV, for widespread ownership of recorders would result in a video recording industry and in the sale, rental, and library loan of recorded television programs of much the same general range as today's audio recordings. The effective differences between commercial television, pay-TV, and video recording can be put this way: no matter how much you might like to see a special television production of Der Freischütz, you are not likely to see it on commercial television. In the improbable event that it does appear, it will do so just once, on a Saturday or Sunday afternoon, and it will be thoroughly fractured by commercials. Your chances of seeing it on pay-TV would probably not be a great deal better. If it should be programmed, there would be no commercials, but you would have to watch it on one of the few days it was being presented. With video recorders and recordings, your chances of seeing Der Freischütz would be quite good. You could rent it without any commercials and watch it any time of the day you pleased.

Unfortunately, however, this agreeable prospect lies some distance in the future—by five, ten, or fifteen years. Right now, the large electronics firms are too busy making color sets for the multitudinous majority who dote on commercial television to worry about making recorders for the minority who do not.

And until video recording or some other alternative is realized, we will continue to be stuck with commercial television, which will continue to grind its repetitive, skillful, profitable way. Television reviewers will angrily scold, instructively praise, and loudly hope. Television producers will brag about hairbreadth advances over mediocrity. Television executives will count their cultural contributions and discuss their frequently magnificent public-information programs. Do not be deceived. Critics and defenders alike are symbiotically linked to the great audience-delivery systems. Those systems are married to cost-per-thousand, compelled to the pursuit of total audience, and—with factories in Hollywood, main offices in New York, gala introductory promotions each fall, and franchised dealers throughout the country—are among America's biggest and most successful mass-production businesses.

Ask NBC to give you just two unbroken hours of fine, honest repertory one evening a week for thirty-nine weeks.

If they will, General Motors will build you an Aston Martin.

JOHN TEBBEL

TV and the Arts:
The Prospect Before Us

We have reached the point in the development of television where the private monopoly in programing enjoyed by the networks has come into direct conflict with the public interest on a number of fronts. Nowhere, perhaps, has this conflict been sharper than on the cultural front. For years the medium has been under heavy attack by people who despise its cultural poverty, and recently there has also been a marked disaffection in the mass audience itself—a boredom with the product. No group is more bored than the young. College students who were glued to the tube as children now turn away from it. To use the most battered word of our times, they do not consider it relevant—politically, culturally, or any other way.

Even movies, upon which television has been relying so heavily, show signs of slipping in popularity. Motion picture audiences in this country are growing steadily younger, but the movies shown on television reflect, in general, the conventional middle-class and middle-aged values which have dominated movie exhibition in small towns for decades. The young prefer the kind of movies shown in art houses in cities and college communities; television does not dare show these films except occasionally and late—and even then, in cut versions—or on a UHF channel which has relatively little to lose. People who do watch movies on television are more and more irritated by the stupefying number of commercials, which often make the picture itself seem almost incidental.

As Jack Gould remarked recently in *The New York Times*, "much more direction and push from New York will be indicated to induce Hollywood

John Tebbel is professor of journalism at New York University. "TV and Arts: The Prospect Before Us" is reprinted from *Saturday Review*, April 26, 1969, with permission. Copyright 1969 Saturday Review Inc.

to forget about formula stuff and use TV as a creative instrument in its own right. Sales-oriented executives, capable in their chosen field but largely numb in terms of venturous theater, still dominate too many decisions at the TV networks."

True, perhaps, but critics and resident intellectuals will likely be one with Nineveh and Tyre before TV is used "as a creative instrument in its own right" by those who presently control it. For television is a *mass* medium, in the truest sense of that abused phrase, and what television's critics sometimes forget is that the history of mass culture shows us that the more the base of a medium is broadened, the lower its cultural level will be. Television has the broadest base of any medium, and by and large, it rests at the lowest cultural level.

What else should we expect? For more than a decade, the critical litany has been that if television's entrepreneurs would only conceive of their medium in the lofty terms everyone envisioned when it first appeared as a factor in national life, everything would be fine. It is asserted repeatedly that the networks underestimate their audiences, that the ratings game is rigged and does not truly represent the national taste, and that programing more closely reflects the commercialism of the network operators than it does the cultural potential of the audience.

One could argue this question endlessly, and indeed that seems to be its fate. It is not difficult to cast doubts on the ratings business; sometimes the business obligingly casts doubts on itself. Nor is it hard to castigate much, or most, of what appears on television; no dead horse has ever been beaten more thoroughly. But had the Caesars given the ancient Romans chamber music instead of bread and circuses, there is no reason to believe that the cultural level of the populace would have been raised appreciably.

If the critics are right, they will have to explain why *Bonanza* was not only the number one show in America for so long, but quickly attained that status in every country where it was shown, in Europe and Asia alike. *Bonanza*, situation comedies of every stripe, audience participation games, daytime serials, old Hollywood movies, new Hollywood movies— all have one thing in common. They are mass entertainments, designed for a mass medium.

As long as television remains a private commercial enterprise instead of a government-sponsored institution, as it is almost everywhere else, it seems idle to condemn the network heads for programing what they know most people will look at, and therefore what these businessmen will be able to sell best. Surely the hope for the future does not lie in trying to persuade or force the networks to purvey something that would result in their economic suicide. Nor does it lie in government ownership or greater federal control. (Curiously, one hears and reads the same criticisms of television in Britain that are so common here.) Recent attempts to force the networks and individual stations to provide a diversity of programing on FM channels have met with failure, except in a handful of cases.

Would it not be more rational to accept the fact that there is a mass audience with concurrent tastes, to which commercial television is going to cater despite whatever vicissitudes of programing it may pass through as public taste fluctuates within a necessarily narrow range? Then would it not be better to proceed from that point and work out ways and means by which minority cultural tastes can be met and satisfied? Is there any valid reason why *Bonanza* cannot coexist with programing for a higher level of taste?

The consensus today seems to be that a viable alternative to commercial television must be provided, if the medium is to have any meaning beyond simple mass entertainment. As matters stand, music lovers cannot turn to it. What was once offered, holding so much promise, has virtually disappeared. . . . FM radio is the only resource for those who want serious music, and even there it is under commercial pressures that are presently diminishing its presence. Similarly, the balletomane finds dance represented only fleetingly in occasional "specials." Looking at art is a growing interest among Americans, as crowded galleries and museums testify, but it is scarcely represented on television. Theater on the tube, which once held the most promise of all, has also been largely relegated to "specials," and many of these are of doubtful quality. Serious, young, creative playwrights no longer turn to television, as they did at its inception.

If we agree that a viable alternative is essential, two formidable questions arise: Who determines what is to be programed? And how is it to be financed?

The second question is the more difficult. Television is by far the most expensive of the media, and there is little reason to believe it will ever be less costly, except at the receiving end. The cost of experimenting, even of trying to establish the best alternative, has brought nearly every reform attempt to the brink of disaster.

In the case of the Ford Foundation-sponsored Public Broadcast Laboratory, one can see how hard it is going to be to answer both questions. The PBL was financed as a two-year experiment to extend and explore the range of viable alternatives to commercial television already being offered by National Educational Television; as such, it was able to use the facilities of NET stations around the country. It had some splendid plans. Yet, from the beginning it had to contend with a wide disparity of ideas, among everyone concerned, about what constituted good public broadcasting. The governing editorial board disagreed with the creative staff; the creative staff often disagreed with itself.

Early in April, with its time running out, PBL was pronounced officially dead, but some of its basic concepts and its production staff were to be preserved in a restructuring of educational television by the Corporation for Public Broadcasting. Remaining would be a two-hour Sunday night show, in which the emphasis would be more on culture and less on public affairs. The PBL experiment cost $12,000,000 for its two-year run, but the expenditure was justified, perhaps, if for no other reason than that it focused at least some public attention on a few of the possibilities for new programing that could be directed toward the audience which NET has established.

Clearly, foundations cannot carry the burden of alternative broadcasting alone. As matters seem to be working out in the case of PBL and elsewhere, the Corporation for Public Broadcasting may become the major factor in noncommercial transmission. The Corporation was created by the Public Broadcasting Act of 1968. Its fifteen-member board of directors, composed of distinguished citizens, subsequently appointed John W. Macy, Jr., as president of the Corporation. Macy, a former university vice president, had been chairman of the Civil Service Commission and was the Johnson Administration's principal talent scout for federal jobs. He came to his new job with an open mind, having had no previous broadcasting experience.

After his appointment, Macy observed that public television should be "broadly educational," and expressed the belief that local noncommercial stations should not be dominated by a national network. Some facts have been faced by the new Corporation. Frank Pace, its chairman, has said bluntly that there is no alternative to federal funding, and Macy has laid it down that this funding must not impair "freedom from federal interference." Among those who know Congress best, no bets are being taken. Indeed, the kind of help we may expect from Congress could be seen in the March hearings of the communications subcommittee of the Senate Commerce Committee. The Congressmen were disturbed about violence and sex. They thought a television commercial for shaving cream was too suggestive, and one Senator was offended by the fact that *La Dolce Vita*, a motion picture which has been shown without incident all over the world, was exhibited on a Washington station, where presumably the air is purer.

On the subject of violence, the subcommittee offered the novel proposition that it ought to be removed from television, leaving viewers with no knowledge of it except what could be gleaned from newspapers, books, magazines, and movies, not to mention the streets of any city. Television, of course, is the only medium where violence can be censored by Congress.

But again, the chief problem the Corporation for Public Broadcasting faces is money. When Congress created the Corporation, it gave it a niggardly $5,000,000 on which to operate temporarily. Macy expected to go before Congress sometime this month to ask the House Appropriations Committee for $20,000,000 to cover the fiscal year 1970—an exceedingly modest amount, measured by present television costs.

The Corporation's energies and influence will be directed toward the existing noncommercial alternative—approximately 160 educational stations in the nation, which PBL had helped to pull into a network albeit split at times by dissensions over program content. The Corporation intends to keep its hands off programing. "It is important that we not become a judge of individual programing," Macy has said. "We will never tell a local station what is best for its community." What *will* the Corporation do, then? It would, said Macy, aid the national community effort of educational TV by getting funds, assisting in developing and procuring physical facilities such as color equipment, and in general—through grants and other means—bolster and further resources of NET.

What this means, translated into practical terms, is that the Corporation will make an attempt to provide—at last—adequate financing for the whole educational television system, a large part of which has been gasping for financial air since it began. While it is getting money out of Congress, the Corporation will also act as a buffer between the stations and their probably reluctant benefactors, who may be expected to yield to the temptation to find out if they are getting what, in their opinion, is their money's worth, and if not, to suggest suitable changes.

In announcing the major reorganization of educational television that decided PBL's fate, Macy and Fred W. Friendly, television consultant to Ford Foundation President McGeorge Bundy, made some highly encouraging gestures in the direction of culture. Not only would there be the new two-hour program on Sunday night, devoted to cultural events, but there would be such heartening developments as the creation of a television opera company and a revival of the New York Television Theater, along with better national distribution systems to make this programing accessible to larger audiences.

It was encouraging, too, to note that NET would get approximately $7,600,000 in grants for the coming year, and that the Ford Foundation was granting $5,000,000 directly to fifteen individual stations. Yet this largess only underlined the ultimate problem faced by noncommercial television. Foundation money and private grants, welcome and essential as they are at this stage, cannot sustain alternative television much longer. It will take relatively massive infusions of government money to accomplish what must be done, and the infusions must not be governed by the opinion of Congressmen, individually or even collectively, as to what television should program.

The most likely way to avoid many of noncommercial television's problems appears to be implicit in the report issued late last year by President Johnson's task force on national communications policy. The report focused directly on the diversity of programing, which is the only realistic answer to satisfying all the viewing public all of the time. Briefly, it proposed to give both controversial pay television and comparably controversial cable television equal opportunities to provide the diversity. These opportunities would come not a moment too soon, if they are grasped, because technology, as usual, has outstripped the planners and bureaucrats alike, creating a potentially chaotic situation that might take years to sort out.

Broadly, the report accepts the fact that viewers are going to be bombarded with communications signals ranging all the way from international broadcasting via satellites (turning loose a new set of formidable problems) to communities which will be absorbing not only the familiar commercial variety of TV but specialized programs for special audiences via cable and pay television. Without federal regulation and control of some kind, there is not the slightest doubt that all these endeavors will wind up eventually in the enormous pockets of a national or possibly an international commercial agglomerate.

To oversee this incipient monster and guide it in the public interest, the report advocates creating a major new federal agency, under the Executive branch, which would not replace but rather supplement the FCC. A single corporation under federal regulation would govern international satellite communications, as well as cables and high-frequency radio. There will, of course, be no satellite system at all unless the Government invests in one. Most significantly, cable television is to be given a green light, although with cautionary provisions which at the moment have virtually stalled it.

The conflict will immediately center here. The commercial networks have already worked hard trying to destroy pay television, and they are well aware that cable television is an even better device to break their monopoly. It is also "the other woman" capable of ending the happy marriage between commercial TV and the movies, and the motion picture companies are already investigating whether transmission of motion pictures by cable companies is a violation of copyright. Fleets of lawyers have steamed into the cable TV sea of controversy, and no one knows when this legal blockade will be broken.

Some encouragement came from the Justice Department early this April, when Richard W. McLaren, Anti-Trust Division chief in a letter to the FCC described cable TV as "the most promising means of achieving greater competition and diversity in local mass media communications," and indicated that his division supported the cable companies.

Again, the question is freedom. If cable television is to provide real diversification, it must be free to transmit all the signals it can gather, even if they come from a distance. The Anti-Trust Division apparently upholds this freedom, since it urges the FCC to relax its present restrictions on cable companies that forbid them to broadcast in large cities competitive programs being carried out of town. The cable companies, however, will have to devise a system of payment for what they distribute. There will also have to be moves to prevent newspapers or television stations in a particular locality from owning cable companies in the same market, although the Justice Department apparently believes it may be all right to have such ownership in other markets.

The idea, obviously, is to give the cable companies an opportunity to provide the diversity that public television alone cannot supply. Their advertising will be directed at selective, specialized audiences rather than mass markets. It will be a tricky business, admittedly, to solve the hard problems of who is going to own the cable companies, how much competition there is going to be, and how to save enough cable service for noncommercial purposes. There are presently twelve television channel systems available. Eight more could be added by cable in the present state of technology. It is easy to see where and how the crisis is going to come.

Television and society face these and a number of other critical questions. How they are answered, and what pattern of broadcasting emerges from these controversies, may well determine in significant measure the quality of life in America for generations to come.

NICHOLAS JOHNSON

What Do We Do
About Television?

*It is not intellectually smart to ignore the most
significant force in our society. Alert yourself to
the medium. Determine what is worth
communicating. Get thinkers together with
creators. Team with professionals and make a
program yourself. Make TV deliver.*

Television is more than just another great public resource—like air and
water—ruined by private greed and public inattention. It is the greatest
communications mechanism ever designed and operated by man. It
pumps into the human brain an unending stream of information, opinion,
moral values, and esthetic taste. It cannot be a neutral influence. Every
minute of television programing—commercials, entertainment, news—
teaches us something.

Most Americans tell pollsters that television constitutes their principal
source of information. Many of our senior citizens are tied to their television sets for intellectual stimulation. And children now spend more time
learning from television than from church and school combined. By the
time they enter first grade they will have received more hours of instruction from television networks than they will later receive from college
professors while earning a bachelor's degree. Whether they like it or not,
the television networks are playing the roles of teacher, preacher, parent,

Nicholas Johnson is a Commissioner of the Federal Communications
Commission and author of *How to Talk Back to Your Television Set*
(Little-Brown/Bantam, 1970). "What Do We Do About Television?" is
reprinted from *Saturday Review*, July 11, 1970, with permission. Copyright 1970 Saturday Review, Inc.

public official, doctor, psychiatrist, family counselor, and friend for tens of millions of Americans each day of their lives.

TV programing can be creative, educational, uplifting, and refreshing without being tedious. But the current television product that drains away lifetimes of leisure energy is none of these. It leaves its addicts waterlogged. Only rarely does it contribute anything meaningful to their lives. No wonder so many Americans express to me a deep-seated hostility toward television. Too many realize, perhaps unconsciously but

"You see, son, I'm afraid the real world out there isn't much like 'Sesame Street.'"
Drawing by D. Reilly;
© 1971
The New Yorker Magazine, Inc.

certainly with utter disgust, that television is itself a drug, constantly offering the allure of a satisfying fulfillment for otherwise empty and meaningless lives that it seldom, if ever, delivers.

Well, what do we do about it? Here are a few suggestions:

STEP ONE: *Turn on.* I don't mean rush to your sets and turn the on-knob. What I do mean is that we had all better "turn on" to television—wake up to the fact that it is no longer intellectually smart to ignore it. Everything we do, or are, or worry about is affected by television. How and when issues are resolved in this country—the Indochina War, air pollution, race relations—depend as much as anything else on how (and whether) they're treated by the television network in "entertainment" as well as news and public affairs programing.

Dr. S. I. Hayakawa has said that man is no more conscious of communication than a fish would be conscious of the waters of the sea. The analogy is apt. A tidal wave of television programing has covered our land during the past twenty years. The vast majority of Americans have begun to breathe through gills. Yet, we have scarcely noticed the change, let alone wondered what it is doing to us. A few examples may start us thinking.

The entire medical profession, as well as the federal government, had little impact upon cigarette consumption in this country until a single young man, John Banzhaf, convinced the Federal Communications Commission that its Fairness Doctrine required TV and radio stations to broadcast $100-million worth of "anti-smoking commercials." Cigarette consumption has now declined for one of the few times in history.

What the American people think about government and politics in general—as well as a favorite candidate in particular—is almost exclusively influenced by television. The candidates and their advertising agencies, which invest 75 percent or more of their campaign funds in broadcast time, believe this: to the tune of $58-million in 1968.

There's been a lot of talk recently about malnutrition in America. Yet, people could let their television sets run for twenty-four hours a day and never discover that diets of starch and soda pop can be fatal.

If people lack rudimentary information about jobs, community services for the poor, alcoholism, and so forth, it is because occasional tidbits of information of this kind in soap operas, game shows, commercials, and prime-time series are either inaccurate or missing.

In short, whatever your job or interests may be, the odds are very good that you could multiply your effectiveness tremendously by "turning on" to the impact of television on your activities and on our society as a whole —an impact that exceeds that of any other existing institution.

STEP TWO: *Tune in.* There are people all over the country with something vitally important to say: the people who knew "cyclamates" were dangerous decades ago, the people who warned us against the Vietnam War in the early sixties, the people who sounded the alarm against industrial pollution when the word "smog" hadn't been invented. Why didn't we hear their warnings over the broadcast media?

In part it is the media's fault, the product of "corporate censorship." But in large part it's the fault of the very people with something to say who never stopped to consider how they might best say it. They simply haven't "tuned in" to television.

Obviously, I'm not suggesting you run out and buy up the nearest network. What I am suggesting is that we stop thinking that television programing somehow materializes out of thin air, or that it's manufactured by hidden forces or anonymous men. It is not. There is a new generation coming along that is substantially less frightened by a 16mm camera than by a pencil. You may be a part of it. Even those of us who are not, however, had better tune in to television ourselves.

Here is an example of someone who *did.* Last summer, CBS aired an hour-long show on Japan, assisted in large part by former Ambassador Edwin Reischauer. No one, including Ambassador Reischauer and CBS, would claim the show perfectly packaged all that Americans want or need to know about our 100 million neighbors across the Pacific. But many who watched felt it was one of the finest bits of educational entertainment about Japan ever offered to the American people by a commercial network.

Ambassador Reischauer has spent his lifetime studying Japan, yet his was not an easy assignment. An hour is not very long for a man who is used to writing books and teaching forty-five-hour semester courses, and there were those who wanted to turn the show into an hour-long geisha party. He could have refused to do the show at all, or walked away from the project when it seemed to be getting out of control. But he didn't. And as a result, the nation, the CBS network, and Mr. Reischauer all benefited. (And the show was honored by an Emmy award.)

There are other Ed Reischauers in this country: men who don't know much about "television," but who know more than anyone else about a subject that is important and potentially entertaining. If these men can team their knowledge with the professional television talent of others (and a network's financial commitment), they can make a television program happen. Not only ought they to accept such assignments when asked, I would urge them to come forward and volunteer their assistance to the networks and their local station managers (or to the local cable television system, many of which have been ordered by the FCC to begin local program origination by January, 1971). Of course, these offers won't always, or even often, be accepted—for many reasons. But sooner or later the dialogue has to begin.

There are many ways you can contribute to a television program without knowing anything about lighting or electronics. Broadcasters in many large communities (especially those with universities) are cashing in on local expertise for quick background when an important news story breaks, occasional on-camera interviews, suggestions for news items or entire shows, participation as panel members or even hosts, writers for programs, citizen advisory committees, and so forth. Everyone benefits. The broadcaster puts out higher-quality programing, the community builds greater citizen involvement and identification, and the television audience profits.

Whoever you are, whatever you're doing, ask yourself this simple question: What do I know or what do I have to communicate that others need to know or might find interesting? If you're a Department of Health, Education and Welfare official charged with communicating vital information about malnutrition to the poor, you might be better off putting your information into the plot-line of a daytime television soap opera than spending a lifetime writing pamphlets. If you're a law enforcement officer and want to inform people how to secure their homes against illegal entry, you might do better by talking to the writers and producers of *Dragnet, I Spy,* or *Mission: Impossible* than by making slide presentations.

STEP THREE: *Drop out.* The next step is to throw away most of what you've learned about communication. Don't make the mistake of writing "TV essays"—sitting in front of a camera reading, or saying, what might otherwise have been expressed in print. "Talking heads" make for poor television communication, as educational and commercial television professionals are discovering. Intellectuals and other thinking creative people first have to "drop out" of the traditional modes of communicating thoughts, and learn to swim through the new medium of television.

Marshall McLuhan has made much of this clear. If the print medium is linear, television is not. McLuhan's message is as simple as one in a Chinese fortune cookie: "One picture worth thousand words"—particularly when the picture is in color and motion, is accompanied by sound (words and music), and is not tied to an orderly time sequence.

Mason Williams, multitalented onetime writer for the Smothers Brothers, is one of the few to see this new dimension in communication. He describes one of his techniques as "verbal snapshots"—short bursts of thought, or poetry, or sound that penetrate the mind in an instant, then linger. Here are some that happen to be about television itself: "I am qualified to criticize television because I have two eyes and a mind, which is one more eye and one more mind than television has." "Television doesn't have a job; it just goofs off all day." "Television is doing to your mind what industry is doing to the land. Some people already think like New York City looks." No one "snapshot" gives the whole picture. But read in rapid succession, they leave a vivid and highly distinctive after-image.

Others have dropped out of the older communications techniques and have adapted to the new media. Those students who are seen on television—sitting in, protesting, assembling—are developing a new medium of communication: the demonstration. Denied traditional access to the network news shows and panel discussions, students in this country now communicate with the American people via loud, "newsworthy," media-attractive aggregations of sound and color and people. Demonstrations are happenings, and the news media—like moths to a flame—run to cover them. Yippie Abbie Hoffman sees this clearer than most:

So what the hell are we doing, you ask? We are dynamiting brain cells. We are putting people through changes. . . . We are theater in the streets: total and committed. We aim to involve people and use . . . any

weapon (prop) we can find. All is relevant, only "the play's the thing."
. . . The media is the message. Use it! No fund raising, no full-page ads
in *The New York Times*, no press releases. Just do your thing; the press
eats it up. Media is free. *Make news.*

Dr. Martin Luther King told us very much the same thing. "Lacking
sufficient access to television, publications, and broad forums, Negroes
have had to write their most persuasive essays with the blunt pen of
marching ranks."

Mason Williams, Abbie Hoffman, Dr. Martin Luther King, and many
others have set the stage for the new communicators, the new media experts. All dropped out of the traditional communications bag of speeches,
round-table discussion, panels, symposia, and filmed essays. And they
reached the people.

STEP FOUR: *Make the legal scene.* Shakespeare's Henry VI threatened:
"The first thing we do, let's kill all the lawyers." Good advice in the fifteenth century perhaps. But bad advice today. We need lawyers. And
they can help you improve television.

Examples are legion. The United Church of Christ successfully fought
two legal appeals to the United States Court of Appeals for the District
of Columbia, one establishing the right of local citizens groups to participate in FCC proceedings, and one revoking the license of WLBT-TV in
Jackson, Mississippi, for systematic segregationist practices. In Media,
Pennsylvania, nineteen local organizations hired a Washington lawyer to
protest radio station WXUR's alleged policy of broadcasting primarily
right-wing political programing. In Los Angeles, a group of local businessmen challenged the license of KHJ-TV, and the FCC's hearing examiner awarded them the channel. There are dozens of other examples of the
imaginative use of rusty old legal remedies to improve the contribution
of television to our national life.

For all their drawbacks, lawyers understand what I call "the law of
effective reform"; that is, to get reform from legal institutions (Congress,
courts, agencies), one must assert, first, the factual basis for the grievance;
second, the specific legal principle involved (Constitutional provision,
statute, regulation, judicial or agency decision); and third, the precise
remedy sought (legislation, fine, license revocation). Turn on a lawyer,
and you'll turn on an awful lot of legal energy, talent, and skill. You will
be astonished at just how much legal power you actually have over a
seemingly intractable Establishment.

STEP FIVE: *Try do-it-yourself justice.* Find out what you can do without
a lawyer. You ought to know, for example, that every three years *all* the
radio and television station licenses come up for renewal in your state.

You ought to know when that date is. It is an "election day" of sorts, and you have a right and obligation to "vote." Not surprisingly, many individuals have never even been told there's an election.

Learn something about the grand design of communications in this country. For example, no one "owns" a radio or television station in the sense that you can own a home or the corner drugstore. It's more like leasing public land to graze sheep, or obtaining a contract to build a stretch of highway for the state. Congress has provided that the airwaves are public property. The user must be licensed, and, in the case of commercial broadcasters, that license term is for three years. There is no "right" to have the license renewed. It is renewed only if past performance, and promises of future performance, are found by the FCC to serve "the public interest." In making this finding, the views of local individuals and groups are, of course, given great weight. In extreme cases, license revocation or license renewal contest proceedings may be instituted by local groups.

You should understand the basic policy underlying the Communications Act of 1934, which set up the FCC and gave it its regulatory powers. "Spectrum space" (radio and television frequencies) in this country is limited. It must be shared by taxicabs, police cars, the Defense Department, and other business users. In many ways it would be more efficient to have a small number of extremely high-powered stations blanket the country, leaving the remaining spectrum space for other users. But Congress felt in 1934 that it was essential for the new technology of radio to serve needs, tastes, and interests at the local level—to provide community identification, cohesion, and outlets for local talent and expression. For this reason, roughly 95 percent of the most valuable spectrum space has been handed out to some 7,500 radio and television stations in communities throughout the country. Unfortunately, the theory is not working. Most programing consists of nationally distributed records, movies, newswire copy, commercials, and network shows. Most stations broadcast very little in the way of locally oriented community service. It's up to you to make them change.

You have only to exercise your imagination to improve the programing service of your local station. Student groups, civic luncheon clubs, unions, PTAs, the League of Women Voters, and so forth are in an ideal position to accomplish change. They can contact national organizations, write for literature, and generally inform themselves of their broadcasting rights. Members can monitor what is now broadcast and draw up statements of programing standards, indicating what they would like to see with as much specificity as possible. They can set up Citizens Television Advisory Councils to issue reports on broadcasters' performance. They can send delegations to visit with local managers and owners. They can, when negotiation fails, take whatever legal steps are necessary with the FCC. They can complain to sponsors, networks, and local television stations when they find commercials excessively loud or obnoxious. If you think this is dreamy, pie-in-the-sky thinking, look what local groups have done during the past year.

Texarkana was given national attention last year when a large magazine reported that the city's population of rats was virtually taking over the city. Of lesser notoriety, but perhaps of greater long-run significance, was an agreement hammered out between a citizens group and KTAL-TV, the local television station. In January 1969, the Texarkana Junior Chamber of Commerce and twelve local unincorporated associations—with the assistance of the Office of Communications of the United Church of Christ —filed complaints with the FCC, and alleged that KTAL-TV had failed to survey the needs of its community, had systematically refused to serve the tastes, needs, and desires of Texarkana's 26 percent Negro population, and had maintained no color origination equipment in its Texarkana studio (although it had such equipment in the wealthier community of Shreveport, Louisiana). But they didn't stop there. Armed with the threat of a license renewal hearing, they went directly to the station's management and hammered out *an agreement* in which the station promised it would make a number of reforms, or forfeit its license. Among other provisions, KTAL-TV promised to recruit and train a staff broadly representative of all minority groups in the community; employ a minimum of two full-time Negro reporters; set up a toll-free telephone line for news and public service announcements and inquiries; present discussion programs of controversial issues, including both black and white participants; publicize the rights of the poor to obtain needed services; regularly televise announcements of the public's rights and periodically consult with all substantial groups in the community regarding their programing tastes and needs.

The seeds of citizen participation sown in Texarkana have since come to fruition elsewhere. Just recently five citizens groups negotiated agreements with twenty-two stations in Atlanta, Georgia, and similar attempts have been made in Shreveport, Louisiana; Sandersville, Georgia; Mobile, Alabama; and Jackson, Mississippi.

In Washington, D.C., last summer a group of students under the supervision of the Institute for Policy Studies undertook a massive systematic review of the license applications of all television stations in the area of Washington, D.C., Virginia, West Virginia, and Maryland. They used a number of "performance charts" by which they evaluated and ranked the stations in amounts of news broadcast, news employees hired, commercials, public service announcements, and other factors. The result was a book that may become a working model for the comparative evaluation of television stations' performances. (IPS, *Television Today: The End of Communication and the Death of Community*, $10 from the Institute for Policy Studies, 1540 New Hampshire Ave., N.W., Washington, D.C.) Citizens groups all over the country can easily follow their example.

I have felt for some time that it would be useful to have detailed reviews and periodic reports about the implications of specific television commercials and entertainment shows by groups of professional psychiatrists, ministers, social scientists, and so forth. They could pick a show in the evening—any show—and discuss its esthetic quality, its accuracy, and its potential national impact upon moral values, constructive opinion, mental health, and so forth. It would be especially exciting if this critical analysis could be shown on television. Such professional comment would be bound to have *some* impact upon the networks' performance. (Last year's *Violence Commission Report* did.) It would be a high service indeed to our nation, with rewards as well for the professional groups and individuals involved—including the broadcasting industry. It is not without precedent. The BBC formerly aired a critique of evening shows following prime-time entertainment. It would be refreshing to have a television producer's sense of status and satisfaction depend more upon the enthusiasm of the critics and audience than upon the number of cans of "feminine deodorant spray" he can sell.

These examples are only the beginning. Television could become our most exciting medium if the creative people in this country would use a fraction of their talent to figure out ways of improving it.

STEP SIX: *Get high (with a little help from your friends).* Have you ever made a film, or produced a TV documentary, or written a radio script? That's a real high. But if you're like me, you'll need help—lots of it—from your friends. If you've got something to say, find someone who's expert in communication: high school or college film-makers, drama students, off-time TV reporters, or local CATV outlets with program origination equipment. Bring the thinkers in the community together with the media creators. CBS did it with Ed Reischauer and its one-hour special on Japan. You can do it, too. Get others interested in television. (A free pamphlet, "Clearing the Air," has just been published by Media Ithaca, Department of Sociology, Cornell University, Ithaca, New York 14850. It explains how average citizens can obtain free air time over radio, television, and CATV.)

STEP SEVEN: *Expand your media mind.* Everyone can work for policies that increase the number of radio and television outlets. and provide individuals with access to existing outlets to express their talent or point of view. Those outlets are already numerous. There are now nearly ten times as many radio and television stations as there were thirty-five years ago.

There are many more AM radio stations, including the "daytime only" stations. There is the new FM radio service. There is VHF television. And, since Congress passed the all-channel receiver law in 1962, UHF television (channels 14–83) has come alive. There are educational radio and television stations all over the country. There are "listener-supported" community radio stations (such as the Pacifica stations in New York, Los Angeles, Houston, and Berkeley). This increase in outlets has necessarily broadened the diversity of programing. However, since the system is virtually all "commercial" broadcasting, this diversity too often means simply that there are now five stations to play the "top forty" records in your city instead of two. In the past couple years, however, educational broadcasting has gained in strength with the Public Broadcasting Corporation (potentially America's answer to the BBC). Owners of groups of profitable television stations (such as Westinghouse and Metromedia) have begun syndicating more shows—some of which subsequently get picked up by the networks.

Cable television (CATV) offers a potentially unlimited number of channels. (The present over-the-air system is physically limited to from five to ten television stations even in the largest communities.) Twelve-channel cable systems are quite common, twenty-channel systems are being installed, and more channels will undoubtedly come in the future. Your telephone, for example, is a "100-million-channel receiver" in that it can call, or be called by, any one of 100 million other instruments in this country.

Cable television offers greater diversity among commercial television programs—at the moment, mostly movies, sports, and reruns—but it can also offer another advantage: public access. The FCC has indicated that cable systems should be encouraged and perhaps ultimately required to offer channels for lease to any persons willing to pay the going rate. In the *Red Lion* case last year, the Supreme Court upheld the FCC's fairness doctrine and, noting the monopolistic position most broadcasters hold, suggested that "free speech" rights belong principally to the audience and those who wish to use the station, not the station owner. This concept— which might raise administrative problems for single stations—is easily adaptable to cable television.

If someone wants to place a show on a single over-the-air broadcast station, some other (generally more profitable) program must be canceled. A cable system, by contrast, can theoretically carry an unlimited number of programs at the same time. We therefore have the opportunity to require cable systems to carry whatever programs are offered on a leased-channel basis (sustained either by advertising or by subscription fee). Time might even be made available free to organizations, young filmmakers, and others who could not afford the leasing fee and do not advertise or profit from their programing. Now is the time to guarantee such rights for your community. City councils all across the nation are in the process of drafting the terms for cable television franchises. If your community is at present considering a cable television ordinance, it is your opportunity to work for free and common-carrier "citizens' access" to the cables that will one day connect your home with the rest of the world.

Television is here to stay. It's the single most significant force in our society. It is now long past time that the professional and intellectual community—indeed, anyone who reads magazines and cares where this country is going—turn on to television.

PAUL KLEIN

The Men Who Run TV
Know Us Better
Than You Think

For nearly twenty years I have been watching people watch television. In my time as a specialist in audience measurement at one of the networks, thousands of ideas for new shows have been kicked around, hundreds of pilot scripts have been shot, several dozen new stars and series have come and gone, and a relative handful of programs have survived more than a few seasons. I have brooded about why some programs get, and why so many more fail to get, an audience of commercially acceptable size. I have reached several conclusions. One of them is that when it comes to television, a lot of you otherwise nice people out there are compulsive liars.

You lie to your friends. "I don't watch television much except for the news, maybe a movie, and an occasional special or sports show," you keep telling them. And you lie to yourselves. "I think I'll watch a little TV tonight," you say to yourself. You don't say, "I think I'll watch a little TV tonight *just like I did last night*," because you cannot admit, even to yourself, the nature and extent of your addiction to TV. Watching television seems to be in our day what sex was in the age of Queen Victoria—a filthy little habit best not spoken of.

Paul Klein is president of Computer Television Inc., which he founded in 1970 after five years as Vice President in charge of Audience Measurement for NBC. He is also President of Schools for the Future, a non-profit group which fights illiteracy in this country and abroad. "The Men Who Run TV Know Us Better Than You Think" is excerpted from *New York Magazine*. Copyright 1970. Reprinted by permission of the author.

Make no mistake, though, you *are* hooked, chained or otherwise enslaved by your vice. No one can say whether television programming is better or worse this year than it ever was. But the audience out there in prime time, between 7:30 and 11 at night, is as big as ever. This year, in fact, it is a little bigger because of:

an increase in color-TV penetration; you are buying more expensive receivers so that you can hate the damned thing in living color;

an increase in community-antenna subscribers; you are signing up for CATV service so that you can get a wider choice of hateful images and see them more clearly in the bargain;

an increase in multi-set homes; you are buying second, third, and even fourth TV sets so that several members of the same family can be bored by different programs simultaneously;

a decrease in competition from other media; the increase in clear, colorful video pictures has denied other vehicles for advertising—magazines, for example—their uniqueness.

This year, as a result, 36 million homes—75 million people—are watching TV in prime time at any given moment, and the three networks command over 91 percent of this huge audience. (Independent and educational channels get the rest.) The bigger a network's share of this audience, the more it can charge for the time it sells to advertisers. The rating points which express share of audience are, in effect, the only way the networks have yet figured out to price their merchandise, which is *your* time and attention.

The single most important thing to know about the American television audience is its amazingly constant size. At any given moment in prime time most of the week it stays at about 36 million sets, whether the network shows at a given hour are strong, weak, so-so, or one of each. It's not the same person in each home watching through the evening. It isn't even the same 36 million homes. The precise composition of the audience is changing every half-hour. The point of nearly every strategy and tactic a network can devise is to get the largest possible share of that audience in each half-hour.

Why does the audience remain so constant even though you say you don't care that much for what's on? After contemplating this curious behavior over the years, I have worked out a theory. I call it the Theory of the Least Objectionable Program. Theory, hell. A few explainable exceptions aside, it has the reliability of natural law. According to my theory, you don't watch particular programs. *You watch television.* The medium. The tube. You turn on the set because it is there—*you can't resist*—and you then settle down to watch that program among all those offered at a given time which can be endured with the least amount of pain and suffering.

You view television irrespective of the content of the program watched. And because the programs are designed to appeal to the greatest number of people—rich and poor, smart and stupid, tall and short, wild and tame—you're probably watching something that is not *your* taste. Nevertheless, you take what is fed to you because you are compelled to exercise the medium. The result, after a night's viewing, is guilt. That's why you lie to yourself and your friends. You keep thinking you should have been reading, or something.

The dynamics of LOP are observable elsewhere. In politics, for example, it is called choosing the lesser of two (or, lately, three) evils. The League of Women Voters demands that you vote, dammit. The act of voting—irrespective of the content voted for—is held to be essential to the preservation of democracy. If you don't vote, you are warned, the lesser evil you voted for last time may disenfranchise you.

LOP is the same demand, only it is a demand we make of ourselves. The alternative to submitting to LOP is to turn the damned set off and finds something else to do. Fat chance. Television viewing, like nail-biting, is something you will stop tomorrow.

The thing I like about my theory is that it explains several phenomena that are otherwise inexplicable. In an age that prizes novelty, LOP explains why some new and even likable faces vanish so quickly and why some old ones hang in there. It explains why New York's taste frequently differs, radically, from national preferences.

Most importantly, LOP explains why some interesting programs die and some stupid programs seem to thrive. Place a weak show against weaker competition, LOP teaches us, and it inevitably looks good; it may even look like a hit—get huge rating and a quality audience if the time period it fills has that audience. Place a strong show against a stronger show and, never mind whether it is far superior to a dozen other shows on the air in other time slots, it will look like a bomb.

The theory of LOP has a corollary that derives directly from it. Since one man's Green Acres is another man's Slough of Despond, you may confidently bet the family jewels that, regardless of quality, the winner in a given time period will be the network that is *counter-programming* that slot. Just as Buckley counter-programmed Ottinger and Goodell and won, a weak *old* folks' show will beat two *young* folks' shows because all the old folks will gather before "their" show while the two youngies must share their audience.

A very old law has also become more and more useful in figuring out program popularity. I didn't discover this one. Sir Isaac Newton did. I mean his First Law of Motion, the one that says that a body at rest tends to stay at rest. Once a viewer chooses his LOP, he may have to fiddle with a lot of knobs should he decide to switch channels, especially if it's an older color set. So, because a viewer in a chair tends to stay in his chair, an LOP renders great service to the program following it. It can become, in the trade's argot, a strong lead-in.

Incredible as it may seem, then, despite the money, creative juices, and intelligence that often go into a quality network program, the payoff is really determined by 75 million different thresholds of pain plus the law of inertia.

The best network programmers understand this. They are not stupid. They like most of the stuff they put on about as much as you do. But they also know that a program doesn't have to be "good." It only has to be less objectionable than whatever the hell the other guys throw against it.

For the October–December period of the 1970–71 season, the National Broadcasting Company—my old outfit—had a very slight lead over the Columbia Broadcasting System in their perennial battle for the largest share of the prime-time audience. On the basis of the latest Nielsen data, NBC is getting 32 percent of the available audience, CBS 31 percent. The third network, the American Broadcasting Company's, is running third, with a 29 share, but ABC is doing interesting things.

Next month, network salesmen will start selling time for the new season starting next September. They will have their hands full. Like the rest of us, programmers and advertisers try to read the future by analyzing the past. . . .

Next season the scheduling of prime-time programs will be a whole new ballgame. The Federal Communications Commission has decided to allow the networks only three hours of prime-time programming. (They had been allowed three and a half hours.) The jockeying for position under the new rule has already begun. However simple it sounds, the decision greatly complicates the networks' lives.

NBC was first to announce which three-hour period it would program. It chose 8 to 11 P.M., thereby returning the 7:30-to-8 P.M. slot to its affiliates to program themselves. I think the decision pleased the stations. They'll undoubtedly find it easier to program 7:30 P.M. than 10:30 P.M.

CBS digested the NBC announcement and then announced that it would program 7:30 to 10:30 P.M., giving its affiliates the 10:30-to-11 P.M. period to program themselves. This, CBS told *Variety*, would give CBS a huge audience lead at 7:30 to 8 P.M., some of which it will keep all night long. Some will remember that ABC started to raise hell with the ratings of CBS and NBC back in the late fifties by programming action-adventure at 7:30 to 8 P.M. At the time, CBS and NBC had been programming network news strips.

CBS' logic is only half right, I think. If ABC goes the same way as CBS,

NBC will get huge audiences at 10:30 to 11 P.M. This audience will lead into the late-night news on all NBC-owned local stations. In New York, for example, this would mean that NBC's news show on Channel 4 would, for the foreseeable future, enjoy very much higher ratings than its competition on CBS' Channel 2 and ABC's Channel 7. This, in turn, would give a huge advantage to Johnny Carson over Merv Griffin (or his replacement) and Dick Cavett (or his replacement). The combination of a strong 10.30-to-11-P.M. half-hour with its naturally good demographics plus the strength accruing to both the local news show and the *Tonight Show* make NBC's 8-to-11-P.M. move a sound one—but, again, only if ABC goes along with CBS at 7:30. If ABC goes at 8 P.M., CBS' lead at 7:30 P.M. may be too great to bear.

A lot also depends on the local programming plugged in at 7:30 P.M. Despite the FCC's interest in opening up prime time for many more program producers, the public may end up with significantly less program choice. An NBC station, for instance, may end up carrying one half-hour program "stripped" across five nights instead of five separate programs on the five nights. We are entering the *Let's Make a Deal* era of prime-time programming. Cheap strip programming, if it can get the audience, is a better economic move for local stations than good films. The quiz/game show is just that kind of programming. And since the FCC has ordered that, beginning in 1972, the top 50 markets must play, in prime time, only original programming (no *Dragnet* repeats), these stations must go the strip route.

But I think many stations will choose to expand their news coverage. I think it would make sound economic sense in the long run. News, well done, with an adequate staff, builds a local program with strong local interest that is more salable to advertisers than bimodal stripped games. In the short run, though, news is risky. If NBC affiliates play news at 7:30 P.M., CBS stations playing network bimodals [appealing to young and old viewers in the same audience] such as *Family Affair* will get huge ratings. It is imperative, therefore, that more people in the business learn about the lingering irrelevancies of ratings.

Ratings have not always had a stultifying effect on TV programming. When television started, those who acquired sets first tended to live in the larger marketing areas, and they tended to be people who had the dough to pay for a 10-inch Dumont. Given the high correlation between money and education, these early TV viewers tended to be high up on various socio-economic scales, and the programs that appealed to them tended to be the more sophisticated visual fare. That's how the so-called "golden-age" of TV (live drama and all that) was possible.

But in the mid-fifties, set ownership proliferated furiously, entering small towns and rural areas. Mindless situation comedies and the Western suddenly became the dominant program types as viewers with decidedly different tastes became the majority audience. They were not a real majority in terms of the population as a whole, but they did the majority of the viewing.

This is all to say that the period after the golden age—the family age— led to rules which executives lived by (sit-com will always beat dramas, for example) which *were* valid and are now increasingly irrelevant. Just how irrelevant they have become has been obscured, however, because by now everyone is addicted to TV.

But people's willingness to settle for the least objectionable program available has made the advertisers who want them *less* secure, not more so. The young-adult and upper-income audiences are a fickle bunch, and programming by the old rules is an increasingly costly and, I believe, ultimately, self-defeating game. Time will tell.

These uncertainties notwithstanding, the three-hour rule is a boon to the networks—at least a temporary one. With cigarettes gone, there will not be enough advertising dollars around to buy all the available time even at distress prices. The forced cutback to three hours of network programming amounts to a forced reduction in inventory. The cut, eliminating one-seventh of all available time, nearly equals the time previously bought up by cigarette dollars. Of course, the cut *adds* inventory to the local stations, which had been sharing in the networks' tobacco revenues. They will now have to pay for their own programming and scrounge around for ad dollars, some of which will inevitably be monies that used to go to the networks. In effect, then, the networks will have a considerable lower gross next season—with a lower profit, if they have any profit at all.

CBS has broken the "minute" dam going to thirty seconds as the basic unit of sale. There used to be three minutes of time to sell in a prime-time half-hour. Now, there are six thirty-second units to sell. This will open up prime-time to small-budget advertisers. In fact, some daytime advertisers will graduate to night time, creating some problems for daytime sales. But you will see a lot more USO, United Fund, and other public-service advertisements on all networks until the inventory is reduced. . . .

In the long run, though, all this may lead to better TV for the addicts among us—that is, just about all of us—because the lowest-priced programming will end up being *reality* programming—news and public-affairs documentaries, and such—which, after all, the networks are uniquely equipped to do well.

PART FOUR

What Popular Art Does to Us

Introduction

Many Americans would probably feel more comfortable about mass culture if they could come to firm conclusions about how—and if—it affects attitudes and behavior. Though there have been countless studies of the relationship between exposure to popular art and behavior, the results have been inconclusive. Probably the sanest comment anyone can make is that heavy exposure to the media is likely to have a long-term cumulative effect.

One view holds that our mass media experiences have a cathartic effect on us, that they relieve our aggressions and other antisocial impulses. Again, the evidence here is contradictory. A review of all the studies conducted for the Commission on Causes and Prevention of Violence by Dr. Richard Goranson in 1969 led to the tentative conclusion that antisocial behavior such as violence probably is stimulated rather than reduced by exposure to such behavior in the mass media.

There are few evidences that what we see, hear, or read in the media has a "hypodermic needle," or instantaneous, effect on our behavior. Generally, we are more likely to accept new ideas or ways of doing things if what is new fits into what we already believe; we tend to either reject or misinterpret those new ideas that don't coincide with our established beliefs.

One view is that the social process prepares the way for media messages. According to this argument, the media have less influence on our opinions and behavior than small, primary groups such as the family, our peer groups, and organizations to which we belong.

Closely related to this view is the "two-step flow" theory, which holds that mass media tend to influence our attitudes mainly through peer group leaders. And the influential leaders tend to be those who pay closest attention and have greatest exposure to what is being printed or broadcast on the subject of their expertise.

Arthur Schlesinger, Jr., says, "the mass media do not create violence. But they reinforce aggressive and destructive impulses, and they may well teach the morality as well as the methods of violence." On the other hand, we may turn Professor Schlesinger's argument around and suggest that mass media *also* reinforce peaceful and constructive impulses, and that they *also* teach the morality and methods of conformity and passivity.

HARRY J. SKORNIA

Values Promoted by Television

On television the mediocre and the great appear side by side. Singing commercials are heard more than great music. Pressed by television, the other media adopt this same approach. Starving children and cigarette models face each other in color. The coexistence of the cheap, the vulgar, the violent, and the sacred, give the impression of almost complete value-lessness. The danger in this is that the listener or viewer himself grows indifferent. As broadcasting does not discriminate between opinions, the listener-viewer also becomes undiscriminating.

If television can be said to have any values at all, it is those of the salesmen, big businessmen, manufacturers, and showmen who control it—essentially materialistic values. And, like those who control it, television shuns everything which does not fit with these values.

Randall Jarrell has noted how the media ignore those things which would be disruptive of the value-systems and "happy" picture promoted by their managers:

> I come to a long row of one-room shacks about the size of kitchens, made out of used boards, metal signs, old tin roofs. To the people who live in them an electric dishwasher of one's own is as much a fantasy as an ocean liner of one's own. But since the Medium (and those whose thought is molded by it) does not perceive them, these people are themselves a fantasy; no matter how many millions of such exceptions to the general rule there are, they do not really exist, but have a kind of anomalous, statistical

Harry J. Skornia is professor of radio and television at the University of Illinois. He has been program director of both commercial and educational broadcasting stations, was president of the National Association of Educational Broadcasters, and is a member of the board of the National Association for Better Radio and Television. From *Television and Society* by H. J. Skornia. Copyright © 1965 by Harry J. Skornia. Used by permission of McGraw-Hill Book Company.

subsistence; our moral and imaginative view of the world is no more affected by them than by the occupants of some home for the mentally deficient a little farther along the road.

Television extols the spender. He is portrayed by the stars. He buys everything. He knows that it is a duty to free enterprise to spend, rather than to save. Unlike the networks, which use the same films year after year, he is told to throw away the old and buy new. Whether he needs a product or not, if he is not to be a saboteur of our economic system, he must buy. This value is used as a lever in various ways, affecting even the respect of son for mother and vice versa. If children do not spend on mother, on Mother's Day, they obviously do not love her. Affection or loyalty, like success, is measured in dollars.

The saboteur of our economy is the tightwad father who wants to use the old car another year, or who objects to the rapidity with which items are made obsolete. Since it is believed that fathers most often exercise a restraining hand on spending, television programs ridicule such fathers as much as possible and hero-worship the woman, who spends more readily.

Another of the conspicuous values taught by television is conformity or adjustment. Viewers and listeners are urged to do as the person on the screen does. "Buy item X. Use like this." Television market research proves that this motivation is very effective—and that people *do* do as they are shown. Television defines the good citizen. He is happy and care-free. He spoils himself. He does not walk when he can ride. The well-adjusted, happy individual goes along with the gang. He does not raise unpopular questions. If the craving an individual has is not satisfied by things, he is obviously a deviate. He who is not satisfied with what the media offer is obviously out of step. He is an enemy.

Television exalts celebrities, treating them as society's most valued members. It is taken for granted that on the basis of both salary and prestige, except for corporation executives, show people are the most important people in the United States. They are paid more and imitated more than scientists, artists, journalists, composers, teachers, doctors, or government employees. The best programs on television are tributes to them. The public knows what products are good by noting what products the stars use.

What kind of values do the stars demonstrate in the roles of hero and heroine which they portray? The Payne Fund film studies indicated that the hero had little reluctance to use violence, or to kill if necessary. The hero was responsible for fifteen of the seventy-one deaths by violence found in one group of films. Even the heroine committed some of the murders shown. The violent and illegal use of weapons and other instruments (such as cars) is promoted by television and films. Lessons in how to use such tools for crime (rather than for hunting or safe driving) are, of course, included. So far as respect for education or serious careers is concerned, in 115 films reviewed, scientific or educational achievement is shown as a desirable goal in only four.

Lest the problem of violence or weapons be oversimplified, however, it should be made clear that the position taken here is not simply that violence is always bad. Nor is the showing of the use of weapons necessarily bad. The situation is not that black and white. Cars may be used as weapons, to kill. Guns, used legitimately for sports, recreation, or law enforcement and crime prevention, are surely not bad in themselves.

As Edgar Dale noted (thirty years ago) in his analysis *The Content of Motion Pictures* in the Payne Fund Studies, revenge (which the NAB Code outlaws as a motive) ranks fourth as a motivation and was found in 25 percent of the films. In the group of films studied, five heroes, eight heroines, and ten villains were moved by revenge. Revenge motivated more heroes and heroines than villians.

One recent shift in the qualities of heroines and heroes, as compared with those found in most of the films reviewed in the Payne Fund Studies, is to be noted. Heroes, especially athletes, used to be associated and identified with wholesome food, regular hours, exercise, and self-discipline. Recently, heroes are shown associated with soft drinks, shaving materials, beer, tobacco, automobiles, and luxuries.

The kind of woman who gets ahead is well illustrated in westerns. Young ladies who wish to succeed may study them each evening on television. The pure and virtuous woman is dull. She is spurned by the marshal, the hero, and other males who are worth having. If a woman wishes to be interesting she must have a past. To have fallen at least once usually qualifies her. In his factual study of the Westerner, Robert Warshow writes: "Those women in the Western movies who share the hero's understanding of life are prostitutes (or, as they are usually presented, barroom entertainers) . . . 'fallen' women." Such a fallen woman can, of course, understand the marshal, or other interesting men, in ways which the wife cannot. The old Anglo-Saxon belief that chastity is important, or a virtue, seems to have been largely modified to meet modern television needs. So is the idea that women should not drink too much. In popular television programs the woman most admired enjoys drinking and knows how. The social graces which television shows as desirable seem related to the various liquor and tobacco interests, which are important sponsors. Skeptics see the suspicion of a payola type of relationship. Just as Hollywood films were a powerful force in securing the repeal of Prohibition, television and Hollywood films now seem to be proving their effectiveness in establishing drinking, smoking, and several types of cosmetic, hair, and clothing practices as uniformly desirable social graces.

How heavily tobacco is promoted on television may come as some surprise to people who think it is promoted only, or principally, in paid commercial time. Before smoking by women was widely accepted, Edgar Dale wrote, in *The Content of Motion Pictures:* "We note that in twenty-six of forty pictures the hero used tobacco in some form; the heroines in about one-third of the pictures. . . . The hero did the major part of the smoking. The heroine smoked more than either the villain or villainess and the villainess tied with children for last rank. . . ." As this is written, TV is on the verge of beginning to show cigars being smoked by women—there is, or so the "message" goes, less risk of cancer and none at all of appearing unladylike.

What constitutes acceptable romance is also an interesting indication of television values. Smartly dressed girls are, of course, most popular, and most likely to find romance. The need for spending on clothes, make-up, perfumes and lotions, and hair preparations is demonstrated frequently and in many ways. This, too, is related to the large expenditures of sponsors (the cosmetic interests) in television advertising. Dressing scenes showing various degrees of nudity appeared in 23 percent and undressing scenes in 30 percent of the films analyzed in the Payne Fund Studies, and still seen on television. Romance appears to be principally a premarital phenomenon, or one experienced with someone else's husband or wife. The pleasures and joys of married life itself are rarely shown. In fact, marriage appears to dampen romantic and love interests considerably. It is a social convention still endured, but with little glamor or enthusiasm.

Enough of the technique of love-making is shown in sufficiently alluring fashion to provide incentives for imitation. Of 252 delinquent girls studied by Professor Herbert Blumer and reported in *Movies, Delinquency and Crime* (one of the Payne Fund Studies), one-quarter of them admitted engaging in sexual relations after being aroused by movies. The boys who were studied reported how "when you see these hot love pictures it makes you feel like going out and having sexual relations." The number of both boys and girls who successfully tried out the techniques shown was substantial. One girl, seventeen, reported how such films taught her how to "kiss, love, drink, smoke, and lead up to intercourse. It makes me all stirred up in a passionate way." Several of the girls found these films useful guidance in party behavior, petting leading up to intercourse, and teaching them how to "lead men on," as one of the girls described it. Of the 252 delinquent girls studied by Blumer, 41 percent traced some or all of their difficulties to such movies. How many others unconsciously were also taught or triggered by such movies is not known. Some, no doubt, would have fallen without such exposure. But delinquent males frequently mentioned the usefulness of films in getting the girls worked up to the point of willing intercourse.

Fredric Wertham who, as Consultant Psychiatrist of Queens Hospital

Center in New York, has devoted many years to this problem, pointed out in the February, 1960, *Ladies' Home Journal:* "The connection between violence and sex, as presented on the screen, is particularly apt to arouse fantasies and/or facilitate the transition from fantasy to action. . . . I have known of cases in which boys as young as eleven have been sexually excited by them. Sadistic daydreams, whether or not accompanied by masturbation, are certainly not good for children and may instill a liking for sadism that will cause serious trouble in later life."

Such are some of the values reflected in current television offerings.

PASSIVITY

One of the most disturbing effects of television appears to be the creation, in some people, of passivity. If this seems contrary to findings just reported, indicating that television is responsible for much delinquency, violence, and the teaching of specific techniques of crime, it is well to recall that this is not a simple problem. Just as children will be differently affected by the same schools, lessons, and teachers, so are children differently affected by television.

The recent passivity of Americans surprises and alarms many of our foreign friends, as well as physical- and mental-fitness authorities in the United States. Social scientists point to endless hours, night after night, year after year, spent before television sets, consuming, drinking in, and vegetating. By taking the citizen away from public affairs—town meetings, citizen councils, neighborhood groups, church and discussion groups —how many vital functions of our nation have been dried up by television? How does television's "freedom" to compete in this way square with its responsibility to contribute to, and not counteract, democratic processes and strengths? Does television not have a responsibility itself to supply the functions of those meetings and activities it starves out by keeping people at home or inactivated?

Political scientists and great psychologists like Carl Jung have warned us that it is the dictator state which keeps citizens passive, reassured, and politically inactivated. How long can democracy survive similar treatment, even if it is imposed by economic rather than political controllers?

Martin Grotjahn, a psychiatrist, has said:

> We can observe the development of a new style of living which I call, for want of a better term, "television living." This is characterized by the assumption that we do not do our living ourselves any more but that, so to speak, "we are lived" by the television screen. All that we have to do is sit passively in front of the screen which lives, thinks, sees and hears for us and gives us the proper conclusion. This leads to such increase of all dependent tendencies that it hampers the free development of people into independent individuals capable and willing to form their own opinions, to develop their own personality, and to live actively. Frequently television

children are at a complete loss for any spontaneous imaginative activity.
. . .

Television has brought a great change in the status of the "idler" in society. Many years ago the nobility was considered to be the idle class. With the coming of industrialization came pool halls and taverns. Those who frequented them were generally treated with contempt by society; loafers were not popular. Today the person who loafs in front of his television set is likely to be admired for he knows more about celebrities and products than most other people. He is the model viewer. Is television creating a huge class of idlers whose productive efforts could more usefully be channeled? Certainly there are dangers which grow out of habits of idleness which need to be taken into account: the effect on relief rolls and taxes, and the extent to which missing exercise and activity affects performance on the job (to mention two obvious ones).

Many researchers, like Schramm, Lyle, and Parker, have noted how television leads many children into a withdrawal and private communion with the picture tube. It is something to which a child surrenders himself, something that is done to him, something that he does not have to work for; he merely soaks it up or absorbs it. Is this effortless satiation related to the increasing effeteness we observe? Certainly such problems deserve study.

Broadcast leaders speak much of the broadcast freedoms. So far as viewers and broadcasters alike are concerned, how permissible is it for a democratic people to have the freedom not to worry, the freedom to abstain from politics, the freedom to be irresponsible, or the freedom to be passive and let others do what needs to be done? Democracy will not survive if those freedoms instead of more responsible and positive ones are promoted. Psychiatrist Eugene David Glynn believes television *can* activate. And he suggests how:

> It must find ways to encourage active audience participation; programs which will not satiate but stimulate its viewers . . . showing not a baseball game, but how to pitch a curved ball; . . . sending its audience on nature hunts, into club activity, to the library for books. . . . With this orientation, television can overcome the dangers pointed out and find its way to being highly growth-promoting. Otherwise it will find itself degraded into an instrument for the shaping of a group man: . . . the natural foil of any authoritarianism, be it left or right.

The shrillness of the competitive appeals for attention in the mass media has become increasingly intense. Such stridencies have forced us, in self-defense, to develop an ability to "tune out," which no previous generations had. Americans have been conditioned to not hear, even while listening, and not see, even while looking.

NER LITTNER, M.D.

A Psychiatrist Looks
at Television and Violence

A great deal has been written and said about the harmful psychological effects of television viewing upon the viewer. Some of it is based on clinical studies of the viewers. Much of it is rhetoric aimed at promoting various personal prejudices of the speaker or writer.

I myself have made no clinical studies of the psychological effects of watching TV. What I am about to say is based entirely on my own observations. Some of my remarks undoubtedly will reflect subjective prejudices that I will try to couch in scientific language. Other remarks will agree or disagree with some of the completed research studies. Still others will be based on what I hope are valid observations of my friends and patients.

The literature on the psychological effects of TV can be used to prove anything you want it to. You can find confirmatory evidence for any personal bias that you wish to promote. This means, in effect, that we really have no clear-cut, persuasive, scientific research studies to guide us, so that we end up reading through the literature with the same point of view with which we started.

This absence of scientifically valid studies in the field does not trace to

Ner Littner is a psychiatrist specializing in the psychoanalytic treatment of children and adults, and Director of the Extension Division and the Child Therapy Training Program, Chicago Institute for Psychoanalysis. Dr. Littner has taught psychiatry at Smith College and at the Universities of Indiana, Illinois, and Chicago. "A Psychiatrist Looks at Television and Violence" is excerpted from *Television Quarterly*, the Journal of the National Academy of Television Arts and Sciences, Vol. VIII, No. 4, Fall, 1969, with permission.

a lack of motivation, but rather to the difficulties involved in trying to do research that is meaningful.

Let me mention just a few of the problems involved in trying to measure the specific psychological effects of TV upon the viewer, *e.g., the psychological impact of violence.*

1. How do you factor out the specific variable you are trying to measure? What is your definition of violence? How do you compare the unreality of the violence in many of the children's shows against the realistic portrayal of a savage beating? How does humor affect the impact? What if the violence is justified? etc., etc.

2. Where do you get a control group to compare and contrast with the group exposed to the violence viewing?

3. How do you measure the full effects of the TV viewing upon the viewer? A human being is a psychosomatic entity. His behavior is only one aspect of his functioning. He also has a body that is subject to physical changes, and a mind that shows changes in such areas as thoughts, emotions, and intelligence. To measure only the *behavior* of a person, after he has been exposed to certain TV scenes, may result in one missing most of the possible effects of the viewing.

4. How can you follow the viewer for the length of time necessary to get full and complete results?

Most of the research on violence tries to *measure the immediate behavior* of people who have been exposed to violent scenes. On the one hand, there is no follow up to see what the long-term effect may be. Many of the traumatic influences on children, for example, may not show their harmful effects for many years: there may be a sort of buried, land-mine result. Comparable is the adult who may not show a psychosis until late in adult life, even though it is a result of severe mishandling in early childhood—the psychotic process lying quietly under cover for many years.

On the other hand, some experimental subjects may show an immediate reaction to a scene of violence, as though they are being made more violent by their watching, but there has been little follow up of these subjects. Conceivably, it results from something prior to the scene. Conceivably, also, the impact is only temporary and there is no carry-over into real life. In still another possibility, repeated exposure to violence may change one's threshold of reaction so that after a while he shows little reaction to scenes of violence.

However, I object to the research on violence mainly because it has not gone on for a long enough period of time. *Valid psychological studies require longitudinal studies that cover three generations.* To tease out the true psychological effects of a single variable, one must follow the effects of that variable across three generations. For example, to understand the effects of a specific childrearing practice, such as toilet training, one must study three generations. First, one psychologically studies the parents who are carrying out the specific toilet-training technique. Then, one studies the child who has been toilet trained in that way, following him and his development as he goes into adulthood. Finally, one studies how *he* toilet trains his own children and how they develop in turn.

There is nothing short term about accurate psychological research. No matter how many research studies we may launch today on the impact of TV violence, we will not know the end results for many years. When William H. Stewart, Surgeon-General, announced the one-year, million-dollar investigation of the impact of TV violence on children, he said his panel of experts would review existing studies and recommend long-range research. One cannot expect definitive results for many years.

5. *How do you accurately determine what is cause and what is effect?* An extreme version of this problem is offered by such a well-known authority as Dr. Frederic Wertham, a psychiatrist who has written extensively on the subject of TV and violence. In a 1962 article, he said that "we are confronted in the mass media with a display to children of brutality, sadism and violence such as the world has never before seen. At the same time there is such a rise of violence among our youth that no peace corps abroad can make up for the violence corps at home." While agreeing with Dr. Wertham about the accuracy of both parts of his premise (the increase in exposure to violence and the increase in violence among youth), I think that he is making a serious mistake in logic when he implies that one is the *cause* of the other. One must not overlook the alternative possibility: that *both* are symptoms of something else.

THE VIOLENCE OF TELEVISION

Many prominent people believe that the violence shown on television has either an immediate or a potential harmful psychological effect on its viewers. Thus, Max Born, the noted atomic physicist who was awarded a Nobel Prize in 1954, has commented on "the dark shadow over everything," specifically the methods of mass destruction and the corruptive influence of mass media, especially television. These are strong words.

Dr. Wertham, whom I have already mentioned, has written extensively on what he considers to be the long-range sleeper effects: callousness, loss of sympathy, becoming accustomed to brutality, and falsely linking sex with violence. (He does not even overlook the problem of the child who suffers from lack of sleep because he watches the late-late show.) Dr. Wertham has some rather strong feelings on the subject of TV and violence. I imagine that you will hear much more about them as the

Surgeon-General's investigation picks up speed. Here is a typical quote from his comments about the harmful effects of television and the mass media:

> There is a tendency to stereotype emotions at the expense of the emotional spontaneity of the individual. The relentless commercialism and the surfeit of brutality, violence, and sadism has made a profound impression on susceptible young people. The result is a distortion of natural attitudes in the direction of cynicism, greed, hostility, callousness, and insensitivity . . . Greed and sadism are perpetuated where they exist, and aroused where they do not . . . Harmful mass media influences are a contributing factor in many young people's troubles.

These are but two of the voices in the recently increasing crescendo of attacks on television violence. . . .

To top it all off, two of the major television networks have accepted a proposal for pre-screening censorship of television shows. They have agreed to allow a broadcasting industry representative to preview television entertainment programs for good taste—this, of course, in addition to the normal government censorship or regulation through the licensing power of the Federal Communications Commission, which is already entrusted with the authority to see that the networks and stations operate in the public interest.

I can summarize my own views of the effects of television violence as follows:

1. I believe that the vast amount of violence on television is *basically a reflection of the violent interests of the viewers;* it is a symptom, not a cause; it graphically portrays the violence in our souls. I doubt that it is a serious cause of much of it.

2. I do not believe that television violence, when *honestly portrayed,* engenders violence in viewers of any age who were not violent already; and I do not believe that it raises violent impulses to an uncontrollable pitch in those who are already violent. (I will discuss later what I mean by "honest" television.)

3. I do think, however, that for some who are already violently disposed, TV violence may provide a model, a *modus operandi,* when they choose to discharge their violent urges. However, a book, a newspaper, or a radio program may provide a violent person with the same type of detailed plan for the expression of his violence.

4. As far as *dishonest* television violence is concerned, I do think that exposure to repeated doses may possibly interfere, to a degree unmeasurable at present, with the normal development of impulse control in normal or disturbed children; but I do not think that "dishonest" television violence has any marked pathological impact on the average adult.

5. Instead of wasting their efforts on such red herrings as censorship, violence, sex, or nudity, I think that both the viewing public and the television industry would be far better off if the television industry would devote its considerable talents and energies to creating conditions that would make it possible to develop and screen television shows specializing in such qualities as excellence, artistic value, creativity, originality, honesty, and integrity. If *these* were the hallmark of our television shows, we would not have to worry about possible censorship of their violence, sex, or nudity.

Let me now outline the thinking that undergirds these five points.

As an introduction, I would like to remind you of the law of the land as repeatedly spelled out by the U.S. Supreme Court on the subject of censorship and particularly as it applies to motion pictures. Television is presumably covered by the same constitutional guarantees as freedom of speech and of the press with regard to censorship. . . .

The U.S. Supreme Court has frequently reaffirmed its position that all forms of communication can be censored on only one ground, namely *obscenity:* is the communication obscene or not? *There are no Supreme Court rulings that accept* violence *as grounds for censorship.*

The Supreme Court has also stated that only the effects of the communication on the *average adult* must be considered and that one cannot ban something because it may be harmful to children or to those adults emotionally disturbed. In the 1964 Jacobellis case concerning the picture, *The Lovers,* the Supreme Court quoted Judge Learned Hand who said, as far back as 1913:

> I scarcely think that (man) would forbid all which might corrupt the most corruptible, or that society is prepared to accept for its own limitations those which may perhaps be necessary to the weakest of its members . . . To put thought in leash to the *average conscience* of the time is perhaps tolerable, but to fetter it by the necessities of the lowest and least capable seems a fatal policy . . .

Let us now shift from the legal hat to the psychiatric hat, still focusing our remarks on movies. What is the potential harmful impact of *movie* violence on the viewer?

If we consider the origins of violent feelings in a given person, we recognize that *anger and the wish to be violent are a reaction to feelings either of frustration or of fear.* When a *child* is frustrated or afraid, he becomes angry and wants to hurt violently the person or object frustrating or frightening him. As life is full of frustrating and frightening situations, part of the task of the growing child is to learn how to control and redirect his feelings of anger and violence. The *adolescent* has a particularly difficult time controlling and redirecting these feeling because (1) his size make it possible for him to express them, which frightens him and his environment, and (2) adolescence normally is a time of rebellion and defiance of adults and of authority. The age period from fifteen to twenty is a particularly vulnerable and turbulent period in this respect. Usually, by about twenty-one years of age, adolescent turmoil subsides and normal adult controls over angry and violent feelings become established: the young adult is now socialized.

When a *normal adult* is exposed to scenes of violence, his own violent impulses tend to be stirred up by a process of contagion. This stirring up, in turn, brings his inner controls against violent behavior into action, thus re-establishing his emotional equilibrium.

There are various possibilities as to what can then happen:

1. If the violence to which the adult is exposed is *little or moderate,* he may enjoy it and gain a vicarious, secondhand satisfaction from viewing it, like the audience at a bullfight or a boxing match or a game of lacrosse.

2. If the movie has *one scene of great violence* and it is effectively presented so that it stirs up the destructive, violent impulses of the average adult, he may not enjoy it at all. Instead, the surge of violence within him will frighten him and he will display all the manifestations of fear—a fast pulse and fast breathing, nausea, pallor, diarrhea, etc.

As far as the long-term impact of violent movies is concerned, I think that we must distinguish between the effects on the normal adult and those on the normal child.

I do not believe that the average, normal adult requires any external protection against violent movies.

I believe that the average adult is perfectly capable of protecting himself against any possible psychological damage that may result from seeing one or more violent movies. My reasons for this position are as follows:

1. At any given moment, approximately 90 percent of all adults are functioning within normal emotional limits. Therefore, in line with the Supreme Court philosophy of establishing minimal standards, which are based on the effect of the communication on the "average" adult, we should consider for our purposes that the *average* adult is one who is "normal" emotionally.

2. By the usual definition of normalcy, the adult who is normal emotionally has both the capacity and the ability to protect himself from being harmed by a motion picture that is potentially dangerous to him.

The normal adult already has developed mental resources adequate enough to enable him to use one or more of the following safety valves: he can *ignore* the potentially dangerous violence; he can *reject it* by leaving the movie theatre; or he can *drain off in a safe manner* any potentially harmful tensions aroused by the film.

The normal adult provides his own built-in protection against the potentially dangerous aspects of a film, no matter how violent or depraved it may attempt to be or is.

However, I do not believe that the *average child* is in such a protected position.

Although the U.S. Supreme Court has not authorized any film classification system based on age, it has hinted that it might consider favorably film censorship for children. Also in the 1964 Jacobellis case, the Supreme Court had this to say:

> We recognize the legitimate and indeed exigent interests of states and localities throughout the nation in preventing the dissemination of material deemed harmful to children. But that interest does not justify a total suppression of such material, the effect of which would be to 'reduce the adult population . . . to reading only what is fit for children.' State and local authorities might well consider whether their objections in this area would be better served by laws aimed specifically at preventing distribution of objectionable material to children, rather than at totally prohibiting its dissemination.

I have long advocated movie censorship for children and adolescents, particularly as it concerns violence. My reasons for this advocacy are as follows:

1. A child, by definition, is an immature organism. Even a normal child is not expected to have the wisdom, the judgment, or the maturity of the adult. He is entitled to be protected from situations that may harm him, even though—because of his immaturity, his normal wish to be one of the group, or his normal state of adolescent rebelliousness—he may be attracted, and expose himself, to a potentially dangerous situation. The child is entitled to be protected even from himself.

2. This principle, accepted by all psychiatrists, is also given legal sanction in certain situations. A fifteen-year old may wish to drive a car, a seventeen-year old may wish to marry without a parent's consent, an eighteen-year old may wish to drink alcohol—but the law attempts to protect him in such special circumstances against the potentially dangerous consequences of his own (and sometimes even his parents') wishes.

3. In contrast to other forms of communication, such as books or magazines, films may have a devastating impact upon children and adolescents. This is because:

   a. A well-executed movie may be startlingly realistic, both because of its lifelike nature and because it tends to engage many of the viewer's senses.

b. In addition, a film potentially has a great capacity for capturing and focusing the viewer's attention on specific scenes.

c. Books and magazines can be put aside if they are disturbing, thus diluting their potentially traumatic effect. It is difficult to do so with a movie.

d. Although a child, like an adult, also is able to protect himself from dangerous material by leaving the movie theater, he is less likely to do so because of his immaturity, his fear of being considered "chicken" by his friends, and for economic reasons.

e. Books usually are read in the light, while a movie is viewed in the dark. Darkness tends to rob the child of one of his bases for self-security and self-control. The child may thus be more afraid in the dark, while fears associated with the dark and with nighttime may be more easily aroused.

f. Although the film viewer is usually one of a group physically, psychologically he may be peculiarly alone, cut off and isolated from the person in the next seat both by his own imagination as well as by the darkness.

I have been detailing the reasons for my belief that motion pictures, unlike any other form of communication, should be subject to censorship for their violence, but only as far as children and adolescents are concerned. I make a distinction, however, between violent movies shown in a movie theatre and perhaps the same violent movie shown on television.

From a psychological point of view, there are certain mitigating factors in television viewing that may greatly decrease the traumatic impact of the violence. These include the following:

1. TV viewing is usually with the light on. This absence of darkness provides security and relieves fear for the frightened child.

2. The child, when viewing TV, frequently is not alone; his parents, his family, or his friends may be present. This greatly increases his resistance to the impact of the violence.

3. There are opportunities for better control of what the child sees. The television stations usually make some attempt to show material that is not suitable for children at times that are not convenient for children. Also, the child's parents have greater opportunities for controlling what the child sees on a television screen than what he sees on a movie screen.

4. The inevitable commercials have a mental health value as useful tension-breaking devices. Thus the child has frequent, forced rest periods as far as the build-up of violence-provoked tensions are concerned.

5. The child can also come and go far more readily when watching a TV program than in a movie theater. This also helps him escape from excessively tense situations.

6. Although a child can eat a great deal in the modern movie theater, the opportunities for breaking tension through eating are much greater at home with a television program.

As I do not believe that the average adult can be harmed by the violence in movies, I certainly do not think that television movies will have any greater traumatic effect. As far as television viewing by children and adolescents is concerned, I do believe that there are possible dangers, particularly from viewing programs that are dishonest and lack integrity.

In order to explain what I mean by this, let me discuss for a moment the whole subject of violence on television. There has been until recently an increasing trend to violence on television. I think that this is due to a variety of reasons:

1. We are, and always have been a violent nation. We live in an age of violence. Therefore, to a large degree the violence on television accurately reflects the violence of our times.

2. We are increasingly freer in our acceptance of freedom of expression. The public and the courts are showing greater tolerance of, and are more liberal towards, what can be shown. In a similar way we are far more relaxed about displays of sex and morality. Therefore, more violence is being shown as part of this relaxation of censorship.

3. For some program directors and moviemakers, the showing of violence is a cheap way of producing something that may make money. Instead of relying on art, talent, or creativity, reliance is placed on violence for the sake of violence, of shock for the sake of shock. The shock effect of the violence is being used to sell the movie or the program.

4. Because the portrayal of obscenity is against the law, this sets a limit on the amount of sex that can be safely sneaked in. The portrayal of violence is not against the law and therefore can be used to the extent that audiences will accept it.

These are four reasons (there probably are many more) for the great use of violence on television programs. This is not to say that the showing of violence on television is necessarily bad. Actually, it can have decidedly positive effects on the viewing public, and particularly children. These *positive effects* include the following:

1. An appropriate display of violence tends to present the world as it really is, rather than as we wistfully wish it would be. It is unrealistic to leave it out when it is part of the scene. Therefore, when shown in appropriate amounts it can be of *educational* value.

2. It can also be of *mental health* value, if appropriately done. Like watching a bullfight or boxing match, it can help discharge indirectly various violent feelings of the viewer. This tends to keep the viewer's vio-

lent feelings from boiling over in more dangerous ways. Therefore, in appropriate amounts it can provide a safe catharsis.

On the other hand, the *negative effects* of viewing television include the following:

1. The child or adolescent has not yet settled on his typical behavior patterns for functioning. If exposed to a repetitive display of *violence as a television-approved method for solving problems*, the child may be encouraged in that direction, particularly if he already comes from a family setting where violence also is the way of settling difficulties. . . .

2. The individual, whether child or adult, who already uses violent behavior as a solution, may find worked out for him on television a detailed *modus operandi*. Therefore, the violent viewer may use the detail of the television programs as a way of expressing his violence. Television does not cause juvenile delinquency, but it can contribute techniques for a child already delinquent.

3. If excessive doses of violence are presented on television, it may have sufficient of a shock effect to prevent it being used for catharsis. There is a limit to how much viewing of violence can be used for a safe discharge.

The impact of repeated exposure to excessive violence depends on at least three factors: (a) the age of the viewer; (b) the maturity of the viewer; and (c) the way in which the violence is presented and packaged.

a. *The age of the viewer*

As I have already mentioned, the mature adult will be offended and disgusted by excessive or inappropriate displays of violence. Therefore he can ignore it or turn it off. The *normal adolescent (or the immature adult)* is in a different situation. The excessive display of violence may cause a sympathetic resonance of inner violent feelings in the adolescent to a degree that he cannot handle it. There is no socially acceptable way of discharging excessive violent feelings. Therefore the adolescent may have his normal attempts to come to peace with his violent and rebellious feeling jeopardized. The normal adolescent, unlike the normal adult, will also tend to be attracted to the violence rather than repelled. The *normal pre-adolescent child* may also be disturbed by excessive and inappropriate displays of violence. However, he probably will be less upset than the adolescent because he is not as concerned, as is the adolescent, with problems of violent rebellion against authority.

b. *The maturity of the viewer*

The more emotionally disturbed the viewer is, the more likely it is that he will have difficulty in managing stirred-up violent feelings.

Let us consider an extreme situation where an adolescent, immediately after seeing a TV program in which a juvenile delinquent violently rapes a girl, leaves the TV set and violently rapes the first girl he meets. For such a sequence of events to have occurred, one would have to say that the adolescent probably was seriously disturbed emotionally *before* he saw the TV program. It is highly unlikely that any program, no matter how violent, could have such an effect on a normal adolescent.

One also could not say that it was the viewing of the TV program that "caused" the adolescent to rape the girl. One could only say that the program had two effects. Its first was to *trigger* a previously-existing emotional disorder. The traumatic effect of the program was but one of the many etiological factors which, coming together, resulted in the adolescent's violent action. The second effect would be to provide the disturbed adolescent with a *blueprint* for discharging his violent tensions. These violent tensions, of course, would probably have originated in violent problems within his own family, completely predating his ever seeing the TV program.

Violent television does not make children aggressive; rather, *the aggressive child turns to violent TV*. And, for that matter, TV does not make a child passive; rather, it is the passive child who chooses the TV.

c. *The way in which the violence is presented and packaged*

1. The television violence will be least traumatic if it is completely appropriate and realistic to the story in which it is contained;

2. The television violence will be most traumatic if it is presented dishonestly, if it is being used to sell the program, if it is contrived and inappropriate, if it is unrealistically focused on, if it is presented out of context—in other words, if it is violence for the sake of violence and if the television show is deliberately using violence and brutality to attract and hold a larger audience.

The reason why *dishonest* television violence can be traumatic to the normal child or adolescent is because he feels exploited and used. *He senses he is being taken advantage of.* This tends to reactivate any conflictual feelings he may have about being exploited by his own parents. These reactivated feelings add an additional traumatic impact. In addition, the inappropriateness of the violence makes it harder for the child to deal with it mentally.

There are other packaging factors that help determine the degree of traumatic impact for the normal child or adolescent:

1. The degree of unreality of the characters and the violence may be a modifying factor. Thus cartoon stories, because they are so unrealistic, so caricatured, so bizarre, probably have little traumatic impact. Similarly, western stories, which are usually viewed by the child as being truly

make-believe, also probably have little traumatic impact. On the other hand, the closer the violent action approximates the real thing, and the more vividly and accurately it is portrayed, the greater is the potential harmful effect on children.

2. Humor is also a modifying influence in that it tends to take the edge off the violent impact.

As you will note, I have suggested that a constant diet of violence, when viewed in a movie theatre, may have a harmful effect on the normal child or adolescent. When it is viewed on a television program, I think that the harmful effect on children is limited to those TV programs that are exploitive of the violence and the viewer, programs that lack integrity or are dishonest.

Although a constant viewing diet of dishonest, violent television programs may be harmful to children and particularly to adolescents, it is important that we keep this question in perspective. The viewing of violent TV programs is only one part of a child's life and of the influences upon him. As Jimmy Walker once said, no girl was ever ruined by a book —or, one might add, by a television set. What we do and think at any given moment is the culmination of our entire life history up to that point. When a person commits a crime, he is responding not only to the situation of the moment but to all the events of his entire life and particularly to those of his childhood. When he commits a crime he is responding to all the traumatic experiences he has suffered from the day he was born.

The warm, secure home and satisfactory peer-group relationships provide a highly effective antidote to much of the potential harm that might come from television viewing by children. We know that the roots of all mental illness are anchored solidly in the unhappy experiences of childhood. The vulnerabilities within the adult that cause him to collapse quickly under the vicissitudes of modern living usually were created when he was a child. It is very unlikely that the child who is emotionally healthy will become mentally ill as an adult, or will suffer unduly from being exposed to TV violence.

It has been demonstrated repeatedly that the nature of a child's mothering or fathering in the first five years or so of his life is absolutely crucial. For most children, the adequacy of their care by their parents in these first five years is far more important than all their future television viewing. From the age of six or so, the healthy care or the traumatic pressures on the child—although still quite important—seem to have a decreasing effect in terms of helping him to become either mature or emotionally disturbed. By and large, by the age of six, the major roots of the child's personality and the major props and foundations for his emotional health have all been laid.

This is not to say that experiences and stresses after the age of six may not be of great meaning to the child. Basically, they assist the child in developing along the lines laid down earlier in his life. Good living experiences after the age of six may minimize somewhat the traumatic effects of poor handling prior to the age of six. Usually though, such relatively late corrective experiences have to be fairly intense to outweigh the stunning impact of earlier harmful experiences. Similarly, poor living experiences after the age of six also may retard the child's development of emotional maturity. However, if the child received adequate early care, it will take very hard knocks indeed to tear down his emotional maturity. Of course any child, no matter how healthy he is, may suffer an emotional disorder at any time if the stress and pressure upon him at that point is great enough.

When seen in this greater context, we must recognize that, no matter how harmful television violence may be for children, its traumatic impact is relatively minor compared to possible harmful handling by their parents. Television violence may bore one to death but I doubt if exposure to it will cause anyone to kill someone else. . . .

The violent action story will be with us until the public's taste changes, and there are no indications that a change is around the corner.

To listen to some of the critics of television, one gets the notion that everything would be just fine if only television violence were avoided or censored. Television does not create the desire for violence nor the social nor individual conditions that create it. It only caters to it, to an existing appetite that cannot be legislated or censored away. Violence is appealing to all of us because we all have unacceptable wishes to hurt and be hurt. For the most part, the normal person controls and holds in the direct expression of these wishes, and instead satisfies them indirectly and safely through such a medium as television.

When one observes all the fuss that is being made over television violence, one wonders about the enormously exaggerated statements and accusations. When one considers that our public welfare policies, for example, are doing more damage to the children on welfare than all the television programs put together, yet there is little outcry about the harmful effects of public welfare on children—it begins to make one wonder.

It is my own opinion that we are constantly looking for scapegoats to avoid facing the necessity of dealing with the many complex problems that beset us. We are always looking for an easy answer to what really are enormously complicated difficulties.

There is no such thing as a single simple cause for all cases of violence nor a single simple solution to them. Similarly, a blanket approach to children suffering from a specific symptom is almost useless unless it takes into account the uniqueness of each child.

For example, consider the delinquent child. The notion that every delinquent child has been over-protected and spoiled by his parents and really only requires firmness and punishment is as fallacious as the idea that every delinquent child is emotionally disturbed and requires an extensive psychoanalysis. One might as well prescribe morphine for everyone with a headache. Such a single-track policy would result in many brain tumors being missed and many people over-medicated.

I think that the two television networks that agreed to prescreen censorship have been sucked in by the pressures upon them. In effect, they have confessed to non-existent sins and have helped to drag another red herring across the road to true solutions. The sooner we get off the kick of falsely blaming American violence on American television, the sooner we will start grappling with the true causes of our national violence.

When I read in the papers about the actions of the two television networks, I was most tempted to write them the following letter:

To the two television networks who are willing to have censorship:

I am writing to correct certain misapprehensions you seem to have about the impact of your television shows upon your viewers. I would certainly agree that your programs may be quite entertaining, or even quite dull. They may be most educational, or even the opposite. Their taste may be excellent, or even low. But there is one thing you and your programs are not—they are *not* magical.

You may be the twelfth wonder of the world. You undoubtedly are powerful and wealthy. But as far as your ability to affect the mental health of a developing child is concerned, you are just not in the same league with a mother and father in their ability to help or harm a child's mind and emotions. Don't be so megalomanic. You're really not as omnipotent as you seem to think you are.

Don't be a patsy and get sucked in by those forces in this country that, however unwitting, are constantly looking for instant scapegoats and simplistic answers to what are really highly complex issues. Certainly, through your great potential for education, you can be of great help in our war on mental illness. But mental health is not primarily your thing. Why don't you stick to your thing, and let my colleagues and me worry about the mental health of the developing child.

Yours for greater creativity, artistic values, and imaginative, experimental originality in your programming—.

I haven't yet decided how to sign this letter.

MARYA MANNES

Television: The Splitting Image

A bride who looks scarcely fourteen whispers, "Oh, Mom, I'm so *happy!*" while a doting family adjust her gown and veil and a male voice croons softly, "A woman is a harder thing to be than a man. She has more feelings to feel." The mitigation of these excesses, it appears, is a feminine deodorant called Secret, which allows our bride to approach the altar with security as well as emotion.

Eddie Albert, a successful actor turned pitchman, bestows his attention on a lady with two suitcases, which prompt him to ask her whether she has been on a journey. "No," she says, or words to that effect, as she opens the suitcases. "My two boys bring back their soiled clothes every weekend from college for me to wash." And she goes into the familiar litany of grease, chocolate, mud, coffee, and fruit-juice stains, which presumably record the life of the average American male from two to fifty. Mr. Albert compliments her on this happy device to bring her boys home every week and hands her a box of Biz, because "Biz *is* better."

Two women with stony faces meet cart to cart in a supermarket as one takes a jar of peanut butter off a shelf. When the other asks her in a voice of nitric acid why she takes that brand, the first snaps, "Because I'm choosy for my family!" The two then break into delighted smiles as Number Two makes Number One taste Jiffy for "mothers who are choosy."

If you have not come across these dramatic interludes, it is because you are not home during the day and do not watch daytime television. It also means that your intestinal tract is spared from severe assaults, your credibility unstrained. Or, for that matter, you may look at commercials like these every day and manage either to ignore them or find nothing—given

---

Marya Mannes is a longtime free-lance writer and broadcaster, whose recent book is the novel *They*. "Television: The Splitting Image," from *Saturday Review,* November 14, 1970, is reprinted by permission of Harold Ober Associates, Incorporated. Copyright © 1970 by Marya Mannes.

the fact of advertising—wrong with them. In that case, you are either so brainwashed or so innocent that you remain unaware of what this daily infusion may have done and is doing to an entire people as the long-accepted adjunct of free enterprise and support of "free" television.

"Given the fact" and "long-accepted" are the key words here. Only socialists, communists, idealists (or the BBC) fail to realize that a mass television system cannot exist without the support of sponsors, that the massive cost of maintaining it as a free service cannot be met without the massive income from selling products. You have only to read of the unending struggle to provide financial support for public, noncommercial television for further evidence.

Besides, aren't commercials in the public interest? Don't they help you choose what to buy? Don't they provide needed breaks from programing? Aren't many of them brilliantly done, and some of them funny? And now, with the new sexual freedom, all those gorgeous chicks with their shining hair and gleaming smiles? And if you didn't have commercials taking up a good part of each hour, how on earth would you find enough program material to fill the endless space/time void?

Tick off the yesses and what have you left? You have, I venture to submit, these intangible but possibly high costs: the diminution of human worth, the infusion and hardening of social attitudes no longer valid or desirable, pervasive discontent, and psychic fragmentation.

Should anyone wonder why deception is not an included detriment, I suggest that our public is so conditioned to promotion as a way of life, whether in art or politics or products, that elements of exaggeration or distortion are taken for granted. Nobody really believes that a certain shampoo will get a certain swain, or that an unclogged sinus can make a man a swinger. People are merely prepared to hope it will.

But the diminution of human worth is much more subtle and just as pervasive. In the guise of what they consider comedy, the producers of television commercials have created a loathsome gallery of men and women patterned, presumably, on Mr. and Mrs. America. Women liberationists have a major target in the commercial image of woman flashed hourly and daily to the vast majority. There are, indeed, only four kinds of females in this relentless sales procession: the gorgeous teen-age swinger with bouncing locks; the young mother teaching her baby girl the right soap for skin care; the middle-aged housewife with a voice like a power saw; and the old lady with dentures and irregularity. All these women, to be sure, exist. But between the swinging sex object and the constipated granny there are millions of females never shown in commercials. These are—married or single—intelligent, sensitive women who bring charm to their homes, who work at jobs as well as lend grace to their marriage, who support themselves, who have talents or hobbies or commitments, or who are skilled at their professions.

To my knowledge, as a frequent if reluctant observer, I know of only one woman on a commercial who has a job; a comic plumber pushing Comet. Funny, heh? Think of a dame with a plunger.

With this one representative of our labor force, which is well over thirty million women, we are left with nothing but the full-time housewife in all her whining glory: obsessed with whiter wash, moister cakes, shinier floors, cleaner children, softer diapers, and greaseless fried chicken. In the rare instances when these ladies are not in the kitchen, at the washing machine, or waiting on hubby, they are buying beauty shops (fantasy, see?) to take home so that their hair will have more body. Or out at the supermarket being choosy.

If they were attractive in their obsessions, they might be bearable. But they are not. They are pushy, loud-mouthed, stupid, and—of all things now—bereft of sexuality. Presumably, the argument in the tenets of advertising is that once a woman marries she changes overnight from plaything to floor-waxer.

To be fair, men make an equivalent transition in commercials. The swinging male with the mod hair and the beautiful chick turns inevitably into the paunchy slob who chokes on his wife's cake. You will notice, however, that the voice urging the viewer to buy the product is nearly always male: gentle, wise, helpful, seductive. And the visible presence telling the housewife how to get shinier floors and whiter wash and lovelier hair is almost invariably a man: the Svengali in modern dress, the Trilby (if only she were!), his willing object.

Woman, in short, is consumer first and human being fourth. A wife and mother who stays home all day buys a lot more than a woman who lives alone or who—married or single—has a job. The young girl hell-bent on marriage is the next most susceptible consumer. It is entirely understandable, then, that the potential buyers of detergents, foods, polishes, toothpastes, pills, and housewares are the housewives, and that the sex object spends most of *her* money on cosmetics, hair lotions, soaps, mouthwashes, and soft drinks.

Here we come, of course, to the youngest class of consumers, the swinging teen-agers so beloved by advertisers keen on telling them (and us) that they've "got a lot to live, and Pepsi's got a lot to give." This affords a chance to show a squirming, leaping, jiggling group of beautiful kids having a very loud high on rock and—of all things—soda pop. One of commercial TV's most dubious achievements, in fact, is the reinforcement of the self-adulation characteristic of the young as a group.

As for the aging female citizen, the less shown of her the better. She is useful for ailments, but since she buys very little of anything, not having a husband or any children to feed or house to keep, nor—of course—sex appeal to burnish, society and commercials have little place for her. The same is true, to be sure, of older men, who are handy for Bosses with Bad

Breath or Doctors with Remedies. Yet, on the whole, men hold up better than women at any age—in life or on television. Lines on their faces are marks of distinction, while on women they are signatures of decay.

There is no question, in any case, that television commercials (and many of the entertainment programs, notably the soap serials that are part of the selling package) reinforce, like an insistent drill, the assumption that a woman's only valid function is that of wife, mother, and servant of men: the inevitable sequel to her earlier function as sex object and swinger.

At a time when more and more women are at long last learning to reject these assumptions as archaic and demeaning, and to grow into individual human beings with a wide option of lives to live, the sellers of the nation are bent upon reinforcing the ancient pattern. They know only too well that by beaming their message to the Consumer Queen they can justify her existence as the housebound Mrs. America: dumber than dumb, whiter than white.

The conditioning starts very early: with the girl child who wants the skin Ivory soap has reputedly given her mother, with the nine-year-old who brings back a cake of Camay instead of the male deodorant her father wanted. (When she confesses that she bought it so she could be "feminine," her father hugs her, and, with the voice of a child-molester, whispers, "My little girl is growing up on me, huh.") And then, before long, comes the teen-aged bride who "has feelings to feel."

It is the little boys who dream of wings, in an airplane commercial; who grow up (with fewer cavities) into the doers. Their little sisters turn into *Cosmopolitan* girls, who in turn become housewives furious that their neighbors' wash is cleaner than theirs.

There is good reason to suspect that this manic obsession with cleanliness, fostered, quite naturally, by the giant soap and detergent interests, may bear some responsibility for the cultivated sloppiness of so many of the young in their clothing as well as in their chosen hideouts. The compulsive housewife who spends more time washing and vacuuming and polishing her possessions than communicating to, or stimulating her children creates a kind of sterility that the young would instinctively reject. The impeccably tidy home, the impeccably tidy lawn are—in a very real sense—unnatural and confining.

Yet the commercials confront us with broods of happy children, some of whom—believe it or not—notice the new fresh smell their clean, white sweatshirts exhale thanks to Mom's new "softener."

Some major advertisers, for that matter, can even cast a benign eye on the population explosion. In another Biz commercial, the genial Eddie Albert surveys with surprise a long row of dirty clothes heaped before him by a young matron. She answers his natural query by telling him gaily they are the products of her brood of eleven "with one more to come!" she adds as the twelfth turns up. "That's great!" says Mr. Albert, curdling the soul of Planned Parenthood and the future of this planet.

Who are, one cannot help but ask, the writers who manage to combine the sales of products with the selling-out of human dreams and dignity? Who people this cosmos of commercials with dolts and fools and shrews and narcissists? Who know so much about quirks and mannerisms and ailments and so little about life? So much about presumed wants and so little about crying needs?

Can women advertisers so demean their own sex? Or are there no women in positions of decision high enough to see that their real selves stand up?

Do they not know, these extremely clever creators of commercials, what they could do for their audience even while they exploit and entertain them? How they could raise the levels of manners and attitudes while they sell their wares? Or do they really share the worm's-eye view of mass communication that sees, and addresses, only the lowest common denominator?

It can be argued that commercials are taken too seriously, that their function is merely to amuse, engage, and sell, and that they do this brilliantly. If that were all to this wheedling of millions, well and good. But it is not. There are two more fallouts from this chronic sales explosion that cannot be measured but that at least can be expected. One has to do with the continual celebration of youth at the expense of maturity. In commercials only the young have access to beauty, sex, and joy in life. What do older women feel, day after day, when love is the exclusive possession of a teenage girl with a bobbing mantle of hair? What older man would not covet her in restless impotence?

The constant reminder of what is inaccessible must inevitably produce a subterranean but real discontent, just as the continual sight of things and places beyond reach has eaten deeply into the ghetto soul. If we are constantly presented with what we are not or cannot have, the dislocation deepens, contentment vanishes, and frustration reigns. Even for the substantially secure, there is always a better thing, a better way, to buy. That none of these things makes a better life may be consciously acknowledged, but still the desire lodges in the spirit, nagging and pulling.

This kind of fragmentation works in potent ways above and beyond the mere fact of program interruption, which is much of the time more of a blessing than a curse, especially in those rare instances when the commercial is deft and funny: the soft and subtle sell. Its overall curse, due to the large number of commercials in each hour, is that it reduces the attention span of a people already so conditioned to constant change and distraction that they cannot tolerate continuity in print or on the air.

Specifically, commercial interruption is most damaging during that 10 percent of programing (a charitable estimate) most important to the mind and spirit of a people: news and public affairs, and drama.

To many (and among these are network news producers), commercials have no place or business during the vital process of informing the public. There is something obscene about a newscaster pausing to introduce a deodorant or shampoo commercial between an airplane crash and a body count. It is more than an interruption; it tends to reduce news to a form of running entertainment, to smudge the edges of reality by treating death or disaster or diplomacy on the same level as household appliances or a new gasoline.

The answer to this would presumably be to lump the commercials before and after the news or public affairs broadcasts—an answer unpalatable, needless to say, to the sponsors who support them.

The same is doubly true of that most unprofitable sector of television, the original play. Essential to any creative composition, whether drama, music, or dance, are mood and continuity, both inseparable from form and meaning. They are shattered by the periodic intrusion of commercials, which have become intolerable to the serious artists who have deserted commercial television in droves because the system allows them no real freedom of autonomy. The selling comes first, the creation must accommodate itself. It is the rare and admirable sponsor who restricts or fashions his commercials so as to provide a minimum of intrusion or damaging inappropriateness.

If all these assumptions and imponderables are true, as many suspect, what is the answer or alleviation?

One is in the course of difficult emergence: the establishment of a public television system sufficiently funded so that it can give a maximum number of people an alternate diet of pleasure, enlightenment, and stimulation free from commercial fragmentation. So far, for lack of funds to buy talent and equipment, this effort has been in terms of public attention a distinctly minor operation.

Even if public television should, hopefully, greatly increase its scope and impact, it cannot in the nature of things and through long public conditioning equal the impact and reach the size of audience now tuned to commercial television.

Enormous amounts of time, money, and talent go into commercials. Technically they are often brilliant and innovative, the product not only of the new skills and devices but of imaginative minds. A few of them are both funny and endearing. Who, for instance, will forget the miserable young man with the appalling cold, or the kids taught to use—as an initiation into manhood—a fork instead of a spoon with a certain spaghetti? Among the enlightened sponsors, moreover, are some who manage to combine an image of their corporation and their products with accuracy and restraint.

What has to happen to mass medium advertisers as a whole, and especially on TV, is a totally new approach to their function not only as sellers but as social influencers. They have the same obligation as the broadcast medium itself: not only to entertain but to reflect, not only to reflect but to enlarge public consciousness and human stature.

This may be a tall order, but it is a vital one at a time when Americans have ceased to know who they are and where they are going, and when all the multiple forces acting upon them are daily diminishing their sense of their own value and purpose in life, when social upheaval and social fragmentation have destroyed old patterns, and when survival depends on new ones.

If we continue to see ourselves as the advertisers see us, we have no place to go. Nor, I might add, has commercial broadcasting itself.

PART FIVE

Finessing the Censor

Introduction

Most Americans find the idea of censorship distasteful. Yet the Supreme Court has repeatedly upheld forms of censorship intended to protect social values, including the individual's reputation, national security during war, and the innocence of children.

Still, the Court has stepped more cautiously as the Puritan Ethic seemed to loosen its grip. Definition of obscenity appeared to grow more difficult during the fifties and sixties; language, scenes, and behavior that would have been shocking to most in the thirties are commonplace today.

The very elusiveness of obscenity's definition helps make the problem vexing. The meaning of obscenity varies with different cultures, regions, age groups, and eras. A picture may not be obscene to an artist or biologist, but it may be highly suggestive to a child or to Grant Wood's "American Gothic" farm couple.

We even have trouble if we try to distinguish between ideas and entertainment. The Supreme Court said in 1949 that the "constitutional protection for a free press" did not apply "only to exposition of ideas. The line between informing and entertaining is too elusive. . . . Everyone is familiar with instances of propaganda through fiction. What is one man's entertainment teaches another's doctrine."

Commercial entertainment, especially film, has been an obvious target of pressures for more control. Many argue that the box office morality of the entertainment world bears no resemblance to the real world and complain about attempts to "thrust box office morality" on the general public.

In the fall of 1970, a Presidential Commission on Obscenity and Pornography recommended repeal of all "federal, state and local legislation prohibiting the sale or distribution of sexual material to consenting adults." In the flurry of controversy that rose before Congress buried the Commission's report, most readers failed to note the recommendation for new laws to protect young people against salacious and obscene materials.

From the early 1920s until the fall of 1968, the motion picture industry tried to protect itself against outside attempts at censorship through a "code of self-regulation." Adopted in 1922, the code was modified in 1956 and again in 1966. During the Code's forty-six years, the major producers insisted that no censorship was needed since they were regulating themselves.

Portrayal of sex was, of course, the main target of those who wanted censorship. Lustful love, nudity, suggestive words or gestures, premarital or extramarital intercourse were all specifically prohibited by the Code. Its rules also sought to uphold symbols of morality, virtue, and patriotism, and to discourage portrayal of violence or "vulgarity."

By the mid-1960s, it was clear that the Code was no longer working. More than fifty countries in Europe and elsewhere in the world had adopted government systems of film classification designed primarily to protect the innocence of children. After denouncing the idea of classification for half a century, the MPAA announced a rating system in October, 1968.

The rating system was a voluntary version of compulsory government classification programs in effect elsewhere in the world. It left the producers free to make almost any kind of movie they wanted. The rating system, the MPAA emphasized, was to be administered entirely by the local theatre manager, acting voluntarily. The ratings were intended to be a set of signals to parents who might be concerned about the content of films their children wanted to see.

Adoption of the rating scheme came at a time when movies were introducing more and more explicit sex, in effect thumbing their noses at the old Code and its administrators. The Hollywood giants feared that the trend toward what many critics called obscenity in films might lead to a backlash in the form of government censorship or licensing. The rating system was intended as a hedge against such a backlash. To anyone who complained about obscenity, the reply could now be, "You were warned."

On the surface, the rating system is simple enough. A film rated G is for a general audience—anybody, of any age. If rated GP, all ages are also admitted, but "parental guidance is suggested." If rated R, or Restricted, the film cannot be seen by anyone under seventeen unless accompanied by "parent or adult guardian." And if tagged X, the film can be seen only by "adults," meaning—in most states—those over seventeen.

Many people believe movie-makers deliberately seek the X rating in hopes of boosting box-office take. Figures gathered by the Obscenity Commission showed only 15 X-rated films in the top 222 during the first half of 1970. These 15 drew only 7.2 percent of the gross receipts. Films rated GP numbered 69 and grabbed 33½ percent of the receipts. These figures may help explain the scramble of Hollywood producers for "another *Love Story*" after they saw early box office returns on Erich Segal's movie. Indeed, as the first years of the seventies passed, there was more and more pressure from theatre managers and their organizations for fewer "sexploitation" films and more G and GP movies.

Pressures were also coming from religious groups for more honesty in ratings. In mid-1971, both the Catholic and Protestant agencies that evaluate movies withdrew their support from the rating system, arguing that too many films that should have been rated "R" were being rated "GP."

The continuing battles over censorship may be a sign of society's good health. Writer and critic Malcolm Cowley says artists defend originality, freedom, and "social change, or the possibility of change, since we look to our artists for new perceptions and the first expression of new values." On the other hand, he adds, those who want to censor are "defending older values and established institutions against what they regard as the threat of moral chaos."

DAVID DEMPSEY

Social Comment
and TV Censorship

When the Smothers Brothers gave their farewell show last spring, Tom Smothers told their fans that three-fourths of the program had been censored to some degree by the Columbia Broadcasting System. Ever since the show went on the air in January 1967, the elder of the brothers (Tommy the Militant, as his friends call him) had engaged in a running battle with the network's Department of Program Practices, headed by William H. Tankersley (or Tankersley the Timid, as he is known to many writers and producers in Hollywood). A sketch written and performed by Elaine May dealing with censorship was censored. Ditto Harry Belafonte singing a medley of calypso songs before a newsreel backdrop of the Democratic convention (with scenes of Mayor Daley and the Chicago police). Ditto again when Dr. Benjamin Spock made a guest appearance. Joan Baez could say that her husband had gone to jail, but she wasn't allowed to say why (for refusing draft induction).

The show had seemingly committed the unpardonable sin of making social comment within an entertainment format. Dan Rowan, of *Laugh-In,* points out that Tom and Dick Smothers used comedy as a platform for doctrine, whereas he uses doctrine as a platform for comedy. The Smothers Brothers work from a youthful, anti-Establishment, often sophomoric point of view. Rowan and Martin tell jokes about the Establishment from a neutral position. ("Let's make peace in Vietnam and not tell Martha Raye" isn't the same as Tom Smothers getting off a crack at the very idea

David Dempsey is a free-lance writer, formerly with the *New York Times* and a frequent contributor to the *Saturday Review*. "Social Comment and TV Censorship" is reprinted from *Saturday Review*, July 12, 1969, with permission. Copyright 1969 Saturday Review, Inc.

of the war.) Moreover, *Laugh-In*'s humor flies by so fast that half the audience gets the joke but not the message. Watching the Smothers show, viewers got the message—and sometimes a little smut—but frequently wondered what happened to the joke. The brothers' transgressions, moreover, were simply not offset by a high enough rating in competition with NBC's popular *Bonanza* in the same time slot.

For whatever reasons, public sympathy was with the network. Forty-seven percent of those questioned by Lou Harris pollsters agreed that CBS was right in cancelling the show; 19 percent disagreed. (The remaining 34 percent had no opinion.) By 55 percent to 32 percent, the same group expressed a negative view of the program's contents.

Yet, when the smoke had cleared, millions of Americans had, perhaps for the first time, become aware of the pervasive infrastructure of television's tastemakers; the men, day in and day out, in New York, Washington, Hollywood, and London who decide what shall be shown and what shall not. Thanks to their efforts, viewers are protected from dirty jokes, crooked prize shows, commercials for unworkable toys, racial slurs, nudity, vulgarity, and the three great taboos of television—sin, sex, and sacrilege.

As an entertainment medium with the largest single audience in history (45 million persons at one sitting for some prime-time shows), television is under constant pressure to exercise "good taste," and is at the mercy of its sponsors if it strays into unpopular or controversial territory. For its lapses, it is recurrently threatened with punitive action by Congress. Last winter, Senator John A. Pastore, chairman of the Commerce Committee's Communications Sub-committee, cranked up a new investigation of "sex and violence" in TV programing. As a result, networks have tightened up their standards. CBS announced that it has "achieved a 30 percent reduction over the preceding season in the number of violent incidents in our prime-time programs." NBC has dropped all of its "action adventure" shows, and ABC is currently planning to do only one next season.

ABC also cut out a bikini contest in its *Wide World of Sports*, officially because of the poor quality of the film—and who knows, maybe that was the reason. The line between censorship and editorial acceptability in TV, as in other media, is a thin one. In any case, there will be no bikini contest sharing footage with Alpine skiers and log-rolling demonstrations on *Wide World of Sports*.

The new mood of caution comes at a time when American society is groping toward a more permissive, less hypocritical set of moral standards. In the arts, pornography is gaining an accepted place as a bedfellow of rectitude. The sex act is described freely in books, and the theater of nudity flourishes under the protection of the First Amendment.

Almost anything goes in the movies; profane—even obscene—language is tolerated as a literary right. Shock has become a catalyst for artistic and social change.

In this disturbing context, millions of Americans find prime-time entertainment a nostalgic sanctuary—perhaps the only one left—where few men swear, everyone is politically neutral, the church is never criticized, men and women do not live together out of wedlock, the happy ending is assured, the criminal brought to trial, and the little disturbances of life are usually resolved in favor of the status quo. Critics of television, including many of its own creative personnel, point out that the fallacy of playing to these "accepted moral standards" is that they are not the true standards of most communities, but rather those which the community wants to think are true. By eliminating the unpleasant, the controversial, and the "immoral," TV helps to sustain a mass illusion that is false to the society which gives the medium its franchise.

Yet, no one expects television to emulate the printed page or the theater in matters of frankness. The question isn't whether there should or should not be censorship, but rather how much and to what end. "It's a rare entertainer," writes Steve Allen, "who will willingly eliminate the funniest parts of his act when working a television show, if instructed only by his own conscience."

The conscience of television, on the working level, is embodied in some eighty-five network representatives who must have a thorough knowledge of the National Association of Broadcasters Code—seventy-three do's and don'ts (mostly don'ts) that comprise the parameters of acceptable programing—a high degree of tact, and the ability to delete objectionable material without making their cuts seem too obvious. "We are—to use that harsh and emotive term—censors," Bill Tankersley told a Midwest broadcast group recently. "The inescapable fact is that broadcasters are fully and finally responsible for everything that is broadcast over their facilities, and that responsibility cannot be delegated to anyone."

With this in mind, the censor almost always has the last word in any dispute with a producer. The code itself is a product of the industry's self-regulation, and although adopted in 1952, most of its provisions have gone unchanged over the years. Many of these are common-sense reflections of social decency involving ethnic prejudice, respect for the law, and demeaning references to the handicapped. More inhibiting is what constitutes "anti-social behavior"—illicit sex relations ("not to be treated as commendable") and drunkenness ("should never be presented as desirable or prevalent"). "My job is to move in if a program oversteps the boundaries," declares code-enforcer Stockton Helffrich, a fifty-year-old former NBC staff member who has worked in broadcasting since 1936. During the past year, the NAB screened 455 programs, 7 percent of

which were found questionable in some respect. Not all questionable programs are censored, however. When *The Avengers,* a British import, came
under scrutiny because of its mayhem, a psychiatrist called in to review
the series reported that the show was so highly stylized, and the means of
killing so bizarre, that viewers were not likely to identify with what they
saw. For whatever reason, *The Avengers* ground to a natural death this
spring.

Although the code authority has tightened up on violence, especially in
children's programs, it is moving toward a more liberal stance in the
areas of "taste" and "morals." Helffrich's office found no objections to a
showing of *Never on Sunday* (illicit sex), although admittedly the film's
frankest scene was missing. In any event, the code is not binding, and 35
percent of all TV stations do not belong to the NAB. The code does, however, constitute the Holy Writ whereby a network censor can effectively
snuff out any flame that burns too brightly on the home screen.

At ABC, all programs go through a five-step sanitizing process that begins with a review of the script and proceeds to a consultation with the
producer. A rough cut of the tape is then viewed, followed by another
screening before a different set of editors. A final screening is held with
the commercials in place. (They, too, are subject to being censored.) ABC
is the only network that keeps a full-time censor in London, where several
of its shows are produced. Partly for technical reasons, and because program standards are more lenient in England, ABC will frequently turn
out a separate—and less censored—version for the British market. *This is
Tom Jones,* for example, reaches the United States more fully clothed.
"For this production," declares Miss Grace Johnsen, the network's Director of Broadcast Standards and Practices, "our man in London pins ruffles
on the girls in all the proper places."

Similarly, editors at NBC work with a program from the first outline
right up to the finished product. The network's popular *Laugh-In* keeps
the censors on the *qui vive,* but aside from some suggestive lines, the
show is relatively free to do what it pleases. Gags about the pill, the
church, campus unrest, and politics abound, but they are jokes, not serious satire. Even so, NBC's mail on this program runs about two-to-one
against. The rating No. 1, however, is what counts.

Of all the networks, CBS has the largest staff of censors (twenty-five in
New York and sixteen on the West Coast) and the toughest reputation
among writers and producers. Nevertheless, attitudes here, as elsewhere
—despite Senator Pastore's admonitions—are being liberalized in many
areas. Mild profanity is now permitted in dramatic shows if justified by
character and situation; as violence declines on television, language is becoming more "realistic." The undraped female form is also seen (from the
rear) as the cutoff point—formerly the bra line—has been lowered to the

hip line. Sex is smuggled into TV by all the networks via the movies. However, the bolder these get, the more they are bowdlerized. *The Chapman Report* was so heavily censored that many viewers found it incomprehensible. *The Apartment* lost twenty minutes in its video version. Yet, the fact that they were shown at all marks a step forward.

Humor and satire still remain the touchiest area in entertainment programing; the problem here is not so much the joke as who tells it. Jack Benny once remarked of Bob Hope that although he gets off a lot of political humor, "he doesn't mean it." Benny's own freedom goes uncensored because "I'm not mad at anybody." Tom Smothers, on the other hand, gave the impression of meaning what he said. And unlike Hope, he is not a defender of the status quo in his private life. "Bob . . . is a millionaire Republican who owns the flag in the way that Danny Thomas owns the Cross," Steve Allen has pointed out.

As a "public utility," TV is especially vulnerable to pressure groups. Programs involving physicians, for instance, are usually "cleared" with a committee set up for this purpose by the AMA. Churches, humane societies, ethnic groups, patriotic and veterans' organizations all wield a powerful, if indirect, blue pencil. Even more powerful is the sponsor, whose fear of consumer backlash may lead him to avoid "controversial" programs. In the opinion of Robert Bendick, a former NBC producer, now an independent, this commercial concern is far more restrictive than the code or the networks' own standards. "The knowledge of what is acceptable to a sponsor and what isn't," he says, "is where censorship begins."

Scriptwriter Ernest Kinoy echoes this complaint when he says: "Basic censorship is that which doesn't get bought in the first place." The shrinkage of the big dramatic specials during the past few years has meant a decline in programs dealing with the "live nerve" of society. "Most of them were loss leaders, easily censored and easily dropped," Kinoy remarks. And the popular "talk" shows, as they have become successful, have become less controversial and have been "frightened into being a nice program," Bendick points out, "with a loss of the searching quality that once made them distinctive."

In a major policy statement five years ago, the Federal Communications Commission forswore the power to censor "provocative" programs merely because they might offend some listeners. "Even programs that some find sexually or politically disturbing are not subject to censorship for that reason alone," the commission declared. The code authority specifically encourages controversial programing and urges its members to "broaden the horizons" of the viewer. In this respect, the discrepancy between entertainment TV and the turbulent contemporary world as it is seen on public affairs programs and newscasts is growing wider and more inexplicable as the latter deal increasingly with the very issues that prime time avoids.

On this score, the networks are criticized for showing too much: "the coverage is blamed for the event," says Reuven Frank, head of NBC News, pointing out that to be "current, relevant, and involved" invites the partisan factions of our society to make themselves relevant to maximum TV coverage in pursuit of their aims. In many "demonstrations," the crowds are rehearsed well in advance, partly to make sure that the performance is up to television standards.

Much of this has occurred because entertainment TV, directed at the middle aged and the middle class, has locked out the young, the minorities, and the discontented. This is implicit censorship on a broad, built-in scale. The industry's value to the "have nots" in America is primarily to show them what they can't have. Noting that television heroes and stars, "are the physically attractive, glib, and wealthy," FCC Commissioner Nicholas Johnson contends that the "ideas and life-styles endorsed and purveyed by American television are truly 'popular' only with those Americans fortunate enough to be native-born-white-Anglo-Saxon-Protestant-suburban-dwelling-middle-class-and-over-thirty."

If this is true, TV's responsibility for civil disorder is probably greater than it is willing to admit, for the dissenters can get a hearing only by making themselves "newsworthy" in a way never before possible without the immediate and vast audience provided them—free of charge—by the picture tube. More than in most communications media, good news is no news on television; the militants make sure that the news is bad.

But the prime time goes on being good, censored, and largely irrelevant. It reflects not so much society as the image of society that TV has been instrumental in creating. The entertainer who challenges this image is in trouble; Mark Twain would have had a rough time on the networks, although Hal Holbrook's re-creation of Twain is acceptable because the satire is aimed at another era.

Many writers and producers aren't concerned with the trivia of censorshop—language, blue humor, sex taboos—but the idea content of their shows. A new generation has grown up on both sides of the TV screen that is no longer satisfied with Las Vegas gags. Challenging the complacency of the medium, they have been victims of a censorship never envisioned by the code or the FCC. What they ask for is a chance to compete, to let the public decide what it likes. "The ultimate censorship," says Tommy Smothers, "is the flick of the dial."

STANLEY KAUFFMANN

The Film Rating System

. . . *Last Summer* is rated X under the new rating system of the Motion Picture Association of America . . . presumably because it has a rape scene. X means that those under sixteen are not admitted. (In New York. Elsewhere the age may be a bit higher.) This is an example of one of the easily predictable stupidities of the rating system. I can't even figure out a consistent rationale in the MPAA ratings. *Goodbye, Columbus* is R, which means that those under sixteen may see it if accompanied by elders, although it contains much nudity of happy lovers in bed and lots of sexy talk. Is it rape that makes the difference? But surely the last thing that the Perry's rape scene does is to incite the viewer to some rape of his own. It's much more credible that the sex scenes in *Goodbye, Columbus* would incite him to some jolly intercourse. Maybe the MPAA is trying to tell us something?

This and other instances of stupidity do not prove to me that the MPAA system was a bad move—at this moment in our history. There have been silly ratings since last November. Since last November, there have also been the election of Nixon, the appointment of Warren Burger as Chief Justice, the reelection of Sam Yorty in Los Angeles, and the New York mayoral primaries, to select a few out of many events in recent months that, no matter how they are rationalized, are not cheery news for libertarians. In the climate that seems to be coming, I still think it possible (repeat: possible) that the rating system will prove more helpful than otherwise, something of a bulwark against the flatfooted legal censorship that is already being discussed in many places.

Stanley Kauffmann is a veteran film critic now writing a regular column for *The New Republic*. © 1969, 1971 by Stanley Kauffmann. Originally published in *The New Republic* July 12, 1969, reprinted by permission of the author.

In April the American Civil Liberties Union issued a policy statement on the MPAA system, a statement that I think is highly questionable. It notes that the ACLU has long criticized the picture industry's Code, that the new system is admittedly an improvement over the Code, that it is designed to ward off governmental censorship. Then the statement says:

> Nevertheless, our analysis of the voluntary rating system leads to the conclusion that it acts as a prior restraint on the creative process and denies film makers access to the free market-place where the public, the ultimate arbiter of film fare, can make its judgment.

To support this conclusion, the ACLU refers to the "myriad instances [in the past] where local moralists have insisted on the withdrawal of films

"He's on a scholarship from Paramount." Drawing by Joseph Farris from *Saturday Review*, April 10, 1971. Copyright Saturday Review, Inc., 1971. Reprinted with permission.

they regarded as objectionable" and, through various pressures, got their way. The ACLU fears that "the power of the boycott group can be so great as to pressure exhibitors against taking any X-rated film." This conclusion ignores the intent of the ratings, imperfectly though they may function. Their purpose is to undercut boycott by clearly labeling the product, by making audience deception or surprise impossible, and by excluding children from X films. If a boycott group protests an X film, they cannot, on the face of it, contend that they are protecting minors; nor can they contend that an adult will see the picture without being aware that —in someone's view, at least—it is considered morally daring. The system can be said to facilitate the showing of such films, rather than the contrary; and my own small field-check, in various parts of the country, shows that, to some degree, this has been the result.

The ACLU worries that X films will not run on television. The worry seems premature, since these films will not be available to TV for some years, and who would have predicted *Laugh-in* five years ago? But if TV mores do not themselves change, what difference will the absence of an X make to network censors? Anyway, the subject of TV is irrelevant, since it involves a quite different audience, which gets the material in a quite different way and place.

The only instance of "prior restraint" cited by the ACLU is a statement by Robert Aldrich, the producer-director of *The Killing of Sister George.* He says that, in his new contract with his backers, he has had to guarantee that his future films will not receive X ratings. But even Aldrich does not object to the ratings as such. He specifically states that "lack of adequate education by the MPAA on the true meaning of X-ratings has set the stage for economic censorship. . . ." This is an indictment of the poor explanation of the system, not of the system itself. From this, one can infer that Aldrich sees that the X-rating was intended as an empowerment, not a restriction, and that it is being misunderstood.

I deplore, with the ACLU, the fact that the X-rating interferes with the right of a parent to take his child to any film he chooses. I said so in my first article, where I also deplored (like the ACLU) the silly and inconsistent age limits. But if I am forced to choose—and such a choice looms— between the right of those under sixteen to see X-rated pictures and the possibility that pictures now rated X might be completely suppressed, I have no hesitation in choosing.

In its last paragraph the ACLU says:

> The voluntary rating system now in effect, no matter what its avowed purpose, levels a deadening hand of sterility and conformity on creative people.

The only instance given of this "deadening hand" is Mr. Aldrich. But he concedes that the backers of *Sister George* had the right to edit his picture without his consent, a right granted long before the rating system was instituted. The backers' final control is very much more the rule than the exception in American films—a fact not apparent in the ACLU's airy statements about the freedom of creative film people. (How about an ACLU policy statement protesting *that* peonage of American directors?)

The rating system is not responsible for the deadening hands in our film world.

It may even lighten those hands. For what is happening at the box-office with such X-rated films as *Last Summer* and *Midnight Cowboy?* So far they seem to be prospering. Aldrich's backers will not have missed that news. And there is plenty of evidence of pictures now in preparation that, far from suffering from prior restraint, mean to benefit from the true intention of the labeling.

It feels strange to be arguing in favor of classification. But there seems to be a war shaping up, and a faulty weapon is better than none. In any civilized view, the rating system is shameful; but the conditions that make it possibly necessary and possibly helpful are more shameful.

There is a humorous, pragmatic side to the question. In the *Educational Forum* (March, 1969) Martin S. Dworkin says:

> It is unlikely that the worldlings of the movie business really believe in the real authority of parents of the 1960s over the viewing habits of children of moviegoing age, especially older adolescents. What they obviously do believe in is some display of reliance on parental power, while theater managers do something *in loco parentis*—enough, at least, to hold off action by local censorship authorities. . . .

Basically, that's all I hope for, I guess: that the rating system will prove a useful fraud.

RUTH BRINE

Pornography Revisited:
Where to Draw the Line

Manhattan newsstands are so crowded with displays of *Call Girl, Gay Party, Ball* and *Desire* that it is sometimes the New York *Times* that is sold under the counter. The situation is similar in many big cities. Detroit newsstands even have dildos and whips for sale, bestselling books vie with each other in sexual explicitness and vulgarity and there are no off limits at all in the theater. Around Times Square, exhibitions of simulated intercourse can be seen afternoons and evenings for $5 and up. Skin flicks and their ilk, which used to be limited to a few hundred city theaters, are now shown in about 2,000 moviehouses, many of them in suburbs and small towns, while the criteria by which commercial films are rated are flickering rapidly skinward. What was once R is now GP, and what was X only a year ago is now R. As such ratings and audience thresholds change, so does the borderline of legal obscenity, which is partially defined by "contemporary community standards" that are constantly getting lower.

The national Commission on Obscenity and Pornography recommended —for a variety of reasons—the repeal of dozens of anti-obscenity laws. Judging by the violent reactions that the report provoked, its recommendations are not likely to be widely adopted; on the contrary, signs of a new restrictive mood toward pornography have begun to appear. The publishers of an explicitly illustrated edition of the pornography commission's report itself were indicted by grand juries in Dallas and San Diego. The New York City Criminal Court convicted the editor and publisher of

Ruth Brine is an associate editor of *Time*. "Pornography Revisited: Where to Draw the Line," from the April 5, 1971, issue, is reprinted by permission from *Time*, The Weekly Newsmagazine; Copyright Time Inc., 1971.

Screw, the nation's No. 1 underground sex tabloid, of publishing obscenity. In San Francisco, where everything conceivable has been seen for several years, the D.A. recently got convictions against three porno filmhouse proprietors, one of them for showing a movie in which a woman had intercourse with a dog, a stallion and a hog. The Supreme Court split 4 to 4 in a decision on the obscenity of the film *I Am Curious (Yellow),* which had the effect of upholding the ban on the film in Maryland. Although legal sophisticates realized that this was due to the abstention of Justice William Douglas, some of the more censorious nevertheless took heart.

Meanwhile, a new round of discussion has opened, much of it in favor of some sort of censorship.

QUESTION 1: DOES PORNOGRAPHY REALLY DO ANYONE ANY HARM?

The liberal position, of course, is that "no girl has ever been seduced by a book." That statement is erroneous, according to Poet-Librarian Felix Pollak—or at least he hopes it is: "For the saying doesn't do the cause of literature any good, or the intellectual cause in general. If one denies the power of the word to do evil, one denies the power of the word to do good. In effect, one denies the power of the word. I prefer the healthy fear and awe of the written and spoken word, evidenced by censorious zealots, to the wishy-washy neutralism of the liberalist anti-censors."

But how can one prove the evil effects of words or pictures? Never had there been such a concerted effort to answer this question as was made by the pornography commission with its $2,000,000 budget. In one study that became notorious, measuring devices were attached to twenty-three penises while the owners were exposed day after day to erotica. The resulting data proved only what one might suspect: that men can become satiated. According to the majority report, pornography cannot be proved to cause crime, sexual deviancy, or severe emotional disturbances. This is a conclusion somewhat at odds with that reached by the national Commission on the Causes and Prevention of Violence, whose behavioral studies indicated that exposure to violence does cause harm. The violence commission therefore recommended more restraint, while the pornography commission recommended less.

A dispassionate look at the tangle is provided by Harvard Government Professor James Q. Wilson in the quarterly *The Public Interest.* Wilson found the obscenity studies "unexceptionable within their limited framework." But, he said, "one cannot simulate in the laboratory the existence or nonexistence of a lifelong exposure to or preoccupation with obscenity, any more than one can simulate a lifelong exposure to racist or radical opinions." His major thesis is that proof of harm is largely beside the point. Even if behavioral studies could not prove that individual Negroes are harmed by being denied access to public facilities, reasons Wilson, he would still want them to have that access. Violence and obscenity are moral issues, he believes, and judgments about them must rest on political and philosophical, not utilitarian considerations.

QUESTION 2: DOES PORNOGRAPHY HAVE A DELETERIOUS EFFECT ON THE MORAL CLIMATE AS A WHOLE AND ON VALUES GENERALLY?

A highly theoretical argument for censorship is made by University of Toronto Government Professor Walter Berns. Democracy, more than any other form of government, requires self-restraint by its citizens, he maintains, and self-restraint can be partially achieved by laws governing public amusements. Pornography makes people shameless, he believes: "Those who are without shame will be unruly and unrulable; having lost the ability to restrain themselves by obeying the rules they collectively give themselves, they will have to be ruled by others." Therefore pornography leads to tyranny, Berns concludes.

Whatever else it does or does not do, pornography makes strange bedfellows. New Left Philosopher Herbert Marcuse is as censorious of it as is Berns. While Berns fears that pornography makes men unrulable, however, Marcuse thinks that it makes them tame. Marcuse objects to sexual permissiveness because he thinks it is a safety valve that keeps people from exploding and breaking up the System. To him, the relaxation of sexual taboos is a sort of capitalist plot. "Desublimation," as he calls it, is therefore repressive.

Many observers are most concerned about the sadistic component of much current pornography. "No civilization, with the possible exception of the Aztec, could produce an art whose sexual ferocity would rival that of the West," according to Mexican Poet-Diplomat Octavio Paz. In Western pornography, "death spurs pleasures and rules over life. From Sade to the *Story of O*, eroticism is a funeral chant or a sinister pantomime." Reading about sadism can have a cumulative effect, according to Psychoanalyst Ernest van den Haag. *Der Stürmer*, a Hitlerite journal that mixed anti-Semitism and sex, contributed to the general atmosphere that made it possible to slaughter Jews, Van den Haag believes. Similarly, he says, today's sadistic pornography contributes to a general atmosphere in which sadism becomes generally permissible.

There is, however, the question of what comes first. Maybe pornography circulates freely because public standards have already changed; maybe people read about sadism because they are already sadistic. Political Scientist Wilson Carey McWilliams argues this point well: "Degeneracy becomes socially visible, emerging from underground, only when it has reason to expect a welcome. Certainly this is the case in relation to sexuality. Our verbal sexual morals had become nothing more than cant some time ago. Worse, they were a form of hypocrisy which discouraged respect for law."

QUESTION 3: DOES THE FIRST AMENDMENT, WHICH GUARANTEES FREE SPEECH, PROTECT OBSCENITY?

Not until 115 years after the first federal obscenity law was passed did the Supreme Court address itself directly to the constitutionality of such laws. Then, in the Roth case of 1957, it held them, in general, to be constitutional. "Obscenity is not within the area of constitutionally protected speech or press," the majority decided. And what is obscenity? A three-part test soon evolved: 1) the dominant theme of the material taken as a whole must appeal to a prurient interest in sex; 2) the material must be patently offensive because it affronts contemporary community standards; 3) the material must be utterly without redeeming social value.

Whereas the Roth decision generally upheld anti-obscenity laws, the succeeding interpretations of it usually knocked them down. They have, for the moment at least, virtually abolished literary censorship. A further liberalizing decision was made two years ago in Stanley v. Georgia. The court concluded that obscenity, when it is read or viewed at home, is protected by the Constitution. This decision, it is now argued, implies the right to buy or receive obscenity. In short, decision after decision has opened wider the umbrella of the First Amendment.

However, at the same time, a few cases snapped that umbrella shut—under specific circumstances. One involved sales to minors. In Ginsberg v. New York, the court held that states may make it a crime to sell "to minors under seventeen years of age material defined to be obscene to them whether or not it would be obscene to adults." The court's reasoning was that "the well-being of its children is a subject within the state's constitutional power to regulate." And Ginzburg v. United States makes it possible to prosecute publishers for "pandering to the widespread weakness for titillation by pornography," even if the obscenity of the material being pandered is in doubt.

Thus the law on obscenity is bewildering, even to many lawyers, though some are gamer than others in defending it. "The landmark case of Roth," wrote Earl Warren Jr. recently, "is still valuable, and in fact has gained viability with each succeeding interpretation, even though it now bears little resemblance to what we originally thought it to be."

QUESTION 4: CAN OBSCENITY LAWS BE ENFORCED?

Stanford Law Professor Herbert Packer declares flatly that a vigorous campaign of law enforcement against pornography "would involve costs in money, manpower and invasions of privacy that we as a society are unwilling to pay." One of the pornography commission's best arguments for repealing many existing laws was that they have not worked. The trouble begins with definitions. Justice Potter Stewart says that he cannot define hard-core pornography, but he knows it when he sees it. This is understandable, but is scarcely a practical basis for criminal indictments.

Nor has the courts' three-part test been much help. How big is the community? A town, a state, the nation? What is prurient interest? What about "utterly without redeeming social importance"? Even if something is of value only to masochists, asks Justice Douglas, how can it be said to be utterly without social importance? Others argue, in effect, that no law is perfect; society must do the best it can. "The Sherman antitrust law forbids monopolies," says Political Scientist Reo Christenson. "What is a monopoly? What is an unfair trade practice? When is guilt proved beyond a reasonable doubt? Those indignant over the lack of specificity in obscenity laws are quite complacent about vagueness in laws they approve."

QUESTION 5: WHAT CAN BE DONE ABOUT PORNOGRAPHY?

Where should the line be drawn against pornography, or should it be drawn at all? Given the narrow scope left by the courts to the legal definition of obscenity, strict laws banning pornographic material from adults will not stand up in court unless the Supreme Court eventually changes its position. In its eyes, the dangers of inhibiting freedom of expression are far greater than those presented by pornography. Beset as we are so suddenly with mountains of pornographic trash and with well-meaning arguments for doing away with it all, it is easy to forget the crimes against political freedom, science and the arts that have been committed in the name of morality. Books by Aristophanes, Defoe, Rousseau, and Voltaire have been seized by U.S. customs, and Hemingway, Dreiser, and Sinclair Lewis were once banned in Boston. Such past errors certainly do not constitute a conclusive argument against censorship, but they do underline one fact: no apparatus of censorship has ever been devised, or probably can be devised, subtle enough to assure the freedom of the arts or of ideas. Nor does the new freedom necessarily mean that the wave of smut will further engulf the nation. Denmark's experiment in legalizing pornography, for instance, by all accounts has resulted in a decline of the Danes' own interest in it, as well as in the number of reported minor crimes like exhibitionism.

It seems wrong to keep pornography from adults who want it; certainly the attempt is also impractical and wasteful of time, money, and effort. But this does not mean that nothing at all should be done. If some have a right to pornography, others have an equal right not to have it foisted on them. The New York State legislature last week passed a law that, if signed by the Governor, ought soon to clamp down on Times Square. This kind of regulation would not put pornography back under the counter but it would at least remove it from the shop windows and posters. As for obscene mail, another unpleasant invasion of privacy, 500,000 orders have already been received by the Post Office to block specific advertising material, and 15,000 requests a week are now coming in to stop all sexually oriented ads, under a new law that went into effect Feb. 1.

Equally important, there are legal, enforceable ways of keeping pornography away from minors—those under eighteen, seventeen, or possibly sixteen, whatever age each community decides—and in fact the pornography commission drafted sample legislation for the states. Logically, of course, if pornography cannot be proved to be bad for anyone, there is no more reason to protect minors from it than to protect adults. But there are strong emotional and cultural arguments for doing so. In order to be effective, however, new laws must be specific.

Any regulation at all is anathema to some civil libertarians, who have a respectable and logical position. It was easier to agree with them when pornography was young and reasonably clean—for instance, back in 1949, when Judge Curtis Bok inveighed against censorship. "I should prefer that my own three daughters meet the facts of life in my own library than behind a neighbor's barn," he wrote. But with pornography what it is today, parents may wonder whether their daughters are not actually better off behind the barn than in the library or at the movies. Even liberal Americans may want to set firmer limits on what their daughters—and sons—will be able to see and read. This should be possible without otherwise blocking the free traffic of ideas.

REO M. CHRISTENSON

Censorship of Pornography? YES

Tougher censorship laws for America? Speaking as a liberal and long-time member of the American Civil Liberties Union (ACLU), I believe stronger pornography legislation is clearly needed.

To most intellectuals these days, censorship in sexual matters is firmly identified with prim little old ladies, country bumpkins, Bob Jones College, backwater conservatism, cultural yahoos—and Puritans in general. (A Puritan is someone whose views on sex are less permissible than yours.) Historian Barbara Tuchman (*The Guns of August*) has observed that prominent writers who favor some censorship where sex is concerned are afraid to speak out openly. Attorney Richard Kuh documents the point in a book which has received far too little attention—*Foolish Figleaves.* (Kenyon political scientist Harry Clor's *Obscenity and Public Morality* deserves a bow, also.)

The case for stricter censorship of pornography runs as follows. More than three-fourths of the American people want it, according to a Gallup Poll in June, 1969. They are affronted by books, magazines, movies, plays, erotic displays, pictures, and records which vulgarize, desecrate, and cheapen sex, or which encourage or glamorize deviant sexual behavior. The Middle Americans—and many others—have a deep-rooted suspicion that all of this will undermine certain moral restraints believed to be essential to the public weal.

There is no way of proving whether this suspicion is or is not well-founded. But the public's fears about excessive sexual permissiveness are supported more than they are challenged by such inadequate empirical evidence that we have. In *The Sexual Wilderness,* Vance Packard summarizes the findings of those academicians who have given the most at-

Reo Christenson is a professor of political science at Oxford University, Miami, Ohio. "Censorship of Pornography? Yes" is reprinted from *The Progressive,* September, 1970, with permission.

tention to the relation between sexual permissiveness and the progress of society as a whole. He cites *Sex and Culture* by Former Oxford Professor J. D. Unwin, whose massive studies of eighty primitive and civilized societies reveal a distinct correlation between increasing sexual freedom and social decline. The more sexually permissive a society becomes, Unwin says, the less creative energy it exhibits and the slower its movement toward rationality, philosophical speculation, and advanced civilization.

Harvard sociologist Pitirim Sorokin agrees with Unwin that sexual restraints promote cultural progress; in *The American Sexual Revolution* he contends that immoral and anti-social behavior increases with cultural permissiveness toward the erotic sub-arts. In an article in *The New York Times* magazine entitled "Why I Dislike Western Civilization," May 10, 1964, Arnold Toynbee argued that a culture which postpones rather than stimulates sexual experience in young adults is a culture most prone to progress.

In another article in *The New York Times* magazine, Bruno Bettelheim, the noted psychoanalyst, recently observed: "If a society does not taboo sex, children will grow up in relative sex freedom. But so far, history has shown that such a society cannot create culture or civilization; it remains primitive." Sorokin asserts ". . . there is no example of a community which has retained its high position on the cultural scale after less rigorous sexual customs have replaced more restricting ones."

Many social scientists doubt that contemporary research skills are capable of either affirming or denying these charges. The Middle American, then, can hardly be blamed for concluding that, in the absence of scientific proof one way or the other, majority views should prevail. In *The Common Law*, the late Oliver Wendell Holmes, celebrated Justice of the United States Supreme Court, declared that "the first requirement of a sound body of law is that is should correspond with the actual feelings and demands of the community, whether right or wrong." And Justice John M. Harlan, in *Alberts v. California*, declared, "the state can reasonably draw the inference that over a long period of time the indiscriminate dissemination of materials, the essential character of which is to degrade sex, will have an eroding effect on moral standards." Harlan has thus established the crucial link between dubious practices and reasonable law.

But should majorities deprive minorities of free expression, whatever their fears may be? When the First Amendment says, "Congress shall make no law . . . abridging freedom of speech or press," should it not mean what it says—*no law?*

The First Amendment does not really mean "no law" and never has. We have had a score of respectable laws abridging freedom of speech and press, some dating back to the earliest days of our republic. A few of these forbid libel, perjury, contempt of court, incitement to violence, disrespect toward command officers, and copyright violation. The First Amendment itself limits free expression; by implication, the "establishment of religion" clause forbids the advocacy of religious doctrines in public schools. The true meaning of the First Amendment is that Congress may place no *unreasonable* restraints on freedom of speech and press. Our entire history attests to this view.

The drafters of the Constitution probably and properly intended an absolute ban on efforts by the Government to forbid the dissemination of any political, economic, religious, or social ideas. John Stuart Mill and others have made an overwhelming cogent case for such freedom; no equally persuasive case has been made for the unlimited freedom of commercial entertainment. There is a right, therefore, to advocate the most disgusting forms of sexual perversion—so long as the proponent is clearly attempting to persuade rather than to entertain commercially. But commercial entertainment cannot logically claim the same constitutional protection as normal political discourse.

To the extent that entertainment and persuasion are combined, the case for constitutional protection is proportionately enhanced. But no one has yet demonstrated that the effective dissemination of ideas demands the use of pornographic techniques. The latter are conceivably of peripheral persuasive value but surely no more than that. The marginal loss of free speech involved in sensible pornography legislation, as with other reasonable restrictions on free speech, is more than counterbalanced by the protection of children and the creation of an environment, especially for children, which is more conducive to responsible sex behavior.

The ACLU takes no absolutist position on the First Amendment, but it does oppose limitations on speech and press unless it can be proved that a given expression creates a clear and present danger that it will trigger an act which society has a right to forbid. The ACLU is also convinced that no scientifically valid proof exists that the consumption of pornography produces criminal behavior.

Obviously, the ACLU wants society to consider only short-term effects since it regards long-term effects unknowable. The truth is that short-term effects are also unknowable. The difficulties of delving into the depths of human motivations and sorting out from the richly tangled psychic undergrowth those strands which "cause" a criminal act are so formidable that root causes or even the relative importance of contributory factors may never be satisfactorily established.

Unhappily, all of the major premises on which our society rests derive from the realm of intuition—the viscera. Can anyone *prove* that the family is a desirable institution? That higher education promotes human welfare? That technology makes men happier? That love is better than hate? That democracy is superior to dictatorship? None of these is provable. But this does not stop us from acting on our best judgment, knowing that all human judgment is fallible. If, then, the regulation of pornography comes down to a matter of visceral hunches, why should not the majority of viscera pervail?

Is "pornography" such an imprecise term that it lacks sufficient clarity to meet the "due process" test?

Current state laws could be updated and made more explicit if they were refined to forbid actual or simulated exhibitions of sexual intercourse or sexual perversion on stage or screen—or pictorial representations thereof in other media—when such exhibitions or pictorial representations are primarily intended for commercial entertainment rather than for education.

If the emerging vogue for making a fast buck by portraying such scenes on stage and screen is not an example of moral degradation, that term must be bereft of all meaning. There *are* limits of human decency, and these limits are being transgressed more blatantly year after year in the shameless commercial exploitation of man's baser instincts. Admittedly a few playwrights or motion picture directors may be able to handle these scenes in a sensitive and illuminating manner, but for every artist who can do so, a hundred entrepreneurs will use such themes in a fashion which can only cheapen and coarsen sex. The interests of the general American public are considerably more important than gratifying the erotic-esthetic yearnings of the avant-garde.

Next, the U.S. Supreme Court should modify the interpretation which holds that censorable material must be "utterly without social importance" (*Jacobellis v. U.S.*, 1964). "Utterly" should be stricken, since it invites dealers in pornographic literature to "redeem" their noxious wares by introducing just enough literary "quality" or moral substance to pass judicial muster. The Court should substitute a test of the "predominant" character of challenged material.

Even with these clarifications, the statutory-judicial definition of pornography remains rather vague. But the same applies to numerous other laws. The Sherman anti-trust law forbids monopolies. What is a monopoly? When one firm—or an oligopoly—controls thirty percent of the output in a field? Fifty percent? Seventy-five percent? Ninety percent? No one knows, and the Supreme Court has never been able to tell us.

What is an "unfair trade practice"? What is a merger which "substantially" reduces competition? What is "negligent" manslaughter? When is guilt proved beyond a "reasonable" doubt?

In terms of imprecision, then, pornography statutes are no more defective than many other well-accepted and adjudicable laws. At one end of their administered continuum, it is clear that a publisher or dealer has not broken the law and no one will take him to court. At the other end, he has so clearly broken the law that he will not bother to appeal the case. But movement toward the center leads to more difficult decisions, until a middle zone is reached in which it is anyone's guess whether the courts will find the defendant guilty. Decisions in this zone inevitably entail a certain amount of arbitrariness and raw subjectivity. Yet those indignant over the lack of specificity in obscenity laws are quite complacent about vagueness in laws they approve.

It is often argued that judges have no special expertise on sexual proprieties. True enough, but if they can bring no special wisdom to bear, they are likely to bring moderation to bear. And that is no mean asset. Furthermore, citizens will accept decisions by judges which they would not so readily accept from others. In brief, entrusting these decisions to the judiciary is a good practical solution to the problem.

Since negative judicial decisions on pornography are sure to be subjected to scathing attacks by civil libertarians—as judges well know —there is much more likelihood of judicial lenience than of excessive restraint. Perhaps it is best to err on the side of leniency, while imposing sufficiently severe penalties where guilt is found to discourage those who specialize in exploring and exploiting the margins of decency.

It is easy to produce a long list of worthwhile books which have been banned and to make censors look ridiculous in the light of modern opinion. But each generation has a right to set its own standards, and if pornography criteria change from time to time, the same is true of legal criteria in other fields. A thousand examples could be cited, including such notable constitutional clauses as "equal protection of the laws" and "the establishment of religion."

Of course, critics are inclined to evaluate censorship solely by its "failures," the banning of works of genuine merit. But it is unfair to exhibit the "failures" of censorship without considering the other side of the coin. If all of the loathsome materials which officials have confiscated and the law has discouraged were balanced against the mistakes, the overall results would look much less damning of censorship than many English professors would have us believe.

Opponents of pornography censorship sometimes contend that the state should not try to be the moral custodian of the people. Nor should a majority seek to impose its moral standards on a minority, it is said.

Yet *every* criminal law represents a moral judgment. And laws typically constitute a coercion of the minority by the majority. Presumably bigamists resent laws against bigamy, polygamists oppose laws against polygamy, and sexual exhibitionists dislike laws against indecent exposure. Their objections are not decisive once society regards these restrictions as reasonable. The same is true of pornography laws.

If the home, the church, and the school provided adequate sex education and moral training, there would be less need for pornography laws. But the law must deal with social realities, not Utopian visions. Since millions of children receive virtually no moral training, or sex education, the nation is obliged to rely partly upon law for their protection.

Those who say, "Don't tell *me* what *I* can see or read," are consulting their impulses rather than the larger interests of society. A socially responsible person will forego the indulgence of a desire if the policy permitting that indulgence jeopardizes the well-being of others.

Most of us, it should be emphasized, welcome today's freedom to discuss sexual questions and seek greater sexual satisfactions through increased education and scientific knowledge. Nor will the censorship envisaged herein interfere with this salubrious development. It is a mistake, however, to believe that the commercial exploitation of sex frees us from crippling inhibitions and promotes a healthy attitude toward sex. Pornography is more likely to deposit ugly images in the consciousness or subconsciousness of the young than it is to contribute toward the formation of a wholesome attitude toward sex.

The New York Academy of Medicine declared in 1963 that reading salacious literature "encourages a morbid preoccupation with sex and interferes with the development of a healthy attitude and respect for the opposite sex." Certainly if young people are stimulated to experiment with forms of perversion before they understand their implications, traumatic experiences may occur which leave them psychologically scarred for life. Parents who strongly oppose the introduction of unsolicited pornography into their homes display an eminently sensible attitude toward the protection of their children. This outrage, reported to affect more than a million children a year, obviously must be halted.

Sexually abnormal persons who "need" pornography probably need psychiatric care even more. However, since they are unlikely to get the latter, it would probably be unwise to try to eliminate all pornography. If dealers do not solicit or sell to children, do not advertise their wares, and limit their sales to adults who seek them out, perhaps it is best to leave such traffic alone. Sometimes it is prudent to temper the administration of law with a realistic regard for human weakness. The Greek rule applies—"nothing too much."

Are pornography laws unenforceable? Do they tend to make pornography more attractive, since it becomes forbidden fruit?

Enforcement is admittedly difficult. We have not been able to prevent drunken driving, either, or supermarket theft, or income tax evasion, but we do not proceed to make them legal. Instead, we seek more effective enforcement measures.

Laws may make pornography somewhat more attractive to certain persons; so do laws against vandalism and speeding and heaven knows how many other misdeeds. In any case, the repeal of pornography laws would not eliminate the social disapproval associated with the behavior involved. This social disapproval would continue the "forbidden fruit" effect, even in the absence of law.

As for oft-cited Denmark, which has repealed all prohibitions against written pornography (and against pictures sold to persons over sixteen years old), the trial period is far too short to enable us to draw any firm conclusions. Certain kinds of pornography have experienced declining sales; other kinds are flourishing even more. *Newsweek* has called Copenhagen "a veritable showcase of pornography," bristling with shops specializing in every conceivable form of erotic lingerie, sadomasochistic devices, sexual stimulators, and pornographic jewelry. This may be an appealing demonstration of the delights of a free and liberated society, but a dissenting view is also conceivable.

Paradoxically, the existence of censorship probably assures greater freedom in America than its absence. Morris Ernst, the noted civil liberties lawyer, in *Censorship: The Search for the Obscene,* agrees that the decline of governmental censorship has led to an increase in private vigilantism. If, somehow, the tiny minority (Gallup estimates about six percent) which wants no censorship were to have their way, it would be an open invitation for vigilante groups to take over. Outraged at the irresponsibles, the Middle American would employ extralegal pressures as a substitute for law. And a sorry substitute they would be. Controlling pornography by legal means and orderly institutions gives us the best assurance that society's concern will be dealt with in a civilized manner.

To those in the entertainment world, freedom is the supreme value. Whatever makes men more free is believed *ipso facto* good. But freedom is not, standing alone, the *summum bonum* of human society. If it were, we would need no government. Men once saw *laissez-faire* as the culmination of economic progress, only to discover that commercial greed was not quite an adequate guide for achieving human welfare. When freedom is not accompanied by a reasonable amount of self-restraint and social responsibility, it can become a destructive force. I see neither this self-restraint nor this sense of social responsibility being manifested in much of the entertainment world. The most profound (although often subliminal) message which much of modern music, movies, and literature convey to the young is, "Let 'er rip."

A society can tolerate only so much emotional turmoil, so much disruption, so many assaults upon its sensibilities and its mores. At some point, the public's patience becomes exhausted; it cries, "Enough." This denouement may not be far off in America. When it comes, the entertainment industry should be assigned its full share of responsibility in the area of pornographic presentations for the general repression which follows. (Those who condone gross social injustices and those who employ violence for political ends admittedly deserve a large share of blame.)

For the record, I find much to applaud in our revolutionary age: the refusal to support a senseless war; the challenge to the military budget and to certain military assumptions; the so-called "equality revolution," the demand for justice to the blacks and the poor; the call for sweeping educational reforms; the insistence on higher standards of public morality. But the stresses and strains involved in these movements are hard enough for the body politic to bear. Add to these a dubious sexual revolution powerfully stimulated by the entertainment industry, and society may be bearing an overload of tension.

A final word. Maybe all the "dumb people" are not so dumb after all. Maybe they are right in sensing that sex needs to be treated with some caution, that sexual privacy needs to be preserved from commercial contamination, that sexual relations must not be divested of all sanctity, all mystery, and reduced to the level of leer and titter.

It is a disturbingly democratic idea that the common man just might be smarter, now and then, than many of our avant-garde intellectuals.

DISCUSSION AND ESSAY QUESTIONS

1. Make up a list of five standards that represent the ways in which you make judgments about programs you like or dislike on TV.

2. How do you, personally, define what writer Richard Schickel calls the New Class? Do you consider yourself a member? If so, what kinds of things do you do or think that distinguish you as a member?

3. Can you think of five movies you've seen which were not particularly great, or even good, but which had enough story and good dialog to keep you entertained for two hours?

4. If you had a choice between watching a TV program on which your city council debated a red-hot issue or a serious TV drama, which would you select? Why?

5. A few press councils have been organized to hear public complaints about newspapers in this country, and more seem in the offing. Do you think similar councils would help in the radio and television industry?

6. The FCC is now trying to stop newspapers from buying radio or TV stations in the same community. Do you think that's a good idea? Explain your reasons.

7. If you were to organize a Citizens Television Advisory Council, as Nicholas Johnson of the FCC suggests, how would you go about setting up standards to rate a broadcaster's performance?

8. Do you agree with Johnson's statement, "What the American people think about government and politics in general, as well as a favorite candidate in particular, is almost exclusively influenced by television"? Explain your answer.

9. Let's say that a viewer suddenly realized he is spending more time than he really wants to spend watching television. What strategies could he adopt in order to become more selective in his viewing?

10. Do you know anyone who is a TV addict in the sense that he watches the set for several hours every night, regardless of the programs being broadcast? Are his behavior or attitudes unusual?

11. If you were a television writer, plotting a one-hour drama, what characteristics would you want your hero and heroine to portray? Try to "create" an imaginary hero or heroine.

12. Do you think there would be less violence on television and in films if there were less violence in society?

13. Discuss the argument that men are presented on television in a more favorable light than women, regardless of age. Give examples from programs or commercials that you have seen.

14. In your opinion are talk shows, such as those featuring Johnny Carson and Dick Cavett, too bland, too careful about avoiding real controversy?

15. Do you feel that pornography is harmful? Discuss your answer.

16. What are the problems of arriving at a workable legal definition of obscenity?

17. Do you agree with the American Civil Liberties Union that the voluntary rating system restricts the creative process of film makers? What is your reasoning?

18. Can you give four or five examples of TV programs you watch for reasons of escapism? Do they include both low culture "kitsch" and high culture?

19. Do you see signs of a decline in admiration for European movies and increased respect for American-made films? What are the signs?

20. Are older people—those, say, in their thirties or forties—more, or less, likely than young people to be influenced by TV in attitudes and behavior?

21. Discuss the question whether TV violence may have a different effect on a child or adolescent who has a warm, secure home life than it has on a youngster whose home life is troubled.

22. Do you think many TV watchers pay attention to commercials? Is it possible that the proportion varies with both program content and advertised product?

23. "Mild profanity" is now allowed in TV network programs. Are there any words, in your opinion, that should be banned, regardless of the plot?

24. Make a list of four or five recent movies and/or books which have been popular even though they were considered by some to be pornographic. Do you think they should have been censored?

25. Do you think it is necessary for some films to be spiced with sex and/or violence in order to succeed at the box office? Discuss.

Conclusion

THEODORE PETERSON

Why the Mass Media
Are That Way

In the past few years a good many persons have been lining up, like sailors at a shooting gallery, to draw a bead on the various mass media of communication. A. J. Liebling, for one, has published his essays about our "monovocal, monopolistic, monocular press." Newton Minow has spoken about television fare with such vehemence and frequency that he has given the term "wasteland" a currency that T. S. Eliot never did. And Robert Lekachman, in the greatest heresy of all, has charged that our good magazines, our *Harper's* and *Atlantic* and *Nation,* are not good enough, are not the equal of their British counterparts.

Editors, publishers, and broadcasters have learned to live with this criticism, but they have seldom learned to like it. Their reactions have varied from surprised hurt and mild petulance on the one hand to red-faced indignation and savage counterattack on the other.

I cannot agree with those publishers and broadcasters who seem to think that finding fault with the mass media is somehow un-American, like setting out poisoned Ken-L-Ration for Lassie. My aim is not to argue that the American mass media are the best in the world, although I think they are. It is evading the issue to say that our media are the best or even good. The word "good," after all, has many meanings, as G. K. Chesterton reminds us with his remark that a man who shoots his grandmother at five hundred yards may be a good shot but not necessarily a good man.

The truth is that I sometimes agree with what the critics have to say about press performance. But when I do, I often have the uneasy feeling that they are right for the wrong reasons and that one may as well look to

Theodore Peterson is head of the Journalism Department of the University of Illinois. "Why the Mass Media Are That Way" is reprinted from *Antioch Review,* Vol. XXIII, No. 4, 1964, with permission.

Dr. Seuss for richness of character and complexity of plot as to look to them for sensible prescriptions. So what I propose to do is to touch on a major stream of press criticism that I think is bound to be futile, to examine its assumptions and shortcomings, and then to suggest, a little hesitantly, a direction that I think holds greater promise.

The strain of criticism that strikes me as essentially futile blames publishers and broadcasters for all of the shortcomings of the mass media. In its many variations, this line of criticism sees the men who own and operate the media as merely foolish, as irresponsible, or as downright evil. The common denominator of the variations is that the media are bad because the men who own and operate them are in some way bad.

That idea is almost as old as printing itself. In the sixteenth century, even before the newspaper came to England, critics were grumbling about the half-penny chroniclers who scampered off to scribble verses for its precursor, the broadside. When newspapers did appear, the men who ran them came in for some abuse. Samuel Johnson, who had opinions on all subjects worth having opinions about and on a good many that were not, delivered his views on newsmen in 1758: "The compilation of Newspapers is often committed to narrow minds, not qualified for the task of delighting or instructing; who are content to fill their pages with whatever matter, without industry to gather, or discernment to select." His observations were mild compared with the American variety, especially those in the period of bitter partisan journalism in the late eighteenth and early nineteenth centuries, when the press deserved all of the criticism it got. James Ward Fenno, an old newspaperman himself, said in 1799:

> The American newspapers are the most base, false, servile, and venal publications, that ever polluted the fountains of society—their editors the most ignorant, mercenary and vulgar automatons that ever were moved by the continually rusting wires of sordid mercantile avarice.

In our own century, by far the great bulk of press criticism, I think, has blamed the owners and operators for the shortcomings of the media. A good deal of it arises from what we might call the conspiratorial theory of press malfunction—the notion that publishers and broadcasters have conspired with big business to promote and to protect their mutual interests, that in exchange for suppressing and distorting media content they share in such handsome rewards as advertising contracts, social position, and political prominence.

Will Irwin set the themes for much of such criticism in a series of articles about newspapers that he wrote for *Collier's* back in 1911. Advertisers had come to realize their power over the press, he said, and in some instances they had been taught it by the newspaper themselves. To attract customers for advertising space, some papers had made concessions to advertisers. In time advertisers came to take these concessions as special privileges—insertion of publicity; biased news accounts; suppression of news harmful to the advertiser, his family, his associates and his business interests; and, in rare instances, a complete change in editorial policy. Irwin was perceptive enough to recognize that many shortcomings of the newspaper arise not from the harmful influence of advertising but from the commercial nature of the press, and he observed that simply because publishers are businessmen, the newspapers they control might be expected to reflect the viewpoint of business.

Irwin was followed by a succession of critics who reiterated his charges, although not always with his perception. In 1912, after he had already clubbed the packing industry with his wooden prose, Upton Sinclair brought out *The Brass Check,* which likened the press to a vast brothel in which truth was the virtue for sale. *The Brass Check* has been almost as durable as its author, who has written a book for each of his eighty-four years, for it went through several editions and was revised in 1936. Sinclair's pitch was that the "Empire of Business" controls journalism by four devices—by direct ownership of the press, by ownership of the owners, by advertising subsidy, and by direct bribery.

The "empire of business" idea was a favorite one in the Depression of the 1930s, when businessmen were low in popular esteem, and critic after critic described how knights of that empire worked hand in hand with the press to thwart the common good. Harold L. Ickes contended that publishers made up America's House of Lords, a body enriching and enhancing the power of the economic royalists whose ideology had a well-filled purse as its core. George Seldes saw the lords of the press as polluting the fountain of truth by suppressing news or distorting it and plotting evil behind closed doors at meetings of the American Newspaper Publishers Association. Ferdinand Lundberg wrote scathingly of Imperial Hearst, and other writers did portraits of other publishers in acid.

Today critics seldom speak of "lords of the press," a term that sounds a little dated, but they sometimes do number media owners among "the power elite." And quite a few critics evidently do assume that Sinclair and Seldes and Ickes were right in blaming the owners and operators for a good share of what is wrong with the media.

Their line of thought, let me confess, is rather appealing. For one thing, there is enough truth in it to make it seem valid. The media *are* big business, and their outlook *does* tend to be that of big business generally. For another thing, the way to improvement is then comparatively easy: Somehow, through punishment or persuasion, we must make the media owners pure of heart; then the press will be as great as publishers say it is during National Newspaper Week, and television will become man's greatest achievement since the pyramids. Charles Dickens had a similar explanation for the ills of nineteenth-century England, and his solution was equally simple: Let evil-doers be shown their errors, and they will join their nobler fellows in a merry dance of brotherhood around the Christmas tree.

Criticism that does little more than blame the men who own and operate the mass media is bound to be futile, I think, for it rests on debatable if not downright erroneous assumptions.

One is that most owners and operators lack a sense of social responsibility. Now, some publishers do show a deeper concern over what paper costs than over what they print on it, and some broadcasters do regard the public airwaves as their personal, exploitable property. Even so, I am prepared to argue that most publishers and broadcasters have a greater sense of public responsibility than a good many critics gave them credit for having—one as high as that of most leaders in business and government, and perhaps higher. At times their standards of performance may not be the ones that most intellectuals would set if they were running the media, but the eggs that make one man's soufflé make the next man's omelet.

A second assumption is that the nature of the communications system is determined primarily by the men who now own and operate the media. They of course do have a good deal to say about what the mass media pump out. But in one sense what they choose to include and omit, as I will try to show, is not entirely of their own doing.

Let me make it abundantly clear that I am not suggesting that publishers and broadcasters are sacrosanct, like Harvard, J. Edgar Hoover, and the Marines. I am not defending the shortcomings of the media for which they can be held accountable. What I am saying is this: Criticism that concentrates on them and their motives at best can explain only a small part of reality and at worst can obscure a genuine understanding of why the mass media are what they are.

Jay Jensen, in an article in the *Journalism Quarterly*, argued that genuine criticism of the press must begin with an understanding of the mass media as an institutional order.* His approach enables us to see the mass media from an entirely different perspective. It changes our focus from the transitory, short-term effects of the media to the relationships of the communication system to society in their most fundamental form. It enables us to see that the communication system performs certain objective functions quite irrespective of the intents and interests of the men who operate it.

For criticism to be valid and fruitful, Jensen said, it must meet three re-

* Jay W. Jensen, "A Method and a Perspective for Criticism of the Mass Media," *Journalism Quarterly* 37 (Spring 1960), 261–66.

quirements. First, it must be objective. It must be conducted without bias or censure arising from ideological presuppositions. Second, it must take into account the influence of social, political, and cultural forces in the historical development of the media. And finally, it must put the media into the context of their environment; it must take note of the demands, values, aspirations, and life interests of the society in which the media operate.

Criticism meeting those three tests can come about, he said, if we will look at the mass media from an institutional perspective. Man has devised various institutions to help solve different aspects of the problem of human existence. Each institution is a complex pattern of values and behavior designed to meet some persistent and pressing social need. The family exists to sustain life, the church to give it meaning and direction. An institutional order is simply a larger and more complex pattern of values and behavior, for it is made up of several institutions by which man attacks the overall problem of existence. In that functional sense, then, the mass media are an institutional order. They are a way of dealing with one phase of existence—the necessity for social communication. So wrote Jensen.

In a sense, human societies arose from and are maintained by communication. What makes man unique among all creatures is his capacity for creating symbols. Throughout history, in all societies, mankind has had certain fundamental means of communicating—gesture, imitation, what Sapir calls social suggestion, language. Using them, both primitive man and civilized man have surrounded themselves with a web of symbols.

Man, in fact, seems to have some inner compulsion to create symbols. They give him his image of himself and locate him in the vast stream of time. As Kenneth Boulding reminds us, a dog has no idea that there were dogs before him and that there will be dogs after him. But man, through his symbolic creations, has a sense of the past that stretches centuries behind him and a concept of the future. Symbols are man's chief means of communicating with his fellow man, the carrier of the social process. Through them, he can express his fears, his hopes, his plans, his ideas of the world he lives in, and through them he achieves the consensus that is necessary if he is to get along with his fellow men. They are the means whereby man copes with his environment and gives meaning to his existence.

Man's propensity for creating symbols has given human beings a whole new environment. For man, alone of all creatures, reacts not just to his physical surroundings but to a pseudo-environment, a symbolic environment, and it may be more important than the actual one in governing what he thinks and does. Only with comparative rarity does man deal with physical reality at first hand; for the far greater part, he deals with ideas about reality. In short, he interposes a symbolic system between himself and his purely physical universe. This is not to say, of course, that he moves in a world of utter fantasy. The symbols he has developed are his attempts to organize his sensations and experiences into some meaningful form, to bring some order and meaning to his existence, and thus to deal with his environment. And indeed through the use of symbols man can alter and shape his environment.

What one sees from the institutional perspective is that the mass media are but one aspect of human communication in general. Like the semaphore and tribal drum, they are technical extensions of this primary social process that I have been talking about. As purveyors of symbols, the mass media help society to function. They are carriers of the values, the beliefs, the distinctive tone of the society in which they operate. As Walter Lippmann observed some forty years ago, they interpose a sort of pseudo-environment between man and physical reality. But if they are a force for stability, they are also a force for change. And because they are technical extensions, they can transmit their message across vast sweeps of space and time.

What one further sees from his institutional perspective is that the mass media are not really autonomous but are adjuncts of other orders. Looking back through history, one sees how various dominant institutions, unwittingly or by conscious design, have used the media to maintain and strengthen their power. So it was when the church used the printing press to reinforce and extend its influence. So it was when the Crown held the press of England in thrall. So it is today in Soviet Russia, where the mass media are an adjunct of the political order, or in the United States, where they are an adjunct of the industrial.

What one sees still further, however, is that the media are a force for disrupting the status quo as well as for perpetuating it. Under the bejeweled but firm hand of Queen Elizabeth I, the press was a means of consolidating the power of the Crown and of achieving the nationalism that echoes so gloriously through the chronicle plays of Shakespeare. Yet in the hands of dissidents the press became a powerful weapon for wresting the scepter from the monarch and reducing his presence on the throne to the largely ceremonial. Or consider another instance. When printing came along, its immediate effect seems to have been to disseminate and perpetuate the very superstitions that scientists were trying to combat. In the November 1962 issue of *The American Behavioral Scientist*, Livio C. Stecchini summarized the effects in this way:

> In the sixteenth century books of geography consolidated the outmoded conceptions, just when navigators and discoverers were revealing completely new worlds. The press was greatly responsible for the general wave of

opposition to the Copernican doctrine. Copernicus' book *De revolutionibus orbium coelestium,* published in 1543 A.D., was not reprinted for twenty-three years, while in the interval there appeared a cataract of popular works on astrology. Not until the beginning of the seventeenth century did the non-academic public, reading in vernacular, become sufficiently enlightened to make it possible for Galileo to impose his views by appealing especially to them. The surprising epidemic of witch trials which began in the sixteenth century can be blamed partly on enterprising publishers who discovered that there was an excellent market for books on magic and witchcraft.

Yet true as all of that may be, few persons would dispute the subsequent influence of the press on the dissemination and advancement of learning.

If we look at the press from an institutional perspective, we should be especially concerned, I think, with the forces that have helped to make our mass communications system what it is. From here on, I would like to talk about two environments in which our communications system grew up. Both of those environments, as I will try to show, have played a tremendous part in determining the nature of our communications system. On the one hand, the mass media have been conditioned by an environment that exists largely in the minds of men. They have been profoundly influenced, that is, by the way we have answered such fundamental questions as the nature of man, the ideal relationship of man to the state, and the nature of truth and knowledge. On the other hand, the media have been shaped by such powerful social and economic forces as the rise of democracy, urbanization, and the industrial and technological revolution.

The classical libertarian theory of the press derived from the ideas of the Enlightenment, and among its several assumptions are these: That man is a creature of reason who wants to know the truth and will be guided by it, that he can find truth by applying his reason, that he is born with certain inalienable natural rights, and that he forms governments of his own volition to protect those rights, and that hence the best government is that which governs least.

In brief, the libertarian theory of the press came to be something like this: The press must have only the most minimum of restraints imposed upon it because man can find truth only if there is free trade in information and ideas. No one need worry about the wide arena of freedom, though, for the natural working of things provides certain built-in correctives and safeguards. If some parts of the press lie and distort, if some parts abuse their freedom, other parts will find it expedient or profitable to expose them. And, after all, man puts all information and ideas to the powerful test of reason. He may find some truth amidst falsehood, some falsehood amidst truth, but over the long pull truth will prevail.

The government should keep its hands off the press for several reasons. For one thing, free expression is a natural right, one the state must preserve and protect. For another, the state has traditionally been a foe of liberty and is always likely to use the press for its own selfish purposes. For yet another thing, the state by intervening would surely upset the delicate dialectic by which truth emerges. The press, then, is best left in private hands, to make its own way in the market-place, free from the pressures of any one group or interest. In short, freedom under libertarian theory consists simply of the absence of restraint; to put it another way, a negative freedom is an effective freedom.

As that theory evolved, certain social functions came to be ascribed to the press. The press, for instance, is charged with enlightening the public and providing it with some entertainment. It is charged with servicing the political system by carrying the information and discussions that the electorate needs for its decisions. It is charged with protecting individual rights by sounding the alarm whenever they are threatened or infringed. It is charged with servicing the economic system, largely through advertising, and with earning its own financial support.

In the twentieth century especially, many of the assumptions of traditional theory have been seriously challenged if not indeed actually undermined, and some of us have found signs that a new theory of the press, a social responsibility theory of the press, has begun to emerge. But social responsibility theory is still largely theory, and our traditional ideas still guide a good deal of thinking about the press and still influence its workings in many ways. Let me give just one rather detailed example.

One tenet of Anglo-American theory is that the government should stay out of the communications business. My purpose is not to debate whether or not that idea is a good one. My point is that the idea has profoundly affected the nature of our communications system, although someone from another society may find it as quaint as we find the Yurok salmon fisherman's belief that he must not eat in his boat. From his parochial viewpoint, the Yurok has good reason for that bit of dietary abstinence: eating on the water violates his tribe's belief that various channels of nature must be kept apart. From our parochial viewpoints, so ingrained are the laissez faire doctrines of Adam Smith and the experiences of men who fought for press freedom in the past, we think we have good reason for keeping the government's hands off communications; for control necessarily follows support, we reason, and the government can weigh the scales on which truth is measured. In each case, a sacrosanct belief has affected life's crucial affairs—getting enough to eat in one, communicating with our fellows in the other.

Let me give just one illustration of how our faith in laissez faire has affected our communications system. Broadcasting depends upon the use of a limited number of channels, and other countries have handled the ownership of radio and TV facilities in various ways. The assumption is that the airwaves belong to the people. There is nothing in the nature of the medium demanding that it be left to private entrepreneurs, or, if it is, that its programs be surrounded by and punctuated with pleas to buy this product or that.

But broadcasting costs money, and someone has to pick up the tab. In our society the financing, described crudely, goes something like this: Broadcasters pay for programing and all of the equipment for transmitting it, but they are more than reimbursed by advertisers. Presumably the advertisers are not out of pocket, though, for they are reimbursed by listeners and viewers, who also must invest in receiving equipment. So ultimately the consumer bears the cost of broadcasting, but his money is channeled through private rather than governmental hands. True, the government regulates broadcasting, but the Federal Communications Commission has severe legal and practical limitations on its powers.

So strong is the conviction that communications must be kept in private hands that the federal government was reluctant to assign frequencies for educational and other non-commercial broadcasting. When it did, it acted in accord with the negative tradition of our press theory. It simply granted schools and communities permission to operate stations, but it made no provision for getting them on the air or keeping them there. Many stations got their money from state funds, a form of government support that was only partially taboo, since the cause was "education."

Once a year the Yurok suspends his tribal taboos, and in 1962 Congress waived one by authorizing the expenditure of $32,000,000 to encourage the growth of educational TV. Even though that sum was only about 60 percent of what Procter & Gamble spent on network TV in 1961, Congress hesitated for months before actually appropriating just a small part of it.

Although critics have found fault with our system of broadcasting, attack is not my aim here. My object is simply to show how an idea, central to public thinking about the press, has contributed to the nature of the system.

It is not just ideas, however, that have given us the sort of communications system we have. Social, economic, and political forces shaped the media too, and a combination of ideas and these other things made the media what they are.

In a way, it is not surprising that the mass media should be described as an adjunct of the industrial order. The rise of journalism paralleled the rise of capitalism, and printing itself was one of the earliest forms of mass production. Many early printers in England and America were primarily businessmen. Indeed, the fight for press freedom in England arose not just from political causes and the philosophical principles of free inquiry; it also came about from the trade demands of London printers and stationers who wanted to pursue wealth without state interference.

Today our communication system is characterized by bigness, fewness, and costliness. Small units have grown into huge ones. The *Reader's Digest*, for instance, began publication in a Greenwich Village basement in 1921 with a capital of $5,000 and a list of 1,500 charter subscribers. Today it publishes more than forty editions around the world, and its domestic edition alone reaches slightly more than one in four of U.S. adults. As the media have grown, there has been need for fewer of them. Three networks serve the great majority of TV stations, and two major wire services supply the great bulk of international, national, and regional news to the nation's dailies. As the media have grown, they also have become costly. A century ago one could start a metropolitan daily like the New York *Times* for $50,000 to $75,000. Today one can spend more than a million getting a daily going in a medium-sized town such as Jackson, Mississippi, and then have it fail.

In all of those things, the media are not much different from other businesses and industries. Bigness, fewness, and costliness are characteristics of much of our economic order. The electronics industry is dominated by a few huge complexes, and the automotive industry has its short list of giants. Most cities have a few large department stores, and it would be about as quixotic to establish a new one as to run a Republican in an Alabama election.

What happened is that the media were moulded by forces that conditioned American industry generally and that tremendously affected other social, economic, and political institutions. These forces wrought a powerful revolution that affected virtually every aspect of American life, especially after the Civil War, although their foundations were laid long before that.

Those forces, closely interrelated, were the rise of democracy, the spread of popular education, the industrial and technological revolution, urbanization, and, in this century, the redistribution of income.

In the nineteenth century, the electorate broadened as restrictions on voting gradually broke down, although it was not until 1920 that women got the right to vote. Meanwhile, qualifications on the right to hold office were giving way; no longer did a candidate need to own property or meet religious tests before he could hold office. One result of all of this was that the common man, for the first time in history, achieved effective political power. Another was that he was called upon, at least in theory, to make innumerable decisions that once had been made for him, decisions that required information, decisions that countless special pleaders were anxious to help him make.

A concomitant of universal suffrage was the spread of free popular education. By 1850, in principle if not in practice, the issue of a common-school education for all children at public expense was settled in the North and in parts of the South. In the half-century after 1860, the number of high schools increased a hundredfold, from 100 to 10,000, and a growing proportion of children entered their classrooms. After the Civil War, assisted by the land-grant movement, colleges began a period of expansion that has made the bachelor's degree a commonplace. All of this gave the media a vast audience equipped at least with the rudimentary tools of literacy and at best with far-ranging intellectual interests.

Between the end of the Civil War and the start of the new century, industrialization and mechanization hit America with all the force of revolution. So pervasive were the changes they brought about that a man of George Washington's time would probably have been more at home in the Holy Land of Jesus Christ than in the America of Teddy Roosevelt. A web of shiny rails held the nation together, and factories sprouted up where once corn had grown. Inventor after inventor came up with machines and gadgets to do the tasks that man once had performed by hand. Steam power replaced water power; electricity and the internal-combustion engine replaced steam. In the sixty years after 1850, the average manufacturing plant increased its capital more than thirty-nine times, its number of wage earners nearly seven times, the value of its output more than nineteen times.

Beneath much of that change, of course, lay a system of mass production and mass distribution. The system depended upon standardization and mass consumption; so long as consumers would accept goods tailored to averages instead of to individual preferences, they were treated to a profusion of products at relatively low cost. Mass production changed the conception of markets from areas to people. The typical manufacturer no longer produced only for his own locality; he sought out buyers wherever they lived. Now, all of the characteristics of mass production—greater use of product, standardization, and so on—had implications for the mass media, as I plan to show.

But one is so important that I wish to mention it now—the development of advertising. For one thing, mass production and mass distribution needed some kind of inexpensive mass salesmanship. For another thing, the media and appeals that worked when markets were regional or local did not suffice when markets became widely-scattered consumers. For still another thing, manufacturers had no great need of advertising when their production was barely above subsistence level. But as assembly lines turned out a seemingly endless flow of products of seemingly endless variety, as consumption became essential to keeping the stream of goods flowing, manufacturers had to make consumers conscious of dimly-sensed needs and desires, had to channel human drives to exploit the psychic values of their wares, had to make the consumer want to consume. For yet another thing, as unlabeled merchandise gave way to the brand-name product, the manufacturer saw the financial advantage inherent in his name and trademark. If he could convince the consumer that his product was more desirable than all others, he could charge a premium for it. Advertising grew, and as it did the media clutched at it for financial support.

Along with the industrial and technological revolution came the crowding of Americans together in cities. Farm workers put down the plow to tend the machines of the factory. Boat after boat brought immigrants seeking new opportunities—some 11½ million of them in the thirty years before 1900—and although many of them huddled together on the coast, many others ventured inland, some no doubt encouraged by the special rail fares that let them journey from New York to Chicago for as little as a dollar. All in all, the nation's population just about doubled between 1870 and 1900, and the city became home for an increasing proportion of it. Gathered in one place, people were natural markets for the media. And the immigrant, in many ways, had an influence on the media. The foreign-language newspaper, for instance, provided a link with the homeland and with others from it, helped adjustment to a strange land but also encouraged reading of regular American dailies. The early movies, low in price and heavy on pantomime, were an ideal medium for the foreign-born struggling with a new tongue and wanting escape from the drudgery of the factory.

In our own century, we have seen a redistribution of income so apparent that it probably is unnecessary to document it. It is true, of course, that despite all of our talk about the affluent society, poverty stubbornly exists and that many Americans still live in actual want. It is also true that disparities of income still exist, although not on the grand scale of 1900 when Andrew Carnegie's personal tax-free income of $20,000,000 was at least 20,000 times that of the average workingman. The middle-class American is considerably better off financially than he was in 1900, and that point is important to the mass media, not only because he has money for TV sets, transistor radios, and newspaper and magazine subscriptions but also because he has money for the advertisers' washing machines, hi-fi sets, and automobiles.

My little excursion into history has turned up little that is unfamiliar, I am sure. I have dwelt on the past at such length because critics have looked back to it surprisingly little when they have tried to explain why the media are what they are. My pitch is that the communications industries, like other industries, were affected by the social and economic forces

I have just outlined; they changed, in short, from personal craft industries to impersonal mass-production industries, and today they share many of the characteristics of other mass-production enterprises.

First, the mass media usually carve out little markets of their own, much as manufacturers and retailers do. The publisher of a confessions magazine no more expects every literate American to curl up with his tales of sin and redemption than an overalls manufacturer expects every American to wear his blue jeans. Each has a pretty clear idea of who is a good prospect for what he turns out, and he fashions his product accordingly.

Usually the market of a medium coincides with that of its advertisers. A newspaper typically concentrates its circulation in the trade area served by local retailers, for instance, and a magazine like *Farm Journal* aims at people who buy the tractors and chemical fertilizers extolled on its advertising pages. Even TV programers do not necessarily expect the people who guffaw at the Beverly Hillbillies to sit entranced by Meet the Press.

Media that do not carry advertising quite often pick out specialized markets, too. The book clubs neatly illustrate the point. Sired by that middle-aged grandfather, the Book-of-the-Month Club, their tribe has multiplied to include clubs for antique collectors, gardeners, cooks, farmers, educators, salesmen, executives, Civil War buffs and other amateur historians, Irishmen, outdoorsmen, drama and art lovers, science fans, yachtsmen, writers, Catholics, Jews, Lutherans and other Protestants, young children, teenagers, and grapplers of prose in its original French and Spanish.

A second consequence is what we might rather grandiosely call a democratization of content. In simple words, the mass media as a whole turned from a class audience to a mass audience and adjusted their content accordingly. Newspapers began their transition from sober organs for the mercantile class to lively sources of news for quite literally the man on the street in the early nineteenth century. Magazines began their change about a half-century later. Movies, radio, and television, born into a world of cities and technology, went after a mass market from the start.

As I have already said, the media seek out their own little publics. But in speaking to those publics, the media tend to address themselves to some center point, to some common denominator of taste, interest, and capability. In the nature of things a publisher or broadcaster must conduct his business pretty much as any other manufacturer must. A magazine publisher and a refrigerator maker, say, both want maximum saturation of their chosen markets. The media need audiences to exist, and to get and hold them they must please the majority of their chosen market. They can no more tailor their product to the specifications of a single individual or tiny group than can the dressmakers in New York's garment district. Overall, then, they tend to reflect the concerns, values, beliefs, and tastes of the great majority, and therein lies their essential conservatism.

Third, the mass media have become standardized in content and in technique. Newspapers across the land are pretty much alike in size, format, and overall appearance; in the ways in which they get their news; in the ways in which they write it, headline it, and present it; even in the relative play they give to national and international events. Magazines depend upon a pattern of content that carries over from issue to issue, and the big ones play a relatively small scale of major themes. Television programs are remarkable more for their basic sameness than their variety; the past season offered more than a dozen series in which Western badmen found death on the dusty streets of frontier towns, for instance, and depending on how one counted them, between twenty-three and thirty situation comedy series. And TV programs themselves, as any viewer knows, are developed in familiar, standardized ways. This standardization seems an almost inevitable result as the media increased their reach, their speed, and their efficiency by adopting such techniques of mass production as division of labor and mechanization, but consumer convenience and expectation also have probably played some part.

Fourth, as content became democratized, as technological advances enabled speedy output, there has been an increased use of the media. Today the typical American spends more time looking at and listening to the mass media than at anything else except his work or sleeping, and the typical youngster leaving high school has spent more time in front of a TV set than in the classroom. Newspapers, magazines, radio, and television all penetrate deep into the population.

Fifth, the media have become more efficient, just as many other massproduction enterprises have. The telegraph, wireless, train, and plane have enabled the media not only to take the entire world for their beat but to cover it with astonishing swiftness. Until the middle of the last century, England was still two or three weeks away, and at home news was slow in traveling from one part of the country to another.

When Andrew Jackson successfully defended New Orleans in the War of 1812–14, New Yorkers did not read about the outcome until a month afterwards. And as they learned from their papers five days later, the battle itself had been fought two weeks after the peace treaty was signed in London. But when the Korean War broke out in June, 1950, Jack James's United Press dispatch reached Washington almost at once—several minutes before the State Department's own cable, in fact.

New means of communication and improvements in the old ones have made possible vast audiences for the media. High-speed presses and mechanical typesetting allowed newspapers and magazines to seek their large circulations, and the electronic media have put a speaker into instantaneous touch with millions of persons. We often forget how very recent some of these changes are. In my own childhood, in 1919, when President Woodrow Wilson wanted to sell the Treaty of Versailles to the nation, he spent twenty-seven days traveling more than 8,000 miles in seventeen states to deliver forty formal speeches and many more informal talks, only one of them with benefit of public address system. In December, 1962, when three TV networks carried "Conversation with the President," John F. Kennedy was in instantaneous touch with an estimated 21,960,000 American homes, according to A. C. Nielsen figures.

Finally, the mass media, like other industries, have used the assembly-line technique of division of labor. Once even the publisher of a metropolitan daily could operate as James Gordon Bennett did in 1835, when he gathered his own news, wrote it up, handled business affairs, and waited on customers at a desk made of two barrels with a plank across them. By the 1870s those days were largely gone, and by the 1890s the large-city dailies had staffs about as specialized as they are today. All of the other media, too, have come to depend upon a variety of specialists to put together the finished product. As they have, the individual employee has lost most of whatever chance for self-expression he ever had. He became one of a team turning out mass-produced images, and too large an investment rides on his efforts for him to produce with anything but the market in mind.

Those, then, are the forces that have joined to give us the sort of communication system we have, and in large measure they are responsible for the many strengths we too often take for granted. They have contributed to the development of a communication system that reaches virtually the entire population and that in the aggregate makes available an astonishing amount of entertainment and an astonishing array of information, viewpoint, and interpretation on a wide array of subjects with incredible swiftness and superb technical skill. They have contributed to the important part that the media have played in bringing about our high material standard of living.

But in large measure those forces also are responsible for the faults that have sent many a critic reaching for his thesaurus of epithets. They have contributed to the superficiality, the sameness, the blandness, and the blindness that characterize a good deal of media content. They have contributed to the bigness, fewness, and costliness that some critics see as jeopardizing the free trade in information and ideas, putting control of a powerful social instrument into the hands of the few and converting the personal right of press freedom into a property right.

All of what I have said, I immodestly think, has some implications for those who are serious in their criticism of the mass media.

First, those who examine the press should try to achieve objectivity in two meanings of the term. On the one hand, as they set out to discover what the mass media are and why they are what they are, they should leave their ideological baggage behind, much as a good cultural anthropologist does. They should look deep into the past for clues to present understanding. They should examine the interrelationships of the media with other parts of society. On the other hand, they should explore the objective social functions that the media perform, quite apart from those ascribed by normative press theory. As Jensen suggested, the media have a reality of their own. Although they are man-made creations, they have developed certain objective functions distinct from the tasks assigned them by their operators and by society. Desirable or not, those functions exist, and it is the duty of the serious critic to understand them.

Second, critics should put up for serious examination our traditional theory of the press, which in many ways seems out of joint with the times. That theory may have been adequate in the eighteenth and nineteenth centuries, when both the world and the communication system were far less complex than today, but one might ask if it is in accord with contemporary thought and reality. Some such examination has already begun; and as publishers and broadcasters themselves have discarded parts of traditional theory as outmoded, there are indications that a new theory of social responsibility is emerging. As a part of this intellectual overhaul, which should begin with the questioning of basic assumptions, I hope we could also re-examine some of the notions that have long surrounded traditional theory. For instance, are we right in the notion that although the media have a responsibility to enlighten the public, the public has no special responsibility to be enlightened? Are the media right in their notion that in enlightening the public, the demands of the market are the best test of how well the job is being done? Are we right in the notion that bigness is necessarily badness? Does a multiplicity of communications units necessarily mean a multiplicity of viewpoints? Are small media operators necessarily more socially responsible than large ones? Does control necessarily follow financial support?

In conclusion, let me say that I am not proposing that we grant the media absolution for all their sins, venal or otherwise. Some, I know, will read my message that way. In looking at the press from an institutional perspective, some will conclude that publishers and broadcasters are swept inexorably along by powerful, impersonal social and cultural forces and that there is nothing that they or we can do about it. That conclusion implies a degree of predestinarianism I am quite unwilling to accept. Man with brain and hand has given the media the milieus in which they operate, and man if he will can change them.

Bibliography

PERIODICALS

The student interested in current media developments will frequently find articles in *Harper's, Atlantic, Saturday Review, Time, Newsweek, Nation, New Republic, New York Times Magazine,* and *TV Guide.*

There are numerous professional journals; many college libraries subscribe to *Journalism Quarterly, Public Opinion Quarterly, Nieman Reports, Quill, Columbia Journalism Review, Editor and Publisher, Broadcasting, Television Quarterly, Variety,* and others.

THE NEWS MEDIA

General

Berlo, David K., *The Process of Communication.* New York: Holt, Rinehart & Winston, Inc., 1960.

Commission on Freedom of the Press, *A Free and Responsible Press.* Chicago: University of Chicago Press, 1947.

De Fleur, Melvin L., *Theories of Mass Communications.* New York: David McKay & Co., Inc., 1970.

Lane, Robert E., and David O. Sears, *Public Opinion.* Englewood Cliffs, N.J.: Prentice-Hall, Inc., 1967.

O'Hara, Robert, *Media for the Millions: The Process of Mass Communication.* New York: Random House, Inc., 1961.

Rivers, William, and Wilbur Schramm, *Responsibility in Mass Communications.* New York: Harper & Row, Publishers, 1969.

Rosenthal, Raymond, ed., *McLuhan: Pro and Con.* Baltimore: Pelican Books, 1969.

Siebert, Fred S., Theodore Peterson, and Wilbur Schramm, *Four Theories of the Press.* Urbana: University of Illinois Press, 1956.

History

Barnouw, Eric, *The Golden Web*. New York: Oxford University Press, 1968.

————, *The Image Empire*. New York: Oxford University Press, 1971.

————, *A Tower in Babel*. New York: Oxford University Press, 1966.

Emery, Edwin, *The Press and America: An Interpretative History of Journalism* (3rd ed.). Englewood Cliffs, N.J.: Prentice-Hall, Inc., 1971.

Knight, Arthur, *The Liveliest Art: A Panoramic History of the Movies*. New York: The New American Library Inc., 1957.

Mott, Frank Luther, *American Journalism: A History, 1690–1960*. New York: The Macmillan Company, 1962.

————, *A History of American Magazines* (5 vols.). New York: Appleton-Century-Crofts, 1930 (Vol. 1), and Cambridge: Harvard University Press, 1936–1968 (Vols. 2–5).

Peterson, Theodore, *Magazines in the Twentieth Century*. Urbana: University of Illinois Press, 1964.

Rotha, Paul, and Richard Griffith, *The Film Till Now*. Middlesex, Eng.: Spring Books, 1967.

Stewart, Kenneth, and John Tebbel, *Makers of Modern Journalism*. Englewood Cliffs, N.J.: Prentice-Hall, Inc., 1952.

Talese, Gay, *The Kingdom and The Power—The Story of . . . The New York Times*. New York: The New American Library Inc. in association with Cleveland: The World Publishing Company, 1969.

Tebbel, John, *Compact History of the American Newspaper*. New York: Hawthorn Books, Inc., 1969.

Wood, James Playsted, *Magazines in the United States*. New York: The Ronald Press Company, 1956.

Critics and Defenders

Casey, Ralph D., *The Press in Perspective*. Baton Rouge: Louisiana State University Press, 1963.

Friendly, Alfred, and Ronald L. Goldfarb, *Crime and Publicity: The Impact of News on the Administration of Justice*. New York: The Twentieth Century Fund, 1968.

Gerald, J. Edward, *The Social Responsibility of the Press*. Minneapolis: University of Minnesota Press, 1963.

Hohenberg, John, *Free Press, Free People: The Best Cause*. New York: Columbia University Press, 1971.

————, *The News Media: A Journalist Looks at His Profession*. New York: Holt, Rinehart and Winston, Inc., 1968.

Hulteng, John, and Roy Paul Nelson, *The Fourth Estate.* New York: Harper & Row, Publishers, 1971.

Kirschner, Allen, and Linda Kirschner, *Journalism: Readings in the Mass Media.* New York: Odyssey Press, 1971.

Lacy, Dan, *Freedom and Communications.* Urbana: University of Illinois Press, 1961.

Lindstrom, Carl E., *The Fading American Newspaper.* New York: Doubleday & Company, Inc., 1960.

Lofton, John, *Justice and the Press.* Boston: Beacon Press, 1966.

McGaffin, William, and Erwin Kroll, *Anything But the Truth, The Credibility Gap: How the News Is Managed in Washington.* New York: G. P. Putnam's Sons, 1968.

Tebbel, John, *An Open Letter to Newspaper Readers.* New York: James H. Heineman, Inc., 1968.

Adversaries

Aronson, James, *The Press and The Cold War.* Indianapolis: The Bobbs-Merrill Co., Inc., 1970.

Cater, Douglass, *The Fourth Branch of Government.* Boston: Houghton Mifflin Company, 1959.

Cohen, Bernard C., *The Press and Foreign Policy.* Princeton: Princeton University Press, 1963.

Pollard, James E., *The Presidents and the Press: Truman to Johnson.* Washington: Public Affairs Press, 1964.

Reston, James, *The Artillery of the Press, Its Influence on American Foreign Policy.* New York: Harper & Row, Publishers for the Council on Foreign Relations, 1967.

Rivers, William L., *The Adversaries—Politics and the Press.* Boston: Beacon Press, 1970.

————, *The Opinion Makers—An Inside View of the Washington Press Corps.* Boston: Beacon Press, 1965.

Schlesinger, Arthur M., *Prelude to Independence—The Newspaper War on Britain, 1764–1776.* New York: Alfred A. Knopf, Inc., 1958.

Thayer, Frank, *Legal Control of the Press.* Mineola, N.Y.: The Foundation Press, Inc., 1962.

Weinberg, Arthur, and Lila Weinberg, eds., *The Muckrakers.* New York: Simon & Schuster, 1961.

Wiggins, James Russell, *Freedom or Secrecy.* New York: Oxford University Press, Inc., 1964.

Advocates: Books

Glessing, Robert J., *The Underground Press in America*. Bloomington: Indiana University Press, 1970.

Mungo, Raymond, *Famous Long Ago—My Life and Hard Times with Liberation News Service*. Boston: Beacon Press, 1970.

Advocates: Articles

Brown, Charles H., "The Boundaries of Interpretation," *Quill* (May, 1969).

Deitch, David, "Case for Advocacy Journalism," *Nation* (Nov. 17, 1969).

Diamond, Ed, "The Coming Newsroom Revolution," *Columbia Journalism Review* (Summer, 1970).

Hart, Jim A., "Objectivity: Journalists' Bugaboo," *Grassroots Editor* (Jan.–Feb., 1970).

Holhenberg, John, "The Journalist as Missionary," *Saturday Review* (Feb. 14, 1970).

McHam, David, "The Authentic New Journalists," *Quill* (Sept., 1971).

Madigan, John, and Curtis MacDougall, ed. by George Bailey, "The New Journalism Debate," *Quill* (Sept., 1971).

Merrill, John, "Objective Reporting: A Myth, However Valuable," *Quill* (July, 1969).

Rucker, Bryce W., "Revolt of Journalists' Obligation for Survival," *Grassroots Editor* (Sept.–Oct., 1969).

Sesser, Stanford, "Journalists: Objectivity and Activism," *Quill* (Dec., 1969).

Smith, Howard K., "The Deadly Balance," *Columbia Journalism Review* (Fall, 1965).

Interpreters

Adler, Ruth, ed., *The Working Press*. New York: Bantam Books, Inc., 1970.

Barrett, Dean Edward W., ed., *Journalists in Action*. New York: Channel Press, 1963.

Koch, Howard, *The Panic Broadcast, Portrait of an Event: Orson Welles' and His Mercury Theatre's "The Invasion from Mars."* Boston: Little, Brown and Company, 1970.

MacDougall, Curtis, *The Press and Its Problems*. Dubuque: William C. Brown Company, Publishers, 1964.

Merrill, John C., *The Elite Press*. New York: Pitman Publishing Corp., 1968.

Rivers, William L., Theodore Peterson, and Jay W. Jensen, *The Mass Media in Modern Society*. New York: Rinehart Press, 1971.

Rivers, William L., *The Opinionmakers*. Boston: Beacon Press, 1965.

Advisers and Forecasters

Alsop, Joseph, and Stewart Alsop, *The Reporter's Trade*. New York: The Macmillan Company, 1958.

Clark, Wesley C., ed., *Journalism Tomorrow*. Syracuse: Syracuse University Press, 1958.

Copple, Neale, *Depth Reporting*. Englewood Cliffs, N.J.: Prentice-Hall, Inc., 1964.

Final Report of the National Commission on Causes and Prevention of Violence, *To Establish Justice, To Insure Domestic Tranquility*. Washington, 1969.

Friendly, Fred W., *Due to Circumstances Beyond Our Control*. New York: Random House, Inc., 1967.

Gross, Gerald, ed., *The Responsibility of the Press*. New York: Clarion Books, 1966.

Rossiter, Clinton, and James Lare, eds., *The Essential Lippmann*. New York: Random House, Inc., 1963.

Schramm, Wilbur, *The Impact of Educational Television*. Urbana: University of Illinois Press, 1960.

THE ENTERTAINMENT MEDIA

Popular Art as Entertainer for Millions

Agee, Warren K., ed., *Mass Media in A Free Society*. Lawrence: University Press of Kansas, 1969.

Deer, Irving, and Harriet Deer, *The Popular Arts: A Critical Reader*. New York: Charles Scribner's Sons, 1967.

Hall, Stuart, and Paddy Whannel, *The Popular Arts: A Critical Guide to the Mass Media*. Boston: Beacon Press, 1967.

Jacobs, Norman, ed., *Culture for the Millions?* Boston: Beacon Press, 1964.

Katz, Elihu, and Paul Lazarsfeld, *Personal Influence: The Part Played by People in the Flow of Mass Communication*. New York: The Free Press, 1955.

Mayer, Martin, *Madison Avenue, U.S.A.* New York: Harper & Row, Publishers, 1958.

Rosenberg, Bernard, and David M. White, eds., *Mass Culture: The Popular Arts in America*. New York: Free Press of Glencoe, Inc., 1965.

White, David M., and Richard Averson, eds., *Sight, Sound and Society: Motion Pictures and Television in America*. Boston: Beacon Press, 1968.

White, David Manning, *Pop Culture in America*. New York: Quadrangle Books, 1970.

The Film as High, Middle, and Low Culture

Griffith, Richard, and Arthur Mayer, *The Movies*. New York: Simon & Schuster, Inc., 1957.

Manvell, Roger, *The Film and the Public*. Middlesex, Eng.: Penguin Books Ltd., 1955.

Ross, Lillian, *Picture*. New York: Holt, Rinehart and Winston, Inc., 1952.

Seldes, Gilbert, *The Public Arts*. New York: Simon & Schuster, Inc., 1956.

Talbot, Daniel, *Film: An Anthology*. New York: Simon & Schuster, Inc., 1959.

Television: Mass Culture

Arlen, Michael, *The Living Room War*. New York: The Viking Press, Inc., 1969.

Carnegie Commission on Educational Television, *Public Television: A Program for Action*. 1967.

Cole, Barry, ed., *Television*. New York: The Free Press, 1970.

Kendrick, Alexander, *Prime Time*. New York: Avon Books, 1970.

MacNeil, Robert, *The People Machine*. New York: Harper & Row, Publishers, 1968.

Skornia, Henry J., and Jack W. Kitson, *Problems and Controversies in Television and Radio*. Palo Alto: Pacific Books, Publishers, 1968.

Steiner, Gary, *The People Look at Television: A Study of Audience Attitudes*, New York: Alfred A. Knopf, Inc., 1963.

What Popular Art Does to Us

Backman, Jules, *Advertising and Competition*. New York: New York University Press, 1967.

Baker, Robert K., and Sandra J. Ball, *Violence and the Media*. Staff Report of the National Commission on Causes and Prevention of Violence, 1969.

Bogart, Leo, *The Age of Television*. New York: Frederick Ungar Publishing Co., Inc., 1956.

Johnson, Nicholas, *How to Talk Back to Your Television Set*. New York: Bantam Books, Inc., 1970.

Kerner Report, *Report of the National Advisory Commission on Civil Disorders*, 1968.

Larsen, Otto N., *Violence and the Mass Media*. New York: Harper & Row, Publishers, 1968.

Sandage, Charles H., and Vernon Fryburger, *The Role of Advertising: A Book of Readings*. Homewood, Ill.: Richard D. Irwin, Inc., 1960.

Schramm, Wilbur, J. Lyle, and E. B. Parker, *Television in the Lives of Our Children*. Stanford: Stanford University Press, 1963.

The Walker Report to the National Commission on Causes and Prevention of Violence, *Rights in Conflict*. 1968.

Finessing the Censor

Carmen, Ira H., *Movies, Censorship and the Law*. Ann Arbor: University of Michigan Press, 1966.

Gillmor, Donald M., and Jerome A. Barron, *Mass Communications Law: Cases and Comment*. St. Paul: West Publishing Co., 1969.

Hachten, William A., *The Supreme Court and Freedom of the Press*. Ames: Iowa State University Press, 1968.

McKeon, Richard, Robert K. Merton, and Walter Gellhorn, *The Freedom to Read: Perspective and Programs*. New York: R. R. Bowker Co., 1957.

The Report of the Commission on Obscenity and Pornography. New York: Bantam Books, Inc., 1970.

Schumach, Murray, *The Face on the Cutting Room Floor*. William Morrow & Co., Inc., 1964.

CONCLUSION

Final Report, Commission on Causes and Prevention of Violence, *To Establish Justice, to Insure Domestic Tranquility*. 1969.

Gross, Gerald, ed., *The Responsibility of the Press*. New York: Clarion Books, 1966.